Norms *for* Priestly Formation

Volume I • *November 1993*

National Conference of Catholic Bishops

In its 1993 planning document as approved by the general membership of the National Conference of Catholic Bishops in November 1992, the Bishops' Committee on Priestly Formation through its Secretariat was authorized to compile for publication a compendium of official documents of the Chruch relating to priestly formation. This two-volume compendium of documents, including those of Vatican Council II and subsequent documents published by the Holy See, has been approved by the Bishops' Committee on Priestly Formation and authorized for publication by the undersigned.

Monsignor Robert N. Lynch
General Secretary
NCCB/USCC

November 12, 1993

Cover adapted from design for *Program of Priestly Formation* by Ted Jarkiewicz Studio, Baltimore, Maryland.

Text design and layout by Mack Rowe Visual Communications, Ltd., Alexandria, Virginia.

Note: The documents in this compilation have been edited for consistency in format and style. In no way has this editing affected the meaning of the original documents.

Decree on the Training of Priests and *Decree on the Ministry and Life of Priests* are taken from *Vatican Council II: The Conciliar and Post-Conciliar Documents,* copyright © 1975 by Costello Publishing Company, Inc., and Reverend Austin Flannery, OP, and are used with permission of the copyright owner.

This two-volume series of publications: ISBN 1-55586-619-0

Contents

Decree on the Training of Priests

Second Vatican Council
1965

Paul, Bishop, Servant of the Servants of God,
together with the Council Fathers,
for a permanent record

Decree on the Training of Priests [a]

(Optatam totius)

Introduction

The Council is fully aware that the desired renewal of the whole Church depends in great part upon a priestly ministry animated by the spirit of Christ[1] and it solemnly affirms the critical importance of priestly training. It lays down certain fundamental principles, wherein regulations already tested by the experience of centuries are reaffirmed, and new regulations are introduced, in harmony with the constitutions and decrees of the sacred Council and the changed conditions of our times. Because of the unity of the Catholic priesthood, this priestly formation is required for all priests, secular, religious and of every rite. Hence, although these directives are immediately concerned with the diocesan clergy, they should with due qualification be adapted to all.

I. Priestly Training in Different Countries

1. Since only regulations of a general nature can be made, owing to the wide diversity of peoples and countries, each nation or rite should have its own *Program of Priestly Training*. This should be drawn up by the episcopal conference[2] and should be revised at regular intervals and approved by the Holy See. In every such program, the general regulations will be adapted to the circumstances of time and place, so that priestly training will always answer the pastoral requirements of the particular area in which the ministry is to be exercised.

II. More Intensive Fostering of Priestly Vocations

2. The duty of fostering vocations[3] falls on the whole Christian community, and they should discharge it principally by living full Christian lives. The greatest contribution is made by families which are animated by a spirit of faith, charity and piety and which provide, as it were, a first seminary, and by parishes in whose abundant life the young people themselves take an active part. Teachers and all who are in any way involved in the education of boys and young men — and this applies especially to Catholic societies — should endeavor to train the young entrusted to them to recognize a divine vocation and to follow it willingly. All priests should show their apostolic zeal by fostering vocations as much as possible, and should draw the hearts of young men to the priesthood by the example of

3

their humble, hardworking and happy lives, as well as by their mutual charity and fraternal cooperation.

It is the duty of bishops to encourage their people to foster vocations, and to see that all their energies and undertakings are closely coordinated, sparing themselves no sacrifice in their efforts to help, as fathers, those who in their judgment have been called to God's service.

Such active collaboration by all God's people in the task of fostering vocations is a response to the action of divine Providence, which endows with appropriate qualities and helps with divine grace those who have been chosen by God to share in the hierarchical priesthood of Christ. Divine Providence entrusts to the lawful ministers of the Church the task of judging the suitability of candidates seeking this exalted office with right intention and full liberty, and, after they have been approved, of calling and consecrating them with the seal of the Holy Spirit to the worship of God and the service of the Church.[4]

The Council, first of all, recommends the traditional aids towards this general cooperation, such as: unceasing prayer,[b] Christian penance and progressively more advanced instruction for the faithful, wherein the necessity, nature and excellence of the priestly vocation will be set forth by preaching, catechetics and the various means of social communication. The Council also directs that the organizations for promoting vocations which have been — or are about to be — set up in the various dioceses, regions or countries, in accordance with the relevant pontifical documents, should coordinate and systematize all pastoral work for vocations and develop them with as much discretion as zeal, making full use of the aids provided by modern psychological and sociological teaching.[5]

The work of fostering vocations should be done generously. It should cross the boundaries of individual dioceses, countries, religious congregations and rites and, with the needs of the universal Church in view, should assist especially those areas for which workers are required with special urgency for the Lord's vineyard.

3. In minor seminaries founded to nurture the seeds of vocation, students should be prepared by a special religious formation and, especially, by suitable spiritual direction, to follow Christ the Redeemer with generous souls and pure hearts. Under the fatherly supervision of the superiors, the parents too playing their appropriate part, let them lead lives suited to the age, mentality and development of young people. Their way of life should be fully in keeping with the standards of sound psychology and should include suitable experience of the ordinary affairs of daily life and contact with their own families.[6] Furthermore, all that is laid down in the following paragraphs for major seminaries should be adapted to the minor seminary also as far as is suitable to its purpose and character. Courses of studies should be so arranged that pupils may be able to continue them elsewhere without inconvenience, should they embrace another state of life.

The same care should be taken to foster the seeds of vocations in those special institutes which, in keeping with local conditions, take the place of minor seminaries, and also among boys educated in other schools or according to other systems. Colleges for late vocations and other undertakings for the same purpose should be diligently promoted.

III. Major Seminaries

4. Major seminaries are necessary for priestly training. In them the whole training of the students should have as its object to make them true shepherds of souls after the example of our Lord Jesus Christ, teacher, priest and shepherd.[7] Hence, they should be trained for the ministry of the Word, so that they may gain an ever increasing understanding of the revealed Word of God, making it their own by meditation, and giving it expression in their speech and in their lives. They should be trained for the ministry of worship and sanctification, so that by prayer and the celebration of the sacred liturgical functions they may carry on the work of salvation through the eucharistic sacrifice and the sacraments. They should be trained to undertake the ministry of the shepherd, that they may know how to represent Christ to men, Christ who "did not come to have service done to him, but to serve others and to give his life as a ransom for the lives of many" (Mk. 10.45; Jn. 13.12-17), and that they may win over many by becoming the servants of all (1 Cor. 9.19).

Hence, all the elements of their training, spiritual, intellectual, disciplinary, should be coordinated with this pastoral aim in view, and all superiors and teachers should zealously cooperate to carry out this program in loyal obedience to the bishop's authority.

5. The training of students depends not only on wise regulations but also, and especially, on competent educators. Seminary superiors and professors should therefore be chosen from among the best[8] and should receive a careful preparation in sound doctrine, suitable pastoral experience and special training in spirituality and teaching methods. To provide this training, special colleges should be established, or at least suitable courses should be organized, as well as regular meetings of seminary directors.

Superiors and professors should be keenly aware of the extent to which their mental outlook and conduct affects the formation of their students. Under the guidance of the rector they should cultivate the closest harmony of spirit and action, and should form with one another and with the students such a family as corresponds to our divine Lord's prayer: "that they may be one" (cf. Jn. 17.11), and quickens in the students' hearts a sense of joy in their vocation. The bishop with his constant and affectionate interest should encourage those engaged in seminary work and show himself a true father in Christ to the students. Furthermore, all priests should regard the seminary as the very heart of the diocese and give it their willing support.[9]

6. Each candidate should be subjected to vigilant and careful inquiry, keeping in mind his age and development, concerning his right intention and freedom of choice, his spiritual, moral and intellectual fitness, adequate physical and mental health, and possible hereditary traits. Account should also be taken of the candidate's capacity for undertaking the obligations of the priesthood and carrying out his pastoral duties.[10]

Notwithstanding the regrettable shortage of priests,[11] due strictness should always be brought to bear on the choice and testing of students. God will not allow his Church to lack ministers if the worthy are promoted and those who are not suited to the ministry are guided with fatherly kindness and in due time to adopt another calling. These should be directed in such a way that, conscious of their Christian vocation, they will zealously engage in the lay apostolate.

7. Where individual dioceses are unable to provide adequate separate seminaries out of their own resources, common seminaries should be established and maintained. These common seminaries could meet the needs of a group of dioceses or of an entire region or nation. By their means better provision will be made for the solid training of the students, which is of paramount importance in this matter. These seminaries, regional or national, are to be controlled according to regulations drawn up by the bishops concerned,[12] and approved by the Holy See.

In large seminaries, the students should be suitably organized in smaller groups, to enable more personal attention to be given to each student, while retaining unity of discipline and scientific training.

IV. Greater Attention to Spiritual Training

8. Spiritual formation should be closely associated with doctrinal and pastoral formation, and, with the assistance of the spiritual director in particular,[13] should be conducted in such a way that the students may learn to live in intimate and unceasing union with God the Father through his Son Jesus Christ, in the Holy Spirit. Those who are to take on the likeness of Christ the priest by sacred ordination should form the habit of drawing close to him as friends in every detail of their lives.[14] They should live his Paschal Mystery in such a way that they will know how to initiate into it the people committed to their charge. They should be taught to seek Christ in faithful meditation on the Word of God and in active participation in the sacred mysteries of the Church, especially the Eucharist and the Divine Office,[15] to seek him in the bishop by whom they are sent and in the people to whom they are sent, especially the poor, little children, the weak, sinners and unbelievers. With the confidence of sons they should love and reverence the most Blessed Virgin Mary, who was given as a mother to the disciples by Jesus Christ as he was dying on the cross.

The exercises of piety which are commended by the venerable practice of the Church should be strongly encouraged, but care must be taken that spiritual formation does not consist in these alone, nor develop religious sentiment, merely. The students should learn, rather, to live according to the standard of the Gospel, to be firmly established in faith, hope and charity, so that the practice of these virtues may develop in them a spirit of prayer,[16] may strengthen and protect their vocation and invigorate their other virtues, intensifying their zeal for winning all men to Christ.

9. The students should be thoroughly penetrated with a sense of the Mystery of the Church, which this holy Council has set particularly in relief. Their sense of the Church will find expression in a humble and filial attachment to the Vicar of Christ and, after ordination, in their loyal cooperation with the bishop, in harmony with their fellow-priests. By this means they will bear witness to that unity which draws men to Christ.[17] They should learn to participate with enthusiasm in the life of the Church as a whole, keeping in mind the words of St. Augustine: "A man possesses the Holy Spirit in the measure in which he loves the Church."[18] Students must clearly understand that it is not their lot in life to lord it over others and enjoy honors, but to devote themselves completely to the service of God and the pastoral ministry. With special care they should be so trained in priestly obedience, poverty and a spirit of self-denial,[19] that they may accustom themselves to living in conformity with the crucified Christ and to giving up willingly even those things which are lawful, but not expedient.

Students should be informed of the obligations which they are undertaking, and no difficulty of the priestly life should be concealed from them. They should not, however, be almost completely taken up with the element of danger in their future apostolate, but should rather be trained to strengthen their spiritual life as fully as possible in the very exercise of their pastoral activity.

10. Students who follow the venerable tradition of priestly celibacy as laid down by the holy and permanent regulations of their own rite should be very carefully trained for this state. In it they renounce marriage for the sake of the kingdom of heaven (cf. Mt. 19.12) and hold fast to their Lord with that undivided love[20] which is profoundly in harmony with the New Covenant; they bear witness to the resurrection in a future life (cf. Lk. 20.36)[21] and obtain the most useful assistance towards the constant exercise of that perfect charity by which they can become all things to all men in their priestly ministry.[22] They should keenly realize with what a sense of gratitude they should embrace this state, not only as a precept of ecclesiastical law, but as a precious gift of God which they should ask for humbly and to which they should hasten to respond freely and generously, under the inspiration and with the assistance of the Holy Spirit.

Students should have a proper knowledge of the duties and dignity of Christian marriage, which represents the love which exists between Christ and the Church (cf. Eph. 5.32). They should recognize the greater excellence of virginity consecrated to Christ,[23] however, so that they may offer themselves to the Lord with fully deliberate and generous choice, and a complete surrender of body and soul.

They should be put on their guard against the dangers which threaten their chastity, especially in present-day society.[24] They should learn how, with suitable natural and supernatural safeguards, to weave their renunciation of marriage into the pattern of their lives, so that not only will their daily conduct and activities suffer no harm from celibacy, but they themselves will acquire greater mastery of mind and body, will grow in maturity and receive greater measure of the blessedness promised by the Gospel.

11. The standards of Christian education should be faithfully maintained and they should be supplemented by the latest findings of sound psychology and pedagogy. A prudent system of training will therefore aim at developing in the students a proper degree of human maturity. This will be chiefly attested by a certain stability of character, the ability to make carefully weighed decisions, and a sound judgment of events and people. The students should learn self-control,[c] develop strength of character, and in general value those good qualities which are esteemed by men and make Christ's minister acceptable.[25] Such qualities are sincerity, a constant love of justice, fidelity to one's promises, courtesy in deed, modesty and charity in speech.

The discipline of seminary life should be regarded not only as a strong protection for community life and charity, but as a necessary part of the complete system of training. Its purpose is to inculcate self-control, to promote solid maturity of personality and the formation of those other traits of character which are most useful for the ordered and fruitful activity of the Church. But it should be applied in such a way as to develop in the students a readiness to accept the authority of superiors out of deep conviction—because of the dictates of their conscience, that is to say (cf. Rom. 13.5) — and for supernatural reasons. Standards of discipline should be applied with due regard for the age of the students, so that while they gradually acquire self-mastery, they will at the same time form the habit of using their freedom with discretion, of acting on their own initiative and energetically,[26] and of working harmoniously with their confreres and with the laity.

The whole program of the seminary should be so organized that, with its atmosphere of piety and silence and its concern for mutual cooperation, it should already be an initiation to the students' future lives as priests.

12. To provide a more solid foundation for the students' spiritual formation, and enable them to decide upon their vocation with full deliberation, it will rest with the bishops to set apart a suitable interval of time for a more intensive spiritual preparation. It is for them also to consider carefully the advantage of arranging some interruption of studies, or of providing suitable training in pastoral work, so that better provision can be made for testing the fitness of candidates for the priesthood. It will be for the bishops likewise, keeping in mind the special conditions of each country, to determine if the age at present required by the common law for the reception of sacred orders should be raised, and to discuss whether it be opportune to make a ruling that at the end of the theological course students should work for a time as deacons before being raised to the priesthood.

V. The Revision of Ecclesiastical Studies

13. Before seminarians commence their specifically ecclesiastical studies, they should already have received that literary and scientific education which is a prerequisite to higher studies in their country. In addition they should acquire a knowledge of Latin which will enable them to understand and make use of so many scientific sources and of the documents of the Church.[27] The study of the liturgical language of their own rite should also be considered a necessity and the acquisition of an adequate knowledge of the languages of holy Scripture and Tradition should be warmly encouraged.

14. In the revision of ecclesiastical studies the main object to be kept in mind is a more effective coordination of philosophy and theology so that they supplement one another in revealing to the minds of the students with ever increasing clarity the Mystery of Christ, which affects the whole course of human history, exercises an unceasing influence on the Church, and operates mainly through the ministry of the priest.[28]

This vision should be communicated to the students from the very first moment of their training; their ecclesiastical studies, therefore, should begin with an introductory course of appropriate duration. In this course the mystery of salvation should be presented in such a way that the students may understand the meaning, arrangement and pastoral aim of ecclesiastical studies, and may be helped at the same time to make faith the foundation and inner principle of their entire personal lives, and be strengthened in their resolve to accept their vocation with joyful heart and complete personal dedication.

15. Philosophical subjects should be taught in such a way as to lead the students gradually to a solid and consistent knowledge of man, the world and God. The students should rely on that philosophical patrimony which is forever valid,[29] but should also take account of modern philosophical studies, especially those which have greater influence in their own country, as well as recent progress in the sciences. Thus, by correctly understanding the modern mind, students will be prepared to enter into dialogue with their contemporaries.[30]

The history of philosphy should be taught in such a manner that students may grasp the fundamental principles of the various systems, retaining those elements which are proved to be true, while being able to detect and refute those which are false.

The teaching method adopted should stimulate in the students a love of rigorous investigation, observation and demonstration of the truth, as well as an honest recognition of the limits of human knowledge. Careful attention should be paid to the bearing of philosophy on the real problems of life, as well as to the questions which engage the minds of the students. The students themselves should be helped to perceive the connection between philosophical arguments and the mysteries of salvation which theology considers in the higher light of faith.

16. Theological subjects should be taught in the light of faith, under the guidance of the magisterium of the Church,[31] in such a way that students will draw pure Catholic teaching from divine revelation, will enter deeply into its meaning, make it the nourishment of their spiritual life,[32] and learn to proclaim, explain, and defend it in their priestly ministry.

Students should receive a most careful training in holy Scripture, which should be the soul, as it were, of all theology.[33] After a suitable introductory course, they should receive an accurate initiation in exegetical method. They should study closely the principal themes of divine revelation and should find inspiration and nourishment in daily reading and meditation upon the sacred books.[34]

The following order should be observed in the treatment of dogmatic theology: biblical themes should have first place; then students should be shown what the Fathers of the Church, both of the East and West, have contributed towards the faithful transmission and elucidation of each of the revealed truths; then the later history of dogma, including its relation to the general history of the Church;[35] lastly, in order to throw as full a light as possible on the mysteries of salvation, the students should learn to examine more deeply, with the help of speculation and with St. Thomas as teacher, all aspects of these mysteries, and to perceive their interconnection.[36] They should be taught at all times in the ceremonies of the liturgy,[37] and in the whole life of the Church. They should learn to seek the solution of human problems in the light of revelation, to apply its eternal truths to the changing conditions of human affairs, and to express them in language which people of the modern world will understand.[38]

In like manner the other theological subjects should be renewed through a more vivid contact with the Mystery of Christ and the history of salvation. Special care should be given to the perfecting of moral theology. Its scientific presentation should draw more fully on the teaching of holy Scripture and should throw light upon the exalted vocation of the faithful in Christ and their obligation to bring forth fruit in charity for the life of the world. In the same way the teaching of canon law and Church history should take into account the mystery of the Church, as it was set forth in the Dogmatic Constitution *De Ecclesia,* promulgated by this Council. Sacred liturgy, which is to be regarded as the first and indispensable source of the true Christian spirit, should be taught as prescribed in articles 15 and 16 of the Constitution on Sacred Liturgy.[39]

With due regard to the conditions of different countries, students should be introduced to a fuller knowledge of the Churches and ecclesial communities separated from the Holy See, so that they may be able to take part in promoting the restoration of unity between all Christians according to the decisions of the Council.[40]

They should also be introduced to a knowledge of whatever other religions are most commonly encountered in this or that region, so that they may recognize more clearly how much goodness and truth they possess through the Providence of God, and learn how to refute their errors and bring the light of truth to those who are without it.

17. Doctrinal training should not have the mere communication of ideas as its objective, but a genuine and profound formation of the students. Teaching methods, consequently, should be revised. This applies to lectures, discussions and seminars and involves encouraging the students themselves to study, whether privately or in small groups. Great care should be taken to achieve an overall training which is coherent and solid, avoiding over-multiplication of subjects and lectures and omitting problems which have little importance today or which should be left to higher academic studies.

18. It is the bishops' responsibility to send young men of suitable character, virtue and ability to special institutes, faculties or universities, so that the various needs of the apostolate may be met by priests trained to a higher scientific standard in the sacred sciences and in other appropriate subjects. But the spiritual and pastoral training of these young men, especially if they have not yet been raised to the priesthood, should by no means be neglected.

VI. Attention to Strictly Pastoral Training

19. The pastoral preoccupation which should characterize every feature of the students' training[41] also requires that they should be carefully instructed in all matters which are especially relevant in the sacred ministry. These are, principally, catechetics, preaching, liturgical worship and the administration of the sacraments, works of charity, their duty to contact those in error and the unbelievers, and other pastoral duties. They should receive precise instruction in the art of directing souls. They will thus be able, first of all, to form all the members of the Church in a Christian life which is fully conscious and apostolic. They will also instill in them a sense of the obligation of fulfilling the duties of their state. With equal solicitude they should learn how to help religious men and women to persevere in the grace of their vocation and to make progress, according to the spirit of their respective institutes.[42]

In general those aptitudes should be cultivated in the students which are most conducive to dialogue amongst men. They include the willingness to listen to others and the capacity to open their hearts in a spirit of charity to the various needs of their fellow men.[43]

20. They should be taught to use correctly the aids provided by pedagogy, psychology and sociology,[44] in keeping with the regulations of ecclesiastical authority. They should also be carefully taught how to inspire and encourage apostolic action among the laity,[45] and to promote various and more effective forms of apostolate; and they should be filled with that truly Catholic spirit which habitually looks beyond the boundaries of diocese, country or rite, to meet the needs of the whole Church, being prepared in spirit to preach the Gospel everywhere.[46]

21. Students must learn the art of exercising the apostolate not only in theory but in practice and should be able to act on their own initiative and in cooperation with others. To this end, they should be initiated to pastoral work as a part of their course of studies, and also in holiday time, in suitable undertakings. These enterprises should be carried out methodically and under the direction of experts in pastoral work, according to the prudent judgment of the bishops, taking into account the age of the students and local conditions, and always keeping in mind the outstanding power of supernatural helps.[47]

VII. Later Studies

22. Since priestly training, especially in view of the circumstances of modern society, should be continued and perfected after the completion of the seminary course,[48] it will be the task of episcopal conferences in each country to provide the appropriate means for its continuation. Examples of such means are: pastoral institutes cooperating with certain parishes selected for the purpose, the holding of meetings at stated times, and suitable projects by which the junior clergy will be gradually introduced to priestly life and apostolic activity in their spiritual, intellectual and pastoral aspects, with opportunities for constant renewal and progress.

Conclusion

The Fathers of the Council, continuing the work begun by the Council of Trent, confidently entrust to superiors and professors in seminaries the duty of training Christ's future priests in the spirit of that renewal promoted by the Council itself. At the same time, they most strongly exhort those who are preparing for the sacred ministry to develop a keen awareness that the hopes of the Church and the salvation of souls are being committed to them, and urge them by their joyful acceptance of the regulations in this Decree to bring forth most abundant and lasting fruit.

What has been set down in this Decree has been accepted by the Fathers of the Sacred Council in its entirety and in all its parts. And, together with the Venerable Council Fathers, we by the apostolic power granted to us by Christ, approve, decree and establish it, and we order that what has been established in synod be promulgated, for the glory of God.

Given at Rome, at St. Peter's, 28 October 1965.

I, Paul, Bishop of the Catholic Church
(The signatures of the Fathers then follow.)

Notes

a) This translation has been done by Fathers B. Hayes, S.M., S. Fagan, S.M., and Austin Flannery, O.P.

1. It is clear from the words by which our divine Lord appointed the apostles, with their successors and fellow workers, to be the preachers of the Gospel, the leaders of the new chosen people and the dispensers of the mysteries of God, that according to the will of Christ himself the progress of the whole People of God depends in the highest degree on the ministry of priests. This is supported by the statements of the Fathers and saints and by a whole series of papal documents. Cf. especially:

St. Pius X, Exhortation to the Clergy *Haerent animo,* 4 August 1908: St. Pii X Acta IV, 237-264.

Pius XI, Encycl. Letter *Ad Catholici Sacerdotii,* 20 December 1935: *AAS* 28 (1936), especially 37-52.

Pius XII, Apostolic Exhoration *Menti Nostrae,* 23 September 1950: *AAS* 42 (1950) 657-702.

John XXIII, Encycl. Letter *Sacerdotii Nostri primordia,* 1 August 1959: *AAS* 51 (1959) 545-579.

Paul VI, Apostolic Letter *Summi Dei Verbum,* 4 November 1963: *AAS* 55 (1963) 979-995.

2. The whole course of priestly training, i.e. the organization of the seminary, spiritual formation, course of studies, the common life and rule of the students, and pastoral practice, should be adapted to local conditions. The general principles of this adaptation should be decided by episcopal conferences for the diocesan clergy and in a similar manner by the competent superiors for religious (cf. the General Statutes attached to the Apostolic Constitution *Sedes Sepientiae,* art. 19).

3. Almost everywhere one of the chief anxieties of the Church today is the dearth of vocations.

Cf. Pius XII, Apostolic Exhortation *Menti Nostrae:* " . . . both in Catholic countries and in mission territories, the number of priests is insufficient to cope with the increasing demands" (*AAS* 42 [1950] 682).

John XXIII: "The problem of ecclesiastical and religious vocations is a daily preoccupation with the Pope. . . . Vocations are the object of his prayer, the ardent longing of his soul" (from the Allocution to the First International Congress on Religious Vocations, 16 December 1961: *L'Osservatore Romano,* 17 December 1961).

4. Pius XII, Apost. Const. *Sedes Sapientiae,* 31 May 1956: *AAS* 48 (1956) 357. Paul VI, Apost. Letter *Summi Dei Verbum,* 4 November 1963: *AAS* 55 (1963) 984 ff.

b) This could also be rendered "fervent prayer" *(instans oratio).* Several translators have given that rendering.

5. Cf. especially: Pius XII, Motu proprio *Cum nobis,* on the establishment of the Pontifical Work for priestly vocations, 4 November 1941: *AAS* 33 (1941) 479; with the attached statutes and rules promulgated by the Sacred Congregation for Seminaries and Universities, 8 September 1943. The Motu proprio *Cum supremae,* on the Pontifical Work for religious vocations, 11 February 1955; *AAS* 47 (1955) 266; with the attached statutes and rules promulgated by the Sacred Congregation for Religious *(ibid.,* 298-301); Vatican Council II, Decree on the Renewal of Religious Life, n. 24; Decree on the Pastoral Function of Bishops in the Church, n. 15.

6. Cf. Pius XII, Apostolic Exhortation *Menti Nostrae,* 23 September 1950: *AAS* 42 (1950) 685.

7. Cf. Vatican Council II, Dogmatic Constitution *De Ecclesia, n.* 28: AAS 57 (1965) 34.

8. Cf. Pius XI, Encycl. Letter *Ad Catholici Sacerdotii,* 20 December 1935: *AAS* 28 (1936) 37: "In the first place let careful choice be made of superiors and professors. . . . Give these sacred colleges priests of the greatest virtue, and do not hesitate to withdraw them from tasks which seem indeed to be of greater importance, but which cannot be compared with this supremely important matter, the place of which nothing else can supply." This principle of choosing the best men for the seminaries is again insisted on by Pius XII in his Apostolic Letter to the hierarchy of Brazil, 23 April 1947, *Discorsi e Radiomessaggi* IX, 579-580.

9. With regard to this general duty of priests to give their support to seminaries, see Paul VI, Apostolic Letter *Summi Dei Verbum,* 4 November 1963: *AAS* 53 (1963) 984.

10. Cf. Pius XII, Apost. Exhortation *Menti Nostrae,* 23 September 1950. *AAS* 42 (1950) 684; cf. also the Sacred Congregation for the Sacraments, circular letter *Magna equidem* to Bishops, 27 December 1935, n. 10. For religious cf. the General Statutes attached to the Apostolic Constitution *Sedes Sapientiae,* 31 May 1956, art. 33. Paul VI, Apostolic Letter *Summi Dei Verbum,* 4 November 1963: *AAS* 55 (1963) 987 f.

11. Cf. Pius XI, Encycl. Letter *Ad Catholici Sacerdotii,* 20 December 1935: *AAS* 28 (1936) 41.

12. It is decreed that in drawing up the statutes of regional or national seminaries, all bishops concerned will take part, setting aside canon 1357, par. 4, of the Code of Canon Law.

13. Cf. Pius XII, Apost. Exhortation *Menti Nostrae,* 23 September 1950: *AAS* 42 (1950) 674; Sacred Congregation of Seminaries and Universities, *La Formazione spirituale del candidato al sacerdozio,* Vatican City, 1965.

14. Cf. St. Pius X, Exhortation to the Catholic clergy, *Haerent animo,* 4 August 1908: *St. Pii X Acta,* IV, 242-244; Pius XII, Apost. Exhort, *Menti Nostrae,* 23 September 1950: *AAS* 42 (1950) 659-661; John

XXIII, Encycl. Letter *Sacerdotii Nostri primordia*. 1 August 1959: *AAS* 51 (1959) 550 f.

15. Cf. Pius XII, Encycl. Letter *Mediator Dei*, 20 November 1947: *AAS* 39 (1947) 547 ff. and 572 f.; John XXIII, Apostolic Exhortation *Sacrae Laudis*, 6, January 1962: *AAS* 54 (1962) 69; Vatican Council II, Const. *De Sacra Liturgia*, art. 16 and 17: *AAS* 56 (1964) 104 f.; Sacred Congregation of Rites, *Instructio ad exsecutionem Constitutionis de Sacra Liturgia recte ordinandam*, 26 September 1964, nn 14-17: *AAS* 56 (1964) 880 f.

16. Cf. John XXIII, Encycl. Letter *Sacerdotii Nostri primordia*: *AAS* 51 (1959) 559 f.

17. Cf. Vatican Council II, Dogmatic Constitution *De Ecclesia*, n. 28: *AAS* 57 (1965) 35 f.

18. St. Augustine, *In Ioannem tract*. 32, 8: *PL* 35, 1646.

19. Cf. Pius XII, Apostolic Exhortation *Menti Nostrae*: *AAS* 42 (1950) 626 f., 685, 690; John XXIII, Encycl. Letter *Sacredotii Nostri primordia*: *AAS* 51 (1959) 551-553, 556 f.; Paul VI, Encycl. Letter *Ecclesiam suam*, 6 August 1964: *AAS* 56 (1964) 634 f.; Vatican Council II, Dogmatic Constitution *De Ecclesia*, especially n. 8: *AAS* 57 (1965) 12.

20. Cf. Pius XII, Encycl. Letter *Sacra Virginitas*, 25 March 1954: *AAS* 46 (1954) 165 ff.

21. Cf. St. Cyprian, *De habitu virginum*, 22: *PL* 4, 475; St. Ambrose, *De virginibus*, I, 8, 52: *PL* 16, 202 f.

22. Cf. Pius XII, Apostolic Exhortation *Menti Nostrae*: *AAS* 42 (1950) 663.

23. Cf. Pius XII, Encycl. Letter *Sacra Virginitas*, *loc. cit.*, 170-174.

24. Cf. Pius XII, Apostolic Exhortation *Menti Nostrae*, *loc. cit.*, 664 and 690 f.

c) The Latin of the phrase is: '*Alumni propriam indolem recte componere assuescant.*' Translators seem divided as to what exactly it means. Some take it, as we have done, to refer to self-control — thus, the translation published in French by Editions du Cerf: '*Que les seminaristes prennent l'habitude de dominer leur tempérament.*' Others, however, take it to refer to the development of their abilities by the students — thus, the translation edited by Father Walter M. Abbott, S.J. *(The Documents of Vatican II):* 'They should be practised in an intelligent organization of their proper talents' and that published by the English Catholic Truth Society: 'The students should know how to make the most of their own abilities,' and the Italian translation published by the *L'Osservatore Romano:* '*Gli alunni si abituino a perfezionare come si deve la propria indole.*

25. Cf. Paul VI, Apostolic Letter *Summi Dei Verbum*, 4 November 1963: *AAS* 55 (1963) 991.

26. Cf. Pius XII, Apostolic Exhortation *Menti Nostrae, loc. cit.*, 686.

27. Cf. Paul VI, Apostolic Letter *Summi Dei Verbum, loc. cit.*, 993.

28. Cf. Vatican Council II, Dogmatic Constitution *De Ecclesia*, nn. 7 and 28: *AAS* 57 (1965) 9-11, 33 f.

29. Cf. Pius XII, Encycl. Letter *Humani Generis*, 12 August 1950: *AAS* 42 (1950) 571-575.

30. Cf. Paul VI, Encycl. Letter *Ecclesiam suam*, 6 August 1964: *AAS* 56 (1964) 637 ff.

31. Cf. Pius XII, Encycl. Letter *Humani Generis: AAS* 42 (1950) 567-569; Allocution *Si diligis*, 31 May 1954: *AAS* 46 (1954) 314 f.; Paul VI, Allocution in the Pontifical Gregorian University, 12 March 1964: *AAS* 56 (1964) 364 f.; Vatican Council II, Dogmatic Constitution *De Ecclesia*, n. 25: *AAS* 57 (1965) 29-31.

32. Cf. St. Bonaventure, *Itinerarium mentis in Deum*, Prol., n. 4: "Let no one think he will find sufficiency in a reading which lacks unction, an enquiry which lacks devotion, a search which arouses no wonder, a survey without enthusiasm, industry without piety, knowledge without love, intelligence without humility, application without grace, contemplation without wisdom inspired by God" (St. Bonaventure, *Opera Omnia*, V, Quaracchi 1891, 296).

33. Cf. Leo XIII, Encycl. *Providentissimus Deus*, 18 November 1893: *ASS* 26 (1893-94) 283.

34. Cf. Pontifical Biblical Commission, *Instructio de Sacra Scriptura recte docenda*, 13 May 1950: *AAS* 42 (1950) 502.

35. Cf. Pius XII, Encycl. Letter *Humani Generis*, 12 August 1950: *AAS* 42 (1950) 568 f.: "The sacred sciences are being constantly rejuvenated by the study of their sacred sources, while on the other hand that speculation which neglects the deeper examination of the sacred deposit becomes sterile, as we know from experience."

36. Cf. Pius XII, Address to Seminarians, 24 June 1939: *AAS* 31 (1939) 247: "Emulation in seeking and propagating the truth is not suppressed, but is rather stimulated and given its true direction by commending the teaching of St. Thomas." Paul VI, Address in Gregorian University, 12 March 1964: *AAS* 56 (1964) 365: "Let (teachers) listen with respect to the Doctors of the Church, among whom St. Thomas Aquinas holds the principal place. For so great is the power of the angelic Doctor's genius, so sincere his love of truth, and so great his wisdom in investigating the deepest truths, in illustrating them, and linking them together with a most fitting bond of unity, that his teaching is a most efficacious instrument not only for safeguarding the foundations of the faith, but also in gaining the fruits of healthy progress with profit and security." Cf. also his Allocution to the Sixth International Thomistic Congress, 10 September 1965.

37. Cf. Vatican Council II, Const. *De Sacra Liturgia*, nn. 7 and 16: *AAS* 56 (1964) 100 f. and 104 f.

38. Cf. Paul VI, Encycl. Letter *Ecclesiam suam*, 6 August 1964: *AAS* 56 (1964) 640 f.

39. Vatican Council II, Const. *De Sacra Liturgia*, nn. 10, 14, 15, 16; Sacred Congregation of Rites, *Instructio ad exsecutionem Constitutionis de Sacra Liturgia recte ordinandam*, 26 September 1964, nn. 11 and 12: *AAS* 56 (1964) 879 f.

40. Cf. Vatican Council II, Decree *De Oecumenismo*, nn. 1, 9, 10: *AAS* 57 (1965) 90 and 98 f.

41. The perfect ideal of the pastor can be seen in the recent documents of the popes dealing specifically with the life, qualities and training of priests, especially:

St. Pius X, Exhortation to the Clergy *Haerent animo,* St. Pii X Acta, IV, 237 ff.;

Pius XI, Encycl. Letter *Ad Catholici Sacerdotii: AAS* 28 (1936) 5 ff.;

Pius XII, Apostolic Exhortation *Menti Nostrae: AAS* 42 (1950) 657 ff.;

John XXIII, Encyl. Letter *Sacerdotii Nostri primordia: AAS* 51 (1959) 545 ff.;

Paul VI, Apostolic Letter *Summi Dei Verbum: AAS* 55 (1963) 979 ff.

Much information about pastoral training is also given in the encyclicals *Mystici Corporis* (1943); *Mediator Dei* (1947); *Evangelii Praecones* (1951); *Sacra Virginitas* (1954); *Musicae Sacrae Disciplina* (1955); *Princeps Pastorum* (1959), and in the Apostolic Constitution *Sedes Sapientiae* (1956) for religious.

Pius XII, John XXIII and Paul VI have often thrown light on the ideal of the good shepherd in their allocutions to seminarians and priests.

42. As regards the importance of that state which is set up by the profession of the evangelical counsels, see the Dogmatic Constitution *De Ecclesia* of the Second Vatican Council, chapter VI: *AAS* 57 (1965) 49-55; Decree on the Renewal of Religious Life.

43. Cf. Paul VI, Encycl. Letter *Ecclesiam suam: AAS* 56 (1964), *passim,* especially 635 f. and 640 ff.

44. Cf. especially John XXIII, Encyl. Letter *Mater et Magistra,* 15 May 1961: *AAS* 53 (1961) 401 ff.

45. Cf. especially Vatican Council II, Dogmatic Const. *De Ecclesia,* n. 33: *AAS* 57 (1965) 39.

46. Cf. Vatican Council II, Dogmatic Const. *De Ecclesia,* n. 17: *AAS* 57 (1965) 20 f.

47. Very many papal documents sound a warning against the danger of neglecting the supernatural goal in pastoral activity, and of minimizing the value of supernatural means, at least in practice; see especially the documents recommended in note 41.

48. More recent documents of the Holy See urge that special attention be paid to newly ordained priests. The following are specially recommended:

Pius XII, Motu Proprio *Quandoquidem,* 2 April 1949: *AAS* 41 (1949) 165-167; Apostolic Exhortation *Menti Nostrae,* 23 September 1950: *AAS* 42 (1950); Apostolic Constitution (for religious) *Sedes Sapientiae,* 31 May 1956, and the General Statutes attached to it; Address to the priests of the *"Convictus Barcinonensis,"* 14 June 1957, *Discorsi e Radiomessaggi,* XIX, 271-273.

Paul VI, address to the priests of the Gian Matteo Giberti Institute, of the diocese of Verona, 11 March 1964.

Basic Norms for Priestly Formation

Ratio Fundamentalis
Institutionis Sacerdotalis

Sacred Congregation for
Catholic Education
Rome 1985

Edition prepared after
the promulgation of the new *Code of Canon Law*

Basic Norms for
Priestly Formation

Preface

Fifteen years have passed since "The Basic Norms for Priestly Formation" was successfully written and published by the Congregation for Catholic Education, with the cooperation of the Episcopal Conferences, in order to stimulate fittingly the work of conciliar renewal and to place it in the right light through norms and examples of a right plan of acting.

Indeed, the First Synod of Bishops in 1967 had recommended that it be prepared, earnestly desiring that an apt instrument be provided to the Episcopal Conferences for the more convenient completion for their national "Programs of Priestly Formation," according to the norm of the Decree *Optatam totius,* n.1. It was to have appropriate standards for preserving the unity of universal ecclesiastical discipline in this area, and for permitting at the same time healthy variety to the extent that this was required by the different pastoral conditions of various places. For this reason such a document contained only the general themes of ecclesiastical pedagogy, from which a sufficiently clear and genuine mind of the Second Vatican Council shone forth, and the limits within which the life of seminaries could safely progress.

The true usefulness of that very provident enterprise has more than adequately been noted in these last years in such a way that it needs no special mention. For by its help, the national "Programs" are now also more easily worked out, revised, and explained whenever doubts have arisen about the meaning of individual norms. It clearly appears, therefore, that the document not only did not inhibit the work and initiative of each country, but helped and stimulated it as much as possible.

Since, nevertheless, in the new Code of Canon Law, promulgated on January 25, 1983, all the pedagogical and disciplinary material dealing with seminaries and priestly formation was reordered *"ex integro,"* the "Basic Norms," treating the same material, has been deprived of its juridical value. In some way Bishops and Educators have been found bereft of a very good working document which they previously enjoyed in the fulfillment of their tasks.

Moreover, as it was previously noted, very many national "Programs of Priestly Formation" were deeply rooted in the "Basic Norms" (often quoting verbatim various of its paragraphs), and ecclesiastical Superiors themselves readily refer to the same document whenever they must consider or resolve questions not explicitly contained in the new Code.

In consideration of this, the Congregation for Catholic Education has judged it opportune to revise the aforesaid "Basic Norms for Priestly Formation" after the promulgation of the new Code of Canon Law, and to include in it some, indeed, very few emendations, as new circumstances require. As is apparent at the first glance, the new adjustments pertain to footnotes, abundantly enriched in various places, rather than to the text itself of the document which is substantially the same as it was when produced along with the help of the Episcopal Conferences.

With the appropriate approval conferred by the Supreme Pontiff John Paul II, happily reigning, the present edition of the "Basic Norms" is offered to Institutions of priestly formation with the sincere desire that they, relying on its clear and certain norms, may continue successfully to fulfill their very prudent mission for the greater good of souls and of the entire Holy Church.

Given at Rome, from the Halls of the Congregation, on March 19, 1985, the Solemnity of Saint Joseph, Spouse of the Blessed Virgin Mary.

Introduction

By the decree *De institutione sacerdotali* (On Training for the Priesthood), the Second Vatican Council provided the principal and more general rules for today's efforts towards seminary reform, to ensure that these efforts might go forward safely, and produce a salutary increase of piety, learning and pastoral zeal in candidates for the priesthood. Certain further determinations are needed in order that the reforms may be adapted in the best possible way to the special needs of individual nations, and for the preservation of that unity and that image of the Catholic priesthood which it demands of its very nature, and on which the Council earnestly insisted.[1] With this twofold need in view, the Basic Scheme for Priestly Training proposed here has been worked out by the Sacred Congregation for Catholic Education and the delegates of the Episcopal Conferences, in common effort and consultation. Their constant care and sincere prayer, too, was to express in this document the genuine spirit and pastoral purpose of the Second Vatican Council; also that these, expressed in more clearly defined form, might be more effective towards fitting the work of education in Seminaries to the new needs of our times.

1. In what sense the Second Vatican Council confirms the validity of seminary training.

In the Second Vatican Council, the Church decreed that its experience of Seminaries, tried out for many centuries, was to be maintained as valid, affirming that *Seminaries were necessary*[2] as institutions set up for the formation of priests, and provided with these excellent educational features which combined with others can effectively promote the integral formation of future priests.[3] However, while confirming afresh this well-tried path to the priesthood, it by no means wished to pass over in silence the manifold and varied needs arising, in course of time, from out-dated means or changed conditions; it allowed for, or even prescribed not a few changes to increase the power and pedagogical efficacy of this useful institution.

Although the Council differentiated between Seminaries which are called *Major* and those called *Minor,* or Junior, it determined certain principles valid for both."[4] Before the particular problems of each are brought out, however, it is first necessary to give careful consideration to what is in a way presupposed in all that is to be said below: the Seminary, as a community of young men,[5] derives its primary force and fitness to train future priests from its own circumstances and way of life; here the young men live; its air, one may say, they breathe; they themselves have a part in determining and reforming its character. It is a question of various concurrent factors, both internal and external; of the structure of the whole community, and of its spirit, which can check or promote improvement, whose influence is, in varying degrees, apparent in everything.[6]

In this situation, then, the primary duty of the Superiors is to obtain the collaboration of all concerned, in order to produce and perfect this spiritual climate. It should be such as to ensure that whoever enters the Seminary may find there the aids necessary for developing his own vocation and carrying out God's will wholly and entirely.[7] The material setting should not be reckoned as of little importance towards this purpose: the sober and suitable arrangement, that is, of site, buildings, furniture and so on, adequate for the life the young men are leading.

2. The position of modern youth as regards education.

In any sound reform of Seminaries, moreover, present-day circumstances and their special educational needs must certainly be considered.[8] The young men who are called by Divine Providence to exercise the priestly office among men of our time *bring special dispositions* that match the mind and attitudes of modern men. So, as their outlook manifests itself at various times, one observes in them an ardent longing for sincerity and truth; they are noticeably very prone to take up everything new and out-of-the ordinary; they admire the world with its scientific and technical progress; we see them wanting to work their way more deeply into the world to serve it, with a sense of "solidarity" particularly with the poorer classes and the oppressed, and a spirit of community. But besides all this they have clearly a distrust for everything old and traditionally accepted; they cannot make up their minds, and are inconsistent in putting plans into effect; they show a lack of docility—very necessary for spiritual progress—with a disposition difficult and critical towards authority and the various institutions of civil and ecclesiastical society, etc. In his pedagogical work, the educator not only does not neglect these special qualities, but endeavours to understand them, and to turn them, as far as he can, to his purpose of formation, with the cooperation of the future priests themselves: he makes a clear distinction always between what is more useful for better priestly formation and what is less useful, not useful at all, or an actual obstacle. All things considered, it is impossible to ignore the fact that in these last years particularly there are problems, originating from youth or from modern society, which exercise a powerful influence on the whole work of formation, and therefore demand greater efforts from educators.[9]

Two features of modern youth need particular attention: their keener sense of their own dignity as persons and their keener feeling for the things and the men of this world, whether for its undoubted goods or its particular spiritual situation, which displays more perceptibly as the days go by the effects of a neglect of religion.[10] These two factors combine with others in their hearts and create a kind of common mentality, one which requires in Seminaries, besides other remedial measures, a greater esteem for the person and the removal of anything whose reason is an unjustified "convention"; everything must be done in accordance with truth and charity; genuine dialogue must be established among all parties; more numerous contacts with the world must be encouraged, to meet the just needs of right formation; finally, everything that is prescribed or demanded should show the reason on which it is based and should be carried out in freedom.[11]

If these things require the revision of certain elements of training accepted from past practice, they also demand a genuine pedagogical effort, one relying on mutual trust and understanding, with a right notion of freedom, and particularly the knowledge of how to distinguish the means and the ends of education. For if useful dialogue and fruitful enquiry about means can be instituted in collaboration with the students, at all times and from the beginning there should be kept well in view the purpose of the Seminary and of all education, as the basis of all considerations, to which any discussion of this kind must be referred. The more clearly the sublime purpose of their formation is put before the young men, the more willingly will they join forces to seek the means best fitted to attain it. Guided by their resolve to promote the common good, and by the will of God, they will arrive at a true sense of freedom and authority.[12]

3. *The idea of the Catholic priesthood as the proper end of priestly education.*

The proper end of priestly education is based on the idea of Catholic priesthood as it arises from divine revelation, clarified by the constant tradition and magisterium of the Church. This teaching, which must be the formative element in every Scheme of Priestly Training, infusing therein its special force and significance, can be taken from the very words of the Second Vatican Council.

All priestly power and ministry in the Catholic Church derives its origin from the unique and eternal priesthood of Christ, who was sanctified by the Father and sent into the world (cf. *Jn* 10, 36), and made his apostles in the first place, and their successors, the bishops, sharers in the same priesthood. In different ways the various members of the Church share in that one same priesthood of Christ: the general, or common priesthood of the faithful constitutes a certain simple degree of this sharing, the faithful who through baptism and the anointing of the Holy Spirit "receive consecration as a spiritual house, a holy priesthood. It is their task, in every employment, to offer the spiritual sacrifices of a Christian man".[13] Priests share in the priesthood of Christ in a different way: they "do not possess the high dignity of the Pontificate; they are dependent on bishops for the exercise of their power. They are nevertheless united to them in priestly honour. In virtue of the sacrament of order, they are consecrated in the likeness of Christ, high and eternal priest (cf. *Heb* 5, 10; 7, 24; 9, 11-28) as genuine priests of the New Testament, for the work of preaching the gospel, tending the faithful, and celebrating divine worship".[14] For this reason, therefore, the *ministerial priesthood* of priests surpasses the general priesthood of the faithful, since through it some in the Body of the Church are assimilated to Christ the Head, and are promoted" to serve Christ, their Master, Priest and King, and to share his ministry. Thus the Church on earth is constantly built up into the People of God, the Body of Christ and Temple of the Holy Spirit".[15]

"There is an essential difference between the faithful's common priesthood and the priesthood of the ministry or the hierarchy, and not just a difference of degree. Nevertheless, there is an ordered relation between them: one and the other has its special way of sharing the single priesthood of Christ".[16]

When raised to the priesthood, priests enter into manifold *relationships* with their own Bishop, with all other priests, and with the people of God.[17] For "since all priests share one and the same priesthood and ministry of Christ with the Bishops, the very unity of their ordination and function demands their communion in the hierarchy with the Order of Bishops ... Bishops, therefore, must regard their priests as indispensable helpers and advisers in the ministry and office of teaching, sanctifying and nourishing the people of God".[18] Together with their Bishop "they make a single priesthood, though there is a difference in the duties by which it is carried into effect. They render the Bishop present, in a way, in individual local communities. Their association with him is marked by confidence and generosity. To the best of their ability they shoulder his tasks and anxieties and make the exercise of them their daily care".[19]

This true sharing in one and the same diocesan priesthood creates many close ties among the priests themselves: "priests in virtue of their ordination are established in the priestly Order and are intimately united in sacramental brotherhood"[20] "which should be spontaneously and cheerfully demonstrated in mutual help, spiritual and material alike, pastoral and personal; shown too in reunions and a fellowship of life, work and charity";[21] "in this way priests display that unity by which Christ desired his own to be made perfect in one, in order that the world might know that the Son was sent by the Father".[22]

Every priest, however, is taken from among the people of God in order to be appointed on behalf of the same *people*. Though by the sacrament of order they exercise the office of father and teacher, "they too, like the faithful, are our Lord's disciples, and are called by God's grace to share his kingdom. For they are brothers among brothers with all who have been reborn in the font of baptism. They are likewise members of the one same Body of Christ which all Christians are called to build up".[23] Therefore "they must, like fathers in Christ, take care of the faithful, by baptism and instruction (cf. *1 Cor* 4, 15; *1 Pet* 2, 23). Being examples to the flock (*1 Pet* 5, 3), they must take charge of their local community and serve it in such a way that it may deserve to be given the title of the Church of God (cf. *1 Cor* 1, 2; *2 Cor* 1, 1) which is the title that distinguishes the one People of God in its entirety. They must be mindful of their obligation truly *to show the face of the priest's and pastor's ministry* to believers and care; to bear witness to all of truth and life; as good shepherds, to search out even those (cf. *Lk* 15, 4-7) who after baptism in the Catholic Church have fallen away from sacramental practice, or worse still, from belief",[24] that through their tireless work" the Church as the universal sacrament of salvation"[25] may shine out before all men and become the sign of God's presence in the world.[26] "Together with the Religious and their faithful, they should show by their lives and utterance that the Church, merely by its presence here with all that it has to offer, is an inexhaustible source of those virtues which the world needs today".[27] "A priest, however, has a duty not only to his own flock but to the whole community, to which he must strive to give a truly Christian character"[28] which should be penetrated with a genuine missionary spirit and one of Catholic universality.

The *priestly ministry* as expounded by the Second Vatican Council is chiefly *put into practice in the ministry of the word and the word and the work of sanctification.* "Since nobody can be saved without faith, the first duty of priests as fellow workers with the Bishops is to preach the Gospel to all men",[29] carrying out our Lord's command: *Go into the whole world and preach the Gospel to every creature* (*Mk* 16, 16). This they fulfil when "being on good terms with people, they turn them to God; or by preaching openly they proclaim the mystery of Christ to unbelievers; or give Christian instruction or explain the Church's teaching, or endeavour to discuss contemporary problems in the light of Christ's word".[30]

The aim of the ministry of the word is to bring men to faith and the sacrament of salvation, and it attains its peak in the celebration of the Eucharist: "their mightiest exercise of their sacred office is at the eucharistic worship or assembly. There, acting in the person of Christ, they make the proclamation of his mystery; they unite the aspirations of the faithful with the sacrifice of their head; in the sacrifice of the Mass, until the coming of the Lord (cf. *1 Cor* 11, 26), they present and apply the sole sacrifice of the New Testament, the single offering Christ makes of himself as an unblemished victim to the father (cf. *Heb* 9, 11-28). The ministration of reconciliation and relief is their high function on behalf of penitent or sick faithful. They convey the needs of the faithful and their prayers to God the Father (cf. *Heb* 5, 1-3)".[31] Thus the office of preaching has as its special characteristic that it must be completed by the work of sanctification, by which the priest, acting in the person of Christ, cooperates in building up the Church.

The *priest presides* over the people of God when they are gathered together, through the preaching of the Gospel, through the sacraments, and above all through the celebration of the Eucharist. He should, therefore, be such a man as can likewise be recognized by everyone as acting in the place of Christ the Head; for "priests with the authority they have been given carry on the work of Christ their Leader and Shepherd. In the name of the Bishop they gather the family of God together into one united brotherhood. In union with the Holy Spirit they lead them through Christ to God the Father. To enable them to do this, or any other priestly work, priests receive spiritual strength".[32] By this power the priestly or hierarchic ministry differs from the general priesthood of the faithful not only in degree but essentially.[33] For though the faithful can and must have some part in the task of spreading the Gospel and in pastoral duties,[34] only the man who has received the sacred order of priesthood can fully exercise the sacramental ministry, above all that of the Eucharist, from which the other ministries derive, and to which they are directed. And so, *set apart for the Gospel of God (Rom* 1, 1) he should not hesitate to dedicate his whole life to the service of God and man, indeed to lay down his life for his sheep.[35]

4. The activity and life of the priest in present-day conditions.

The *priestly office,* as essentially defined by the Church, is today carried out *in an entirely new situation,* which comes to light as a result of mankind's new needs, and from the nature of modern civilization.[36]

The main factors today determining mankind's needs arise from the heightened regard for the human person, or the progressive alteration of the religious sense. If not always openly and in fact, at least virtually the dignity of every man is acknowledged, his right to progress, to manifest his mind freely, to have a part in his own development and in that of the material world. As man's dominion in the world grows more complete, in conjunction with great changes in society, less room is granted to traditionally accepted forms of Christian life. While, in the general upheaval, Christian groups display a more personal form of religious life, which shows itself in special reverence for the word of God and the sacred Liturgy, and in the acquisition of a more mature conscience, the number is daily increasing, too, of those who are partly or wholly losing their due familiarity with the Church, and leaning towards a natural sort of religion and ethic. Indeed, all too often they go to such lengths that atheism—once restricted rather to philosophers—is becoming ever more common, little by little affecting the minds of great numbers of people. These various features of modern civilization must be constantly borne in mind, since the life and activity of the priest, and his preparation for his task, must have reference to them.[37]

Through the various ways of social communication, young men who today enter a Seminary are closely attached to that kind of society, and their outlook is affected by problems concerning religion, especially priestly activity and life. They often approach theological studies with a sincere will to serve God and men in the priestly life, without, however, what was formerly the normal thing, a confident and clear grasp of the benefits of religion, of which they must at sometime become the heralds and administrators. These things from time to time cause grave difficulties to arise in the Seminary, yet they form the true and principal object of education, to which Superiors must give special care and attention. In their method of formation they should first of all try, not so much to remove these various obstacles by some sudden, radical intervention, but rather step by step to purify minds and intentions. In particular they should employ prudent judgement and moderation, to ensure that the sound element in the young men's aims may steadily grow and gain strength; thus their priestly life and work may in future bear richer fruit.

The generous and keen spirit of the young men will help towards this end, and their zeal to be of use to human society, even at times also the doubts they must overcome and their critical examination of the faith; since the people to whom they will be sent as priests, whose religious outlook is full of doubt and uncertainty, will not accept a priest's teaching authority easily and without reaction; nor are they going to believe and hold uncritically and without prejudice the doctrine which the priest tries, *ex officio,* to teach them.

The young men, then, must be so trained that this particular situation, which they at present experience with the whole Church, may not only not lead them into any danger of spiritual collapse, but in fact stimulate them, with firm hope and faith in God, to try new ways and means of easier communication with the men of today. For the world "now entrusted to the pastors of the Church to cherish and serve, was so loved by God that for its sake he gave his only-begotten Son (cf. *Jn* 3, 16). Indeed this world, held down by many sins, does in fact possess abundant possibilities and could provide the living stones (cf. *1 Pet* 2, 5) with which to build a dwelling place for God in the Spirit (cf. *Eph* 2, 22). The same Holy Spirit, while urging on the Church to open up new approaches to the world of today, inspires and fosters timely adaptations for the priestly ministry".[38]

This up-to-date adjusting of priestly activity and life is at present causing anxious concern in many minds, and raising all kinds of questions every-where. Hence, too, much discussion and writing, and many proposals about the priest himself, his nature, his proper place in society, his style of life, his better preparation for more effective fulfillment of his task.[39] The Seminary, obviously, must never be unaware of these things nor ever neglect them; but on the other hand it must carefully guard and preserve what the priesthood possesses of certain and lasting good. The task of this *Ratio Fundamentalis* will be to safeguard this acquired good; the Episcopal Conferences, with full freedom, will see to the adaptation to the needs of time and place of other contingent elements.

I
General Rules[40]

1. The Scheme for Priestly Training drawn up by an Episcopal Conference in accordance with no. 1 of the Decree *Optatam totius* and canon 242, par. 1 of the *Code of Canon Law*, is approved by the Sacred Congregation for Catholic Education first of all "ad experimentum", for trial.

If within the period of trial some urgent need arises to adapt the Scheme in any part to fresh circumstances, such changes are not excluded so long as the Holy See is informed in good time.

Before the period of trial is finished, the Episcopal Conference's Scheme will be revised in the light of experience by the Episcopal Commission for Seminaries,[41] with the help of experts, and will be submitted for fresh approval of the Sacred Congregation.

Such revision and approbation will afterwards be repeated at certain times, as shall seem necessary or useful to the individual Episcopal Conferences.[42]

The right and duty of drawing up a Scheme for Priestly Training in their own nation or region, and of approving special experimentation as may seem opportune, belong to the Episcopal Conference alone, and not to individual Bishops.

2. The rules of a Scheme thus worked out are to be observed in all the Seminaries for diocesan clergy, whether regional or national;[43] their particular adaptations will be determined by the competent Bishops in the Rule of Life proper to each Seminary.[44]

Training Schemes of Religious Institutes are also to be adapted to these rules, comparing like with like.[45]

Where Seminary students carry out their philosophical and theological studies in Faculties or other Institutions of Higher Studies, for what pertains to studies, reference should be made to the rules laid down by the Apostolic Constitution *Sapientia Christiana* in Art. 74, par. 2.

3. The Scheme embraces basic priestly training under its human, spiritual, intellectual and pastoral aspects: these parts must be aptly fitted together to ensure that the priest is prepared for the needs of our time.

4. It is of primary importance that all priestly training, while taking account of the document of the Holy See concerned with the formation of students, should conform to the spirit and norms of the Second Vatican Council, as they clearly appear in the Decree *Optatam totius* and in the other Constitutions and Decrees which touch on the education of clerics,[46] as well as conforming to the current norms of Canon Law.

II
The Pastoral Care of Vocations

5. Vocation to the priesthood has its setting in the wider field of Christian vocation, as rooted in the sacrament of baptism, by which the People of God "is founded by Christ for a fellowship of life, charity and truth; it is taken up by him as the instrument of salvation for all men; it is sent on a mission to the world at large as the light of the world and the salt of the earth (cf. *Mt* 5, 13-16)".[47] This vocation, aroused by the Holy Spirit, "who dispenses his gifts in variety, for the Church's advantage, according to his wealth and the requirements of the ministries (cf. *1 Cor* 12, 1-11)",[48] is aimed at the building up of the Body of Christ in which "there exists a diversity of members and functions".[49]

6. As manifestations of the unsearchable riches of Christ (cf. *Eph 3, 8*) in the Church, all vocations claim high esteem and therefore must be developed with all care and concern towards their maturity and increase. It is, then, for the whole Christian community,[50] but in a special way for priests, "as educators in the faith, themselves or through others, to train each of the faithful to follow his vocation according to the Gospel, and practice sincere and fruitful charity. They must show the faithful by the light of the Holy Spirit how to use that liberty with which Christ has made us free"[51] so that they "may reach their Christian maturity".[52]

7. Among the many vocations unceasingly aroused by the Holy Spirit in the People of God, the vocation to a state of perfection, and above all the vocation to the priesthood, has a special importance. By the latter a Christian is chosen by God[53] to share in the hierarchical Priesthood of Christ "to nourish the Church by the word and grace of God."[54] At the different stages of life this vocation shows itself in different ways: in youths, in men of more mature years, and also, as the constant experience of the Church testifies, in boys—in whom it not infrequently shows itself, like a "seed", in company with a distinct piety, an ardent love of God and neighbor, and a leaning towards the apostolate.[55]

8. From consideration of the great needs of Christ's faithful and an understanding of our Divine Saviour's invitation to all: "Pray the Lord of the harvest to send labourers into his harvest (*Mt* 9, 38; *Lk* 10, 2), it is obviously a serious duty for the whole Christian community continually and in faith to foster religious and especially priestly vocations. Therefore in every Diocese, region, or nation, a Vocations Organization should be established and built up, in accordance with the Pontifical documents on the matter. Its function is the due coordination of all that belongs to pastoral action for the fostering of vocations, neglecting no suitable means, and to promote this work with equal prudence and zeal.[56]

"This vigorous collaboration of all God's People springs up in response to the initiatives of Divine Providence, which endows with the natural qualities they need those whom God has chosen to share the hierarchic Priesthood of Christ, and assists them by his grace. At the same time, God leaves the rightful minister of the Church to designate as acceptable those candidates whose acknowledged fitness is combined with the complete freedom and honest purpose essential in those who seek so great a role. Once she has accepted them, the Church then dedicates them by the seal of the Holy Spirit for the worship of God and the service of the Church".[57]

To promote the Organization and foster vocations, Bishops should take the greatest care to make use of the combined efforts of priests, religious and lay people, especially of parents and teachers, and also of Catholic associations, on the pattern of any general, organically coordinated pastoral care.[58]

9. Everything necessary to obtain vocations from God should be encouraged, in the first place the prayer demanded by Christ himself (cf. *Mt 9, 39, Lk* 10, 2). Private prayer is called for, and prayer in common at suitable times in the liturgical year, and on solemn occasions fixed by ecclesiastical authority. This is the primary purpose of the *World Day for Vocations,* instituted by the Holy See, to be kept every year by the Church throughout the world.[59] Everything, too, should be encouraged that can rouse and open men's minds to recognize and welcome a divine vocation. The example of priests "who openly manifest true paschal joy";[60] well-organised pastoral care of youth in the dioceses; sermons and catechesis that treat of vocation; spiritual preparation such as retreats: all should be regarded as important features of this pastoral work.[61]

This activity should observe the laws of sound psychology and pedagogy, and must be aimed at men of different ages; but nowadays fresh effort is urgently needed: more men show a vocation at a more mature age (sometimes after practicing a career); special undertakings and programmes are demanded to detect, develop and form vocations.[62]

10. The fostering of vocations should be done in a generous spirit, not only for each one's diocese and nation, but also for other dioceses and other nations: the needs of the Universal Church should be remembered, and the action of God who calls individuals to different tasks: to the secular priesthood, or missionary work, or to the religious institutions. To make this end easier of attainment, single Centres are desirable in the individual dioceses, which may be expressions of the cooperation and unity existing between both clergies, diocesan and religious, in favour of all vocations.[63]

III

Minor Seminaries[64] and Other Institutions Founded for the Same Purpose

11. The specific purpose of the Minor Seminary is to help boys who seem to show the initial signs of vocation to recognize this vocation more easily and clearly, and to respond to it. In a matter demanding so much prudence and judgement, which can be dealt with only by the light and guidance of the Holy Spirit, who distributes his gifts as he wills (cf. *1 Cor* 12, 11), candidates should be led by Superiors, parents, the parish community, and others concerned, to respond faithfully to the intentions of divine Providence; to live up to their baptismal consecration ever more completely, and fulfil it; and to advance in the spirit of the apostolate; thus in the end they may be better prepared to see the sublime gift of their vocation in its real nature, and if lawful authority approves, to embrace it freely and gladly.[65]

A vocation to the priesthood, though a supernatural and entirely gratuitous gift, is necessarily based on natural endowments: if any is lacking, it is to be doubted if a vocation is really there. Hence the young students must be carefully examined as regards their families, their physical, psychological, moral and intellectual qualities, in order that sure factors for a judgement of their fitness may be had in good time.[66]

12. The Minor Seminary should be given due importance in the life of the diocese. It must be prudently open to this life and form part of it. Then it may not only attract the ready cooperation of faithful and clergy, but also—as the centre of pastoral care for vocations—exercise a beneficent and effective influence on the young students, promoting their spiritual progress. From this opportune contact with the outside world, they should learn, according to their ability, to grasp the more important problems of the Church and of human life, and to interpret them in a Christian spirit, and in this way they will make steady progress in the spirit of the Church and of her mission.[67]

Due and necessary contacts should be maintained also with their own families and contemporaries, as they need these contacts for a sound psychological, and particularly emotional development. The right sort of spiritual help should be given to their families to enable them to take ever more effective care of vocations, working in union with the Seminary.[68]

13. The young seminarians should lead a life suited to their age and development, in line with the sound rules of psychology and pedagogy. Carefully to be avoided is anything that could lessen in any way their free choice of state; and it must always be borne in mind that among them there are some who see the priesthood clearly as their goal, others who admit it as a possibility, and others who show themselves hesitant and doubtful about their vocation, yet are well gifted and do not cause all hope to disappear of their ability to reach the priesthood.[69]

All these factors demand in the Minor Seminary a lively familiar trust towards Superiors and brotherly friendship among the students, so that all may grow into one family, with the possibility of developing their own natural selves in the right way and in accordance with the plans of divine Providence.[70]

14. In his spiritual formation, every student should be helped by suitable direction, in order to develop in harmony his physical, moral, intellectual and emotional faculties; to be inspired also with an increasing sense of justice, of sincerity, and of brotherly friendship; with appreciation of truth, of just freedom, and with a sense of duty. With all the elements of his natural self developed with proper care as well,[71] he may be the more easily disposed to follow Christ our Redeemer with a generous and pure heart, and serve Him in an apostolic life.[72]

The principal and necessary factor in this spiritual formation of the student is the life of the liturgy, in which they should take part with growing appreciation as they grow in age; and likewise other devotional exercises, either of daily practice or to be fixed for specified times in the Seminary Rule. These practices should be designed for Christian youths, and they should carry them out gladly and willingly.[73]

15. The Seminary should have its own rules for the other elements of its life, too, suitably arranging the various duties of the students and their activities throughout the day and the whole year.[74]

16. The students should complete the curriculum of studies which is demanded in their own country as a preliminary to studies of university standard;[75] but so far as the programme of studies allows, they should also cultivate the studies that are necessary or useful for candidates for the priesthood. As a general rule they should endeavour to acquire a public certificate of studies, so as to be on a par with other young people, and have the possibility of taking up another way of life should they be found not to have a priestly vocation.[76]

17. These studies should be done either in the seminary's own school, or if the

Bishops judge it better, for local conditions, and it can be done prudently, in Catholic schools outside, or even in others.[77]

18. The same purpose is served by Institutions that have been established in various places, colleges, schools, etc., in which budding priestly vocations are cared for and developed alongside other students. Similar rules should be laid down for these Institutions, to provide for the solid Christian education of their pupils, and the right training needed for higher studies; to cater also for their interest in apostolic work through various associations and other aids.[78]

19. As the needs of each nation demand, there should be built and developed Institutions destined for the formation of those who are called to the priesthood at a more advanced age. With the help of the Bishops of the region or of the country, these houses for special priestly formation should be planned and equipped to correspond fully with their established purpose.[79]

Such foundations ought to have their own Rule of devotional practice, disciplines and studies: its aim, taking into account the previous training of the individual students, is to ensure them through suitable methods of teaching and training, the spiritual and scientific formation which may appear necessary as a preliminary to ecclesiastical studies.

With reference to local conditions, it will have to be decided whether the students should be set to normal Seminary curricula after completing a suitable period of school work, or placed in special philosophical and theological schools.

IV
Major Seminaries[80]

20. The Major Seminary accepts students who, after finishing Grammar School or High School studies, desire strictly priestly training. The aim of the Seminary is the more explicit and fuller development of a vocation; and, after the example of our Lord, Jesus Christ, Teacher, Priest and Pastor, to form and produce true pastors of souls for the ministry of teaching, sanctifying and ruling the people of God.[81]

21. A Major Seminary cannot be set up and kept in being without the following elements: a suitable number of students; superiors soundly prepared for their office and united in brotherly cooperation; professors sufficient in number and quality, where the institution includes a school of philosophy and theology; and suitable buildings, equipped with a library and the other aids needed for an establishment of its level and kind.[82]

Where these conditions cannot be had in the one diocese, it is necessary to set up an interdiocesan (or Regional, Central, National) Seminary.[83] As local circumstances suggest, the brotherly collaboration of diocesan with religious clergy is called for: the rights and duties of both bodies being safeguarded as they should be, by their joint forces suitable places for ecclesiastical studies may be more easily established. The students of both clergies could attend these centres while receiving spiritual and pastoral formation in their own places of residence.[84]

22. Seminary training and education have as their aim to bring the candidates, once they are made sharers in the one priesthood and ministry of Christ, into hierarchic communion with their own Bishop and the rest of their brethren in the priesthood, forming the one single *Presbyterium* of the diocese. It is therefore very desirable that right from Seminary years close links should bind students to their own Bishop and the diocesan clergy, based on mutual charity, frequent conversation, and cooperation of every kind.[85]

23. To assist the right formation of each student, depending on their numbers, it can be useful to form separate groups, in the same building, or in houses near one another to avoid loss of regular communication. However, an effective unity of régime, spiritual direction, and scientific teaching must be retained.[86]

In all cases, students should have the pedagogical benefit of experiencing the larger community.

The individual groups should have their own priest-director, one well prepared for his task. He should maintain close and constant contacts with the Seminary Rector, with the students of his own group, and with the directors of other groups: through this close collaboration the progress may be assured of everything conducive to first class training.[87]

24. The cooperation of students with Superiors should be encouraged, to obtain the best order and efficiency in the life of the Seminary and to foster the students' industry and sense of duty. This cooperation should gradually increase in extent and quality as the students grow in maturity. While they all work together, however, the different responsibility of Superiors and students should be kept clearly defined.

Mutual trust between teachers and students, therefore, is to be fostered in every way, leading to a genuine and effective dialogue, so that decisions, which by right belong to the Superiors, may be made after a fair enquiry into the common good (cf. no. 49).[88]

25. In every Seminary there must be a Rule *(disciplinae Ordinatio)* approved by the Bishop (or by the group of Bishops in the case of an interdiocesan Seminary) in which are set out the important points of discipline affecting the students' daily life and the order of the whole institution.[89]

26. All should observe, generously and willingly, the regulations laid down in the Rule or in other decisions, acting through conviction of how necessary this is for a genuine community life, and for the unfolding and strengthening of each man's own character. So the rules affecting community or private life, which should leave fair room for freedom, are not just to be suffered passively, or by coercion, but accepted cheerfully and without hesitation, out of deep conviction and charity. As time goes on and the maturity and sense of duty of the students increases, the rules should gradually be diminished so that the men may learn, as they go along, to be their own guides.[90]

V

Superiors

27. Following local practice, in every Seminary there should be a staff of men responsible for its direction, consisting, for example, of Rector, Vice-Rector, Spiritual Director or Directors, Prefect of Studies,[91] Pastoral Director, Prefect of Discipline, Bursar, Librarian. The functions, rights and duties of each, and their just emoluments, should be clearly defined.

There is no strict need in Seminaries of smaller size and number of students to allot individual men to each individual task.

28. The Superiors are nominated by the Bishop[92]—unless the statutes of the Seminary prescribe otherwise—after careful consultation. They should all be genuinely concerned for the progress of the Seminary, welcoming frequent dialogue with the Bishop and the students, the better to discover the common good and steadily perfect their pedagogical work.[93]

29. The principal and most serious task in the direction of the Seminary is undertaken by the Rector.[94] It is his part to keep the staff together, and he should work closely with them in brotherly charity, always religiously respecting the forum of conscience, to ensure harmonious progress in the work of training the students. Community life among the Superiors can contribute very much to this end. They should often—once a month for example—meet to arrange their communal activity, to assess the Seminary's affairs and problems, and find fitting solutions.[95]

30. Superiors should be chosen with the greatest care and should be men of deep priestly and apostolic spirit, fit to work with one another in their common task of education, in a fraternal collaboration. They should be open and alert to grasp the needs of the Church and of civil society; taught by pastoral experience in parish ministry or elsewhere, and outstanding in their clear understanding of young minds.[96]

The task of Seminary Superiors is the most excellent of all arts, one which cannot tolerate an off-hand or chance mode of action. Of necessity, therefore, besides natural and supernatural gifts, they must have, as each one's duty demands, due spiritual, pedagogical or technical training, which they would best have acquired in special Institutions founded, or to be founded, for this purpose in their own or in other areas.[97]

31. The Superiors' preparation should also be completed by being regularly brought up-to-date through attendance at conferences or courses, such as are held to review progress in spiritual or pedagogical sciences, or to learn about new methods and recent experience. The various experiments and undertakings through which Superiors can better know, and in the light of faith solve modern problems, particularly those of youth, should not be neglected.[98]

VI

Professors

32. A suitable number of Professors should be provided, taking into account the subjects to be taught, the method of teaching and the number of students; where philosophical and theological teaching is given, there should be a regular list of the Professors who are needed in the various courses and subjects.

33. As a general rule, Professors for the sacred subjects ought to be priests. All should willingly work with the rest in brotherly association; and they should be of the quality to show the students an example of Christian or priestly life, according to their status. Unless it is otherwise provided, they are appointed by the Bishop, or in the case of Regional Seminaries by the Bishops in charge of those Seminaries, after consultation with the Rector and the body of Professors, who can propose suitable candidates.[99]

34. The Professors should be genuinely expert, each in his own subject, and with a reasonable knowledge of kindred subjects.[100] So they must have had proper preparation and attained the requisite academic degrees: to teach sacred sciences and philosophy, they ought to have at least the Licentiate or its equivalent, and for the other subjects fitting academic qualifications.[101]

35. They should possess the art of teaching, so care is to be taken to ensure to them due preparation in this matter also. Training in active teaching methods is required, which will enable them to teach their students through group work and discussions.[102]

36. It must be the Professors' own concern to keep their scientific preparation up-to-date by reading periodicals and new books, by frequent discussion with men of learning, and by taking part in study conferences.[103]

37. They ought not to undertake duties which will hinder them from carrying out their proper tasks; for this reason they should be given a just remuneration, to enable them to devote themselves entirely to their own important office. However, a moderate amount of pastoral ministry is commendable: by pastoral experience they can be helped to a fuller knowledge of modern problems, those of youth in particular, and can present their own subjects to better advantage for the training of future pastors of souls.

38. As they carry out their work, let them think of themselves as educators in the proper sense of the word; hence they must keep in view the rules about presentation of doctrine and methods of teaching which are mentioned below. They should be concerned for the training and whole priestly formation of each individual student, to ensure his real progress in learning and in the spiritual life. Frequent meetings, once a month for example, should be held to go over scholastic matters in common, to promote the instruction and formation of the students by serious and united effort.

They should keep up a close collaboration with the Superiors of the Seminary too, in order to make a more effective contribution not only to the scientific but also to the whole priestly formation of the students.[104] Superiors and professors, lastly, should make up a single community of educators, to present together with their students the genuine image of one family, which fulfills the prayer of our Lord "that they may be one" (*Jn* 17, 11).[105]

VII
Students

39. Right training demands not only prudent selection of students[106] but also serious trial of individuals during their course of studies, to be made with the advice of experts, in order to reach certainty about the will of God regarding their vocation. In this sincere search for the will of God, the candidates on trial themselves should readily be asked to share, the more quickly and surely to obtain their greater spiritual good.

Consideration is to be given to the young men's human and moral qualities (e.g. sincerity, emotional maturity, good manners, keeping their word, steady concern for justice; feeling for friendship, for just freedom and responsibility; industry, the will to work with others, and so on); to their spiritual qualities too (e.g. love of God and neighbour, spirit of fellowship and self-denial, docility, well-tried chastity; appreciation of the faith and the Church, apostolic and missionary concern); and intellectual qualities (e.g. correct and sound judgement; sufficient ability to complete ecclesiastical studies; a right notion of the priesthood and of what it involves, etc.). Such consideration makes it possible to judge whether they are suited for priestly ministry.[107]

Likewise as a general rule their physical and mental health should be examined, if the case merits it, by expert doctors and others competent in psychological science; possible inherited traits should also be given attention.[108] Bishops have a grave obligation to investigate especially the cases of those who were dismissed from another seminary or religious institute.[109]

The first thing is to help the students seriously and sincerely to ponder before God whether they can really believe themselves called to the priesthood, and make them able to sort the motives of their intention. So, if God wills, they may proceed to the priestly office with a right and free will.[110]

40. Every student's personal position should be examined at certain times, with his own cooperation. In that way the Rector and his advisers may discover the unsuitable, and invite them, in all kindness, and help them to take up a different state of life, for the good of the Church and their own. This definite choice of a state of life should be obtained in good time and as soon as possible, to prevent any harm to the candidate from too long and useless delay.[111]

41. Special importance is to be given to the assessments (*scrutinia*) prescribed before the taking of Holy Orders. As a duty of conscience arising from his office, the Rector should himself, with the help of others who know them well, gather accurate information about each candidate. Parish priests, other priests and selected lay people may help him — the forum of conscience being always religiously respected. The Rector should send this information to the Bishop, so that he can make a safe judgement about the candidate's vocation. Should a doubt persist, the safer opinion is to be followed.[112]

42. To improve the training of the students and give them a more mature preparation for Holy Orders, the Episcopal Conferences should consider the opportuneness of introducing in their own regions special experiments or tests, for all students, or for some individuals, as their own Ordinary may judge fitting.[113]

The following experiments, among the various possibilities, are suggested by way of example:

a) At the beginning of the philosophy-theology course, a special period can be given for serious thought about the excellence of the priestly vocation, its nature, and the obligations connected with it: this is to initiate the students to mature decision, through very careful consideration and really intense prayer.

This initiation, which can be of varying length, is normally combined aptly with the introduction to the mystery of Christ and the history of salvation which the Council prescribed for the beginning of the philosophy-theology course.

b) During the said course, an interruption of residence in the Seminary is possible, e.g., for a year or six months, during which the student breaks off either studies and life in the Seminary together, or just his life in the Seminary while pursuing his studies (of philosophy-theology) elsewhere. During this interval, under the guidance of a skilled priest, he gives help in the pastoral ministry, learns about men and the problems and difficulties among which he will have to work, and tries out his own fitness for the priestly life and ministry. Trials of secular life in manual work or in military service, where that is obligatory, are not ruled out.

Or after the first year of the Major Seminary the students may be given permission either to enter the second year, or to take up secular studies in a University, or to pursue study of some special subject outside the Seminary: in this way the student, after completing his first experiences in the Seminary, will be offered a period of real freedom both interior and exterior to develop his vocation more solidly and with greater effort.

c) Having finished the philosophy-theology course, they will be able to work as Deacons for one or more years. This work, under the direction of a competent priest, should let them acquire a fuller maturity and strengthening of their vocation; they should better assimilate the pastoral teaching which they learned as young men in the Seminary, and so pass on more smoothly and easily to the ministry of a priest.

The experiments described under b) and c) should have their terms of reference properly defined to ensure a safe and successful result.

43. The Episcopal Conference should also consider whether, with reference to local conditions, the age required by the common law for Holy Orders should be raised.[114]

VIII
Spiritual Training[115]

44. The end of spiritual training is the perfection of charity, and it should lead the student, not just by dint of his ordination, but from the intimate fellowship of his whole life, to become in a special way another Christ; deeply penetrated by His spirit, he should truly realize what he is doing when celebrating *the mystery of the Lord's death,* should imitate what he is handling, and follow Him *who came not to be ministered to but to minister* (cf. *Mt 20,* 28).[116]

45. While the pastoral purpose of all priestly formation should constantly be borne in mind, the spiritual life of the student, with the help of the Spiritual Director,[117] should develop in an orderly way in its various aspects.[118] Together with the virtues most esteemed among men, the young students should endeavour to bring the grace of their baptism to perfection; they should have an ever clearer and more definite appreciation of their special priestly vocation, and so make themselves better able to acquire the virtues and habits of priestly life.

46. The community should also be given its due weight in spiritual formation: here the students, as members, should get used to putting aside their own will, and with common purpose and effort seek the greater good of their neighbour. In this way they do their best to perfect both their own lives and the common life of the whole Seminary, like the early Church, in which the whole group of believers was united, heart and soul (cf. *Acts, 4,* 32). For by charity the community enjoys God's presence, observes the law in its fullness, attains the bond of perfection, and puts into practice great apostolic virtue.[119]

47. Their community life in the Seminary should prepare candidates for the priesthood, so that in the end, raised to Holy Orders, they may be united in a "sacramental brotherhood with the wider community of the diocesan *Presbyterium,* by the bond of charity, prayer, and manifold cooperation, in order to build up the Body of Christ, a task demanding, in our days particularly, many duties and up-to-date reforms".[120] So the students should gradually be introduced to the actual conditions of the diocese (cf. above no. 22), in order to be aware of the situation and needs of clergy and faithful, and be able to carry out their future pastoral duties with greater success.[121]

48. The Church of the Latin rite has established the rule, which claims respect from long usage, of choosing for the priesthood only those who by the grace of God are willing freely to embrace celibacy for the Kingdom of God's sake.[122] This way of life is rooted in the teaching of the gospel and the authentic tradition of the Church, and in many ways matches the priesthood. The entire mission of the priest is dedicated to the service of the new human race which Christ, Victor over death, raises up in the world by his Spirit; it is a state by which priests "more easily stay close to Christ with undivided heart, more freely dedicate themselves to the service of God and man ... and so are better fitted to receive their fatherhood in Christ with great generosity..." In this way, then, choosing the state of virginity for the Kingdom of Heaven's sake, *(Mt 9,* 12) "they are made a living sign of that world to come which is present now through faith and charity", "in which the children of the resurrection do not marry" (cf. *Lk 20,* 35-36).[123]

Therefore those who are preparing for the priesthood should recognize and accept celibacy as a special gift of God; by a life unstintingly devoted to prayer, to union with Christ, to sincere fraternal charity, they should create the necessary conditions in which they can fully and joyfully preserve their celibacy, anxious always for the sincerity of their gift of self.[124]

In order that the choice of celibacy may be really free, a young man must be able to see the evangelical force of this gift by the light of faith, and at the same time rightly esteem the good of the married state.[125] He should enjoy full psychological freedom, both interior and exterior, and have the necessary degree of emotional stability in order to appreciate and live his celibacy as his personal fulfillment.[126]

Adequate education in matters of sex is required for this.[127] In students of some maturity, this education consists rather of formation leading to a chaste love of people than in an anxiety to avoid sins, a thing at times very disturbing. Such formation must prepare them for the future involvements of the pastoral ministry. Gradually, then, with sound and spiritual discretion, the young men should be asked and guided to experience and show, in groups and in various areas of the apostolate and of social cooperation, a love that is sincere, human, fraternal, personal, and offered to God after the example of Christ; a love for all men, but above all for the poor and the distressed, and for their fellows. In this way they will overcome any sense of loneliness. They should expose this love openly and with confidence to their Spiritual Directors and Superiors, and learn to judge it in the Lord with their help. They should, however, avoid individual relationships, particularly any of a solitary and protracted nature, with people of the opposite sex. They ought rather to endeavour to practice a love open to all and therefore truly chaste. This they should habitually ask for as a gift from God.

The nature of this gift being clearly of a special order, *from above, coming down from the Father of light* (*Jas* 1, 17), candidates for the priesthood must rely on God's help without too much confidence in their own strength, and "should practice mortification and custody of the senses. They should not leave aside the natural means favourable to mental and physical health. Thus they will not be disturbed by false teachings which represent perfect continence as impossible or hurtful to human development; and they should reject, by a kind of spiritual instinct, everything that leads their chastity into danger".[128]

49. The student should aim at a close and friendly relationship with the person and mission of Christ, who completed his task (cf. *Jn* 4, 34) in humble submission to the will of the Father. This relationship of necessity demands that a candidate for the priesthood should know how to "dedicate his own will, by obedience, to the service of God and his brethren",[129] with sincere faith. One who wishes to have a part with Christ crucified in the building up of His Body is under a grave obligation not only to learn to accept the Cross, but also to love it, and to take up in a willing and pastoral spirit all the heavy tasks required to carry on his apostolic mission.

So it lies with the Superiors to train the young men to true and mature obedience in reliance on Christ,[130] who indeed required obedience from his followers, but first showed Himself as the exemplar of this virtue, and by his grace made Himself the principle of obedience in us. The Superiors, then, must exercise authority with prudence and respect for persons. In this matter the young men will surely offer their cooperation, so long as obedience is put forward in its true light, i.e., if it is made clear how all must join in pursuing the common good, and how authority is designed for this (cf. no. 24).

The students should show this full and sincere obedience first of all to the Pope, the Vicar of Christ, with humble service and filial piety; and to their own Bishop in the same spirit, so that through the priesthood they may become his faithful co-workers, generously and freely giving their help in fellowship with the other priests of the *Presbyterium*.[131]

50. The spirit of poverty, so much demanded from the Church these days, and itself necessary for fulfilling the work of the apostolate, is what the students should learn to foster by deeds and not just by words: relying on the Father's providence, they may thus know both how to have plenty and to how *to have plenty and to be in want* (*Phil* 4, 12) like the Apostle without anxiety. Although not obliged like Religious to renounce material goods completely, still they should as spiritual men strive to acquire the liberty and docility of the children of God, and attain that spiritual restraint which is necessary for finding a right attitude towards the world and worldly goods.[132] Following the example of Christ, *who became poor for our sakes though he was rich (2 Cor 8, 9)*, they should consider the poor and the less well-off to be their own special charges:[133] by a simplicity and austerity of life, let them be able to bear witness to poverty, with self-denial of superfluous goods already a habit.[134]

51. Spiritual formation should take in the whole man (cf. nos 14, 15). Grace does not take away nature, but raises it to a higher level, and no one can be a true Christian unless he has and exercises the virtues befitting a man, and demanded by charity which has to animate and make use of them. The future priest, then, must learn to practice sincerity, a constant concern for justice, good manners in dealing with people; he must keep to his word, be controlled and kind in conversation;[135] must have a spirit of fellowship and service and of readiness to work, and the ability to work with others, etc. With these qualities he may reach that harmony in reconciling human with supernatural good which is needed for the true witness of Christian life in modern society.

A priest must preach the gospel to all men, and therefore the candidate for the priesthood must do his best to develop his ability for forming right relationships with men of different sorts. He should learn in particular the art of speaking to others in the right way, of listening patiently, and of making himself understood. In this respect he must treat all men with great reverence, filled with the spirit of humble charity, so that he may reveal to others the mystery of Christ living in the Church.[136]

52. Daily celebration of the Eucharist, which is completed by sacramental communion received worthily and in full liberty, should be the centre of the whole life of the Seminary, and the students should devoutly take part in it. Sharing in the sacrifice of the Mass, "source and culmination of all Christian life,"[137] they share in the charity of Christ, drawing from this richest of sources supernatural force for their spiritual life and apostolic labour.

Therefore the Eucharistic sacrifice, - and indeed the whole Sacred Liturgy, as the Constitution *Sacrosanctum Concilium* wishes, should occupy the place in the Seminary which will truly reveal it as "the peak point towards which the activity of the Church tends, and at the same time the source from which its strength flows".[138]

A sound variety in the manner of participation in the Sacred Liturgy should be provided for, so that the students may not only realize greater spiritual progress themselves, but also be prepared practically, from their Seminary years, for their future ministry and liturgical apostolate.[139]

53. With formation for Eucharistic worship there should be closely combined formation for the divine Office, by which priests "pray to God in the name of the Church for the entire people entrusted to them, and indeed for the whole world",[140] Students should learn the Church's method of prayer by means of a suitable introduction to Sacred Scripture, the Psalms, and other prayers of scriptural content; also by frequent recitation in common of part of the Office (e.g. Lauds or Vespers), so they may with more understanding and reverence know the Word of God speaking in the psalms and in all the Liturgy, and be trained at the same time for faithful observance in their priestly life of the obligation of divine Office.[141]

This liturgical instruction will lack completeness unless it reveals to the students the close connection between the Sacred Liturgy and their daily working life, with its needs of apostolate and of sincere witness that reveals a living faith acting through charity.[142]

54. To live the life of a priest uprightly and loyally, the students should gradually attain, corresponding with their own age and maturity, a firm pattern of life, safeguarded by solid virtues, without which they will not be able to persevere in a genuine close attachment to Christ and the Church.

For the following must be features of the priest's life:

a) he must learn "to live in familiar and constant company with the Father through his Son, Jesus Christ, in the Holy Spirit;[143]

b) he ought to be able to find Christ habitually in the intimate communion of prayer;

c) he should have learnt to keep by his side the word of God in Sacred Scripture, with an affection rooted in faith, and to give it others;

d) he should be willing and happy to visit and adore Christ sacramentally present in the Eucharist;

e) he ought, as the Church desires, to have a fervent love for the Virgin Mary, Mother of Christ, who was in a special way associated with the work of Redemption;[144]

f) he should readily consult the documents of sacred tradition, the works of the Fathers, and the examples of the saints;

g) he must know how to examine and judge himself, his conscience and his motives, with honesty and sincerity.

The priest will keep to all these duties only if in his Seminary days he has faithfully practiced the devotional exercises that have long proved their worth, and are sanctioned by the Rule of the Seminary; and if he has correctly grasped their importance and force. If it should be necessary to adapt one or other of these practices to modern needs, its inherent and essential purpose should carefully be kept in mind so that it may be attained in some other suitable way.[145]

55. To follow Christ in the spirit of the gospel is an intention certainly to be renewed every day. The virtue of penance, then, should be instilled into future priests. Penitential acts made in common may be used, which serve both for personal formation and for mutual instruction. Students should strive to acquire a real enthusiasm for a life crucified with Christ, through love of Him, and for purity of heart. They should therefore pray fervently for the help of the grace they need; frequent recourse to the sacrament of penance should become a habit: there everyone's efforts are in a sense consecrated; moreover each should have his spiritual director to whom he may humbly and confidently open his conscience, so as to be guided safely in the way of the Lord.[146]

The students are to choose their spiritual director and confessor with full freedom, from among those appointed as fit for the task by the Bishop.[147]

56. The only way to the priesthood is by stages: these stages give their meaning to the institution of the liturgical rite of admission and of the ministries of lector and acolyte, which appoint a man to definite functions in the Church, after duly completed training and spiritual preparation.[148] In fact the spiritual training of the students proceeds by degrees, and needs to be adapted to the age, experience, and ability of individuals. Its efficacy is considerably helped by fixed periods of more intensive training, for example when men first enter the Seminary, at the beginning of the theology course, or at the approach of priestly ordination, and so on. Besides the spiritual direction of individuals, the students should also be given, at fixed times as each Seminary's Rule determines, a spiritual instruction or conference suited to the situation and outlook of modern youth: their efforts in the spiritual life receive in this way a regular fresh impulse, and can be directed towards the gaining of a genuine mature priestly spirituality, according to the mind of the Church. Self examination, regular periods of recollection and other exercises of the kind should also have their place. Every year all should spend some days in retreat.

57. In the midst of his daily labours Christ used readily to seek solitude, in order to pray to his Father without distraction: following his example and counsel (cf. *Mt* 6, 6; 14, 13; *Mk* 6, 30, 46) students should try to develop "a life hidden with Christ in God (cf. *Col* 3, 3) from which arises irrepressibly the love of one's neighbour, directed towards the salvation of the world and the building up of the Church".[149] They ought, therefore, to be concerned about the keeping of external silence, without which there is no interior silence of soul, and which is needed for thought and for the work and the repose alike of the whole community.[150]

58. Much good will result from communication with their fellow-men, among whom Christ was sent by the love of the Father (cf. *Jn* 4, 9) and there accomplished his work of redemption. This will allow the student to be trained in observing correctly the signs of the times[151] and judging events by the light of the gospel; also to interpret accurately the various circumstances and exigencies of human life which contain the true "seeds of the Word hidden in themselves",[152] and demand "to be illuminated by the light of the gospel; to be set free and brought back under the sway of God our Saviour".[153] As regards this mixing with the world, it should be carefully noted that all experiences of this sort are designed for the pastoral purpose of the Seminary, and for the spiritual preparation of the students, to ensure that their future activity will be not an obstacle but a help towards the development and strengthening of their own spiritual life.[154]

IX

Intellectual Formation in General

59. The purpose of the intellectual formation is to enable the students to acquire, along with a general culture which is relevant to present-day needs, an extensive and solid learning in the sacred sciences such as can give a firm foundation to their faith, enable it to mature, and can equip them to proclaim the teaching of the Gospel effectively and make it part and parcel of the culture of modern man.[155]

This formation includes:

a) after finishing the curriculum of studies mentioned in n. 16, the completion, where necessary, of their education in the Arts and Sciences;

b) philosophical formation;

c) theological formation.

60. There are three main ways of providing this:

a) in three distinct and successive periods of time the Arts and Sciences where necessary—the study of Philosophy—the study of Theology;

b) Arts and Sciences along with Philosophy (cf. *American College*); then Theology;

c) The Arts and Sciences followed by a combined course of Philosophy and Theology. If this is done, care must be taken to present Philosophy as a separate entity having its own special method, and not reduce it to a fragmentary consideration of problems arising from questions in Theology.

These are to be taken merely as examples, and do not exclude other methods of arranging the studies. In their Scheme for Priestly Training the Episcopal Conference should indicate what systems they choose to approve, and, in doing so, they should take into account their local conditions.

61. Whatever study arrangement be adopted, the following principles should be carefully observed:

a) it should always commence with an introductory course in the Mystery of Christ, such as will be found described in the following section;[156]

b) if Philosophy and Theology are taught at separate times, an attempt should be made to coordinate subjects in Philosophy with those of Theology, particularly Natural Theology with the Tract in Dogma concerning God, Ethics with Moral Theology, the History of Philosophy with Church History and the History of Dogmatic Theology, etc.;[157]

36

c) the time devoted to studies of a particularly philosophical nature should be equivalent to at least two years (or, where certain countries use a system of computing the length of studies by hours per term, the equivalent number of such hours); the time devoted to theological studies should equal at least four years (or the equivalent number of hours per term), so that the study of Philosophy and Theology should take no less than six years (or the equivalent number of hours normally requiring six years to cover).[158]

62. The Introduction into the Mystery of Christ and Salvation History which is to inaugurate the course of Philosophy and Theology is designed to enable the students to appreciate the idea which lies behind ecclesiastical studies, their general plan and connection with the apostolate. At the same time it should help to give roots to their own faith, to understand at greater depth their priestly vocation, and consequently to commit themselves with greater awareness.

The programme and length of this course should be regulated for in the Scheme for Priestly Training. Before doing so, account should be taken of the experiments which have already taken place in the country concerned and in the Church abroad, and care is needed to link the course properly with the rest of the theological studies. It should also continue afterwards especially by means of Scripture Reading under the direction of professors.[159]

63. The professors, as a body, when teaching their own subject, must be concerned for the internal unity and harmony of the whole corpus of doctrine about the Faith which is being taught (cf. n. 90). This they can do by emphasizing the salvation aspect of their particular subject. But to really do the job properly, as the course of studies comes to an end—or, if the Bishops' Conferences prefer, after a few years of pastoral experience—time might be set aside, even a fairly lengthy period, when the students can be directed in a methodical way and in the light of what they have already learned, to examine the Word of God, contemplate it as it were and experience it, simply from the point of view of its unity, the unity of its message of salvation in the way it is to be put over to the faithful, and thus mould together into one the main points of each subject which have been taught as separate entities. This time set aside for a final round-up is to be highly recommended. It can prevent acquired pieces of knowledge from remaining out on a limb and isolated from each other. It enables the priest to see everything wedded to one aim: the spiritual development of his people. It creates that harmony which is necessary for his own spiritual maturing, and enables him to see the use of the knowledge he has acquired and thus give him a greater love of theological learning.

If individual Bishops, or their Conferences as a whole, should decide to restore the exercise of the Diaconate for a year or so after the completion of studies (cf. n. 42c),[160] this general unification, or knitting together, of the different branches of Theology would be more usefully transferred to the time when the deacons return to the Seminary to prepare themselves for the Priesthood. But the period will have to be sufficiently long to make it a really effective and immediate preparation.

64. An overriding consideration to be borne in mind is that the whole of the intellectual formation of students must take into account their differing backgrounds. They have to be capable of understanding and expressing Christ's message in a form which has meaning for them. They are products of a certain culture, and they have to translate the Christian life into terms which will be relevant to their own cultural ethos.

Therefore, professors of Philosophy and Theology should always draw comparisons between Christian teaching and the particular ideas about God, the world, and man which are enshrined in popular traditions that are held as sacred by the people concerned, and as far as possible, use these notions to enrich the wisdom of the philosophers and the understanding of the faith.[161]

X
Studies in the Arts and Sciences

65. Before the students embark on their specific studies for the Priesthood they must have completed the schooling which is required in their own country as a necessary qualification for commencing University studies, and, if possible, have obtained a State-recognized diploma of proficiency.[162]

66. On the completion of these studies, any deficiency in knowledge which is required in a priest must be made good either before or during the study of Philosophy, as n. 60 indicates. An example would be that reasonable proficiency in Latin which the Church continually and insistently demands.[163] A list and programme of these studies should be included in the Schema for Priestly Training.

67. Students should learn, apart from their own language, whatever languages are deemed necessary or useful for their future pastoral ministry.[164] In this matter the civil programme of education should also be observed. But in addition they should be taught how to express themselves in an idiom acceptable to modern people, how to communicate in the spoken and the written word, and how to get to the heart of the meaning of a question, an art which is so necessary for the priest. A training in the appreciation of art and music, whether sacred or profane, would also be an advantage for them.[165]

68. Nowadays people receive their information and convictions, not only from books and teachers, but more and more through audio visual aids. It is of the utmost importance, therefore, that priests should be versed in these methods. They should, however, have the right attitude towards them; be ready to use them critically, not be merely passive spectators or listeners. This demands that they be used, with moderation and with prudence, for experimental teaching purposes in the Seminary under expert guidance. Their controlled use should enable the students to exercise restraint themselves and teach others the same, while availing themselves of their usefulness for the apostolate.[166]

69. Right from their first Seminary years, and increasingly as they grow older and more mature, the students should be introduced to the social problems of their own country in particular. Their studies, their contact with people and the world around them, and the events of daily life should make them acquainted with questions and disputes of a social order, and they should come to grips with them, with their real significance, the pros and cons, problems and consequences inherent in them and learn to see where, in the light of the natural law and the precepts of the Gospel, just and equitable solutions are to be found.[167]

XI
Studies in Philosophy and Kindred Subjects[168]

70. Studies in Philosophy and kindred subjects— no matter how they may be distributed over the years (cf. n. 60). — must be equivalent to a two-year course. Their purpose is to form the students as human beings by sharpening their judgement and refining their appreciation of the wisdom of the ancients and moderns with which the human family has been enriched through the course of the centuries. At the same time the method of teaching these subjects should assist the student to a deeper awareness and a more intense living out of his faith. They should also be a preparation for his theological studies and for the right performance of his apostolic ministry which requires him to be properly trained for dialogue with people of this day and age.[169]

71. *Systematic Philosophy* and its component parts should be regarded as of particular importance in leading one to the acquisition of a solid and coherent understanding of man, the world, and God.

This training in Philosophy must be based on that always valid philosophical patrimony[170] whose witnesses are the great Christian philosophers. They are the ones who have handed down those first philosophical principles which have a constant value since they are founded in nature itself. Granted such a philosophical basis, the students' attention should be directed towards contemporary Philosophy, and, in particular, to the schools of thought which exercise special influence in their own country, and to recent scientific progress. In this way they will be in a position to view the modern age in its right perspective and be adequately prepared for dialogue with society.[171]

72. The *History of Philosophy* must also be taught to show the origins and development of the great problems which have faced mankind. From an understanding of the different solutions which have been proposed to these problems over the centuries, students will be able to discern the truth, detect error, and refute it.[172]

73. *Related sciences* should also be taught; the natural sciences, for instance, and mathematics, insofar as they are related to Philosophy. But a due sense of proportion should be observed: their purpose is not to produce superficial and encyclopedic minds, but to be of real complementary value to the principal subjects.[173]

74. The matter and manner of presentation in all subjects should take cognizance, not only of the intrinsic importance of each question, but also of its relevance to present day circumstances, whether of the students or local conditions.[174]

75. In National Schemes for Priestly Training (or, in an Appendix) an outline should be given of all the subjects taught in the Philosophy curriculum and a brief note of the programme, number of years or terms and hours per week given in class to each subject.

If, for one reason or another (e.g., because different systems are employed in a large country), this be too difficult or impossible to do, some examples at least of study-programmes should be included, which could provide a clear indication of what is in progress and be of help to everyone.

XII
Theological Studies

76. The whole of four years at least must be devoted to theological studies.[175] Their purpose is to enable the students to make as profound a study as possible of the teaching of Divine Revelation in the light of faith and under the guidance of the authoritative magisterium, nourish their own spiritual lives with what they have learned, guard it in their priestly ministry, and proclaim and expound it for the spiritual good of the faithful.[176]

77. No matter under which aspects (ecumenical, missiological, etc.)[177] theological subjects be treated, they should be so taught as to clearly reveal their interrelation[178] and their proper place in the setting of the mystery of the Church.[179] Moreover, each subject in its own way should be seen to fit in neatly with the overall pattern of explaining the history of salvation as it continues to be worked out, among the ups and downs of the world, in the life of the Church.[180]

78. The whole of Theology finds its soul in Sacred Scripture which is to be the inspiration of every part of Theology.[181] For this reason due importance should be accorded to biblical studies. Students should be introduced into the correct methods of exegesis after a suitable introduction and with the support of auxiliary courses. In accordance with their needs, the professors should explain what the main problems are and their solution and really help them acquire a vision of the whole of Sacred Scripture with a clear insight into the principal chapters of the history of salvation. Moreover they should give their divinity students a theological synthesis of divine revelation which is necessary for their spiritual life and future preaching, since these require a firm basis.[182]

79. *Sacred Liturgy* is now to be regarded as one of the principal subjects. And it is to be presented, not so much in its juridical aspect, as in a theological and historical context, and, on the spiritual and pastoral plane, it should be linked up with the other subjects in order that the students may realize how the salvation mysteries are rendered present and operative in the liturgical ceremonies. Texts and rites of Oriental and Western liturgies should be explained in order to illustrate the eminent place which, theologically speaking, the Sacred Liturgy occupies in expressing the faith and spiritual life of the Church.[183]

They should have the norms governing the restored liturgy explained for a better understanding of the adaptations and changes which the Church has decided. They also ought to be capable of evaluating what is legitimately optional, and, while we are in the middle of the present heated debate of more serious and thorny problems, they should be able to draw a clear line between what is changeable and what is, by divine institution, liturgically immutable.[184]

Dogmatic Theology should be presented in full and systematically. It should begin with an exposition of its biblical sources, followed by an explanation of the contribution which the Oriental and Latin Fathers have made to the formulation and handing down of the truths of revelation, and how dogma has developed through historical progression. Finally, there should be a full, speculative study, based on St. Thomas, of the mysteries of salvation and their interrelation. Students should be taught to recognize how the mystery of salvation is present and operative in the liturgy. They should learn to look for solutions to human problems in the light of Revelation, and not only have an insight into the eternal, embodied in the changeable conditions of this world, but also be able to communicate these eternal truths to modern man.[185]

There is no objection to the teaching of dogmatic Theology by the so-called *regressive method,* which begins with conciliar definitions and works backwards through the Fathers to Sacred Scripture, if in this way one can learn to read and understand Scripture in the light of the living tradition of the Church.[186]

Right from the beginning of a theological training it is important that solid doctrine based on theological sources be imparted.[187] And although it now needs to be adapted to this ecumenical age and to the circumstances of the day, one should not neglect what is called *Apologetics* which is concerned with the preparation necessary for the gift of faith and with the rational foundations of a living faith in relation to the sociological conditions which influence the Christian life in a particular way.[188]

Moral Theology should also be animated by the teaching of Sacred Scripture. It has to demonstrate how the Christian's vocation is founded on charity and give a scientific explanation of the obligations incumbent on the faithful. It should endeavor to discover the solution to human problems in the light of Revelation and make eternal truths relevant in a changing world. It should seek the assistance of reliable and modern anthropology in its efforts to restore a sense of virtue and of sin to men's consciences.[189] The teaching of morals is completed by a study of *Spiritual Theology* which, apart from anything else, should include a study of the theology and spirituality of the Priesthood and of a life consecrated to God by the following of the evangelical counsels, in order that spiritual direction can be given according to one's state of life.[190]

40

Pastoral Theology has to explain the theological principles of action—of the action by which God's salvific will though the various ministries and institutions in the Church of today is actually realized.[191]

However, since a solid training in social questions is of considerable importance in making for a successful pastoral ministry, efforts should be made to reserve a definite number of lectures, as many as are necessary, for the *Social Doctrine of the Church* in order that the students may learn the means of adapting the teaching and the principles of the Gospel to the life of society.[192]

Church History should explain the origins and progress of the People of God as it unfolds itself in time and space. It should be scientific in weighing its historical sources. It will be necessary to pay attention, in the course of the treatment of the subject matter, not only to the development of theological doctrine, but also to social, economic and political factors, their theories and doctrines, which have had the greatest influence over the course of Church History, since the evolution of one cannot be explained except through its dependence and connection with the other. The History of the Church is also the story of a wonderful partnership between God and man, and it should inculcate in the students a genuine sense of the Church and Tradition.[193] Due attention should also be paid to the history of their own country.

Canon Law should be taught in relation to the mystery of the Church as more profoundly understood by the Second Vatican Council. While explaining principles and laws, the point should be made plain, apart from anything else, how the whole system of ecclesiastical government and discipline is in accord with the salvific will of God, and, in all things, has as its scope the salvation of souls.[194]

80. Ancillary subjects and special courses ought also to be determined, and which of them are obligatory or not. Likewise the students should be offered the opportunity of learning Hebrew and Biblical Greek[195] to enable them to tackle the original biblical texts, and understand and explain them.

But, on the other hand care must be taken to avoid multiplying the number of courses. Rather insert new questions, or new ways of looking at things, into the courses which are already provided where this is possible.[196]

Means should be found of leading the students to a fuller understanding of the Churches and ecclesial communities separated from the Apostolic See as a step to the reestablishment of unity,[197] which is provided for in the Decree *De Oecumenismo* and the *Directorium Oecumenicum* published by the Holy See.[198] Facilities should also be provided for them to get to know other religions which may be more prominent in certain areas; to recognize what is good and true in them, what errors are to be refuted, and to communicate the full light of the truth to those who do not possess it.[199]

Equal attention should be paid to questions concerning modern atheism in all its aspects, so that as priests they can be better qualified to tackle the grave pastoral responsibilities which arise therefrom.[200]

81. In the National Schemes for Priestly Training (or in an Appendix) an outline should be given of all the subjects taught in the Theology curriculum with a brief note made of the programme and the number of years or terms and hours per week given in class to each subject.

If, for one reason or another (e.g., because different systems are used in a large country), this be too difficult or impossible to do, there should be included at least some examples of study programmes as an indication of the general pattern of studies approved by the Episcopal Conference.

XIII
Specialized Studies
in Preparation for Particular Offices

82. The apostolate of today demands that, besides a general formation which is common to all church students, there should be some special preparation provided with a view to the various tasks to be performed in the future by each priest.[201]

83. Having established the principle of a general philosophical and theological formation for all, the specialization can take two forms:

A) One useful for priests who will be engaged in pastoral activities and which can be organized in the Seminary, particularly in the final year, without any attendance necessary at a special Institute: for instance, preparation for an apostolate among a certain class (industrial workers, farming communities, etc.)

B) Training for a particular post requiring its own preparation in specialized Institutes; e.g., training to teach sacred or secular subjects.

84. As regards A) the aim should be to provide this special preparation during the six years' course of Philosophy and Theology. This can be done:

a) if special courses are properly organized, particularly in the latter years, within the scholastic year, so long as they are not disproportionate to the principal subjects and fit into the scheme of general formation. Alternatively, such courses might be arranged for the vacation period;

b) by concentrating on giving all, or the majority, of the general course in the first five years, and in the sixth year giving a full and intensive specialized training in a special course of subjects.

Through schemes like these, different groups of students will be able to receive a varied specialized formation according to their aptitude, and, in particular, according to what the Bishop decides are the peculiar needs of the diocese. In its Scheme for Priestly Training the Episcopal Conference should state what it has decided for each region and for each Seminary faculty.

85. As regards B) it is essential that the general formation be first completed and also some pastoral experience be had before sending candidates to higher Institutes or Universities where they can obtain the specialized training along with their degrees or diplomas.

Only those should be chosen for this purpose who are really suitable from the point of view of character, virtue and intelligence, and it is of the utmost importance that their spiritual and pastoral formation, particularly if they are not yet ordained priests, should be fully completed.[202]

Episcopal Conferences in each country should make suitable provisions in this matter.[203] Moreover, where Major Seminaries have their theological studies organized on a scientific basis, they should see if they cannot have them affiliated to a University faculty of Theology in order to enable a number of Seminary students to gain a first degree (baccalaureate) in Theology within the University system.

Seeing the unique importance of the Roman Colleges,[204] on account of their being able to offer a wide choice of specialized courses, the Episcopal Conferences should preserve close links with these, their own Colleges. By their joint effort they can promote their special function, and increase the contribution which they can make to the new needs which face their countries and the Universal Church.

XIV

The Type of Teaching to be Given

86. God's Revelation is the foundation and real scope of the whole formation of a priest, since of this students must become devoted and trustworthy ministers. Therefore, both professors and students must adhere faithfully to the written and unwritten Word of God. They must love it, make it their careful study, and in it find their spiritual nourishment.[205] Tradition and Sacred Scripture form one sacred deposit of God's word and this is committed to the Church's care.[206] Consequently students should have a lively appreciation for this Tradition as it is found in the works of the Fathers, and should pay special attention to the doctrine of the Fathers and of the other Doctors who are renowned in the Church.[207] They should regard St. Thomas as one of the Church's greatest teachers while still esteeming authors of more recent times.[208]

87. Professors of the ecclesiastical sciences hold a very honorable position in the Church, but also one which entails great responsibility: they teach, not in their own, but in the Church's name, since it is from the Church that they have received their commission. They should keep before their eyes the special place they occupy in the Body of Christ, and ever manifest a spirit of respect and submission to the Church's magisterium. In this way they will play their part in the building up in faith of their students and the faithful.[209]

88. Professors should take into account present trends and state of doctrine. They should use their rightful freedom of enquiry and of speaking their minds, but, as true cooperators of the truth,[210] they should always approach new questions with the prudence and seriousness which the weight of their office, their responsibilities towards the truths of Revelation, demand.

In view of the fact that there exist different degrees of theological certainty, professors should make it clear in their teaching what is proven doctrine of faith and what is so by the consent of theologians. For this to be done properly a basic and reliable text is essential. Only when doctrine which is certain has been fully expounded should they turn their attention to an unemotional exposition of what is only probable or novel or their own personal theories.[211]

89. While candidates for the priesthood are to concentrate on the Church's teaching in their studies, efforts should be made to make them open, in moderation and for the right motives to modern culture. With this in mind, their teachers should strive to make them into men of balanced mind and mature judgment.[212] Students for the priesthood are to learn to be men of discernment, to read with a critical eye, to know what to approve and what to reject of the culture of today. A very useful method is group reading of the Press and of books followed by a critical discussion in the company of professors.

XV

The Programme of Teaching[213]

90. The programme of studies should be revised at stated intervals so that obsolete questions can be omitted from the curriculum and the teaching of questions which are still in vogue can be improved and be given more detailed treatment.

New courses—as already mentioned (cf. n. 80)—should not be lightly introduced; rather, new questions should be fitted into the already existing subjects where possible.

Professors should realize that they are, and should be eager to be, a unified teaching body. It is only when this unity is present in the teaching staff that there will be the desired unity in teaching.

They must be concerned for the interrelationship and unity of the subjects they teach, so that the students themselves realize that they are learning, not many, but the one science of the Faith and the Gospel.[214]

In order to facilitate this unification, someone in the Seminary should be in charge of integrating the course of studies.

91. Teaching methods should also be revised, but, as a premise to this revision, the following should be borne in mind:

a) Professors must be agreed upon a definite number of lectures for all formal courses which are necessary to cover the presentation and explanation of the main topics to be taught, the general direction of the students' private study, and useful reading lists.

b) There should be a system of *seminars* and practical exercises to encourage the active participation of the students; professors whose task it is to direct these activities should be aware of the seriousness of their work which demands as much of them as do formal lectures.[215]

c) Work in small groups with a master in charge should also be encouraged; likewise, private study under the direction of professors with whom they can have frequent discussions. Ways like these teach the students a personal method of study.

d) Finally, appropriate surveys might be undertaken by candidates for the priesthood to study scientifically the pastoral problems affecting their dioceses.[216] A joint study of a theological nature to examine events and factors more clearly connects their life with their spiritual formation and their formal classroom learning. Apart from this, it imparts to the students a fuller theological preparation.

However, to satisfy all these requirements in teaching-methods and the demands of personal study, professors must be sufficiently numerous and well-trained for their duties.

92. A library is an indispensable instrument for study, both for the professors and the students. Each major Seminary should have one carefully arranged and looked after by a qualified librarian. It should be kept continually well stocked with books: for this purpose an annual allowance should be generously allotted and the assistance of all who use it should be enlisted.

Students should be taught the modern methods of making use of a library.

93. The Episcopal Conferences are to determine definite standards of attainment required of their students, whose progress should be ascertained at stated intervals by means of discussions and written essays and examinations.

XVI
Strictly Pastoral Formation[217]

94. The entire training for the Priesthood must have a thoroughly pastoral slant, because the purpose of the Seminary is to form pastors of souls (cf. n. 20), and consequently the pastoral aspect must receive special emphasis in all the subjects which are taught.[218]

Special pastoral training, however, is also to be given adapted to local conditions which vary according to whether the Christian way of life is flourishing, neglected, or is simply non-existent, or whether it is a country with confessional differences or a plurality of religions. In particular, this pastoral training should include catechetics and homiletics, the administration of the

Sacraments, spiritual direction according to the varying states of life, parochial administration, pastoral joint-action with non Catholics and non-believers, and other questions necessary for the building up of the Body of Christ.[219]

Together with all this the students should be trained how to acquire the ability to involve themselves with true pastoral concern in the lives of the faithful. The study of psychology, pedagogy, and sociology are of great assistance in the acquisition of this fuller knowledge of people and their problems, which, however, should always be taught according to correct methods and the rules established by ecclesiastical authority.[220]

95. The students are also to be trained in the various forms of the modern apostolate: Catholic Action and its associate bodies, working with deacons, enlisting the support of the laity to encourage and develop their own special apostolate and promote their greater active cooperation,[221] methods of assisting all men without distinction as needs and local conditions require, and the art of entering into worthwhile dialogue with then.[222]

Particular attention should be paid to the preparation of students for a correct and healthy relationship with women. This will involve instruction in the character and psychology of women as it is affected by the sort of life they lead and by their age. The purpose of this is to enable them as priests engaged in the pastoral ministry to undertake a more effective spiritual care of women and behave towards them with the normality and prudence which befit ministers of Christ.[223]

96. Students should be imbued will a true spirit of Catholicity which transcends diocesan and national boundaries and barriers imposed by differences of rite, and be openheartedly disposed to be of assistance to others. They should, therefore, be instructed in the needs of the whole Church, as for instance, in the problems of ecumenism or of the missions, and anything else which is a matter of urgency in various parts of the world.[224] With special care they should be prepared for dialogue with non-believers.[225]

97. Throughout the whole of the scholastic year, as well as in vacation time, provided the Bishops think it fit, practical works of the apostolate, which form a necessary part of the strictly pastoral training, should be introduced in accordance with the age of the students and local conditions.[226]

Since it often happens nowadays that students go abroad during their holidays in order to gain pastoral experience, it would be as well if the Episcopal Conferences concerned were to lay down, by common consent, suitable provisions to ensure that the experience intended is really obtained.

98. A selection should be made of the more suitable practical activities, taking into consideration where the Seminary is, the number of students involved, and any other circumstances which can be undertaken during the scholastic year: for instance, giving religious instruction, taking an active part on feast-days in the parish' liturgy, visiting the sick, the poor, prisoners, helping priests engaged in youth-work, etc.

Due proportion, however, should be observed between the time given to these practical exercises and the demands of study. Moreover, they should be performed in the light of theological principles and under the direction of experts and wise priests who will assign each one his work, teaching them how to go about it, be at hand while the work is being done, and arrange for a review of its performance afterwards with the students in order that they may reflect on what the experience has taught them and receive elective advice. This is the right way of ensuring that these activities are a help, not a hindrance, to their spiritual and doctrinal formation.

99. These exercises can be more easily performed during vacation time if arrangements are made by the Seminary Superiors. They might help priests in their pastoral work, or assist workers, etc., but always under the direction of experts as explained in the foregoing section.

XVII.
Post-Seminary Training

100. Priestly training, of its nature, is such that it must be continued and increasingly perfected throughout the whole of a priest's life, but more particularly during the first years after Ordination.[227] It is for this reason that the Decree *Optatam totius,* n. 22 prescribes that post-Seminary priestly training should be maintained and developed in the spiritual, intellectual and, above all, pastoral fields, so that new priests may be better equipped to undertake and perform the duties of the apostolate. One might here recommend team-work for priests which, particularly today, has much to offer for the pastoral ministry.[228]

101. As a means towards the realization of a post-Seminary training, the Scheme for Priestly Training should indicate the practical measures which the Episcopal Conference proposes and recommends. A few examples which are already in use are suggested:[229]

a) a pastoral year or biennium in which new priests live together and divide each week between a few days of classroom work and pastoral studies and the rest of the week in parish work;

b) pastoral training given to young priests over a number of years while they are engaged in the ministry. This involves one or two days a week of school and pastoral studies;

c) vacation courses or courses given at an opportune time when the younger priests are given pastoral questions for consideration and study, and in which they prepare for triennial examinations;

d) a "Priests' Month" after about five years of priestly ministry, during which young priests renew themselves spiritually by a retreat and bring themselves up-to-date in doctrine and pastoral matters by means of special courses and the study of pastoral problems under the guidance of experts.

None of these projects, however, will come up to expectations and be successful unless there is coordination between the Seminary and the post-Seminary courses, nor unless they are organized by a priest who is genuinely outstanding in intellectual ability, virtue and experience.

Finally, the fraternal cooperation of parish priests and of priests of mature age and experience is needed. They are responsible for furthering the pastoral formation of the younger clergy. But, at the same time, they must also encourage that brotherhood of priests which the Decree *Presbyterorum Ordinis* (n. 8) recommends, and make sure that there is no division between the new and older generations of priests.

This edition of the "Basic Norms for Priestly Formation" according to the norms of the new Code of Canon Law, has been ratified, confirmed and ordered to be published by the Supreme Pontiff, John Paul II, by Divine Providence Pope.

Given at Rome from the office of the Congregation on the Solemnity of Saint Joseph, Spouse of the Blessed Virgin Mary, 19th March, 1985.

William Cardinal Baum, *Prefect*

+ Anthonio M. Javierre Ortas,
Tit. Archbishop of Meta
Secretary

Notes

1. Vatican Council II, Decree *Optatam totius*, Preface; Decree *Presbyterorum Ordinis*, nn.1, 2, 7 and passim; cf. Synod of Bishops, document *Ultimis temporibus* (on the ministerial priesthood), Nov. 30, 1971: AAS, 63 (1971), pp. 903-8.

2. Vatican Council II, Decree *Optatam totius*, n. 4; cf. John Paul II, Letter *Magnus dies* to all the Bishops of the Church on the occasion of Holy Thursday, April 8, 1979: AAS 71 (1979), p.392; cf. in addition, *Insegnamenti di John Paul* II, II, 2, p.479, p.585 (hereafter *Insegnamenti* of the reigning Pontiff); Synod of Bishops, Final Declaration of the Special Synod of Dutch Bishops, January 31, 1980: AAS 72 (1980) p. 224, n.26; John Paul II, Address *Nao vos surpreendereis*, to the seminarians of Portalegre, July 5, 1980: AAS 72 (1980), pp.904-905, n.5; Address *Après avoir*, to the Professors of the Theology Faculty of Freiburg (Switzerland), June 13, 1984: *Insegnamenti*, VII, 1, p.1717; Address *Notre rencontre*, to the Bishops of the Swiss Episcopal Conference assembled in the Abbey of Einsiedeln, June 15, 1984: *Insegnamenti*, VII, 1, p.1784.

3. Vatican Council II, Decree *Optatam totius*, nn.4-6; John Paul II, Address *Oggi si celebra*, to the faithful assembled in St. Peter's Square, January 14, 1979: *Insegnamenti* II, II, 1, pp.68-69.

4. Vatican Council II, Decree *Optatam totius*, n.3.

5. Cf. note 80 for a more accurate description of a seminary.

6. Pius XII, Apostolic Exhortation *Menti Nostrae*, September 23, 1950: AAS 42 (1950), p.685; Paul VI, Address *Non è senza*, on the inauguration of the new building of the Pontifical Lombard College, Rome, November 11, 1965: *Insegnamenti*, III, pp.604-605; Sacred Congregation for Catholic Education, *A Guide to Formation in Priestly Celibacy*, April 11, 1974, nn.70 ff.

7. John XXIII, Address *E grande*, to the first national Italian convention on vocations, April 21, 1961: AAS 53 (1961), p.311; John Paul II, Address *One of the Things*, to seminarians in Philadelphia, October 3, 1979: AAS 71 (1979), pp.1189ff.

8. Vatican Council II, Decree *Gravissimum educationis*, Introduction; Pastoral Constitution *Gaudium et spes*, chapter II; Paul VI, Address *Salutiamo con vivissima*, to the leaders of the Italian Catholic Adult Scout Movement, November 5, 1966: *Insegnamenti*, IV, pp.538ff.; Address *A voi giovani*, to young people of all nations assembled in Rome, March 23, 1975: *Insegnamenti*, XIII, pp.242ff.; Address *Una grande*, to the pupils of the Catholic Schools of Rome, February 25, 1978: *Insegnamenti*, XVI, pp.152ff.; John Paul II, Address *Sono assai grato*, to the Sacred College of Cardinals, December 22, 1979: *Insegnamenti* I, II, 2, pp.1490ff.; Address *Merci, merci*, to the young people of Paris, June 1, 1980: *Insegnamenti*, III, 1, pp.1608ff.; Address *Je désire d'abord*, to UNESCO in Paris, June 2, 1980: *Insegnamenti* II, III, 1, pp.1636ff.; Address *Wenn Christus*, to the young people of Munich, November 19, 1980: *Insegnamenti*, III, 2. p.1346ff.; Address *Sim*, to the young people of Lisbon, May 14, 1982: *Insegnamenti*, V, 2, p.1668ff.

9. Paul VI, Address *Libenti fraternoque animo*, to the Delegates of the Episcopal Commissions for Seminaries assembled in Rome to deliberate the *Ratio fundamentalis*, March 27, 1969: AAS 61 (1969), pp.253-256.

10. Cf. Vatican Council II, Pastoral Constitution *Gaudium et spes*, nn. 24, 26, 41; Paul VI, Address *Salutiamo con vivissima*, cf. note 8.

11. Cf. Vatican Council II, Pastoral Constitution *Gaudium et spes*, n. 31.

12. Sacred Congregation for Catholic Education, *Circular Letter concerning Some of the More Important Aspects of Spiritual Formation in Seminaries,* January 6, 1980, part II, 3, The Word of the Cross: Spiritual Sacrifices - Obedience.

13. Vatican Council II, Dogmatic Constitution *Lumen gentium*, n.10.

14. *Ibid.* n.28. Cf. in addition John Paul II, Letter *Novo incipiente Nostro*, to all priests of the Church, Holy Thursday, April 8, 1979: AAS 71 (1979), pp.393ff.; Synod of Bishops, Document *Ultimis temporibus* (on the ministerial priesthood), November 30, 1971: AAS 63 (1971), pp.898ff.; Sacred Congregation for the Doctrine of Faith, Declaration *Mysterium Ecclesiae*, concerning the Catholic Doctrine of the Church against Certain Errors of the Day, June 24, 1973: AAS 65 (1973), p.405f., n.6; Declaration *Inter insigniores*, on the Question of the Admission of Women to the Ministerial Priesthood, October 15, 1976: AAS 69 (1977), pp.98ff.; Letter *Sacerdotium ministeriale*, to the Bishops of the Church on some questions concerning the ministry of the Eucharist, August 6, 1983: AAS 75 (1983), pp.1001ff.

15. Vatican Council II, Decree *Presbyterorum Ordinis*, n.1.

16. Vatican Council II, Dogmatic Constitution *Lumen gentium*, n.10.

17. This is to be taken into account especially in the spiritual and pastoral formation of students (cf. chapters VIII and XVI).

18. Vatican Council II, Decree *Presbyterorum Ordinis*, n.7.

19. Vatican Council II, Dogmatic Constitution *Lumen gentium*, n.28.

20. Vatican Council II, Decree *Presbyterorum Ordinis*, n.8.

21. Vatican Council II, Dogmatic Constitution *Lumen gentium*, n.28.

22. Vatican Council II, Decree *Presbyterorum Ordinis*, n.8.

23. *Ibid.* n.9.

24. Vatican Council II, Dogmatic Constitution *Lumen gentium*, n.28.

25. *Ibid.* n.48.

26. Cf. Vatican Council II, Decree *Ad gentes divinitus*, n.15.

27. Vatican Council II, Pastoral Constitution *Gaudium et spes*, n.43.

28. Vatican Council II, Decree *Presbyterorum Ordinis*, n.6.

29. Vatican Council II, Decree *Presbyterorum Ordinis*, n.4; Dogmatic Constitution *Lumen gentium*, n.28.

30. Vatican Council II, Decree *Presbyterorum Ordinis*, n.4.

31. Vatican Council II, Dogmatic Constitution *Lumen gentium*, n.28.

32. Vatican Council II, Decree *Presbyterorum Ordinis*, n.6.

33. Vatican Council II, Dogmatic Constitution *Lumen gentium*, n.10.

34. *Ibid.* nn.11, 12.

35. Vatican Council II, Decree *Presbyterorum Ordinis*, n.13; Paul VI Address *Venire in questo*, to the clergy of the diocese of Rome, February 20, 1971: *Insegnamenti*, IX, pp.119ff.; Address *Questo nostro incontro*, to the Lenten preachers and pastors of Rome, February 17, 1972: *Insegnamenti*, X, pp.157ff.; John Paul II, Address *E solene esta ora*, during the ordination of priests in Rio de Janeiro, July 2, 1980: *Insegnamenti*, III, 2, pp.54ff.; Address *I greet you*, to the priests and seminarians of Cebu (Philippines), February 19, 1981: *Insegnamenti*, IV, 1, pp.401ff.; cf. above, note 14.

36. This new situation in which the priest exercises his apostolate is more accurately described in the documents of Vatican Council II and of recent popes, e.g.: Vatican Council II, Pastoral Constitution *Gaudium et spes*; John XXIII, Encyclical Letter *Pacem in terris*, April 11, 1963: AAS 55 (1963), pp.257ff.; Encyclical Letter *Mater et Magistra*, May 15, 1961: AAS 53 (1961), pp.401ff.; Paul VI, Encyclical Letter *Ecclesiam Suam*, August 6, 1964: AAS 56 (1964), pp.609ff.; Encyclical Letter *Populorum progressio*, March 26, 1967: AAS 59 (1967), pp.257ff.; Address *Benedicamus Domino*, to the Bishops of Latin America participating in the Second General Episcopal Conference at Medellin, August 24, 1968: *Insegnamenti*, VI, pp.403ff.; Address *Questo annuale incontro*, to the Lenten preachers and pastors of Rome, February 17, 1969: *Insegnamenti*, VII, pp.116ff.; John Paul II, Address *Desidero ringraziare*, to the clergy of the diocese of Rome, November 9, 1978: *Insegnamenti*, I, pp.112ff.; Address *Esta hora*, to the Episcopal Conference of Latin America participating in the Third General Conference at Puebla, January 28, 1979: AAS 71 (1979), pp.187ff.; Encyclical Letter *Redemptor hominis*, March 4, 1979: AAS 71 (1979), pp.257ff.; Encyclical Letter *Dives in misericordia*, November 30, 1980: AAS 72 (1980), pp.1177ff.; Encyclical Letter *Laborem exercens*, September 14, 1981: AAS 73 (1981), pp.577ff.; Address *Os invito*, to the Episcopal Conference of Latin America (CELAM) at Port-au-Prince, March 9, 1983: *Insegnamenti*, VI, 1, pp.690ff.; Congregation for the Doctrine of Faith, Instruction *Libertatis nuntius*, on some problems regarding the "Theology of Liberation", August 6, 1984: AAS 76 (1984), pp.876ff.

37. Vatican Council II, Pastortal Constitution *Gaudium et spes*, nn.4-10; Paul VI, Homily *Hodie Concilium*, on the occasion of the IX session of Vatican Council II, December 7, 1965: *Insegnamenti*, III, pp.720ff.

38. Vatican Council II, Decree *Presbyterorum Ordinis*, n.22.

39. Synod of Bishops, Document *Ultimis temporibus* (on the ministerial priesthood), November 30, 1971: AAS 63 (1971), pp.899-903; John Paul II, Address *Unsere heutige denkwurdige*, to the Bishops of the German Episcopal Conference, November 17, 1980: *Insegnamenti*, III, 2, pp.1287ff.

40. These norms propose to Episcopal Conferences some general lines to guide the preparation of their national programs (*Rationes*) for priestly formation.

41. Or the Commission or Secretariat to whom seminaries are entrusted: such Commissions or Secretariats, as also the technical Commissions of *experts*, were particularly recommended by the Synod of Bishops in 1967: The Episcopal Conference is to determine their composition, duty and competence.

42. Code of Canon Law: Can. 242, par 1.

43. *Ibid.* Can. 242, par 2.

44. *Ibid.*: Can. 243; Sacred Congregation for Bishops, *Directorium*, on the pastoral ministry of Bishops, February 22, 1973, n.191.

45. Cf. Code of Canon Law, Can. 659, par 3; Vatican Council II, Decree *Optatam totius*, Preface; Paul VI, Motu proprio *Ecclesiae Sanctae*, August 6, 1966: AAS 58 (1966), p.781; with regard to mission territories, cf. Decree *Ad gentes divinitus*, n.16.

46. For example: Decree *Presbyterorum Ordinis*; Declaration *Gravissimum educationis*; Decree *Perfectae caritatis*; Dogmatic Constitution *Lumen gentium*; Pastoral Constitution *Gaudium et spes*; Decree *Unitatis redintegratio*; Constitution *Sacrosanctum Concilium*; Decree *Apostolicam actuositatem*, etc.

47. Vatican Council II, Dogmatic Constitution *Lumen gentium*, n.9; cf. Paul VI, Address *Nostro desiderio*, to the General Audience on May 5, 1965: *Insegnamenti*, II. pp.928ff.

48. Vatican Council II, Dogmatic Constitution *Lumen gentium*, n.7.

49. *Ibid.*

50. Vatican Council II, Decree *Optatam totius*, n.2.

51. Vatican Council II, Decree *Presbyterorum Ordinis*, n.6.

52. *Ibid.*; cf. Decree *Christus Dominus*, n.15.

53. Cf. Vatican Council II, Decree *Optatam totius*, n.2.

54. Vatican Council II, Dogmatic Constitution *Lumen gentium*, n.11.

55. Cf. Vatican Council II, Decree *Presbyterorum Ordinis*, n.11; Pius XII, Apostolic Constitution *Sedes sapientiae*, May 31, 1956: AAS 48 (1956), pp.357ff; Paul VI, Apostolic Letter *Summi Dei Verbum*, November 4, 1963: AAS 55 (1963), pp.984ff.; cf. Address *Il grande rito*, on the occasion of the fourth centenary of the institution of seminaries by the Council of Trent, November 4, 1963: *Insegnamenti*, I, pp.288-290; Address *Vous nous offrez*, to the altar servers of Europe, March 30, 1967: *Insegnamenti*, V, pp.126-127; John Paul II, Homily *Je suis heureux*, to the altar servers of Europe, April 9, 1980: *Insegnementi*, III, 1, pp.847ff.

56. Vatican Council II, Decree *Optatam totius*, n.2; Decree *Perfectae caritatis*, n.24; Decree *Christus Dominus*, n.15; Decree *Ad gentes divinitus*, nn.16, 39; cf. Pius XII, Motu proprio *Cum nobis*, for the constitution of the Pontifical Work for Priestly Vocations, attached to the Sacred Congregation for Seminaries and Universities, November 4, 1941: AAS 33 (1941), p.479, with the connected *Statutes and Norms*, promulgated by the same Sacred Congregation, September 8, 1943; Motu proprio *Cum supremae*, for the Pontifical

Work for Religious Vocations, February 11, 1955: AAS 47 (1955), p.266, with connected *Statutes and Norms*, promulgated by the Sacred Congregation for Religious (*ibid.*, pp.298-301).

57. Vatican Council II, Decree *Optatam totius*, n.2; Pius XII, Apostolic Constitution *Sedes sapientiae*, May 31, 1956: AAS 48 (1956), p.357; Paul VI, Apostolic Letter *Summi Dei Verbum*, November 4, 1963: AAS 55 (1963), pp.984ff.

58. Code of Canon Law, Can. 233, par 1; Vatican Council II, Decree *Optatam totius*, n. 2; Decree *Presbyterorum Ordinis*, n.11; Dogmatic Constitution *Lumen gentium*, n.11; Decree *Perfectae caritatis*, n.24; Decree *Apostolicam actuositatem*, n.11; Decree *Christus Dominus*, n.15; Pastoral Constitution *Gaudium et spes*, n.52; Decree *Ad gentes divinitus*, n.39; Pius XII, Apostolic Exhortation *Menti Nostrae*, September 23, 1950: AAS 42 (1950), p.683; John XXIII, Address *E grande*, at the First Italian National Congress on Vocations, held in Rome, April 21, 1961: AAS 53 (1961), pp.308-314; Address *Quod spectaculum*, to the participants at the First International Congress for Vocations, May 26, 1962: AAS 54 (1962), pp.451-453; Paul VI, Apostolic Letter *Summi Dei Verbum*, November 4, 1963: AAS 55 (1963), pp.985ff.; John Paul II, Homily *Queste parole di Maria*, at the Mass for the pupils of the Roman Minor Seminary, March 20, 1983: *Insegnamenti*, IV, 2, pp.1170ff.; Address *La Vostra visita*, to the parents of the pupils of the Roman Minor Seminary, March 20, 1983: *Insegnamenti*, VI, 1, pp.770ff.; Sacred Congregation for Seminaries and Universities, *La preminente*, Instruction concerning the cooperation of Catholic Action in the promotion of priestly vocations, October 1, 1960; Sacred Congregation for Bishops, *Directorium*, on the pastoral ministry of Bishops, February 22, 1973, n.197; Sacred Congregation for Catholic Education, *Developments in the pastoral care for vocations*, May 10-16, 1981, n.57.

59. Letter from Cardinal A.G. Cicognani, Secretary of State, to Cardinal G. Pizzardo, Prefect of the Sacred Congregation for Seminaries and Universities, January 23, 1964; Paul VI, Radio Message *Pregate il Padrone*, April 11, 1964: *Insegnamenti*, II, pp.204ff.; Letter *Il felice esito*, to Cardinal Giuseppe Pizzardo, Prefect of the Sacred Congregation for Seminaries and Universities, and Cardinal Ildebrando Antoniutti, Prefect of the Sacred Congregation for Religious and Secular Institutes, April 26, 1965: AAS 57 (1965), pp.504ff.; Messages for the World Day of Prayer for Vocations: 1966: *Insegnamenti*, IV, p.748; 1967: *Insegnamenti*, V, pp.669ff.; 1968: *Insegnamenti*, VI, pp.133ff.; 1969: *Insegnamenti*, VII, pp.1270ff.; 1970: *Insegnamenti*, VIII, pp.188ff.; 1971: Insegnamenti, IX, pp.358ff.; 1972: *Insegnamenti*, X, pp.263ff.; 1973: *Insegnamenti*, XI, pp.247ff.; 1974: *Insegnamenti*, XII, pp.373ff.; 1975: *Insegnamenti*, XIII, pp.282ff.; 1976: *Insegnamenti*, XIV, pp.87ff.; 1977: *Insegnamenti*, XIV, pp.1117ff.; 1978: *Insegnamenti*, XVI, pp.256ff.; John Paul II, 1979: *Insegnamenti*, II, pp.937ff.; 1980: *Insegnamenti*, III,1, pp.951ff.; 1981: *Insegnamenti*, IV, 1, pp. 1057ff.; 1982: *Insegnamenti*, V, 1, pp.1265ff.; 1983: *Insegnamenti*, VI, 1, pp.302ff.; 1984: *Insegnamenti*, VII, 1, pp.369ff.

60. Vatican Council II, Decree *Presbyterorum Ordinis*, n.11; Decree *Optatam totius*, n.2.

61. John Paul II, Address *Desidero ringraziare*, to the clergy of the diocese of Rome, November 9, 1978: *Insegnamenti*, I, p.117; Address *Cristo pronuncia*, to the Episcopal Conference of Italy, May 15, 1979: *Insegnamenti*, II, pp.1127; Address *Sono sinceramente lieto*, to representatives of the Major Superiors of Italy, February 16, 1980: *Insegnamenti*, III, pp.394ff.; Homily *Nella quarta Domenica*, at the inauguration of the II International Congress on Vocations, May 10, 1981: *Insegnamenti*, IV, 1, pp.1147ff.; Sacred Congregation for Catholic Education, Developments in the pastoral care of vocations, May 10-16, 1981.

62. Code of Canon Law, Can. 233, par 2; 385; Vatican Council II, Decree *Optatam totius*, n.2; cf. the documents reported in footnote 58; concerning adult vocations, cf. Apostolic Exhortation *Menti nostrae*, September 23, 1950: AAS 42 (1950), p.684; Sacred Congregation for Bishops, *Directory*, on the pastoral ministry of Bishops, February 22, 1973, n.196; Sacred Congregation for Catholic Education, *Circular Letter, to the Presidents of Episcopal Conferences*, July 14, 1976.

63. Vatican Council II, Decree *Optatam totius*, n.2; Decree *Presbyterorum Ordinis*, nn. 10-11; Sacred Congregation for Bishops, *Directory*, on the pastoral ministry of Bishops, February 22, 1973, n.197.

64. Vatican Council II affirmed the necessity of the major seminary as the institution immediately directed towards and necessary to the priesthood, referring also to the institution called the minor seminary, which had been common until then. The Council certainly established that it - the minor seminary - must be completely renewed, but it affirmed that it is still a valid institution for our times, well adapted for the nourishing of vocations. The Council also established some norms which, though few, are very apt in helping the minor seminary perform its important role in the present circumstances, that it have a specific structure which is consonant with its nature and purpose, and that it not be a major seminary in miniature in which one could not provide the necessary care and freedom for vocations. The Council, while recommending the minor seminary, did not deny the possibility of experimenting with other methods of fostering vocations, provided that the institution of the minor seminary not be damaged by them, and that the new methods prudently serve their purpose and not hide the renunciation of the minor seminary. The Church holds, in fact, from her doctrine, experience and practice, that even in childhood the signs of a divine vocation may be discerned and that they require diligent and appropriate fostering.

65. Code of Canon Law, Can. 234; Vatican Council II, Decree *Optatam totius*, n.3; Pius XII, Apostolic Exhortation *Menti Nostrae*, September 23, 1950: AAS 42 (1950), p.685; Apostolic Constitution *Sedes sapientiae*, May 31, 1956: AAS 48 (1956), pp.358ff.; Address *C'est une grande joie*, to the pupils of the minor seminaries in France, gathered in Rome on pilgrimage, September 5, 1957: AAS 49 (1957), pp.845-849; Sacred Congregation for Catholic Education, Developments in the pastoral care of vocations, May 10-16, 1981, n.53.

66. Vatican Council II, Decree *Optatam totius*, n.6; Pius XII, Apostolic Exhortation *Menti Nostrae*, September 23, 1950: AAS 42 (1950), p.684; Apostolic Constitution *Sedes sapientiae*, May 31, 1956: AAS 48 (1956), p.357; Paul VI, Apostolic Letter *Summi Dei Verbum*, November 4, 1963: AAS 55 (1963), pp.990ff.; cf. the notes to paragraphs numbered 39-40.

49

67. Vatican Council II, Decree *Optatam totius*, n.9; Pastoral Constitution *Gaudium et spes*, n.25; Decree *Ad gentes divinitus*, n.39; Paul VI, Encyclical Letter *Ecclesiam Suam*, August 6, 1964: AAS 56 (1964), pp. 627, 638; Address *L'odierna udienza*, at the general audience of September 2, 1964: *Insegnamenti*, II, pp. 517-519.

68. Vatican Council II, Decree *Optatam totius*, n.3; Declaration *Gravissimum educationis*, n.3; cf. Pius XII, Apostolic Exhortation *Menti Nostrae*, September 23, 1950: AAS 42 (1950), p.685; John Paul II, Apostolic Exhortation *Familiaris consortio*, November 22, 1981: AAS 74 (1982), pp.145ff.; nn.53, 54.

69. Vatican Council II, Decree *Optatam totius*, n.3; Declaration *Gravissimum educationis*, n.1; Pius XII, Apostolic Exhortation *Menti Nostrae*, September 23, 1950: AAS 42 (1950), p.687; Apostolic Constitution *Sedes sapientiae*, May 31, 1950: AAS 48 (1956), p.357; Paul VI, Radio Message *La quinta giornata*, on the occasion of the fifth World Day of Prayer for Vocations, 1968: *Insegnamenti*, VI, pp.134-135.

70. Vatican Council II, Decree *Optatam totius*, n.5.

71. Vatican Council II, Declaration *Gravissimum educationis*, n.1; cf. Pius XII, Apostolic Constitution *Sedes sapientiae*, May 31, 1956: AAS 48 (1956), pp.359-360.

72. Vatican Council II, Decree *Optatam totius*, n.3.

73. Vatican Council II, Decree *Optatam totius*, n.8; Constitution *Sacrosanctum Concilium*, nn.13, 14, 17; cf. Declaration *Gravissimum educationis*, nn. 2, 4; Pius XII Apostolic Exhortation *Menti Nostrae*, September 23, 1950: AAS 42 (1950), pp.671, 689; Paul VI, Address *Il Concilio*, to the Bishops of Italy, December 6, 1965: *Insegnamenti*, III, p.710; Sacred Congregation for the Sacraments, Instruction *Postquam Pius*, to Bishops on daily communion in seminaries and other ecclesiastical institutes, December 8, 1938; Sacred Congregation for Rites, Instruction *Inter oecumenici*, on the correct implementation of the Constitution on the Sacred Liturgy, September 26, 1964, nn.14, 15, 17, 18: AAS 56 (1964), pp.880-881; Instruction *De cultu mysterii eucharistici*, May 25, 1967: AAS 59 (1967), pp.539-573; Sacred Congregation for Catholic Education, *Instruction on Liturgical Formation in Seminaries*, June 3, 1979.

74. Code of Canon Law: Can. 243; John XXIII, Address *Questo incontro*, to Spiritual Directors assembled in Rome, September 9, 1962: AAS 54 (1962), p.676; Sacred Congregation for Bishops, *Directorium* on the pastoral ministry of Bishops, February 22, 1973, n.191; Sacred Congregation for Catholic Education, *Circular Letter on Some of the More Urgent Aspects of Spiritual Formation in Seminaries*, January 6, 1980, p.20.

75. Code of Canon Law: Can. 234, par 2.

76. Vatican Council II, Decree *Optatam totius*, n.3; cf. Pius XII, Apostolic Exhortation *Menti Nostrae*, September 23, 1950: AAS 42 (1950), p.687; Apostolic Constitution *Sedes sapientiae*, May 31, 1956: AAS 48 (1956), pp.361-362.

77. Sacred Congregation for Bishops, *Directorium* on the pastoral ministry of Bishops, February 22, 1973, n.194.

78. Vatican Council II, Decree *Optatam totius*, n.3; cf.n.13.

79. Code of Canon Law: Can. 233, par. 2; Vatican Council II, Decree *Optatam totius*, n.3; Sacred Congregation for Bishops, *Directorium* on the pastoral ministry of Bishops, February 22, 1973, n.196; Sacred Congregation for Catholic Education, *Circular Letter, to the Presidents of Episcopal Conferences*, July 14, 1976.

80. Vatican Council II affirmed the necessity of major seminaries (*Optatam totius*, n. 4) and prescribed many norms for their renewal in their various aspects. In order to satisfy this clear desire and to meet the new necessities arising, it is necessary to clarify perfectly ideas about this institution: that is, what is - and what is not - of the essence of a major seminary, according to the mind of the Church.

Its identity and essential characteristics can be deduced from the documents and the constant thought of the Church : a community filled with the true spirit of charity, open to the necessities of the world today, systematically organised, in which the authority of the legitimate superior is responsibly and effectively exercised, according to the example of Christ, and in such a way that with the help of others the human and Christian maturity of the students is promoted; it offers the possibility of beginning to experience the priestly state by means of fraternal and hierarchically dependent relationships; the doctrine of the priesthood and the life of the priest in all the circumstances in which he finds himself are clearly explained by superiors delegated by the Bishop himself so that the students gradually come to know and accept both that which pertains to faith and doctrine and that which pertains to the conduct of life; it offers the opportunity for tying a vocation and for confirming it with signs and sound qualities which can offer the Bishop a certain judgement on the suitability of the candidate.

81. Vatican Council II, Decree *Optatam totius*, n. 4.

82. Code of Canon Law: Can. 239; 253, par. 2; cf. Vatican Council II, Decree *Optatam totius*, nn. 5, 9.

83. Code of Canon Law: Can. 237, par. 2; 242, par. 2; Vatican Council II, Decree *Optatam totius*, n.7; cf. Pius XI, Apostolic Letter *Officiorum omnium*, August 1, 1922: AAS 14 (1922), pp.456-457; Encyclical Letter *Ad Catholici Sacerdotii*, December 20, 1935: AAS 28 (1936), pp.38-39; Sacred Congregation for Bishops, *Directorium*, on the pastoral ministry of Bishops, February 22, 1973, n.193.

84. Sacred Congregation for Religious and Secular Institutes-Sacred Congregation for Bishops, *Notae directivae*, on the mutual relations between Bishops and Religious in the Church, May 14, 1978: AAS 70 (1978), p.473, nn.31, 42.

85. Code of Canon Law: Can. 245, par. 2; Vatican Council II, Decree *Presbyterorum Ordinis*, n.8; Dogmatic Constitution *Lumen gentium*, n.28; Pius XII Apostolic Exhortation *Menti Nostrae*, September 23, 1950: AAS 42 (1950), p.690; Sacred Congregation for Bishops, *Directorium*, on the pastoral ministry of Bishops, February 22, 1973, n.191.

86. Vatican Council II, Decree *Optatam totius*, n. 7.

87. John Paul II, Allocution *Nao vos surpreendereis*, to seminarians living in the city of Porto Alegre, July 5, 1980: *Insegnamenti*, III, 2, p. 134 s., n. 8.

88. Code of Canon Law: Can. 239, par. 3; cf. Vatican Council II, Decree *Optatam totius*, n. 11; Paul VI, Encyclical Letter *Sacerdotalis caelibatus*, June 24, 1967: AAS 59 (1967), p. 684, n. 68; Address *Libenti fraternoque animo*, to the delegates of the Episcopal Seminary Commissions meeting in Rome to work out the *Ratio Fundamentalis*, March 27, 1969: AAS 61 (1969), pp. 253-256; Sacred Congregation for Catholic Education, *Circular Letter concerning Some of the More Urgent Aspects of Spiritual Formation in Seminaries*.

89. Code of Canon Law: Can. 243; John Paul II, Allocution, *One of the things*, to the seminary students of Philadelphia, October 3, 1979: AAS 71 (1979, pp. 1189 ss.; Allocution *Nel rivolgervi*, to the governing staff of the major seminaries of Italy, January 5, 1982: *Insegnamenti*, V, 1, pp. 34-35; Sacred Congregation for Bishops, *Directorium* on the pastoral ministry of Bishops, February 22, 1973, n. 191; Sacred Congregation for Catholic Education, *Directorium, A Guide to Formation in Priestly Celibacy*, April 11, 1974, n. 74; *Circular Letter Concerning Some of the More Urgent Aspects of Spiritual Formation in Seminaries*, January 6, 1980, p. 20.

90. Vatican Council II, Decree *Optatam totius*, n. 11; cf. Pius XII, Apostolic Exhortation *Menti Nostrae*, September 23, 1950: AAS, 42 (1950), p. 686; John XXIII, Address *Questo incontro*, to Spiritual Directors meeting in Rome, September 9, 1962: AAS 54 (1962), p. 676; Paul VI, Encyclical *Sacerdotalis caelibatus*, June 24, 1967: AAS 59 (1967), p. 684, no. 67.

91. Code of Canon Law: Can. 239.

92. Code of Canon Law: Can. 259, par. 1.

93. Cf. Vatican Council II, Decree *Optatam totius*, n. 5; Pius XI, Encyclical Letter *Ad Catholici Sacerdotii*, December 20, 1935: AAS, 28 (1936), p. 37; Paul VI, Apostolic Letter *Summi Dei Verbum*, November 4, 1963: AAS 55 (1963).

94. Code of Canon Law: Can 260.

95. Cf. John XXIII, Address *L'incontro odierno* to the Rectors from all Italy who took part in the Congress on training students by up-to-date method, July 29, 1961: AAS 53 (1961), p. 562; Address *Questo incontro*, to Spiritual Directors meeting in Rome, September 9, 1962: AAS 54 (1962), p. 673.

96. Vatican Council II, Decree *Optatam totius*, n. 5; cf. Decree *Perfectae caritatis*, n. 18; Pius XI, Encyclical Letter *Ad Catholici Sacerdotii*, December 20, 1935: AAS 28 (1936), p. 37; cf John XXIII, Address *E grande*, to the members of the Congress held in Rome from all Italy for the fostering of priestly vocations, April 21, 1961: AAS 53 (1961), p. 311; Sacred Congregation for Bishops, *Directorium*, on the pastoral ministry of Bishops, February 22, 1973, n. 192.

97. Cf. *Question no. IV* in the Synod of Bishops (a. 1967) put forward by the Cardinal Prefect of the Sacred Congregation for Catholic Education: "Should it be prescribed that the teachers of future clergy must be given special preparation, through regular attendance at some Institute or School of Higher Studies set up or approved by the Episcopal Conference, or at least by taking part in some courses arranged for the purpose". The Fathers voted on the question as follows: placet 120, non placet 8, placet iuxta modum 51, with 3 abstentions.

Cf. John XXIII, Address *Questo incontro*, to Spiritual Directors meeting in Rome, September 9, 1962: AAS 54 (1962), p. 674.

98. Cf. Vatican Council II, Decree *Christus Dominus*, n. 16; John XXIII, Address *L'incontro odierno*, to Seminary Rectors from all Italy present at the Congress on bringing students' education up-to-date, July 29, 1961: AAS 53 (1961), p. 560; Address *La vostra vibrante*, to Catholic teachers meeting in Rome, September 22, 1962: AAS 54 (1962), pp. 713-714; Paul VI, Motu proprio *Ecclesiae Sanctae*, August 6, 1966: AAS 58 (1966), p. 786; III, n. 3.

99. Code of Canon Law: Can. 253, par. 2; Vatican Council II, Decree *Optatam totius*, n. 5; Decree *Perfectae Caritatis*, n. 18; Paul VI, Allocution, *Questa Nostra*, to delegates of the faculties of studies of academic ecclesiastics, December 1, 1976; *Insegnamenti*, XIV, pp.998-999; Sacred Congregation for the Doctrine of Faith, *Normae*, on the conditions on which those serving as priests are reduced to the lay state, January 13, 1971: AAS 63 (1971), p. 308; Sacred Congregation for Bishops, *Directorium*, on the pastoral ministry of bishops, February 22, 1973, n. 192.

100. Pius XII, Apostolic Constitution *Sedes sapientiae*, May 31, 1956: AAS 48 (1956), p. 362.

101. Code of Canon Law: Can 253, par. 1; Sacred Congregation for Catholic Education, *Letter on The Theological Formation of Future Priests*, February 22, 1976, nn. 117-119 (La formazione teologica dei futuri sacerdoti).

102. Cf. above note 99.

103. Cf. Paul VI, Motu proprio *Ecclesiae Sanctae*, August 6, 1966: AAS 58 (1966), p. 786; III, n. 3.

104. Code of Canon Law: Can. 261, par. 1.

105. Vatican Council II, Decree *Optatam totius*, n. 5; cf. Pius XII, Apostolic Constitution *Sedes sapientiae*, May 31, 1956: AAS 48 (1956), pp. 362-363; John XXIII, Allocution *E grande*, to the First Italian Congress for the fostering of vocations held in Rome, April 21, 1961: AAS 53 (1961), p. 311; John Paul II, Allocution *Dopo le recenti*, to the professors and students of the Pontifical Lateran University, February 16, 1980: *Insegnamenti*, III, i, pp. 408 ss.

106. Code of Canon Law: Can. 241.

107. Sacred Congregation for Catholic Education, *Directorium, A Guide to Formation in Priestly Celibacy*, April 11, 1974, n. 38.

108. Paul VI, Encyclical Letter *Sacerdotalis caelibatus*, June 24, 1967: AAS 59 (1967), pp. 682-683, n. 63; Sacred Congregation for the Holy Office, Admonition *Cum compertum*, on some erroneous opinions about sins against the 6th commandment and on psychoanalysis, July 15, 1961: AAS 53 (1961), p. 571; Sacred Congregation for Religious and Secular Institutes, Instruction *Renovationis causam*, on reform of training for the religious life, January 6, 1969: AAS 61 (1969), p. 113, n. 11; Sacred Congregation for Catholic Education, *Directorium, A Guide to Formation in Priestly Celibacy*, April 11, 1974, n. 38.

109. Code of Canon Law: Can. 241, par. 3.

110. Code of Canon Law: Can. 1026; 1029; Vatican Council II, Decree *Optatam totius*, n. 6; Pius XI, Encyclical *Ad Catholici Sacerdotii*, December 20, 1935: AAS 28 (1936), p. 41; Pius XII, Apostolic Exhortation *Menti Nostrae*, September 23, 1950: AAS 42 (1950), p. 684; Sacred Congregation for the Sacraments, Letter *Magna equidem*, sent to local Ordinaries, December 27, 1955, n. 10; for religious, cf. *Statuta Generalia* appended to the Apostolic Constitution *Sedes sapientiae*, May 31, 1956, art. 33; John XXIII, Encyclical Letter *Princeps Pastorum*, November 28, 1959: AAS 51 (1959), pp. 842-843; Address, *Ad vobiscum*, at the second session of the Roman Synod, January 26, 1960: AAS 52 (1960), p. 224 seq.; PAUL VI, Apostolic Letter *Summi Dei Verbum*, November 4, 1963: AAS 55 (1963), p. 987 seq.; Encyclical Letter *Sacerdotalis caelibatus*, June 24, 1967: AAS 59 (1967), pp. 682 seq.

111. Sacred Congregation for the Sacraments, Letter *Magna equidem*, to local Ordinaries, December 27, 1955, nn. 4 seq.

112. Code of Canon Law: Can. 1051; 1025, par. 1; 1029; Pius XI, Encyclical Letter *Ad Catholici Sacerdotii*, December 20, 1935: AAS 28 (1936), pp. 39 seq; Sacred Congregation for Bishops, *Directorium* on the pastoral ministry of Bishops, February 22, 1973, n. 191.

113. Vatican Council II, Decree *Optatam totius*, n. 12; Paul VI, Encyclical Letter *Sacerdotalis caelibatus*, June 24, 1967: AAS 59 (1967), p. 685, n. 71.; cf. Sacred Congregation for Religious and Secular Institutes, Instruction *Renovationis causam*, on the reform of training for religious life, January 6, 1969: AAS 61 (1969), pp. 109, 115 s., nn. 5, 23, 24.

114. Code of Canon Law: Can 1031, par. 3; Vatican Council II, Decree *Optatam totius*, n. 12; cf. Sacred Congregation for Religious and Secular Institutes, Instruction *Renovationis causam*, January 6, 1969: AAS 61 (1969), p. 110, n. 6 (in regard to solemn vows).

115. This chapter treats some guidelines for the priest's spiritual life. They should be developed step by step in the life of seminarians. They can be summarised as follows:

The spiritual life of the students takes its main pattern from Christ the Priest, with whom future priests have a special relationship through their vocation. Since they must share "in the one priesthood and ministry of Christ" (*Presbyterorum Ordinis*, no. 7), they must be conformed to Him not only through sacred Ordination, but with their whole heart, gradually by daily effort taking up the life taught by the gospel. They must dedicate themselves to Christ in a special way and follow Him "who in virginity and poverty (cf. Mt 8, 20; Lk 9, 58) by his obedience unto the death of the Cross (cf. Phil 2, 8) redeemed and sanctified mankind" (*Perfectae caritatis*, n. 1).

Growing ever more strong in faith, hope, and charity, they should open their minds to the light of the Holy Spirit, and endeavour to acquire the habit of prayer particularly from the Liturgy and from contemplation of God's Word. Drawing nourishment from regular use of the sacraments, they should try to develop all virtues harmoniously. Thus they can become worthy "ministers of Christ the Head" (*Presbyterorum Ordinis*, n. 12) in his mystical Body. They will in that way be guided to a sense of the Church, be prepared for their future apostolic work, and be able to cooperate with the diocesan clergy under the authority of the Bishop, in a spirit of service, humility and fellowship. Pastoral charity should help them to grasp quickly and intelligently how human society is changing, to interpret the signs of the times, and to unite their interior life with their external activity in the light of God's will (cf. *Presbyterorum Ordinis*, n. 14). Through the faithful carrying out of their apostolate they may then attain holiness, and though living in this world may show that they are not of it (cf. *Lumen gentium*, n. 41).

116. Vatican Council II, Decree *Optatam totius*, nos. 4, 8; Dogmatic Constitution *Lumen gentium*, no. 28; Decree *Presbyterorum Ordinis*, nn. 4, 5, 6; Pius XII, Apostolic Exhortation *Menti Nostrae*, September 23, 1950: AAS 42 (1950), pp. 660ff.; John XXIII, Encyclical Letter *Sacerdotii Nostri primordia*, August 1, 1959: AAS 51 (1959), pp. 545 ss.; Paul VI, Apostolic Letter *Summi Dei Verbum*, November 4, 1963: AAS 55 (1963), pp. 979ff.; Sacred Congregation for Catholic Education, *Circular Letter concerning Some of the More Urgent Aspects of Spiritual Formation in Seminaries*, January 6, 1980.

117. Code of Canon Law: Can. 239, par. 2; 246, par 4; Vatican Council II, Decree *Optatam totius*, n. 8; John XXIII, Apostolic Letter *Pater misericordiarum*, August 22, 1961: AAS 53 (1961), p. 677; Address, *Questo incontro*, to Spiritual Directors meeting in Rome, September 9, 1962: AAS 54 (1962), pp. 673-674; John Paul II, Address, *Nel rivolgervi*, to the superiors of the major seminaries of Italy, January 5, 1982: *Insegnamenti*, V, 1, pp. 33-34.

118. Vatican Council II, Decree *Optatam totius*, n. 11; Decree *Presbyterorum Ordinis*, n. 3; cf. Pius XII, Address *Magis quam*, to Discalced Carmelites, September 23, 1951: *Discorsi e Radiomessaggi*, XIII, p. 256; Apostolic Constitution *Sedes sapientiae*, May 31, 1956: AAS 48 (1956), pp. 358-360; Paul VI, Address *Il 12 dicembre*, given at the opening of the new South American College Buildings, Rome, November 30, 1963: *Insegnamenti*, I, p. 352; Encyclical Letter *Sacerdotalis caelibatus*, June 24, 1967: AAS 59 (1967), pp. 683-684, nn. 65-67.

119. Code of Canon Law: Can 245, par. 1; cf. Vatican Council II, Decree *Perfectae caritatis*, n. 15.

120. Vatican Council II, Decree *Presbyterorum Ordinis*, no. 8.

121. Code of Canon Law: Can 245, par. 2; Pius XII, Apostolic Exhortation *Menti Nostrae*, September 23, 1950: AAS 41 (1950), pp. 686-687; cf. also John XXIII, Encyclical Letter *Princeps Pastorum*, November 28, 1959: AAS 51 (1959), p. 842; John Paul II, Address *Je ne pouvais achever*, to the students of the major seminary of Paris at Issy-les-Moulineaux, June 1, 1980: *Insegnamenti*, III, 1, p. 1606.

122. Vatican Council II, Decree *Optatam totius*, no. 10; Decree *Presbyterorum ordinis* , n. 16; Paul VI, Encyclical Letter, *Sacerdotalis caelibatus*, June 24, 1967; AASS 59 (1967), pp. 657-697; John Paul II, Encyclical Letter, *Redemptor hominis*, March 4, 1979; AAS 71 (1979), pp. 319-320, n. 21; Letter *Novo incipiente nostra*, to all priests on the occasion of Holy Thursday, April 9, 1979: AAS 71 (1979), pp. 405-409, nn. 8,9; Synod of Bishops, Document *Ultimis temporibus*, on the ministerial priesthood, November 30, 1971: AAS 63 (1971), pp. 915 ff.

123. Vatican Council II, Decree *Presbyterorum Ordinis*, no. 16.

124. Code of Canon Law: Can 247; Paul VI, Encyclical Letter *Sacerdotalis caelibatus*, June 24, 1967: AAS 59 (1967), pp. 686-690, nn. 72-82.

125. Vatican Council II, Decree *Optatam totius*, n. 10.

126. Paul VI, Encyclical Letter *Sacerdotalis caelibatus*, June 24, 1967: AAS 59 (1967), p. 683, nn. 65,66.

127. Cf. Vatican Council II, Declaration *Gravissimum educationis*, n. 1; cf. Pius XII, Address *Magis quam*, to Discalced Carmelites, September 23, 1951: *Discorsi e Radiomessaggi*, XIII, p. 257; Encyclical Letter *Sacra Virginitas*, 25 March 1954: AAS 46 (1954), pp. 183-186; Sacred Congregation for Catholic Education, *Directorium*, A Guide to Formation in Priestly Celibacy, April 11, 1974; *Educational Guidance in Human Love (Orientamenti educativi sull'amore umano)*, November 1, 1983.

128. Vatican Council II, Decree *Perfectae caritatis*, no. 12; cf. John XXIII, Encyclical Letter *Sacerdotii Nostri primmordia*, August 1, 1959: AAS 51 (1959), pp. 554-556; Address *Questo incontro*, to students from some Italian Seminaries, November 22, 1959: AAS 51 (1959), pp. 904-905; Paul VI, Encyclical Letter *Sacerdotalis caelibatus*, June 24, 1967: AAS 59 (1967), pp. 684-685, n. 70; Sacred Congregation for the Doctrine of Faith, Declaration *Persona humana*, on certain questions concerning sexual ethics, December 29, 1975: AAS 68(1976), pp. 77 ss.; Sacred Congregation for Catholic Education, *Educational Guidance in Human Love*, November 1, 1983, nn. 94-105.

129. Vatican Council II, Decree *Presbyterorum Ordinis*, no. 15.

130. Sacred Congregation for Catholic Education, *Directorium*, A Guide to Formation in Priestly Celibacy, April 11, 1974, n. 74; *Circular Letter concerning Some of the More Urgent Aspects of Spiritual Formation in Seminaries*, January 6, 1980, pp. 20 s.

131. Code of Canon Law: Can. 245, par. 2; Vatican Council II, Decree, *Optatam totius*, nos 9, 11; Decree, *Presbyerorum ordinis*, nos. 7, 15; Dogmatica Constitution, *Lumen gentium*, no. 28; cf. Pius XII, Apostolic Exhortation, *Menti Nostrae*, September 23, 1950: AAS, 42 (1950); John XXIII, Encyclical, *Sacerdoti Nostri primordia*, August 1, 1959: AAS, 51 (1959), pp. 556-558; Paul VI, Allocution, *Libenti fraternoque*, to the delegates from Episcopal Commissions for Seminaries meeting in Rome to work out the "Ratio Fundamentalis," March 27, 1969: AAS, 61 (1969), pp. 253-256; John Paul II, Allocution, *Potete immaginare*, to the students of Roman major seminaries, October 13, 1979; *Insegnamenti*, II, 2, pp. 744ff.

132. Vatican Council II, Decree *Presbyterorum Ordinis*, no. 17.

133. *Ibid.*, no. 6.

134. Vatican Council II, Decree *Optatam totius*, no. 9; cf. John XXIII, Encyclical Letter *Sacerdotii Nostri primordia*, August 1, 1959: AAS 51 (1959), pp. 551-554; Paul VI, Address *Siamo particolarmente*, to the priests attending the Congress of the association "Federazione Associazioni del Clero Italiano", June 30, 1965: *Insegnamenti*, III, pp. 385-386; Address *Benedicamus Domino*, to the South American Prelates about to take part in the second general Assembly at Medellin, August 24, 1968: *Insegnamenti*, VI, pp. 411-412; Address *Se vogliamo*, to the faithful in audience, October 2, 1968: *Insegnamenti*, VI, pp. 943 ss.; Apostolic Exhortation *Evangelii nuntiandi*, December 8, 1975: AAS 68 (1976), pp. 25 ss., nn. 29 ss.; John Paul II, Address *Esta hora*, to the Bishops of Latin America gathered at the III plenary conference at Puebla, January 28, 1979: AAS 71 (1979), pp. 198ff.; Encyclical Letter *Redemptor hominis*, March 4, 1979: AAS 71 (1979), pp. 289ff., no. 16; Encyclical Letter *Dives in misericordia*, November 30, 1980: AAS 72 (1980), pp. 1196ff., nn. 6, 11, 12, 14.

135. Cf. Vatican Council II, Decree *Optatam totius*, no. 11; Decree *Presbyterorum Ordinis*, no. 3; Declaration *Gravissimum educationis*, n. 1; cf. Pius XII, Address *Sull'esempio*, prepared for the 50th anniversary of the founding of the Regional Seminary of Apulia, October 1958: *Discorsi e Radiomessaggi*, XX, pp. 446-447; Paul VI, Apostolic Letter *Summi Dei Verbum*, November 4, 1963: AAS 55 (1963), p. 991; cf. also note 118.

136. Cf. Vatican Council II, Decree, *Optatam totius*, no. 19; Decree, *Presbyterorum ordinis*, nos. 6,9; Dogmatic Constitution, *Lumen gentium*, no. 28; Paul VI, Encyclical Letter, *Ecclesiam Suam*, August 6, 1964: AAS 56 (1964)m pp, 640 ff.; Address, *Il Concilio*, to the faithful in audience, October 9, 1968: *Insegnamenti*, VI, pp 959ff.; John Paul II, Letter, *Novo incipiente Nostro*, to all priests on the occasion of Holy Thursday, April 8, 1979: AAS 71 (1979), pp. 400 ff., nn. 5-7.

137. Vatican Council II, Dogmatic Constitution, *Lumen Gentium*, no. 11; cf. Sacred Congregation for the Discipline of Sacraments, *Instructio*, on giving sacramental communion more easily in certain suitable circumstances, January 29, 1973: AAS, 64 (1973), pp. 264 ff.

138. Code of Canon Law, Can. 246, par. 1; Vatican Council II, Constitution, *Sacrosanctum Concilium*, no. 10; cf. Sacred Congregation for Rites, Instruction, *de cultu mysterii Eucharistici*, May 25, 1967: AAS 59 (1967), pp. 539-573; John Paul II, Encyclical Letter *Redemptor hominis*, March 4, 1979: AAS 71 (1979), pp. 309 ff., n. 20; Letter *Dominicae Cenae* to all bishops on the worship of the Most Holy Eucharist, February 24, 1980: AAS 72 (1980), pp. 113 ff.; Sacred Congregation for Sacraments and Divine Worships, Instruction, *Inaestimable donum*, on some norms concerning the worship of the Eucharistic Mystery, April 3, 1980: AAS 72 (1980), pp, 331 ff.; Sacred Congregation for Catholic Education, Instruction, on liturgical instruction in seminaries, June 3, 1979, nn. 22 ff.; *Circular Letter concerning Some of the More Urgent Aspects of Spiritual Formation in Seminaries*, January 6, 1980, pp 14 ff.; Sacred Congregation for the Doctrine of Faith, Letter, *Sacerdotium ministeriale* to the bishops of the Church on some questions concerning the ministry of the Eucharist, August 6, 1983: AAS 75 (1983), pp. 1001 ff.

139. Vatican Council II, Decree *Optatam totius*, no. 8; Constitution *Sacrosanctum Concilium*, nos. 17, 18, 19; Decree *Presbyterorum Ordinis*, no. 5; Decree *Ad gentes divinitus*, no. 19; Sacred Congregation of Rites, Instruction *Inter Oecumenici*, on the implementation of the Constitution on the Sacred Liturgy, September 26, 1964: AAS 56 (1964), nos 14, 15; cf. also Paul VI, Address *Voi avete*, to delegates attending the Congress "XIII Settimana Nazionale di Orientamento Pastorale", Rome, September 6,

1963: *Insegnamenti*, I, pp. 121-122; Encyclical Letter *Mysterium Fidei*, September 3, 1965: AAS 57 (1965), pp. 770 ss.; Sacred Congregation for Catholic Education, Instruction on Liturgical Formation in Seminaries, June 3, 1979, nos. 17, 18, 20, 21.

140. Code of Canon Law: Can. 246, par. 2; Vatican Council II, Decree *Presbyterorum Ordinis*, no. 5.

141. Code of Canon Law: Can. 276, par. 2, sec. 3; Vatican Council II, Constitution *Sacrosanctum Concilium*, nos. 17, 90; Sacred Congregation for Rites, Instruction *Inter Oecumenici*, nos. 14-17; Sacred Congregation for Catholic Education, *Instruction on Liturgical Formation in Seminaries*, June 3, 1979, nos. 11, 28 ss.; Appendix, nn. 68 ss.; *Circular Letter concerning Some of the More Urgent Aspects of Spiritual Formation in Seminaries*, January 6, 1980, pp. 12 f.

142. Vatican Council II, Constitution *Sacrosanctum Concilium*, no. 10.

143. Vatican Council II, Decree *Optatam totius*, no. 8.

144. Code of Canon Law, Can. 246, par 3; Paul VI, Apostolic Exhortation, *Marialis cultus* to all bishops on rightly establishing and promoting the veneration of the Blessed Virgin Mary, February 2, 1974: AAS 66 (1974), p 21 ff; John Paul II, Encyclical Letter, *Redemptor hominis*, March 4, 1979: AAS 71 (1979), pp. 320 ff; n. 22; *Novo incipiente Nostro*, to all priests on the occasion of Holy Thursday, April 8, 1979: AAS 71 (1979), p. 415 f., n. 11; Address *Penso che abbiate*, to students of the major seminaries of Rome, February 12, 1983; *Insegnamenti*, VI, 1, pp. 409 ff.; Sacred Congregation for Catholic Education, *Circular Letter concerning Some of the More Urgent Aspects of Spiritual Formation in Seminaries*, January 6, 1980, p. 21.

145. Cf. Vatican Council II, Decree *Optatam totius*, no. 8; Constitution *Sacrosanctum Concilium*, nos. 12, 13; Decree *Perfectae caritatis*, no. 6; cf. Sacred Congregation for Catholic Education, *A Guide to Formation in Priestly Celibacy*, April 11, 1974, nos. 75 ff.

As regards these preferable means of practicing the spiritual life, cf. John XXIII, Encyclical letter *Sacerdotii Nostri primordia*, August 1, 1959: AAS 51 (1959), p. 560: "There are various practices of priestly piety which bring about and safeguard this constant union with God; the Church has wisely laid down rules prescribing many of the more important: in particular, daily sacred meditation; devotional visits to the Tabernacle; recitation of the Rosary of Our Lady; careful examination of conscience (C.I.C., can. 125). As regards the daily office, priests have undertaken a grave obligation towards the Church binding them to its recital (*ibid.*, can. 135). From neglect of one or other of these rules, we can often perhaps derive the reason why men of the Church are swept away in the whirlpool of exterior realities, gradually cease to give any inspiration of this sacred, and finally, enticed by the attractions of this earthly life, are placed in grave danger, because they are destitute of any spiritual protection".

146. Code of Canon Law, Can. 246, par. 4; Pius XII, Encyclical Letter, *Mystici Corporis*, June 29, 1943; AAS 35 (1943), p. 235; Apostolic Exhortation *Menti Nostrae* September 23, 1950: AAS 42 (1950), p. 674; John XXIII, Encyclical Letter *Sacerdotii Nostri primordia*, 1, c., pp. 574-575; Paul VI, Apostolic Constitution *Paenitemini*, November 17, 1966: AAS 59 (1966), pp. 177 ff.; Address *Noi non dobbiamo*, to the faithful in general audience, April 3, 1974; *Insegnamenti*, XII, pp. 309 ff.; John Paul II, Encyclical Letter, *Redemptor hominis*, March 4, 1979: AAS 71 (1979), pp. 313 ff., n. 20; Encyclical Letter *Dives in misericordia*, November 30, 1980: AAS 72 (1980), pp. 1218 ff., n. 13; Apostolic Exhortation *Reconciliatio et paenitentia*, December 2, 1984: *L'Osservatore Romano*, December 12, 1984; Sacred Congregation for the Doctrine of Faith, *Normae Pastorales* concerning sacramental absolution given in the general mode, June 16, 1972: AAS, 64 (1972), pp. 510 ff.; Sacred Congregation for Catholic Education, *Instruction* on liturgical formation in seminaries, June 3, 1979, nn. 35,36; *Circular Letter concerning Some of the More Urgent Aspects of Spiritual Formation in Seminaries*, January 6, 1980, pp. 18 ff.

147. Code of Canon Law: Can. 240, par. 1; can 239, par. 2; Vatican Council II, Decree *Perfectae caritatis*, no. 18.

148. Code of Canon Law: Can. 1035; 1034, par. 1; Paul VI, Motu Proprio *Ministeria quaedam*, August 15, 1972: AAS 64 (1972), pp. 529ff.; Sacred Congregation for Catholic Education, Instruction on Liturgical Formation in Seminaries, June 3, 1979, nos. 37, 38; *Circular Letter concerning Some of the More Urgent Aspects of Spiritual Formation in Seminaries*, January 6, 1980, p. 16.

149. Vatican Council II, Decree *Perfectae caritatis*, no. 6.

150. Vatican Council II, Decree *Optatam totius*, no. 11; Paul VI, Allocution *Il grande rito*, on the 4th centenary of the founding of Seminaries by the Council of Trent, November 4, 1963: AAS 55 (1963), p. 1034; Sacred Congregation for Catholic Education, *Circular Letter concerning Some of the More Urgent Aspects of Spiritual Formation in Seminaries*, January 6, 1980, p. 13.

151. Vatican Council II, Pastoral Constitution *Gaudium et spes*, nos. 1-4.

152. Vatican Council II, Decree *Ad gentes divinitus*, no. 11.

153. Ibid.

154. Vatican Council II, Decree *Optatam totius*, no. 11; Decree *Presbyterorum Ordinis*, no. 3; cf. John XXIII, Address *Questo incontro*, to Spiritual Directors meeting in Rome, September 9, 1962: AAS 54 (1962), pp. 675-676; Paul VI, Encyclical Letter *Ecclesiam Suam*, August 6, 1964: AAS 56 (1964), pp. 627, 638; John Paul II, Address *Je ne pouvais achever*, to students of the Major Seminary of Paris at Issy-les-Moulineaux, June 1, 1980: *Insegnamenti*, III, 1, pp. 1604 ss.

155. Code of Canon Law: Can. 248; cf Vatican Council II, Decree *Optatam totius*, nos. 13-17; Pastoral Constitution *Gaudium et spes*, nos. 58, 62; Decree *Ad gentes divinitus*, no. 16; Pius XII, Apostolic Constitution *Sedes sapientiae*, May 31, 1956: AAS 48 (1956), pp. 361 f.; Paul VI, Motu proprio *Ecclesiae Sanctae*, August 6, 1966: AAS 58 (1966), p. 786; III, n. 2.

156. Vatican Council II, Decree *Optatam totius*, no. 14.

157. Ibid.

158. Code of Canon Law, Can. 250; Sacred Congregation for Catholic Education, *Circular Letter on the Study of Philosophy in Seminaries*, January 20, 1972, Part III, no. 1c; Letter on the Theological Formation of Future Priests, February 22, 1976, nn. 129, 132; cf. John Paul II, Apostolic Constitution *Sapientia Christiana*: AAS 71 (1979), p. 494, Art. 74, par. 2.

159. Vatican Council II, Decree *Optatam totius*, no. 14; cf Constitution *Sacrosanctum Concilium*, no. 16; Decree *Ad gentes divinitus*, no. 16.

160. Cf. Code of Canon Law: Can. 1032, par. 2; Vatican Council II, Decree *Optatam totius*, no. 12.

161. Vatican Council II, Decree *Ad gentes divinitus*, nos. 16, 19, 22; Pastoral Constitution *Gaudium et spes*, nos. 44, 58, 62; Decree *Unitatis redintegratio*, nos. 4, 17; Decree *Orientalium Ecclesiarum*, nos. 4, 5, 6; cf. Pius XII, Encyclical Letter *Evangelii Praecones*, June 2, 1951: AAS 43 (1951), pp. 521 ss.; John XXIII, Encyclical Letter *Princeps Pastorum*, November 28, 1959: AAS 51 (1959), pp. 843ff.; Paul VI, Homily *Hi amicti sunt*, delivered on the occasion of the canonization of the Ugandan Martyrs, October 18, 1964: *Insegnamenti*, II, pp. 588-589; Motu proprio *Ecclesiae Sanctae*, August 6, 1966: AAS 58 (1966), p. 786, III, n. 2; Apostolic Exhortation *Evangelii nuntiandi*, December 8, 1975: AAS 68 (1976), p. 18, n. 20; Address *Greetings to you*, to all the Bishops of Asia, November 28, 1970: *Insegnamenti*, VIII, pp. 1215ff; John Paul II, Address *Vous etes*, to the African Community in Rome, February 2, 1980: *Insegnamenti*, III, 1, pp. 287ff.; Address *Quelle joie*, to the Bishops of Zaire gathered in Kinshasa, May 3, 1980: *Insegnamenti*, IV, 1, pp. 1084ff.; Address *I am overjoyed*, to the Bishops of Nigeria, February 15, 1982: *Insegnamenti*, V, 1, pp. 463 ss.; Sacred Congregation for Catholic Education, *Circular Letter on the Study of Philosophy in Seminaries*, January 20, 1972, Part III, no. 2; Letter on the Theological Formation of Future Priests, February 22, 1976, nos. 10, 27, 52, 66, 68, 77, 109, 110, 123.

162. Code of Canon Law: Can. 234, par. 2; Vatican Council II, Decree *Optatam totius*, no. 13; cf. no. 3; Pius XII, Apostolic Exhortation, *Menti Nostrae*, September 23, 1950: AAS 42 (1950), p. 687; Apostolic Constitution *Sedes Sapientiae*, May 31, 1956: AAS 48 (1956), pp. 361-362.

163. Code of Canon Law: Can. 249; Vatican Council II, Decree *Optatam totius*, no. 13; Paul VI, Apostolic Letter *Summi Dei Verbum*, November 4, 1963: AAS 55 (1963), p. 993; Apostolic Letter *Studia Latinitatis*, February 22, 1964: AAS 56 (1964), pp. 225 ss; John Paul II, Address *Salvere vos*, to the winners of the "Certamen Vaticanum", December 1, 1980: *Insegnamenti*, III, 2, pp. 1480f.

164. Code of Canon Law: Can. 249.

165. On harmonizing human and civic culture with Christian teaching, cf. Vatican Council II, Pastoral Constitution *Gaudium et spes*, nos. 59, 62. On art and sacred music: Vatican Council II, Constitution, *Sacrosanctum Concilium*, nos. 115, 129; Sacred Congregation for Rites, Instruction *Musicam sacram*, on music in the sacred liturgy, March 5, 129: AAS 59 (1967), pp. 300ff.; cf. no. 52; Sacred Congregation for the Clergy, Circular Letter *Opera artis* to the presidents of episcopal conferences, on the care of the historical-artistic patrimony, April 11, 1971: AAS 63 (1971), pp. 315 ff.; Sacred Congregation for Catholic Education, Instruction, on liturgical formation in seminaries, June 3, 1979, nos. 56, 57; Appendix, nos. 18, 23,

166. Vatican Council II, Decree *Inter mirifica*, no. 16; Pastoral Constitution, *Gaudium et spes*, no. 61; Decree, *Christus Dominus*, no. 13; cf. Constitution *Sacrosanctum Concilium*, no. 20; Paul VI, Radio Message, *Ci rivolgiamo*, on the occasion of the First World Day for the promotion of the right use of the means of social communication, May 2, 1967; *Insegnamenti*, V, pp. 203-206; Apostolic Exhortation *Evangelii Nuntiandi*, December 8, 1975: AAS 68 (1976), p. 35, n. 45; John Paul II, written message *Con sincera fiducia*, on the occasion of the Thirteenth World Day for the promotion of the right use of the means of social communication, May 23, 1979: *Insegnamenti*, II, pp. 1190ff.; Apostolic Exhortation, *Catechesi tradendae*, October 16, 1979: AAS 71 (1979), p. 1314, n. 46; Pontifical Council on the Instruments of Social Communication, Pastoral Instruction *Communio et progressio*, May 23, 1971: AAS 63 (1971), pp. 593ff.; Sacred Congregation for Bishops, *Directorium*, on the pastoral ministry of bishops, February 22, 1973, no. 74; Sacred Congregation for Catholic Education, *Directorium*, on formation for sacred celibacy, April 11, 1974, no. 89; *Instructio* on liturgical formation in seminaries, June 3, 1979, n. 58.

167. Vatican Council II, Decree, *Optatam totius*, no. 20; cf. Pius XII, Apostolic Exhortation, September 23, 1950: AAS 42 (1950), pp. 687, 696-697; John XXIII, Encyclical Letter, *Mater et Magistra*, May 15, 1961: AAS 53 (1961), p. 453; Synod of Bishops, Document, on justice in the world, November 30, 1971: AAS 63 (1971)m p. 923ff.; Paul VI, Encyclical Letter, *Populorum progressio*, March 25, 1967: AAS 59 (1967), pp. 257ff.; Apostolic Letter, *Octogesima adveniens*, May 14, 1971: AAS 63 (1971). pp. 401ff.; John Paul II, Address, *Esta hora* to the Bishops of Latin America participating in the Third General Conference at Puebla, January 28, 1979: AAS 71 (1979), pp. 401ff.; Encyclical Letter, *Redemptor hominis*, March 4, 1979: AAS 71, pp. 282 ff., nn. 13ff.; Encyclical Letter, *Dives in misericordia*, November 30, 1980: AAS 72 (1980), pp. 1210ff., nn. 10-12; Encyclical Letter, *Laborem exercens*, September 14, 1981: AAS 73 (1981), pp. 577ff.; Apostolic Exhortation, *Familiaris consortio*, November 22, 1981: AAS 74 (1982), pp. 81ff.; Address, *Magno cum gaudio*, to the International Theological Commission on the rights and dignity of the human person, December 5, 1983: *Insegnamenti*, VI, 2, pp. 1257ff.; Sacred Congregation for the Doctrine of Faith, Instruction, *Libertatis nuntius*, on some problems regarding the "Theology of Liberation," August 6, 1984: AAS 76 (1984), pp. 886-887.

168. On various counts the present situation demands that a real formation in Philosophy be given. For:

a) the very purpose of studying Philosophy and the present-day circumstances which demand exactness in training give sufficient indication that, not only are these studies not alien to, but have a highly helpful value in the search for faith and the ability to communicate about it. This relationship of reason to faith needs to be increasingly highlighted in the teaching of Philosophy, by *professors of Theology and Philosophy working closely together* and by the *order in which the courses of each department are distributed*. Future priests are not to feel, as it were, removed by force from the love and truth of Christ during their study of Philosophy, but rather experience Christ's influence in their studies. The Second Vatican Council itself in many places, but especially in the Pastoral Constitution *Gaudium et spes*, clearly shows how good philosophical principles assist the preservation of true Christian values in present day social and cultural life, and enable mankind to enjoy and further their benefits (cf. nos. 23 ss., 53 ss.).

b) Leaving aside the necessary question of how and what things are to be taught, the *ultimate purpose* of learning Philosophy is a point which has to be clearly understood, and, as proved by the end-product, it has to be constantly brought to mind. A sense of what is "being", with which alone a firm and unequivocal *yes* can be given to a statement, is essential for a minister of the faith - the ability to discern the truth, to see it for what it is and accept it, irrespective of its provenance. Equally necessary in the priest is a keen power of judgement with which he can see, and make decisions about, the daily problems of life and situations in their true light. These are acquired qualities which equip the priest to teach, to converse and not to be bowled over by every wind which blows - to the ruination of his work. Hence the Church's anxiety, cautious though it be, to discover and experiment with new ways of improving the teaching of Philosophy in Seminaries.

c) The post of professor of Philosophy demands *real preparation*. It not infrequently happens that when there is no really skilled philosopher to teach, the subject is simply not learned, and the students fail to discriminate between the different philosophical opinions, which in turn they may also regard as a kind of game.

d) If the teaching of Philosophy is to be genuinely useful and formative, it must be *closely related to problems which the modern age considers problems*. It must, therefore, be involved in, for example, the present-day growing inclination towards atheism and to the attempts to divorce faith from religion; it must tackle the philosophical principles which endanger the true interpretation of the Word of God and the importance which psychology, sociology, and the human sciences have for modern man.

169. Code of Canon Law: Can 251; Vatican Council II, Decree *Optatam totius*, no. 15; cf. Pastoral Constitution *Gaudium et spes*, nos. 44, 59; Declaration *Gravissimum educationis*, no. 10; Decree *Ad gentes divinitus*, no. 16; cf. Paul VI, Encyclical Letter *Ecclesiam Suam*, August 6, 1964: AAS 56 (1964), pp. 637 ss; Sacred Congregation for Catholic Education, *Circular Letter on the Study of Philosophy in Seminaries,* January 20, 1972.

170. Cf. Pius XII, Encyclical, *Humani generis*, August 12, 1950: AAS 42 (1950), pp. 571-575; Paul VI, Address, *Nous sommes*, to delegates at the Sixth International Thomistic Congress, September 10, 1965: *Insegnamenti*, III, pp. 445ff.; Apostolic Letter, *Lumen Ecclesiae*, to Father Vincent de Cuesnongle, Master General, O.P., on the seventh century since the death of St. Thomas Aquinas, November 20, 1974: AAS 66 (1974), pp. 673ff.; John Paul II, Address, *E con senso* at the Pontifical University of St. Thomas Aquinas, a century after the issuance of the Encyclical Letter, *Aeterni Patris*, November 17, 1979: AAS 71, (1979), pp. 1472ff.; Address, *Con senso* to administration, professors and students of the Pontifical Gregorian University, December 15, 1979: AAS 71 (1979), p. 1542.

171. Vatican Council II, Decree *Optatam totius*, no. 15.

172. *Ibid.*

173. Vatican Council II, Decree, *Optatam totius*, no. 15; Pastoral Constitution, *Gaudium et spes*, nos. 44, 62; Pius XII, Apostolic Constitution, *Sedes Sapientiae*, May 31, 1956: AAS 48 (1956), p. 362; Paul VI, Address, *Siate i benvenuti*, to delegates at the Thirty-sixth Italian Congress of Stomatologists, October 24, 1963: *Insegnamenti*, I, pp. 256-257; Apostolic Letter, *Octogesima adveniens*, May 14, 1971: AAS 63 (1971), p. 427, nos. 38-40; John Paul II, Letter to His Eminence Cardinal Augustino Casaroli on the occasion of the Seventh International Congress on "Studies and Cultural Relations (metaphysics and the human sciences)," Bergamo, September 5, 1980: *Insegnamenti*, III, 2, pp. 541ff.

174. Vatican Council II, Decree *Optatam totius*, no. 15; cf. John XXIII, Encyclical Letter *Princeps Pastorum*, November 28, 1959: AAS 51 (1959), pp. 843f.

175. Code of Canon Law: Can. 250.

176. Code of Canon Law: Can 252; Vatican Council II, Decree *Optatam totius*, no. 16; cf. Pius XII, Encyclical Letter *Humani generis*, August 12, 1950: AAS 42 (1950), pp. 567-569; Apostolic Constitution *Sedes Sapientiae*, May 31, 1956: AAS 48 (1956), pp. 361-363; Paul VI, Address *Incensissimo desiderio*, to the Academic Senate and students of the Pontifical Gregorian University in Rome, March 12, 1964: *Insegnamenti*, II, pp. 178ff.; Address *Libentissimo sane*, to delegates at the International Congress of the Theology of the Second Vatican Council, October 1, 1966: *Insegnamenti*, IV, pp. 443ff.; Address *Gratia Domini*, to the International Theological Commission, October 6, 1969: AAS 61 (1969), pp. 713ff.; JohnPaul II, Address *Con senso* to the professors and students of the Pontifical Gregorian University, December 15, 1979: AAS 71 (1979), pp. 1538ff.

177. Cf. Vatican Council II, Decree, *Unitatis redintegratio*, nos. 4, 5, 6, 10, 17; Decree, *Ad gentes divinitus*, no. 39; Decree, *Orientalium Ecclesiarum*, nos. 4, 6; John Paul II, Address, *E con gioia particolare*, to participants in the school of missiology at the Pontifical Gregorian University, December 2, 1982: *Insegnamenti*, V, 2, pp. 1502ff.; Secretariat for the Promotion of Christian Unity, *Directory*, Part II, nos. 71-74: AAS 62 (1970), pp. 710-712; Sacred Congregation for Evangelization, Circular Letter. *Puisque la Ratio*, on the missionary aspect of formation, Pentecost, 1970.

178. Cf. Vatican Council II, Decree *Optatam totius*, no. 17; Constitution *Sacrosanctum Concilium*, no. 16; cf. Pius XII, Apostolic Constitution *Sedes Sapientiae*, May 31, 1956: AAS 48 (1956), p. 363.

179. Vatican Council II, Decree, *Optatam totius*, no. 16; Dogmatic Constitution, *Lumen gentium*, no. 8 et passim; Constitution, *Sacrosanctum Concilium*, no. 2; Decree, *Ad gentes divinitus*, no. 16; cf. Paul VI, Address, *Salvete, Fratres*, at the beginning of the second session of the Second Vatican Council, September 29, 1963: *Insegnamenti*, I, pp. 172ff.; Sacred Congregation for the Doctrine of the Faith, Declaration *Mysterium Ecclesiae*, concerning the Catholic Doctrine of the Church against certain errors of the day, June 24, 1973: AAS 65 (1973), pp. 396ff.

180. Vatican Council II, Decree *Optatam totius*, nos. 14, 16; Constitution *Sacrosanctum Concilium*, no. 16; Decree *Ad gentes divinitus*, no. 16; cf. PAUL VI, Address *Nous sommes profondement*, to the Observers at the Second Vatican Council, October 17, 1963: *Insegnamenti*, I, pp. 232, 235.

181. Code of Canon Law: Can. 252, par. 2; Vatican Council II, Decree *Optatam totius*, no. 16; Dogmatic Constitution *Dei verbum*, no. 24; cf. Leo XIII, Encyclical Letter *Providentissimus Deus*, November 18, 1893: AAS 26 (1893-1894), p. 283.

182. Vatican Council II, Decree *Optatam totius*, no. 16; Dogmatic Constitution *Dei Verbum*, no. 23; cf. Pius XII, Encyclical Letter *Divino afflante Spiritu*, September 30, 1943: AAS 35 (1943), pp. 310ff.; cf.

Pontifical Biblical Commission, *Instructio de S.Scriptura recte docenda*, May 13, 1950: AAS 42 (1950), pp. 502 f.; Address *Nous remercions*, to delegate attending the 7th International Congress of Old Testament Exegets, April 19, 1968: *Insegnamenti*, VI, pp. 138ff.; Sacred Congregation for Catholic Education, *Letter on the Theological Formation of Future Priests*, February 22, 1976, nos. 79-84.

183. Vatican Council II, Decree *Optatam totius*, no. 16; cf. Constitution *Sacrosanctum Concilium*, nos. 2, 10, 14, 15, 16; Decree *Orientalium Ecclesiarum*, no. 4; Sacred Congregation for Catholic Education, Instruction on Liturgical Formation in Seminaries, June 3, 1979, nos. 43ff.

184. Vatican Council II, Constitution *Sacrosanctum Concilium*, no. 23; Sacred Congregation of Rites, Instruction *Inter Oecumenici*, on implementing the Constitution on the Sacred Liturgy, September 26, 1964: 56 (1964), pp. 879f., nn. 11, 12; Sacred Congregation for Catholic Education, Instruction on Liturgical Formation in Seminaries, June 3, 1979, no. 47.

185. Code of Canon Law: Can. 252, par. 3; Vatican Council II, Decree *Optatam totius*, no. 16; cf. Decree *Gravissimum educ.*, no. 10; cf. Pius XII, Encyclical Letter *Humani generis*, August 12, 1950: AAS 42 (1950), pp. 568-569; Apostolic Constitution *Sedes Sapientiae*, May 31, 1956: AAS 48 (1956), pp. 362 s.; John XXIII, Address *Gaudet Mater Ecclesia*, at the solemn opening of the Second Vatican Council, October 11, 1962: AAS 54 (1962), pp. 791ff.; Paul VI, Address *Siamo particolarmente lieti*, to delegates attending the Meeting concerning the mystery of Original Sin, held at Rome, July 11, 1966: *Insegnamenti*, IV, pp. 364ff.; Address *Incensissimo desiderio*, to the Academic Senate and students of the Pontifical Gregorian University in Rome, March 12, 1964: *Insegnamenti*, II, pp. 178ff.; Sacred Congregation for Catholic Education, Letter on the Theological Formation of Future Priests, February 22, 1976, nos. 89-94.

186. Cf. Vatican Council II, Dogmatic Constitution *Dei verbum*, nos. 8, 9.

187. Cf. Vatican Council II, Dogmatic Constitution *Dei verbum*.

188. Cf. Vatican Council II, Pastoral Constitution *Gaudium et spes*, no. 62; Decree *Ad gentes divinitus*, no. 22; Sacred Congregation for Catholic Education, *Letter on the Theological Formation of Future Priests*, February 22, 1976, nos. 107-113.

189. Vatican Council II, Decree *Optatam totius*, no. 16; Pastoral Constitution *Gaudium et spes*, nos. 52, 62; Decree *Ad gentes divinitus*, no. 22; cf. Pius XII, Address *Animus Noster* to the Academic Senate and students of the Pontifical Gregorian University in Rome, October 17, 1953: AAS 45 (1953), p. 688; Paul VI, Address *Presentia vestra*, to the General Chapter of the Congregation of the Most Holy Redeemer, September 22, 1967: *Insegnamenti*, V, p. 444; Address *Instaurantur Nobis*, to the International Theological Commission, December 16, 1974: *Insegnamenti*, XI, pp. 1300 ff.; John Paul II, Address *Magno cum gaudio*, to the International Theological Commission, December 5, 1983: *Insegnamenti*, VI 2, pp. 1257ff.; Sacred Congregation for Catholic Education, *Letter on the Theological Formation of Future Priests*, February 22, 1976, nos. 95-101.

190. Vatican Council II, Decree *Optatam totius*, no. 19; Decree *Presbyterorum Ordinis*, nos. 5, 6; Decree *Christus Dominus*, no. 15.

191. Sacred Congregation for Catholic Education, *Letter on the Theological Formation of Future Priests*, February 22, 1976, nos. 102-106; specialized pastoral expertise is treated more fully in Chapter XVI.

192. Vatican Council II, Decree *Optatam totius*, no. 20; cf. Pius XII, Address *Animus Noster*, to the Academic Senate and students of the Pontifical Gregorian University in Rome: l.c. pp. 686 f.; John XXIII, Encyclical Letter *Mater et Magistra*, May 15, 1961: AAS 53 (1961), p. 453; Paul VI, Apostolic Letter *Octogesima adveniens*, May 14, 1971: AAS 63 (1971), pp. 401ff.; John Paul II, Address *Esta hora* to the Bishops of Latin America gathered in the third general conference in the city of Puebla, January 28, 1979: AAS 71 (1979), p. 203, n. III, 7; Encyclical Letter *Laborem exercens*, September 14, 1981: AAS 73 (1981), pp. 577ff.; Sacred Congregation for the Doctrine of the Faith, Instruction *Libertatis nuntius*, on Certain Aspects of the "Theology of Liberation", August 6, 1984: AAS 76 (1984), pp. 886ff.

193. Vatican Council II, Decree *Optatam totius*, no. 9, 16; Pius XII, Address *Solemnis conventus*, to seminarians studying in Rome, June 24, 1939: AAS 31 (1939), p. 248; Address *Animus Noster*, to the Academic Senate and students of the Pont. Gregorian University in Rome, October 17, 1953: AAS 45 (1953), p. 689.

194. Vatican Council II, Decree *Optatam totius*, no 16; John Paul II, Apostolic Constitution, *Sacrae disciplinae leges* which promulgated the new Code of Canon Law, January 25, 1983; *Insegnamenti*, VI, 1, pp 228 ff.; Address *Ho desiderato grandemente*, to Cardinals, Bishops, Priests and Distinguished Laity, February 3, 1983: *Insegnamenti*, VI, 1, pp. 308ff.; Sacred Congregation for Catholic Education, Circular Letter on the teaching of canon law given to candidates for the priesthood, April 2, 1975.

195. Vatican Council II, Decree *Optatam totius*, no. 13; Sacred Congregation for Catholic Education, *Letter on the Theological Formation of Future Priests*, February 22, 1976, no. 130.

196. Vatican Council II, Decree *Optatam totius*, no. 17.

197. Vatican Council II, Decree *Unitatis redintegratio*, no. 9; Decree *Ad gentes divinitus*, no. 16; Sacred Congregation for Bishops, *Directorium* on the pastoral ministry of Bishops, February 22, 1973, no. 195.

198. AAS 59 (1967), pp. 574ff. (Part I); AAS 62 (1970), pp. 705ff. (Part II).

199. Vatican Council II, Decree *Optatam totius*, no. 16; Declaration *Nostra aetate*, no. 2; Decree *Ad gentes divinitus*, no. 16; Paul VI, Apostolic Exhortation *Evangelii nuntiandi*, December 8, 1975: AAS 68 (1976), p. 41, n. 53; John Paul II, Address *It gives me* to members of the Secretariat for Non-Christians, April 27, 1979: AAS 71 (1979), pp. 611ff; Secretariat for the Promotion for Christian Unity, Orientations and suggestions in regard to the application of the conciliar declaration *Nostra aetate* (n. 4), December 1, 1974: AAS 67 (1975), pp. 73ff.; Secretariat for Non-Christians, *Notae quaedam* on the Church's relations to followers of other religions, June 10, 1984: AAS 76 (1984), pp. 816ff.

200. Vatican Council II, Pastoral Constitution *Gaudium et spes*, no. 21; Paul VI, Encyclical Letter *Ecclesiam Suam*, August 6, 1964: AAS 56 (1964), pp. 650ff.; Address *Nous sommes* to delegates at the Sixth International Thomistic Congress, September 10, 1965: *Insegnamenti*, III, pp. 445ff.; John Paul II, Address

Soyez remercie to delegates attending the Congress on Evangelization and Atheism, October 10, 1980: *Insegnamenti*, III, 2, pp. 825ff.; Secretariat for Non Believers, *Documentum de dialogo* August 28, 1968: AAS 60 (1968), pp. 692-704; *Nota* concerning the study of atheism and instruction about dialogue with Non Christians, July 10, 1970; Sacred Congregation for the Doctrine of the Faith, Instruction, *Libertatis nuntius*, on some problems regarding the "Theology of Liberation," August 6, 1984: AAS 76 (1984), pp. 890ff.

201. Vatican Council II, Decree *Optatam totius*, nos. 18-20; cf. Decree *Ad gentes divinitus*, no. 16; Decree *Apostolicam actuositatem*, no. 25; Pius XII, Apostolic Constitution, *Sedes sapientiae* May 31, 1956: AAS 48 (1956), p. 364; Paul VI, Address *Voi avete* to delegates at the Congress termed "The Thirteenth National Week of Pastoral Guidance," September 6, 1963: *Insegnamenti*, I, pp. 118-119; John Paul II, Address *Questo incontro* to superiors and students of the Pontifical Universities and Roman Faculties of Ecclesiastical Studies October 21, 1980: *Insegnamenti*, III, 2, pp. 940ff.

202. Vatican Council II, Decree *Optatam totius*, no. 18; cf. Decree *Ad gentes divinitus*, no. 16; Decree *Presbyterorum Ordinis*, no. 19; Sacred Congregation for Bishops, *Directorium* on the pastoral ministry of Bishops, February 22, 1973, n. 195.

203. It is very much hoped that Religious will also agree to the special provisions established by each Conference in this matter.

204. Cf. Pius XII, Address *Le centenaire*, to the Superiors and students of the Pontifical French Seminary in Rome, April 16, 1953: AAS 45 (1953), pp. 287 s.; Paul VI, Address *Due fatti*, given in the Vatican Basilica at a Mass concelebrated with the Superiors of the Roman Colleges, June 6, 1965: *Insegnamenti*, III, p. 330; John Paul II, Address *Consentitemi*, to the members of the Catholic Education Institutes of Rome, April 4, 1979: AAS 71 (1979), pp. 597ff.; Address *Dopo le recenti* to the academic professors and students of the Pontifical Lateran University, February 16, 1980: *Insegnamenti*, III, 1, p. 406.

205. Vatican Council II, Decree *Optatam totius*, no. 16; Dogmatic Constitution *Dei verbum*, nos. 24-26; cf. Pius XII, Encyclical Letter *Divino afflante Spiritu*, September 30, 1943: AAS 35 (1943), p. 321.

206. Vatican Council II, Dogmatic Constitution *Dei verbum*, n. 10.

207. Vatican Council II, Decree *Optatam totius*, no. 16; Dogmatic Constitution *Dei verbum*, nos. 8. 23; Decree *Unitatis redintegratio*, no. 17; cf. Pius XII, Encyclical Letter, *Divino afflante Spiritu*, September 30, 1943: AAS 35 (1943), p. 312; Paul VI, Address *I nostri passi*, to members of the Order of St. Augustine present for the inauguration of the Patristic Institute "Augustinianum" May 4, 1970: *Insegnamenti*, VIII, pp. 436ff.; John Paul II, Apostolic Letter *Patres Ecclesiae*, on the 16th centenary of the death of Saint Basil the Great, January 2, 1980: *Insegnamenti*, III, 1, pp. 51ff.; Sacred Congregation for Catholic Education, Letter on the theological formation of future priests, February 22, 1976, nos. 48-49, 74, 85-88, 92.

208. Vatican Council II, Decree *Optatam totius*, no. 16; Declaration *Gravissimum educationis*, no. 10; Paul VI, Address, *Incensissimo desiderio* to the academic senate and the students of the Pontifical Gregorian University, Rome, March 12, 1964: *Insegnamenti*, II, pp. 178ff.; Address *Nous sommes* at the Sixth International Thomistic Congress, September 10, 1955: *Insegnamenti*, III, pp. 446f.; Apostolic Letter *Lumen Ecclesiae*, to Father Vincent de Cuesnongle, Master General, O.P. on the seventh centenary of the death of Saint Thomas Aquinas, November 20, 1974: AAS 66 (1974), pp. 673ff.; John Paul II, Address *E con senso*, given at the Pontifical University of Saint Thomas Aquinas on the centenary of the Encyclical Letter, "Aeterni Patris," November 17, 1979: AAS 71 (1979), pp. 1472ff.; Address *Sono sinceramente lieto* to delegates attending the Eighth International Thomistic Congress, September 13, 1980: AAS 72 (1980), pp. 1036ff.

209. Vatican Council II, Dogmatica Constitution *Lumen gentium*, no. 25; Pius XII, Apostolic Constitution *Sedes Sapientiae*, May 31, 1956: AAS 48 (1956), p. 362; Paul VI, Address *Libentissimo sane*, to delegates attending the Congress of the Theology of the Second Vatican Council, held in Rome, October 1, 1966: *Insegnamenti*, IV, pp. 443f.; John Paul II, Address *Magno cum gaudio*, to the International Theological Commission, October 26, 1979: *Insegnamenti*, II, 2, pp. 965ff.; Address *Es ist mir* to professors of theology held at Altoetting, November 18, 1980: *Insegnamenti*, III, 2, pp. 1332ff.; Address, *Como en mi viaje*, to the teachers of the Pontifical University of Salamanca, November 1, 1982: *Insegnamenti*, V, 3, pp. 1049ff.; Address, *Ihr seid nach Rom*, to the Bavarian Bishops on their "ad limina" visit, January 28, 1983: *Insegnamenti*, VI, 1, pp. 262f.; Sacred Congregation for the Doctrine of the Faith, Declaration *Mysterium Ecclesiae*, concerning the Catholic Doctrine of the Church against certain errors of the day, June 24, 1973: AAS 65 (1973), pp. 400ff., nos. 3, 4; Sacred Congregation for Catholic Education, *Letter on the Theological Formation of Future Priests*, February 22, 1976, nos. 44-77; 122.

210. Vatican Council II, Decree *Presbyterorum Ordinis*, n. 8; Cf. Pastoral Constitution *Gaudium et spes*, no. 62; Paul VI, Address *Postremam dum*, to the International Theological Commission, October 11, 1973: *Insegnamenti*, XI, pp. 990ff.

211. Pius XII, Encyclical *Humani generis*, August 12, 1950: AAS 42 (1950), p. 572; Apostolic Constitution *Sedes sapientiae*, May 31, 1956, AAS 48 (1956), p. 362; Paul VI, Address *Siamo particolarmente lieto*, to the delegates at the meeting of theologians concerning the mystery of Original Sin, July 11, 1966: *Insegnamenti*, IV, p. 365; Address *Incensissimo desiderio*, to the academic senate and students of the Pont. Gregorian University in Rome, March 12, 1964: *Insegnamenti*, II, pp. 177ff.; Apostolic Exhortation *Quinque iam anni*, to all bishops on the fifth anniversary of the close of the Second Vatican Council, December 8, 1970: AAS 63 (1971), pp. 97ff.; Apostolic Exhortation *Paterna cum benevolentia*, on fostering reconciliation in the Church for the Holy Year, December 8, 1974: AAS 67 (1975), pp. 13ff., no. IV; Sacred Congregation for Bishops, *Directorium* on the pastoral ministry of bishops, February 22, 1973, no. 195; Sacred Congregation for Catholic Education, *Letter on the Theological Formation of Future Priests*, February 22, 1976, nos. 124, 126.

212. John Paul II, Address *C'est avec une joie*, to members of the Pontifical Council on Culture, January 18, 1983: *Insegnamenti*, VI, 1, pp. 147ff.

213. Vatican Council II, Decree *Optatam totius*, no. 17.

214. Code of Canon Law: Can. 254, par. 1; Vatican Council II, Decree *Optatam totius*, nn. 5, 17; cf. Constitution *Sacrosanctum Concilium*, no. 16; Sacred Congregation for Catholic Education, *Letter on the Theological Formation of Future Priests*, February 22, 1976, nos. 69-71, 125.

215. Code of Canon Law: Can. 254, par. 2.

216. Vatican Council II, Decree *Christus Dominus*, no. 17; cf. Decree *Ad gentes divinitus*, no. 16; Sacred Congregation for Bishops, *Directorium* on the pastoral ministry of Bishops, February 22, 1973, no. 102; Sacred Congregation for Catholic Education, *Letter on the Theological Formation of Future Priests*, February 22, 1976, no. 59.

217. As the chapter will show more clearly, this training presupposes that throughout their studies the students, in their love of the apostolate, keep close to Christ the Redeemer, and "are also trained in matters both human and divine to be a real leaven in the world for the strengthening and increase of Christ's Body" (*Perfectae caritatis*, no. 11). Students should, therefore, by degrees acquire a pastoral attitude of mind, and try to develop in themselves, along with a book-knowledge of the subject, those practical abilities which enable them to bring Christ's grace and teaching to all men.

All this demands that worthwhile contacts be established between the Seminary and the world outside, both in the Churches and in lay society. It is there that the real field of the apostolate is to be found. A Seminary is not to be thought of as a hermitage, where the students feel forcibly shut off from the real world and society. Nor is it to be so open that they think they can do exactly what they like. Everything must be done in truth - in other words, in the light of their future priestly life, a life which they understand correctly and accept.

In order to get the most out of this formation, the Superiors should be particularly careful to lay down suitable rules governing the life of study and prayer and for the observance of a correct order of values. These rules should have the primary purpose of training the future priest in the right use of his liberty, and experiments should only be admitted which can genuinely further the specific purpose of forming pastors of souls. Candidates for the priesthood will always accept such rules without difficulty provided they are shown quite clearly what their purpose is - that it is a joint-affair, a searching together that goes on day by day with a love that burns ever brighter, and which becomes clearer through discussion with the Superiors.

A further requirement in this practical preparation for the apostolate is that the students be put to worthwhile work, not only with the diocesan clergy, but also with the laity. In this way they will get a better insight into the pastoral situation of the diocese. They should follow the teaching of the Second Vatican Council which outlined the status of the layman in the Church (*Lumen gentium*, Chap. 4) and described the specific, active part he has to play (*Apostolicam actuositatem*, Chap. 3). Gradually they should make suitable contacts, under the direction of skilled leaders, with lay apostolate groups, and so obtain for themselves a true picture of the laity's distinctive role in the Body of Christ. They should realize the value and need for the apostolate of the laity (*Presbyterorum Ordinis*, no. 9; *Apostolicam actuositatem*, no. 25), and see for what it is the magnificent work which the laity performs in the Church. They should, moreover, learn to appreciate in what consists the service of the laity which is the proper office of the priest: that means bringing home clearly the dignity and the complementary character of the priesthood and the lay state.

218. Vatican Council II, Decree *Optatam totius*, nos. 4, 19; Sacred Congregation for Catholic Education, *Letter on the Theological Formation of Future Priests*, February 22, 1976, no. 26ff., 105, 127.

219. Code of Canon Law, can. 255, 256; Vatican Council II, Decree *Optatam totius*, no. 19; Decree *Ad gentes divinitus*, no. 16; Decree *Perfectae caritatis*, no. 18; Decree *Orientalium Ecclesiarum*, no. 4; cf. Pius XII, Apostolic Constitution, *Sedes sapientiae*, May 31, 1956: AAS 48 (1956), pp. 363f.; Paul VI, Apostolic Exhortation *Evangelii nuntiandi*, December 8, 1975: AAS 68 (1976), pp. 5ff; John Paul II, Apostolic Exhortation *Catechesi tradendae*, October 16, 1979: AAS 71 (1979), pp. 1328ff.; on the duties pertaining to a confessor, cf. Apostolic Exhortation *Reconciliatio et paenitentia*, December 2, 1984: *L'Osserv. Rom.*, December 12, 1984, p. 7, no. 29; Sacred Congregation for the Clergy, *Directorium*, General Catechetics, April 11, 1971: AAS 64 (1972), pp. 97ff.

220. Vatican Council II, Decree *Optatam totius*, no. 20; Decree *Christus Dominus*, nos. 16, 17; Pastoral Constitution, *Gaudium et spes*, no. 62; Paul VI, Apostolic Letter *Octogesima adveniens*, May 14, 1971: AAS 63 (1971), pp. 427ff., nos. 38-40; John Paul II, Address *La gioia*, to academic administration, teachers and students of the Pontifical Salesian University, January 31, 1981: *Insegnamenti*, IV, 1, pp. 200ff., nos. 5, 6; Address *Apres avoir*, to the professors of the theological faculty of Freiburg (Switzerland), June 13, 1984: *Insegnamenti*, VII, 1, pp. 1713f; Sacred Congregation for Catholic Education, *Letter on the Theological Formation of Future Priests*, February 22, 1976, nos. 14, 54ff;, 134; Instruction on liturgical instruction in seminaries, June 3, 1979, no. 50; Appendix, no. 25.

221. Vatican Council II, Decree *Optatam totius*, no. 20; Decree *Apostolicam actuositatem*, no. 25; Decree *Christus Dominus*, no. 17; Dogmatic Constitution *Lumen gentium*, no. 33; cf Pius XII, Exhortation *Menti Nostrae*, September 23, 1950: AAS 42 (1950), pp. 676f.; Paul VI, Address *Salutiamo i Delegati*, to the delegates of the Bishops and priest advisers of the Sodality for Catholic Action, July 9, 1966: *Insegnamenti*, IV, pp. 355ff.

222. Cf. Vatican Council II, Decr. *Christus Dominus*, no. 18; Sacred Congregation for the Clergy, Directory, *De peregrinantibus*, April 30, 1969: AAS 61 (1969), pp. 361ff., no. 21; Paul VI, Motu proprio *Pastoralis Migratorum cura*, August 15, 1969: AAS 61 (1969), pp. 601-603; cf. Sacred Congregation for Bishops, Instruction *De pastorali migratorum cura*, August 22, 1969: AAS 61 (1969), pp. 614-643; John Paul II, Apostolic Exhortation, *Familiaris consortio*, November 22, 1981: AAS 74 (1982), pp. 167, 170 nos. 70. 73; Encyclical Letter *Laborem exercens*, September 14, 1981: AAS 73 (1981), p. 635, n. 23; Pontifical Commission on the Spiritual Care of Migrants and People on the Move, Circular Letter *Chiesa e mobilita umana*, to episcopal conferences, May 26, 1978: AAS 70 (1978), pp. 357ff.; cf. also Vatican Council II, Decree *Presbyterorum Ordinis*, nos. 6, 9.

223. Cf. Pius XII, Apostolic Exhortation *Menti Nostrae*, September 23, 1950: AAS 42 (1950), p. 664; cf. above, n. 48; Sacred Congregation for Catholic Education, *A Guide to Formation in Priestly Celibacy*, April 11, 1974, nos. 57-61; cf. Code of Canon Law: Can. 277, par. 2-3.

224. Vatican Council II, Decree *Optatam totius*, no. 20; Dogmatic Constiution *Lumen gentium*, nos. 17, 23; Decree *Christus Dominus*, no. 6; Decree *Perfectae caritatis*, no. 20; Decree *Orientalium Ecclesiarum*, no. 4; Decree *Ad gentes divinitus*, no. 39; cf. Paul VI, Encyclical Letter *Populorum progressio*, April 2, 1967: AAS 49 (1967), pp. 257ff.; Address *L'odierna udienza*, to students gathered together for missiological studies, September 2, 1964: *Insegnamenti*, II, pp. 517-518; Sacred Congregation for the Clergy, *Notae directivae*, on the promotion of mutual cooperation of particular churches and especially on a more suitable distribution of clergy, March 25, 1980: AAS 72 (1980), pp. 343ff.; Secretariat for the Promotion of Christian Unity, Declaration, *Dans ces derniers temps*, on the mind of the Church on certain questions regarding the Eucharist and common elements between various Christian confessions, January 7, 1970: AAS 64 (1970), pp. 184-188; *Instruction*, on special cases in which other Christians are admitted to eucharistic communion in the Catholic church, June 1, 1972: AAS 64 (1972), pp. 518 ff; Secretariat for Non Christians, *Notae quaedam*, on the Church's relations with followers of other religions, June 10, 1984: AAS 76 (1984), pp. 817ff.

225. Secretarait for Non Believers, *Documentum de dialogo*, August 28, 1968: AAS 60 (1968), pp. 692-704; *Nota*, concerning the study of atheism and instruction on dialoging with Non-believers, July 10, 1970; John Paul II, Address *Soyez remercie*, to delegates attending the Congress on Evangelization and Atheism, October 10, 1980: *Insegnamenti*, III, 2, pp. 825ff.

226. Code of Canon Law: Can. 258; Vatican Council II, Decree *Optatam totius*, no. 21; cf. Pius XII, Apostolic Exhortation *Menti Nostrae*, September 23, 1950: AAS 42 (1950), p. 676; Apostolic Constitution *Sedes sapientiae*, May 31, 1956: AAS 48 (1956), p. 364.

227. Code of Canon Law: Can 279; Vatican Council II, Decree *Presbyterorum Ordinis*, no. 19; Decree *Christus Dominus*, no. 16; Decree *Perfectae caritatis*, no. 18; cf. Pius XII, Motu proprio *Quandoquidem templum*, April 2, 1949: AAS 41 (1949), p. 165; Apostolic Exhortation *Menti Nostrae*, September 23, 1950: AAS 42 (1950), pp. 691-692; Apostolic Constitution *Sedes sapientiae*, May 31, 1956: AAS 48 (1956), p. 364; John XXIII, Allocution *Questo incontro*, to teachers of religion gathered in Rome, August 6, 1966: AAS 58 (1966), p. 761.

228. Cf. Vatican Council II, Decree *Presbyterorum Ordinis*, no. 7.

229. Cf. Sacred Congregation for the Clergy, Circular Letter to the Presidents of the Episcopal Conferences concerning the further education of the clergy, particularly the junior clergy, November 4, 1969, nos. 16-21: AAS 62 (1970) pp. 123ff.

The Theological Formation of Future Priests

Sacred Congregation for
Catholic Education
1976

The Theological Formation
of Future Priests

Introduction

1. Deep cultural and theological changes are among the most conspicuous signs of our time. This ferment involves the whole Church but more especially the theological formation of future priests. Here, as in all branches of education, new fields of research, new methods, new interests and changes of emphasis are evident. In recent years numerous problems have arisen that demand attention and consideration of all responsible.
2. For this reason the Sacred Congregation for Catholic Education feels compelled to address Bishops and their collaborators in priestly formation with the following document on the theological formation of candidates for the priesthood. For many reasons, the matter must be treated seriously and at some length. Some of these reasons are intrinsic to theological formation itself; others, such as the changed circumstances of the times we live in, the conditions of life and of priestly ministry, problems of evangelization, and the general needs of the Church, are extrinsic. At the present time theological teaching holds a position of paramount importance and there is much hope for its fruitful renewal. Now a good theological formation of candidates seems one of the surest means of infusing our seminaries with strength and offering an ever firmer basis for the spiritual renewal of the clergy and their pastoral ministry.
3. To put things clearly and in due order, it is worthwhile here:

I) to explain certain *aspects of the present situation;*

II) to recall certain *demands of theological teaching* derived from the very nature of the proper function of theology;

III) to formulate some *lines for the teaching of theology* in general and its particular disciplines;

IV) to establish *practical norms* to be observed in all institutes to which have been entrusted the formation of future priests.

I. Aspects of
the present situation

I. New Requirements of
the Pastoral Ministry

4. 1) The first reason for devoting special care to the deepening of theological preparation arises from the changed conditions in which priests will have to work. As their numbers decrease owing to the decline in vocations, they will be obliged to undertake greater responsibilities in a pastoral context where certain ministries will be shared with deacons and the faithful.

By virtue of their special character priests will be called upon to share more intimately in the cares of their Bishops, undertaking more complex and general pastoral tasks and at the same time far greater initiatives both within their respective dioceses and outside. Such a great increase of pastoral responsibility demands outstanding competence in theology and sound doctrine.

5. 2) Furthermore, priests will exercise their ministry in a Church moving and seeking to adapt herself to the new needs that are emerging both within herself and in the world. In such circumstances sound theological doctrine constitutes an indispensable pre-requisite both for correctly interpreting the signs of the times and for facing new situations, avoiding on the one hand stagnation and on the other dubious adventures and experiments.

6. 3) Priests of tomorrow will also have to exercise their ministry among people who are more adult, more critical, and better informed, immersed in a world of ideological pluralism where Christianity is exposed to many interpretations and suspicions common to a culture becoming ever more alien to the faith. It will be impossible for priests to serve the faith and the ecclesial community effectively without sound theological formation begun in the seminary and carried on beyond. Nor must it be forgotten that many of the laity have more extensive theological knowledge. Many of them study in schools and faculties of theology. This demands that the clergy must have a high level of theological preparation.

7. 4) It must be borne in mind that the very faith of the priests of tomorrow will be exposed to greater dangers than before. In fact, experience has already shown the difficulty that some priests find in overcoming the prevailing atmosphere of unbelief and the skepticism of the world in which they live. Formation of priests must take account of this difficult situation. How can they stand firm in their faith and strengthen their brothers in it without a theological preparation able to meet this situation?

8. 5) These considerations clearly show that a priest cannot be content with a formation which is predominantly practical and culturally mediocre. Although not every priest is called to be a specialist in theology, there does exist an affinity between pastoral ministry and theological competence. Priests are expected to exercise a true theological ministry in the Christian community, without it being necessary for them to be professional theologians. Priests and Bishops, being pastors, are in fact responsible for official preaching in the Church.

II. New Tasks of Theology

9. Theological formation, the importance of which we have tried to underline, must, therefore, face new situations and problems. Experience and different needs induce emphasis on some of the dimensions of theological research and teaching which seem to be especially urgent in view of the many tasks to be fulfilled today.

10. 1) In the past, theology developed in a world whose culture accommodated it easily, because the faith of the Church inspired culture and customs. Today, on the contrary, society is secular and often indifferent to religious problems and no longer in sympathy with either the faith or the teaching of the Church. It is, therefore, most necessary to work to make the Gospel understood by our contemporaries; so we must find a language adapted to them. But, such a task is too delicate and too serious to be left to improvisation and the initiative of individuals. It is rightly the task of theology to provide a contribution of sound scholarship and clear doctrine.

11. 2) Today ecumenical dialogue weighs heavily on theology, at the same time it encourages new research into the history and sources of our doctrine, eliciting a new climate both in theology and in the whole Church. Above all, it imposes the task of rediscovering the ecumenical dimension of theology and formulating the truths of the faith "more profoundly and precisely, in ways and in terminology which our separated brethren too can really understand." [1]

12. 3) Heavy demands also are made on theology today by the life of the Church, which raises new questions when faced with new practices which need to be analyzed and, if possible, integrated in the faith. Here we can see the importance of pastoral activity, which provokes theological reflection and stimulates teaching so that it becomes more alive and up-to-date without losing authenticity. This function of theology is necessary for the service of the people of God.

13. 4) Furthermore, there are grave problems in the modern world which call upon theology for solution with ever greater insistence. The Constitution *Gaudium et spes [Pastoral Constitution on the Church in the Modern World]* demonstrates the interest which the Church takes in the whole human family. Recent theology has shown itself more sensitive to the economic, social, and political problems of humanity seen in the light of the Gospel. A great awareness of the social implications and consequences of dogma has caused ferment not only on the level of action but also on the level of theological reflection. This cannot be ignored in the formation of the clergy.

14. 5) To fulfill its mission of serving the Church today, theology must come to terms with the human sciences. Certainly, these sciences are no longer ignored by theology; on the contrary, some of their findings have been as it were "canonized" to the extent of having been incorporated in the historical formulations of the faith.

But theology, while convinced that it can derive ever greater advantages from the human sciences, cannot be blind to certain drawbacks which such an encounter might have at the present moment. The greater penetration of the human sciences in today's culture sometimes shows the inadequacies of a certain kind of theological language; further, the enormous prestige that these sciences enjoy today has such an influence in some theological circles that the sacred science is disfigured by them, losing its specific character. What is called theology is often only history, sociology, and the like. It is well to be aware of these difficulties and to bear in mind the urgent need accurately to define the epistemological terrain of theology in relation to other sciences.

15. 6) Another phenomenon that is characteristic of our present situation is the loss of that unity which the teaching of theology once had. Theological disciplines are now open to new problems, new philosophies, and new contributions of science. In consequence of this, religious questions are becoming ever more complex and subject to different interpretations. Thus the way is open to a certain pluralism. It is one of the tasks of contemporary theology to define the legitimate and necessary limits of such a pluralism. This emphasizes the need for a renewal of theological teaching.

16. 7) Finally, in teaching theology today there is ever greater difficulty in reconciling the lack of time available with the enormous development of the particular theological disciplines. It is evident that in such a situation an encyclopedic teaching that offers complete answers to all the questions in dispute is quite impossible. For this reason a new arrangement of all theological teaching is necessary to allow it to give the seminarist a cohesive, global vision of the Christian mystery.

II. The demands of theological teaching

I. The Fundamental Demands

17. Anyone who is engaged in teaching theology cannot possibly ignore the complicated situation described above. Teaching of theology has certain fundamental demands, which derive from the nature of theology itself, and from its function.

1. The nature of theology

18. 1) It is of paramount importance to bear in mind the nature of theology. If theology is to be renewed and adapted to the needs of our times, it must not lose touch with tradition, and it must always be true to itself as *the science of Christian Revelation. Fides quaerens intellectum,* that is, faith, that searches for and develops its self-understanding, reaches its goal in a higher and more systematic form through theology. The object with which theology is concerned *is not the truth acquired by human reason but the truth revealed by God and known by faith.*

The context of faith is essential to theology, and theology can make no progress if it is confused with sciences outside the perspective of faith.

19. 2) Within the ambit of faith, theology responds to what comes from the dynamism of faith itself — "cum assensu cogitare" — , or to the demands of culture, to integrate the faith within the contemporary psychological and social context, in the midst of the fundamental questions and worries of modern man.

20. 3) As a science born from faith and developing within the ambit of faith and in the service of faith, theology uses rational reflection and the data of culture for better understanding of its own object.

Because of this, theology enjoys a special position in the articulation of the various sciences, also religious ones, but, it must not be confused with them nor reduced to their methods.

a) In particular, theology cannot be confused with or reduced to the level of the history of religions or of dogma, to religious psychology or to the sociology of the Church. It must always remain faithful to its own nature and to its specific function, also in the epistemological context of disciplines concerned with religion.

b) In the social and cultural conditions that have been determined by the development of the human and natural sciences, theology adopts the assured conclusions of these sciences, always taking into account the mentality and spirit which they engender amongst men and the interpretation that man gives of himself in every generation.

For this, theology can and, indeed, must develop a dialogue that is well informed, pertinent, and accessible, above all, on points of dogma and morals, regarding the origins, constitution, behavior, development, conditions, and destiny of man, all the time being very careful not to lose sight of the certain and unchangeable data of the word of God.[2]

21. 4) Catholic theology cannot prescind from the doctrine and experience which come from the life of the Church,[3] within which the Magisterium guards and authentically interprets the deposit of faith contained in Sacred Scripture and Tradition. For this reason the Catholic theologian, in the field of exegesis and in his other scientific work, cannot unconditionally follow methods or accept the results of theologies opposed or extraneous to the Church. An uncritical conformism to such theologies neither responds to the specific character of Catholic theology nor is it in the best interests of ecumenism.[4]

22. 5) Since theology has for its object truths which are principles of life and personal commitment,[5] both for the individual and the community of which he is part, it has a spiritual dimension and, therefore, the theologian cannot be purely intellectual in his research and study, but must always follow the requirements of faith, always deepening his existential union with God and his lively participation in the Church.

By its nature, theology has a vital character, which gives it a unique place in the epistemological framework of science.

2. The function of theology

23. As the *science of Christian Revelation,* theology has a specific function in the broad sphere of the activities and ministries of the Church — the community of faith and love to which God has entrusted Christian Revelation and the work of salvation accomplished by Christ.

24. 1) Theology investigates Revelation and studies it in depth; it describes its limits and plays its part in homogeneous development according to the needs of faith[6] and the signs of the times, in which it sees the signs of God.[7] This essential function of theology cannot be put aside or passed over in any contingent situation, especially at the present moment.

25. 2) In developing this function, theology has a very relevant influence on the spiritual life because it clarifies and deepens a sense of the laws of salvation and the way of spiritual progress that Revelation offers to Christian life. This is particularly true in the formation of future priests in an enlightened and solid piety founded upon an understanding of their ministry and an exact appreciation of what the Church asks of them.[8]

26. 3) Here also arises the part theology has to play in the Christian apostolate and especially in the pastoral ministry; it shows their place in the economy of salvation and helps their completion with the resources of doctrine and the practical indications it gives. Hence, the necessity for a first class theological formation for future pastors of souls.[9]

27. 4) For the building up of the "Body of Christ which is the Church" (Col. 1.4), theology is called upon to be constructive in its service to the Magisterium either by elaborating the data of faith and morals provided by Revelation and to be applied to present-day problems, or by a scientific treatment of problems that concern the life and thought of the Church, or, finally, by singling out, clarifying, and solving difficult points which arise on a doctrinal or practical level.[10]

In particular, theology must be able to interpret, encourage, and serve the impetus of the Church's new missionary awareness. It is necessary to establish conditions for dialogue with non-Christian religions and cultures which will lead to new forms of evangelization as people grow closer together.[11]

Within the Christian world, theology should take into account new ecumenical needs, either by the study of sources held in common, or by deeper knowledge of the thought of various churches and Christian communions on controversial points, by the development of the ecumenical dimension of ecclesiology and other areas of theology closely related to the problem of Christian unity. [12]

28. 5) Confronted with the problems of Christians in the world, theology must pick out the human and evangelical elements which they often contain and try to clarify the points where they touch on the Gospel message without attempting to hide differences. Theology should make sure that the solutions today sought for these problems benefit from the superior power of Christianity to clarify and construct. [13] Within the same context, there are problems of the new solidarity between social classes and peoples, the liberation of man from exploitation and alienation, sharing in the life of the state and of international society, the conquest of hunger, disease, and illiteracy, elimination of war as a means of solving quarrels between peoples, and the creation of more effective means of preserving peace. [14]

In this sense, theology has a "political" function that is original and unique, because it throws light on problems and directs action in man's various occupations, according to the indications and precepts of God's word.

II. The Components of Theology

29. By its very nature and function, theology is a unifying science nourished by Revelation, laying bare the data it receives from it *ad lumen fidei,* either by the process of positive investigation or by speculative development. Consequently, theology is both positive and systematic. In fact, the basis of theology is the study of the sources of Revelation for the purpose of establishing what God has revealed. Such a scientific study of the *auditus fidei,* gives rise to *positive theology.* The results of positive theology are the object of further scientific development by means of systematic theology, which according to the demands of the *intellectus fidei* seeks to penetrate the meaning of revealed truths and discover how they are related, thus coordinating the whole in an organic and unifying manner. [15] These two components of theology — historical research and rational reflection — cannot be ever completely separated, because they have a continual reciprocal interaction and their functions are complementary. It is necessary that they remain in continual equilibrium without one dominating the other.

1. The historical dimension of theology

With regard to historical research, which is predominant in the positive part of theology, the directives to be followed are threefold:

30. 1) It must be developed by methods that are in accordance with its own nature. This implies a legitimate freedom of research based upon valid documentation but it does not permit theology to be reduced to mere philology or historical criticism. To stay exclusively on such a level would be to risk positive theology becoming sterile and betraying its proper mission.

31. In fact, positive theology must recognize, as a matter of primary importance, the supernatural character of its object and the divine origin of the Church. Its development cannot be guided only by human reason without the light of faith nor can it dispense with the Magisterium of the Church. It is founded on the theology of Revelation, inspiration, and on the Church. It belongs to the Church to keep faithfully and interpret authentically the Word of God.[16]

32. 2) Since there is an historical dimension of Revelation, of its transmission, and of the Magisterium, which preserves and interprets it, positive theology must have recourse, over and above its traditional methods of research (philology, history, historical criticism) to philosophical and philosophico-theological reflection. Such reflection should be concerned with the nature of the evidence at the disposal of the historian, the relationship that exists between the facts narrated and their interpretation, and also the nature of this relationship, and the relationship between eye-witnesses and the community of believers. Furthermore, the particular character of the times in which the history of our salvation took place should be considered, as well as the historical character of the narratives and of the events narrated.[17]

33. 3) Moreover the need for positive theology to have recourse to philosophy is a consequence of developments of modern hermeneutics which are due to the particular sensitivity of today's culture to historical fact. It is this that attracts the attention of theologians to the historical conditioning of thought in its various expressions and, consequently, to the difference between the way modern man thinks and expresses himself, and what is found in the Bible and in the traditional formulations of faith. It follows that theology should undertake the task of expounding and re-interpreting the content of faith to express it in concepts more readily understood by modern man and separating it from forms of expression which belong to the past and may not be completely accessible today.

In this regard it is worth noting that the substance of the ancient doctrine in the deposit of faith is one thing and its formulation is another.[18] It is important that only its formulation should be conditioned by history, change, and adaptation, leaving the substance unchanged and firm. It is, therefore, essential that the theologian should know how to avoid the hazards of mere positivism and historicism which likes to explain the phenomena of thought and morality solely by historical causes[19] to the point where all permanent and objective truth is reduced to the relativity of historical contingency. Therefore, the theologian, in order to fulfill successfully his grave responsibilities, must allow himself to be guided not only by the Magisterium[20] and the rules of exegesis[21] but also by sound philosophical principles concerning the objective values of human knowledge.[22]

2. Systematic dimension

34. A characteristic of the present situation is a certain disaffection for philosophy; hence, the importance of giving prominence to the nature as well as to the necessity of theological speculation prescribed by the Council. The Decree *Optatam totius [Decree on the Training of Priests]* requires that for "making the mysteries of salvation known as thoroughly as they can be, students should learn to penetrate them more deeply with the help of speculative reason exercised under the tutelage of St. Thomas."[23]

35. 1) Systematic theological reflection *(intellectus fidei)* is the natural and necessary continuation of the positive method, of which it constitutes in a certain manner the fulfillment and climax. It is true that some reflection is present in every phase of the theological process, even in the positive; but this reflection, be it in *exegesis* to determine the meaning of every fact and concept in Scripture or be it in *Biblical theology* to formulate fundamental themes, is not of itself sufficient to give an adequate and properly theological understanding of revealed facts or to give them an organic and complete systematization.

36. 2) Only a more profound and scientifically methodical reflection is capable, with the help of philosophy, of penetrating in any great degree revealed truth so as to set in order various facts and formulate a mature judgement.[24] Such a recourse to speculative reflection is not simply a characteristic of Medieval scholasticism; it satisfies a theological and intellectual need that always tries to understand more and to understand better.

37. 3) Naturally, systematic theological reflection does not pursue "speculation for speculation's sake" but it keeps in living contact with the sources of Revelation and tends to a more organic understanding of the Word of God which is the permanent internal factor of such speculation.

At this stage of theological study, philosophy is called upon to play the role more of an instrument than a master. We are not dealing with purely intellectual activity but with a process that, while being strictly logical according to philosophical principles, is conducted *ad lumen fidei*. In fact, it is this constant reference to the faith that makes it possible to discover the order and the deeper significance of Revelation.

38. 4) Revelation, the object of all theological speculation, is not merely a sum of truths fed to the intellect but also and above all the means by which God has communicated Himself to man.[25] Therefore, every authentic theological reflection should induce an attitude of sympathy and personal commitment towards the object of study as well as a spiritual affinity with revealed truth. Philosophical reflection, if properly conducted, far from suppressing the spiritual dimension of theology, presupposes and needs it.

39. 5) Reason should never cease to be applied to Revelation. It corresponds to fundamental questions of what faith means and of its dialogue with science and human culture. Reasoned reflection makes possible a *theology of the Word* which cannot be substituted by a "theology of practice" which prescinds from all metaphysical commitment and reduces theology to a mere science of man, leading back in consequence to a pure phenomenologism and pragmatism.

40. 6) Today there is a very common tendency to underestimate the contribution of philosophy to theology and, in fact, an aversion to any systematic thought. Nevertheless, it is necessary to insist on the value of speculation in dogmatic and moral theology in order to assure its solidity and cohesion. In fact, well-understood speculation does not make the study of theology dry or divorced from life but confers on it a wholehearted seriousness that is truly vital and personal.

41. 7) Today it is especially desirable to construct and develop a systematic and organic theology that comprises within its scope the data of faith, as the results of historical research and of what the Church proposes; a rational reflection on it in the light of the faith, the interpretation of the results obtained in a more compact synthesis of its fundamental elements; its application and its response to the individual and collective demands of modern life and thought.

42. It is evident, then, that what distinguishes Catholic theology as a science is its constant reference to the faith. The strictly scientific nature of the process, be it positive or systematic, does not exclude but demands the continual presence of the *sensus fidei* which guides and directs theology from within, in the fields of exegesis, patristics, liturgy, canon law, history and systematic and pastoral theology. It is faith which, in agreement with the Magisterium, guides theology and gives it, together with its specific identity, its full meaning and certainty.

III. Some of the Conditions of Theological Work

43. The present situation of theology and the teaching of theology is characterized on the one hand by an intense application to developing Biblical themes and on the other hand by a new attention to modern currents in philosophy, sociology, and psychology. Some believe that they can take from these not only the result of research, analysis, and experiments, but also categories and criteria of thought. This openness to the natural and human sciences and to the problems of the present time, creates in some people a certain estrangement from the Magisterium of the Church and from traditional Christian theology and philosophy. Thus there is a risk of creating a theology without a solid basis which is outside the area of faith. It is, therefore, fitting to make quite clear the conditions of sound theological work. This is related to the Magisterium, to the theological and philosophical patrimony received from ancient times, to philosophy, science, and finally to the problems and values of this world which are of such great interest today. This is to treat once again of a clarification of the epistemological status of theology as the science of Christian Revelation with regard to principles which are enduring and to historical conditions which change.

1. Theology and the Magisterium

44. 1) The faith which theology seeks to understand and examine in depth is the faith of the Church, the faith professed by the body of the Church *(sensus fidelium),* watched over and authentically interpreted by the ordinary and extraordinary Magisterium entrusted to the Apostles and their Successors by Jesus Christ. Both Revelation and the Magisterium form a natural and inseparable union. According to Vatican Council II, "It is clear that the Holy Tradition of the Church and the Holy Scriptures, and the Magisterium of the Church are, by a most wise disposition of God, so united and joined together as to be unable to exist apart."[26] Hence in Catholic theology the ecclesial character of the faith should be made concrete by constant reference to the Magisterium.

45. 2) The Magisterium can be considered both as authority and as service. It is "not superior to the Word of God but serves it," teaching only what it has received and, by divine command, listens to it attentively, reverently keeps and faithfully expounds it, and out of this deposit of faith, it obtains all it proposes for belief as the revealed Word of God.[27]

Because of this, the Magisterium must not be thought of as extraneous to the Church, something that oppresses it. On the contrary, it should be thought of as having a role, a function as a charismatic service in the community and for the community. It follows that the Magisterium is not something external to and outside of theology, but rather an internal inspiration, completely natural to it, not a limitation, but an indispensable help, a *conditio sine qua non* of Catholic theology.

46. 3) The Magisterium can and, indeed, must be presented and considered as:

a) the bearer, interpreter, and guarantor of the *rule of faith* for the sake of the unity of the community of believers;

b) the active proponent of a synthesis of assured and common values which emerge from various opinions and experiences;

c) the power to judge the conformity of the results of research, theological reflection, and the spiritual experience of individuals and groups, and Revelation which has been handed down through the ages by tradition; this the Magisterium looks after, authentically interprets, and proposes to the faithful.

47. 4) The Church has the right and the duty to demand of theologians a loyalty to the Magisterium that, so far from prejudicing legitimate research, guarantees that it will promote an authentic building-up of the Body of Christ which is the Church. In fact the *munus docendi* belongs to the Bishops united in collegiality with the Supreme Pontiff, in the line of apostolic succession;[28] the episcopal Magisterium in theology, as in all forms of catechesis and preaching, cannot be replaced by individual thought, which has the limited function only of investigating, illustrating, and developing objective data which comes from God; this is guarded and proclaimed by the Church.

Theologians have the task of research and critical reflection. They can receive from the Magisterium a share in its *munus docendi (missio canonica docendi)*. However, the Magisterium must maintain its authority to judge the relation of theological speculation to the Word of God. In particular, the task of professors of theology in seminaries, which is to prepare suitable and good ministers of God, future teachers of the faith,[29] requires the greatest loyalty to the Magisterium, both ordinary and extraordinary.

2. Theology and the theological and philosophical patrimony of Christianity

48. 1) In the same context of the Magisterium of the Church, the perennially valid[30] patrimony of Christian thought, and especially of St. Thomas, referred to by the Council,[31] must always be borne in mind, not only for the employment of philosophy in theology, but also for the assessment of the intrinsic dynamism of this, inasmuch as doctrinal patrimony is the expression of the continuity of the life of faith in the Church in particularly intense moments.

In fact beyond the recognized authority of the individual Fathers or Doctors of the Church, the work of these Fathers and Doctors is part of the Church's living tradition, to which providentially they have brought a contribution of lasting value at times which were quite favorable to a synthesis of reason and faith.

49. 2) It is under the impulse of that tradition and in the light of the teaching of St. Thomas that theology can and should progress and its teaching be conducted. Close contact with the dynamism of tradition is a protection against exaggerated individualism and an assurance of that objectivity of thought which the Church particularly holds.

3. Relations between theology and philosophy

50. 1) With reference to the complex problem of the connection, not only extrinsic, but also intrinsic, between philosophy and theology, we should bear in mind two premises:

a) Theology is radically independent of any philosophical system. Its term of reference is, in fact, the reality of faith; every other reference is merely instrumental. It follows from this that theology is free to accept or reject various philosophical theories in the fulfillment of its own research and reflection. It may adopt the contributions of common sense—insofar as they help its rational development—availing itself of all they have to give but without identifying itself with any one of them.

b) It is necessary for theology to take up the critical challenges which any philosophy may present, not only to theology but also to faith. Theology cannot avoid such confrontations without the danger of being undefended and misunderstood by the various philosophies of today. But, it must not blindly close itself to their suggestions and proposals.

51. 2) Given this point of view, it is not difficult to understand the soundness of the Church's attitude on these matters, which is twofold:

a) While remaining open to every new and old philosophy, she will not accept any that cannot be reconciled with Christian belief.

b) Her preference is for a philosophy whose fundamental tenets are in harmony with Revelation, because it is not possible for there to be any contradiction between the natural truths of philosophy and the supernatural truths of faith.

52. 3) Obviously, the Church cannot accept a philosophy whose tenets are in contradiction with Revelation. In certain circumstances the Church can accept a healthy philosophical pluralism[32] arising from different regions, different cultures, and mentalities, and expressed perhaps in different ways, since the same truth can be reached in different ways, and can be presented and expounded in different ways. On the other hand, it is not at all possible for her to accept a philosophical pluralism which compromises the fundamental truths connected with Revelation such as is apt to occur in certain philosophies influenced by historical relativism or materialistic or idealistic immanentism.

Defects of theirs explain why today it is not so easy to realize a philosophical synthesis with these philosophies as St. Thomas did with the philosophical thought of ancient thinkers.

53. 4) For this reason the Council was justified in the emphasis it put on St. Thomas when, in the decree *Optatam totius* (n. 16), it speaks of speculative theology. His philosophy clearly explains and harmonizes the first principles of natural truth with Revelation, not in any static form but with the dynamism that is peculiar to St. Thomas and which renders possible a continual and renewed synthesis of the valid conclusions of traditional thought and the advances made by modern thought.[33]

4. The contribution of the human and natural sciences

54. 1) After philosophy, theology acknowledges the valuable help given by the natural sciences, history, and anthropology. In fact the *man-God* relationship lies at the very center of the economy of salvation, in which Revelation, and hence, theology, are for the sake of mankind. Therefore, each of the sciences, in its own way, offers theology a valuable aid to a better knowledge of man one of the terms of this relationship, at the same time they stimulate it to determine more precisely the meaning of revealed truth that refers to man.

Furthermore, the contact of theology with science enriches it thematically and prevents it becoming culturally isolated in a world such as ours in which science flourishes and arouses universal interest.

55. 2) But the two fields of theology and the natural sciences must be kept very distinct, each respecting the autonomy of the other. In fact, they have different ends. Hence, just as the sciences should not be subject to theological *a priori* affirmation, so theology cannot solve its problems on the basis of scientific hypotheses and results. Theological studies are concerned with things far beyond the province of the research of the sciences: the mystery of the revealed Word of God. But, should a theological problem touch upon a subject that concerns one of the sciences (e.g., the problem of the origin of man and the world, questions of moral and pastoral order) it cannot ignore what the sciences say with certainty on the matter.

56. 3) Theology without interfering in any way with the sciences can yet help them because theology itself has a more complete understanding of man, and of the world, and because of its hierarchy of values which always reminds scientists to direct their life and thought towards the light of divine truth. Substantially it is a contribution of *wisdom*. According to Vatican Council II, "our era needs such wisdom more than bygone ages if the discoveries made by man are to be further humanized."[34]

57. 4) The contributions of the sciences to theology generally (but not necessarily) come to it through the mediation of philosophy, which today, besides other tasks, has also to evaluate and sift the complex problems set by science and by the solutions proposed so as to pick out what has permanent value with regard to human reason and its connection with Revelation. On the basis of this, theology can better evaluate the real contributions of science.

58. 5) From a methodological point of view theology, while remaining faithful to the demands of its *deductive-inductive* method, cannot ignore the *scientific spirit,* so widely diffused in the human natural sciences. It should follow, even in its own work, as far as possible, the laws of positive research, of control of sources, and of the verification of facts, which are common to the sciences.[35] But, so that it may appreciate and use such a method, theology must remain fully aware of its own epistemological status and avoid confusing itself with the other sciences, even on the level of procedure.

5. Application of theology to earthly reality and integration of human values

59. 1) Among the tasks of theology, there is also that mentioned in the decree *Optatam totius* (n. 16) which invites theologians to employ theological method when applying eternal truths to the unsettled conditions of our time, so that students "may learn to search for a solution of human problems in the light of Revelation; and apply eternal truth to the unsettled conditions of this world and communicate it in the appropriate manner to their contemporaries." Furthermore, the same Council, in the Constitution *Gaudium et spes,* has often invited theologians to give more attention to the problems of contemporary culture and science, so as to renew their way of thinking and contribute "ad compositionem culturae cum christiana institutione" (n. 62).

60. 2) It is as if theologians must write a new chapter in theological and pastoral epistemology, beginning — methodologically — with the facts and questions of the present day, rather than the ideas and problems of the past.

The complex cultural and social reality of our times and the changed attitude toward theology and the Church makes this work difficult, but it is a commitment to evangelization which theologians cannot ignore.

61. 3) Theological endeavor in this field leads to the concrete task:

a) of integrating into Christian doctrine and morals all that experience finds of value in earthly reality and the development of human values;[36]

b) of illuminating earthly reality and human values — without altering their identity — in relation to the kingdom of God;

c) of promoting and inspiring such values even on the level of their natural identity, which is better formed if referred to transcendental reality and values;[37]

d) of contributing towards freeing earthly values and realities from the secular and worldly over-valuation that often accompanies them and thus saving their identity.

All this belongs to the ambit of that *"Christian or integral humanism"* [38] which hinges on the principle of *gratia supponens et perficiens (sanans) naturam.*[39]

62. 4) Working in this field does not mean that theology beomes so anthropological or anthropocentric that it ceases to be the science of God and divine things. It is, on the contrary, a matter of giving greater relevance to the problems of mankind by bringing theology more up-to-date without, however, changing the man-God relationship on the metaphysical, gnoseological, or ethical level. This relationship, in fact, lies at the very center of theology and is always resolved in a definite reference to God.

III. Guidelines for the teaching of theology

I. General Guidelines

63. From a consideration of theology and of the theological teaching in seminaries, today some characteristic facts emerge. Among those, to which particular attention should be given, is a plurality of tendencies, opinions, and interests with a relative lack of unity; the narrow scope of some fields of research, of study, of themes, even notions of theology, and of its connection with philosophy and the sciences, outside an organic and constructive synthesis. A correct concern to find an attentive partner in theological dialogue and to find a type of discourse which interests him, not without a tendency to adaptation, could, if pushed beyond certain limits, mean a break with tradition and a distortion of theology.

In this climate, certain methodological requirements for teaching arise which involve the nature and function of theology.

1. Plurality and unity

64. 1) The plurality, so common today, in the theological expression of faith is nothing new. We find it in the early centuries of the Church in the great theological currents of the West and the East. This tendency grew and manifested itself in the variety of theological schools which later developed, each taking its departure from different organizational principles and different fundamental concerns. Each of these "schools" represents an approach to the Christian mystery, an attempt to interpret the reality of Revelation. None of them can identify with the other except on the level of revealed truth which all are trying to understand on the level of the Church which recognizes them.

65. 2) But, theological pluralism today differs from that of the past in that its scope is so wide and so deep that it could be described as radical. From the quantitative point of view, this is due to the enormous amount of material accumulated by each discipline which theology takes into consideration and utilizes by means of a complex articulation of organizational processes. From the point of view of the arrangement and spirit of theology, today's pluralism is due to the diversity of methods employed, the variety of philosophies followed, the different terminologies used, and basic outlooks adopted. These and other characteristics ensure that the new forms of pluralism, which especially have appeared after the Second Vatican Council, can be seen as even qualitatively distinct from earlier forms of pluralism.

66. 3) In the past the Church not only tolerated but also encouraged a pluralism of theological tendencies because they were an indication of attempts to provide new and better explanations of certain themes and problems which were addressed under different aspects. The Church today has not changed. She encourages and favors a certain pluralism for kerygmatic, pastoral, and missionary reasons, provided always that such pluralism is a further enrichment of a doctrine of faith already well and clearly determined and in constant reference to it.[40]

The Church, however, must deplore arbitrary and chaotic pluralism which uses philosophies far removed from faith, and very disparate terminology thus making understanding between theologians ever more difficult, if not impossible. Such a situation can only lead to confusion of language and concepts and a break with the theological tradition of the past. It cannot be considered as favorable for the formation of future priests and so may not be tolerated in theological teaching. [41]

67. 4) It is absolutely essential that candidates for the priesthood — as beginners in learning theology — should, above all, acquire a sound *forma mentis* from the great Masters of the Church. From them they can learn the true science of theology and the true Christian doctrine. Besides, this principle is true of learning and formation in any field of knowledge and culture.

68. 5) For the theological formation of students at any level the following principles concerning pluralism must be applied:

a) The unity of the faith must be safeguarded. For this purpose it is, above all, necessary to distinguish what is a matter of faith, to which everyone is obliged to adhere, and what is the level where the faith permits a choice of opinions.

b) In the area of theological opinion, the common doctrine of the Church and the *sensus fidelium* must be respected. In theology there is a nucleus of affirmations that are certain, common, and which cannot be given up, constituting the basis of all Catholic dogmatic teaching.

These cannot be questioned but only clarified, studied in depth, and better explained in their historical and theological context.

c) With regard to various theological systems, their unequal value should be borne in mind. Above all, it is necessary to see whether they are guided only by restricted interests, limited to some particular aspect of revealed truth, or whether they embrace the whole Christian mystery, systematizing and integrating a great quantity of data in the light of simple principles and of a value bordering on the universal. In any case, a system shall only be judged valid if it ignores none of the essential aspects of reality and is demonstrably capable of assimilating new points of view in an organic and harmonious synthesis. Under this aspect, the thomistic synthesis retains its full value.

Following these principles and criteria the teacher of theology can move safely among the hazards of modern pluralism.

2. Prospects of a synthesis

69. 1) The theology of today in its search for new arrangement and new formulae is marked by a transitory and provisional character. Always in search of a new synthesis, it is like a huge construction site in which the building is only partly completed, while within there is an accumulation of material which must be used in the building.

Consequently the teaching of theology has in many cases lost its unity and compactness, and presents an incomplete fragmentary aspect so that it is often said that theological knowledge has become "atomized." When order and completeness are lacking, the central truths of the faith are easily lost to sight. Therefore, it is not at all to be wondered at, if, in such a climate, various fashionable "theologies," which are in great part one-sided, partial, and sometimes unfounded, gain ground.

70. 2) These difficulties, inherent in the novelty of many of the problems with which theologians are called upon to deal, and in the vastness of their scientific interests as well as in the general climate of opinion, cannot leave indifferent those who are responsible for the teaching of theology, even in the basic courses. The ideal of unity and synthesis, although it seems difficult, should interest both professors and students. It is a matter of the greatest importance on whose solution depend in great part the efficiency, vitality, and practical utility of their studies. It involves:

a) A synthesis of the various doctrines.

b) A synthesis of the different levels of the theological studies, e.g., systematic theology, exegesis.

c) A synthesis of sciences and religious experiences in relation to pastoral activity, etc.

71. 3) Among the indispensable means to achieve this end are the following:

a) At the beginning of the studies, it is necessary "to organize very well the different theological and philosophical disciplines so that they may converge in harmony towards a progressive opening of the mind of the student to the mystery of Christ, which penetrates the whole history of the human race, working always in the Church, and operating chiefly through the priestly ministry." [42] In a special introductory course, "the mystery of salvation should be proposed in a way that students can understand the point of ecclesiastical studies, their structure, and their pastoral aim." [43]

b) It is necessary to have a detailed and coordinated program of studies that guarantees the integrity and internal cohesion of the whole theological course, the completeness of the material to be studied, as well as a solid foundation and coordination of each particular discipline. [44]

c) The personal commitment of the professors is indispensable. They should have a complete understanding of the ideal of unity and of synthesis, and they should be able to embody single parts and fragmentary data in an organic unity which they already possess and to which they can refer partial considerations.

d) From this, the importance of lectures by a master should be evident. They should be sufficient in number and well prepared. The work of the students in groups and "seminars" should aim to give them a better grasp of the synthesis and an introduction to the method of scientific work. In any case, these groups and seminars are no substitute for lectures, and cannot give students a complete and synthetic vision of the material to be studied. [45]

e) In view of completeness of the teaching and of a desirable theological synthesis, it is necessary to establish a fixed canon of principal disciplines and the fundamental and central themes of the faith which it is obligatory to study. The principle of free choice on the level of the basic courses must be limited to certain auxiliary and special matters only, which must be carefully worked out. [46]

f) The pivot of the effort necessary to obtain a greater completeness and synthesis is constituted by the program of studies and by the effective unity of the teaching staff. It imposes, above all, an interdisciplinary coordination and collaboration which must be in some way institutionalized, especially in the drawing up of the programs and in the subdivision of the various tasks. [47]

g) It is necessary to recognize and respect the extremely important role of the prefect of studies, who must be complete master of his job and truly efficient. [48] He should try to keep alive in the teachers a concern for completeness and synthesis, exerting himself together with the teachers to avoid at any cost fragmentary teaching, polarized on certain questions of the day, or limited to incomplete modern theologies (e.g., the theology of development, the theology of liberation, etc.).

3. Vitality and transmission of theological knowledge

72. 1) Perhaps never more than today has theology been so aware of its duty to pass on the Christian message. This awareness was notably accentuated by Vatican Council II, at which Pope John XXIII urged "ut haec doctrina certa et immutabilis, cui fidele obsequium est praestandum, ea ratione pervestigetur et exponatur, quam tempora postulant nostra." [49] On their part, the students themselves like theological teaching to be alive, spiritually effective, pastoral, and social.

73. 2) By its very nature, theology leads to personal contact with God, stimulating those who teach or study it to prayer and contemplation. Spirituality born from a life of faith is a kind of internal dimension of theology to which it imparts supernatural flavor. On the other hand, to have a more intense spiritual life and an adequate pastoral preparation, serious scientific education is also necessary; without it, any adaptation in the ascetic and pastoral life is of no value.

74. 3) The vitality of theology in relation to prayer and contemplation, according to the teaching of Vatican Council II, is to be found in the Word of God, manifest and working in the history of salvation, which finds the center of its life and its synthesis in the mystery of Christ. [50] The truths of the faith become ever more alive as we see in them their profound unity in Christ, encountered in a particular manner in the Fathers and liturgy. For this reason a greater familiarity both with the Holy Scriptures and with the Fathers of the Church and the liturgy can be considered the most effective means of discovering the vital force of a theological formation. For this end, it is clear that all the efforts and means already mentioned in connection with giving theological teaching unity and cohesion will also help to achieve this other result.

75. 4) Spirituality is one of the principal components of pastoral adaptation but of itself it is not enough. In fact, a greater contact with life is also necessary. With this end in view, the professors should have useful contacts with pastoral situations, with priests having the care of souls, with the faithful, and especially with believing and cultured professional men. [51] In this way the teachers can become more aware of the real problems that daily life and scientific progress set out for the faith, and thus should be able to present courses in such a manner "ut alumni hodiernae aetatis indole recte perspecta, ad colloquium cum hominibus accommodate praeparentur." [52]

76. 5) In order to communicate the faith to the man of today, theology certainly supposes and demands an analysis of man's dispositions and perceptive capacities in relation to the truth that must be proposed to him. [53] Therefore, it must formulate the truth in relation to the *forma mentis* of man, so that it can acquire for him a real meaning and a vital relevance, even in connection with the social, political, and cultural problems that most interest the modern world.

In this work the sense of transcendence of the Christian message must not be lost, nor must theology be reduced to a kind of philology or sociology of religion elaborated by a theologian; nor must it abandon the classical tradition of theology nor neglect the true object of theology which is God.

77. 6) This task, mentioned above, obviously presents theologians with a problem of language which is felt today even by the interest taken in modern hermeneutics. Theology should be very sensitive to the language of the modern world if it wishes to be rooted in modern culture and to communicate with modern man. [54] Pope Paul VI *á propos* of this said: "We must look ahead so as to confirm the integrity of the whole of our doctrine—without any instability due to passing fashion—in *the forms of new language,* which must not be precluded except for reasons of absolute loyalty to Revelation and the infallible Magisterium of the Church, with respect for the *sensus fidelium* and for edification in charity." [55]

II. Particular Guidelines
for the Various
Theological Disciplines

78. Having mentioned certain orientations of a general nature and of special importance for the teaching of theology, it is now opportune to define certain methodological orientations with special reference to the theological disciplines which are today at the center of scientific interest and are called upon to confront special problems and difficulties.

Up to now much thought has been given to safeguarding the specific nature of theology, of faithfully respecting its special methodological procedure, of making good use of philosophical reflection, of natural and human sciences, of seeking a greater internal cohesion, of assuring the vitality and practical utility of theological knowledge, in closer contact with the sources of Revelation and with life. All that has a much stronger and more concrete resonance when it is a matter of applying it within disciplines such as exegesis, dogmatic theology, moral theology, patristics, pastoral and fundamental theology, which will be dealt with later. All these disciplines—because of the direct contact they have either with the sources, or with the central nucleus of the Christian mystery, or with life —are today particularly questioned due to conciliar directives and to the general present-day situation.

1. Holy Scripture

79. 1) The first thing which must be taken into account in the teaching of theology is that Holy Scripture is the point of departure, an *enduring foundation* and the life-giving principle and soul of all theology. [56]

It is, therefore, necessary that professors of Biblical studies should develop their teaching with that competence and scientific completeness which the importance of their discipline demands. So as to be faithful to their task, they must work on the level of texts, on the level of the facts contained in it, on the level of the tradition which the text communicates and interprets. The professors of this subject must have recourse to textual, literary, and historical analysis. But, they must also maintain in the souls of the students a sense of the unity of the mystery and of the plan of God. The Scriptures have been handed down by the Church and in part they were born in the Church and, therefore, they must be read and understood in the ecclesial tradition. [57]

80. 2) Such is the principal role occupied by Scripture that it cannot but determine the nature of the connections which exist between itself and theology with its diverse disciplines. This being the case, it cannot be considered one-sidedly in the service of the said disciplines (as a source of *loci probantes*), but the whole of theology is called upon to make its contribution to a better and ever more profound understanding of the sacred texts, that is, of the dogmatic and moral truths that they contain.

It follows from this that the teaching of Sacred Scripture, having dealt with all the introductory matter, should culminate in a Biblical theology presenting a united vision of the Christian mystery.

81. 3) Biblical theology, to serve truly a better understanding of Holy Scripture, must have its own subject matter, elaborated by a specific methodology, and with a certain autonomy, that is to say, with a certain exclusive attention to the character and integrity of Biblical teaching. Such a relative autonomy does not at all mean an independence or antagonism towards systematic theology, which today does sometimes unfortunately happen.

Between the positive and systematic parts of theology — while maintaining the specificity of their respective methods — there should be, on the contrary, a fruitful and continual collaboration. Properly speaking, in theology there are not two phases of work, inasmuch as the speculative part is already present in the positive; the positive is the speculative "in fieri" and the speculative is the positive carried through to its completion.

82. 4) To achieve such an end as this, there must be effective cooperation and coordination between the teachers of the disciplines chiefly involved: that is to say exegesis, fundamental theology, dogmatic and moral theology, so as to arrive at a suitable division of tasks, and also at a more perfect harmony and structure of the matter being taught.

One expects from professors of Holy Scripture a correct openness towards and an understanding of the problems of other theological disciplines, keeping always present the requirements of the integrity and internal coherence of the faith, expressed in the principle of the *analogy of the faith*.[58]

The importance justly given today to the Biblical sciences, while it increases the responsibility of Biblical scholars "vis á vis" those involved in the other disciplines, does not justify an independent and superior attitude. Biblical scholars should be, above all, the servants of the Word of God, bearing well in mind the delicacy of many exegetical problems that, especially in a seminary course, must be treated with the greatest prudence and moderation, also because of the influence they can have on catechesis and preaching.[59]

83. 5) The professor of Sacred Scripture should be aware, above all, of the task that his teaching fulfills for dogmatic, moral and fundamental theology, the pastoral ministry and the spiritual life of future priests. Here it should be enough to call to mind that:

a) with a view toward systematic theology, exegesis should tend toward a true and proper Biblical theology;

b) in fundamental theology, Biblical science requires a scientific "aggiornamento" united to a mentality that is constructive in using sure scientific information to serve faith;

c) in pastoral ministry, it is necessary to offer a vision of Sacred Scripture which is as complete as possible, not overlooking the more serious problems,[60] to guide the students to a wise use of properly interpreted texts;

d) in the spiritual life, the students must be encouraged to respect and love Sacred Scripture[61] and to be trained to profit from the Bible in the liturgy, and in priestly piety and asceticism.

84. 6) To give a formative value to the teaching that begins with Biblical themes, a professor of Holy Scripture must try to coordinate them in one theological-ecclesial synthesis, inspired by the *Profession of the Catholic Faith* that summarizes the understanding that the Church has of Revelation. In this, theology will be linked to the fundamental articles of the Christian faith.

2. Patristics

85. 1) One could say something similar for patristics, although it is clear that what has been said about the Sacred Scriptures cannot be applied wholly to patristics, because of the evident objective differences between the two disciplines.

But in patristics as in the Biblical sciences it is equally necessary:

a) to respect the special character of the method of historical research;

b) to aim at unity in theological teaching, even if this unity must be done by means of partial and gradual syntheses.

86. 2) One of the principal objects in teaching patristics is to outline the picture of theology and the Christian life in the time of the Fathers in its historical reality. To assign to it other objectives runs the risk of fragmenting it and making it sterile.

87. 3) Furthermore, the teaching of patristics should tend to give a sense of the continuity of theology, which corresponds to fundamental data, and of its relative nature, which corresponds to its particular aspects and applications. In this way, it can help theology in a global sense to remain within the faith interpreted and guarded by the consensus of the Fathers.

88. 4) For this reason also, it will be opportune to strengthen the ties that exist between the teaching of patristics and the teaching of Church history, in order that they may contribute to a systematic understanding of the problems, events, experiences, and doctrinal, spiritual, pastoral, and social developments in the Church at various times. [62]

3. Dogmatic theology

89. 1) The genetic method laid down for dogmatic theology by Vatican Council II[63] consists of five stages: Sacred Scripture, the patristic tradition, history, speculation, the liturgical life, and the life of the Church with an application to the problems of today. This guarantees teaching founded on revealed data, unified in the history of salvation, ordered and integrated in a complete vision of the faith, enlivened by a contact with the liturgy and the life of the Church, and open to pastoral needs, thanks to the attention given to the needs of our time.

90. 2) To realize all the possibilities of such a method, as well as to overcome any difficulties it presents, the first condition is to respect and apply the principle of the *continuity of the faith,* while bearing in mind the need for future generations to understand it ever more deeply and in a way ever better adapted to the needs of the world.

For the sake of this continuity the following points should be considered:

a) the need for a constant reference to Revelation, inasmuch as it is the inexhaustible and objective principle of the faith begetting both dogma and the different expressions of the Christian life, particularly *theology;*

b) the intervention of the ecclesiastical Magisterium to fix and define the permanent requirements of faith;

c) the necessity and also the relative nature of theology, which discovers and brings forth the depths of faith;

d) the need of a contemporary understanding of faith, received and professed in its wholeness, in reference to the new cultural situation, and, therefore, to the special task of theology.

91. 3) A good application of the aforesaid method also requires a good relationship between dogmatic theology and Biblical science, a matter which has already been touched upon.

A direct contact with Sacred Scripture makes it possible to have a greater thematic richness and a teaching more active and creative but consequently a much more demanding work for both professors and students.

92. 4) From what has been said, there emerge certain specific tasks for the teacher of dogmatic theology, especially with regard to the positive part of the teaching under a Biblical and a historical-patristic aspect:

a) under the Biblical aspect he must always remember that Holy Scripture does not only serve to supply proofs to support a thesis, but it is also and above all a point of departure and a source of inspiration for all theological teaching;

b) under the patristic-historical aspect dogmatic theology should be able to acquire promising results from the examination and study of the great masters of Christian tradition, to be used not only in the historical part of theology, but also as a guide in Christian reflection and systematic organization.

93. 5) One must always keep in mind the need of a close coordination of disciplines and of an effective cooperation of teachers between the positive and speculative parts of theology, which should be based on two principles:

a) the breadth and the importance of the positive part of the genetic historical method should not lessen in the least the weight that speculative development must have in the teaching of theology;

b) the integrity of the genetic historical method admits of a certain flexibility in consideration of the nature of the themes taught: some in a more positive way (e.g., penance) and others in a more speculative way (e.g., grace and freedom or the internal consciousness of Christ).

94. 6) In the teaching of dogma, besides the substantial integrity of the genetic method, the material integrity of the discipline must be assured so that all the truths of the faith are treated as they should be. Obviously, a judicious choice is taken for granted. In making this, the essential must be distinguished from the unessential. In fact, there exists a "hierarchia veritatum doctrinae catholicae, cum diversus sit earum nexus cum fundemento fidei christianae." [64] But it is evident that in dogma as in all the other principal disciplines of the seminary course all options and premature specialization must be excluded.

4. Moral theology

95. 1) The renewal of moral theology desired by Vatican Council II[65] is a part of the effort that the Church is making to understand better the man of today and to go out to meet his needs in a world that is in the process of profound change.

It is a matter of putting the yeast of the Gospel teaching "into the circulation of the thought, expression, culture, customs, and tendencies of humanity as it lives and moves about the face of the earth today."[66]

The teaching of moral theology contributes most effectively to this task of the Church, and, therefore, it must be renewed and brought to perfection in accordance with these needs.

96. 2) To overcome one-sidedness and fill in the omissions of which moral theology has at times given evidence in the past, due in great part to a certain legalism and individualism, as well as to a certain separation from the sources of Revelation, it becomes necessary to clarify its *epistemological status*.

It remains, therefore, to determine the way in which it must be built up always in close contact with Holy Scripture, Tradition (received through faith and interpreted by the Magisterium), and in reference to the natural law (known by means of reason).

On this basis, a revision and a revaluation of moral theology should be possible, and the same is true of its spiritual, pastoral, and "political" application. In this way it will have a place as authentic theology. Placing it in this position should be of primary concern, so that theology can meet the demands of what is known as "orthopraxis."

97. 3) With this aim in view, it is necessary, above all, to have a lively awareness of the link between moral and dogmatic theology, so that moral questions can be treated as a true and fitting theological discipline, in conformity with all the fundamental epistemological and methodological rules that are valid for all of theology. With regard to this it would be as well to refer to St. Thomas Aquinas, who, like other great masters, never separated moral from dogmatic theology, but, instead, inserted it in a unified scheme of systematic theology, as a part that concerns the process by which man, created in the likeness of God and redeemed by the grace of Christ, tends toward his full realization, according to the demands of his divine calling, in the context of the economy of salvation historically realized in the Church.

98. 4) By virtue of the strict link between moral and dogmatic theology, the specific procedure of theology should be adopted also in morals, developing properly both the positive and the speculative aspect, drawing widely on Revelation and developing every discourse in harmony with the thought and mind of the Church.

It is much to be desired that there should be the same concern for the material completeness of the teaching of this subject as is demanded by dogmatic theology.

99. 5) For moral theology, even more than the other theological disciplines, it is necessary to bear in mind the results of the natural and human sciences, and also of human experience; while these cannot ever find or absolutely create the rules of morality,[67] nevertheless, they can throw much light on the situation and on the behavior of man, encouraging research, revision, the profound understanding of doctrine which lies between the sure and certain principles of reason and faith, and their application to the concrete facts of life.

The mediation between moral theology and the human and natural sciences will be accomplished by profound philosophical reflection, stimulated by Christian Tradition which has never failed to consider the problem of man, with particular reference to his nature, his destiny, and his whole development on his way to God.

100. 6) It is also necessary to introduce into moral theology the dynamic aspect which will provoke the reply that a man must give to the divine call that comes in the process of his growth in love, in the bosom of a community of salvation. In such a way, moral theology will acquire an inner spiritual dimension in response to the demand for fully developing the *Imago Dei* which is in man, and the laws of spiritual development described by Christian ascetics and mysticism. For precisely this reason, moral theology must keep in strict contact with Biblical and dogmatic theology, always bearing in mind the pastoral tasks that future priests must fulfill in directing souls and administering the Sacrament of Penance.

101. 7) In a particular way, the teaching of moral theology to students who are preparing for the priestly ministry brings with it the need for a close contact and relation with pastoral theology, which will encourage it to study the problems posed by the experience of life, and will provide plans of action inspired by the needs of the Word of God and theologically well-grounded and developed. This is the way of renewal indicated by Vatican Council II: "Sub luce evangelii et humanae experientiae."[68]

5. Pastoral theology

102. 1) Particular attention must be given to the teaching of pastoral theology, both as a part of all the theological disciplines[69] and also as a science that interprets and stimulates the genuine needs of the pastoral ministry and guides their fulfillment in contemporary circumstances according to the demands of faith, in the light of Revelation.[70]

103. 2) Pastoral theology keeps in touch with reality, that is to say, with the problems of the ministry and the solutions which have been given to them at various times, especially today, but it is bound to the rest of theology and draws on it in two fundamental ways:

a) it appeals to and stimulates the other theological disciplines (especially moral theology) by putting before them problems that they cannot hope to solve in a purely empirical and autonomous way, because they must be seen in the light of faith;

b) it studies the practical application of theological solutions, always bearing in mind the concrete situation and respecting the plurality of possible choices, when there is room for different opinions.

104. 3) Following these criteria, the teaching of pastoral theology can give an authentic formation and prepare the ground for well-defined action, avoiding on the one hand timidity and frustration and on the other imprudent and rash initiatives, whose defects would be shown up by a sound theology.

105. 4) It will depend on all professors of theology in the basic courses to make the teaching of pastoral theology harmonious, coherent, and formative both as an aspect of the other theological disciplines and as a specific development of matters regarding the ministry. An adequate place should be given to this material in the structure of the course. Encouragement should be given to developing a year's pastoral course, at the end of the institutional course;[71] however, such teaching should not be excluded earlier in the course when local requirements and possibilities will determine the best form for it to take.

106. 5) In any case it should be kept in mind that teaching of pastoral theology must not be omitted, nor can the whole of theology be reduced to it.

6. Fundamental theology

107. 1) Fundamental theology is the basis of the rational procedure of all theology. The object of its study is the fact of Christian Revelation and its transmission in the Church, themes which are at the center of all discussion of the relationship between reason and faith.

108. 2) Fundamental theology is to be studied as an introduction to dogmatic theology and also as a preparation, reflection, and development of the act of faith (the "Credo" of the creedal Symbols) in the context of the requirements of reason and of the relationship between faith, culture and the great human religions. Moreover, it is also a permanent dimension of all theology, which must try to answer the contemporary problems presented by the students and by the world in which they live and in which they will one day have to conduct their ministry.

109. 3) The essential task of fundamental theology is the rational reflection which a theologian, together with the Church and starting from faith, makes on the truth of Christianity as a work of God Who has revealed Himself and made Himself present in Christ, and on the Church herself as the institution willed by Christ to carry on His work in the world.

Besides confronting faith with reason in abstract terms, it is conceived as a theology of dialogue on the borderline with the historical religions (Hinduism, Buddhism, and Islam), with the expression of modern atheism (especially of Marx, Freud, and Nietzsche), with religious indifference in a secular world dominated by technology, industrialism, and economic values, and finally, with the demands of believers, who today face new doubts and difficulties, and ask new questions of theology and catechesis. To answer the needs and experiences emerging from these varied groups, fundamental theology seeks to define the meaning which Christ and His message and His Church have in such a situation, and to arouse and secure the assent of faith as a way to God.

110. 4) These general lines of fundamental theology involve the study and explanation of the relationship of Christianity to history, language, other religious experiences, mysticism, philosophy, science, and the human condition. But, its specific task is to show by reasonable arguments that are valid for believers and non-believers alike how the mystery of Christ present in the Church, not only enlightens but also completes human existence, by uplifting it through the relationship with God which perfects and saves it.

111. 5) Far from fundamental theology being reduced to anthropology, it will have its full meaning inasmuch as it is an introduction to the total mystery of Christ and so to theology.

This introductory function means among other things that the professor also has the task of clearly bringing out the basic elements of theological epistemology in order to give the students an exact idea of the sacred science.[72]

112. 6) It is opportune to add that, in the teacher and student alike, fundamental theology, set forth according to its full dimension, helps to develop a mature personality in the continual confrontation between faith and reason, achieving a superior harmony between them, as may be seen in so many great masters of the Christian tradition. It helps both the theologian and the pastor of souls to overcome all sense of inferiority in the face of the data of culture and more especially of science, which they use as expressions of rational truth but without becoming enslaved to it, according to the methodological criteria used by fundamental theology. Finally, this fundamental theology serves to stimulate in everyone the courage of the faith, without which neither Christian life nor good theology is possible.

113. 7) For these reasons, fundamental theology is to be considered necessary for theological and pastoral formation, and, consequently, its teaching should hold a place in the program of studies that corresponds to its importance.

7. Other theological disciplines

114. Naturally a complete theological formation of future priests goes together with other disciplines of great importance, for example liturgy, canon law, church history, and the ancillary subjects: spiritual theology, the social teaching of the Church, ecumenism, missionary theology, sacred art, sacred music, etc. These either go side by side with the principal disciplines or (as in the case of catechetics and homiletics) belong to the realm of pastoral theology.

115. Regarding these, there are directives given partly in the documents of Vatican Council II (Const. *Sacrosanctum Concilium [The Constitution on the Sacred Liturgy]*, Decr. *Optatam totius, Ad gentes [Decree on the Church's Missionary Activity], Unitatis redintegratio [Decree on Ecumenism], Orientalium Ecclesiarum [Decree on the Catholic Eastern Churches], Inter mirifica [Decree on the Means of Social Communication]*, etc.), and partly in *Ratio fundamentalis institutionis sacerdotalis, [The Basic Plan for Priestly Formation]*, and in various other special documents.[73]

Every one of these disciplines, while carefully attending to its own problems and specific objects, can derive great advantage from this document, above all, insofar as it is concerned with a more lively awareness of present tasks as well as the need to enter constructively into theological discourse, according to the spirit of the faith.

IV. Practical norms

116. To conclude the preceding considerations it seems right to formulate certain norms specifying the duties of authorities set over seminaries, of professors and students.

I. The Duties of Those Responsible for Theological Formation

1. The authorities set over seminaries: Bishops and Episcopal Conferences, Rectors

117. 1) The authorities set over seminaries have the responsibility of testifying that the candidates for the priesthood possess, besides other requisites, a theological preparation that will enable them to carry out their duty of teaching the faith and acting as spiritual guides of the faithful.

118. 2) The preparation of future priests cannot be adequate without an efficient and qualified body of teachers. It follows that Bishops and Rectors of seminaries should not hesitate to allow candidates capable of higher studies the time necessary to obtain academic degrees recognized by the Church.

They should make available to them adequate instruments of work (libraries, books, periodicals) and willingly allow them periods for renewal.[74]

119. 3) The formation of future priests should be considered as one of the most important ministries in a diocese and, in some ways, the most demanding. In fact, the work of teaching unites the professor very closely to the work of Our Lord and Master, who prepared His Apostles to be witnesses of the Gospel and dispensers of the mysteries of God.

120. 4) These norms will be effective only if they are accompanied by strict vigilance on the part of all those responsible.

2. The professors

121. 1) The role of the professor is particularly important in the seminary course. It is, in fact, he who demonstrates the continuity of faith, tradition, and the life of the Church. It is he who assures, in the present pluralistic climate, lasting assent to fundamental truths as well as critical judgment, and a balanced assessment of a situation.

He is the unifying element indispensable for giving a solid basic formation. Therefore, it is necessary to reassess the function of the professor, for whom the Church, quite aware of the difficulty of his mission, wishes to express appreciation and recognition.

122. 2) As the servant of the Word of God, the professor of theology is bound to Christ and to the Church. His teaching should be carried out in the horizon of faith in the Word of our Lord and Savior, and with an outlook of loyalty to the Church and her Magisterium.[75]

123. 3) The plurality of schools of thought in the Church is a common phenomenon and in some ways can be considered beneficial. It was Vatican Council II that recognized its legitimacy and fruitfulness.[76]

Nevertheless such plurality must not become a pluralism of systems that undermine the unity of faith which must always remain intact. It would be lamentable if theological pluralism were to be confused with pluralism of faiths.

124. 4) In his teaching, the professor must show himself abreast of the most recent contributions of theological research, and capable of expounding and evaluating them.

He must guard against that kind of *a priori* thinking which could induce a mentality that holds new ideas and theories as certain simply because they are new, and older ideas as out of date simply because they are less recent.[77]

125. 5) Theology today has become very much aware of the necessity of a collaboration between the disciplines. In theology, just as in the field of profane science, teams of professors dedicate themselves to finding a deeper knowledge of faith. It is greatly to be desired that seminary teachers intensify amongst themselves those exchanges that help interdisciplinary work on the level of both teaching and research.[78]

126. 6) In the interests of a more effective formation and especially of a more systematic theological preparation, which is complete and doctrinally sound, up-to-date textbooks for each of the disciplines are highly to be recommended as the basis of both lectures and private study.[79]

127. 7) Since theological teaching in seminaries has for its principal object the formation of priests for the pastoral ministry, professors must keep this in mind, and, to understand better the needs of the pastoral life, they should keep in touch with parish priests and those who work in the areas of their students' future ministry.[80]

3. The students

128. 1) Students should feel co-responsible for their own theological formation. In fact, today they should take a more active part in the area of doctrine as in other areas of their formation. This is in conformity with the best traditions of teaching, which today are being given their full value.[81]

129. 2) Before students are introduced to theology, they should have the necessary literary[82] and philosophical preparation, unless the philosophical course is integrated with the theological one. Their philosophical formation should not comprise only the history of philosophy but also systematic reflection on the world and on man culminating in the affirmation of a personal Absolute. The philosophical course, according to the norms prescribed, should last at least two years.[83]

130. 3) Students of theology should be ready to approach the sources of theological reflection (in a special way the New Testament, the documents of the Magisterium, the works of the Fathers of the Church and of the great Scholastics), by means of an adequate knowledge of Latin[84] and the Biblical languages[85] and by the use of works of contemporary research (translations and commentaries).

131. 4) Students of the theological course should take pains to attend lectures regularly. In fact it is a case not merely of imparting knowledge but of giving a tradition of faith. In this matter of Christian tradition, contact with the master is indispensable, since he is also bearing witness to the faith which has illuminated and transformed his life.

His teaching thus becomes the discourse of a believing and praying theologian in whom there coincide an understanding of the mystery and intimate joining of it to his life. Theology cannot be taught and studied as if it were a secular subject before which one can remain neutral.

Personal contact between the professors and the students in lectures, written work, seminars, and personal direction is very important.[86]

II. The Arrangement of Theological Studies

132. 1) In all seminaries the basic formation necessary to prepare a man for the priesthood should take at the very least four years of theology, or its equivalent in systems that integrate philosophy and theology.[87] The same applies to religious scholasticates.[88]

133. 2) A seminary course in theology should aim to give a systematic vision of the Christian mystery, including the study of the essential themes of faith and the Christian life. Without such a formation assuring, as it does, the solidity and fruitfulness of every later specialization, the priestly vocation would run the risk of collapsing. It would not be possible even to speak of a solid basic formation, if one or other of the following themes were to be omitted or treated hastily and superficially: Revelation and its transmission by means of Tradition and the Holy Scriptures, the affirmation of one God in Three Persons; of God as the Creator, of the Incarnation of the Son of God and of the Redemption of man (the paschal mystery), the Church and the Sacraments; Christian anthropology (grace and the life of God); eschatology; Christian morals (fundamental and special); the whole of the Sacred Scriptures (the law and the prophets, the synoptics, John and Paul).

Equally important in this vision of the Christian mystery are the studies of fundamental theology, theological epistemology, liturgy, Church history, canon law, pastoral theology, the social teaching of the Church, ecumenism, missionary theology.

134. 3) Without being confused with the human sciences so that it becomes psychology, sociology, or anthropology, contemporary theology, even in a seminary course, cannot overlook the problems posed to the man of today by the development of the human sciences. In fact, theology should be not only an understanding of the Word of God but also the understanding of mankind to whom the Word of God is addressed, and of the conditions under which this Word is heard. It must speak of the Christian mysteries in such a way that it reaches an understanding of what they are in themselves and what they are for us.

135. 4) In teaching the various theological disciplines, the guidelines indicated in the third part of this document (some affirmations of which have been here deliberately repeated and emphasized) should be kept constantly in mind, in such a way as to assure students, whether or not they are candidates for Holy Orders, of a sound and complete formation.

Conclusion

The Sacred Congregation for Catholic Education entrusts this document to the Bishops and to all others responsible for the theological formation of candidates for the priesthood to help them in the serious tasks that they must carry out in today's situation.

An attempt has been made to set forth the true nature and specific mission of the teaching of theology — set in the new outlook initiated by Vatican Council II and by the successive documents of the Supreme Pontiff and the Holy See — to assure the future "masters of the faith" of a doctrinal formation fit for our times. In this way they will be able to *cognoscere quod agunt et imitari quod tractant.*

It is to be hoped that the assimilation of the Word of God and of its saving value will be translated by them into a life in conformity with it, sustaining an authentic priestly spirituality, which will bring the truth into harmony with the needs of pastoral charity, directed to the transmission of the faith of the Church.

Rome, given at the Offices of the Sacred Congregations, February 22, 1976, the feast of Saint Peter's Chair.

Gabriel M. Cardinal Garrone, *Prefect*

Joseph Schröffer
Tit. Archbishop of Volturnum
Secretary

Notes

1. *Decree on Ecumenism*, n.11.

2. Cf. Paul VI, Homily, *Hodie concilium*, in the last session of the Second Vatican Council, 7 Dec. 1965: AAS 58 (1966) 55 ff.; Allocution, *L'homme existe-t-il?* at the International Thomistic Congress, 12 Sept. 1970: AAS 62 (1970) 602 ff.

3. Paul VI, Apostolic Exhortation, *Quinque iam anni*, five years after the Second Vatican Council, to the whole episcopate, 8 Dec. 1970: AAS 63 (1971) 102-103.

4. Cf. *Decree on Ecumenism*, n.11.

5. "'The obedience of faith' (Rom. 16.26; cf. Rom. 1.5; 2 Cor. 10.5-6) must be given to God who reveals, an obedience by which man entrusts his whole self freely to God, offering 'the full submission of intellect and will to God who reveals'" *(Dogmatic Constitution on Divine Revelation*, n. 5).

6. Cf. *Dogmatic Constitution on Divine Revelation*, n. 8.

7. Cf. *Pastoral Constitution on the Church in the Modern World*, n. 4.

8. This aspect of theology must be given special prominence in the introductory course in which "the mystery of salvation is put forward in a way that the students can understand the significance of ecclesiastical studies, their structure and their pastoral goal while at the same time being helped to make the faith the foundation and spirit of their whole life and become strengthened in their embrace of their vocation with a complete personal dedication and joy" *(Decree on the Training of Priests*, n. 14).

9. Cf. *Decree on the Training of Priests*, n. 18; *Decree on the Ministry and Life of Priests*, n. 19; *The Basic Plan for Priestly Formation*, nn. 82-85.

10. Cf. *Pastoral Constitution on the Church in the Modern World*, nn. 46 ff.

11. Cf. *Declaration on the Relation of the Church to Non-Christian Religions*, passim; *Decree on the Church's Missionary Activity*, nn. 11, 22.

12. Cf. *Decree on Ecumenism*, n. 11; cf. as well Secretariat for Promoting Christian Unity, *Ecumenical Directory*, Part II: On ecumenical matters in higher education: AAS 62 (1970) 705 ff.

13. *Pastoral Constitution on the Church in the Modern World*, nn. 46 ff.

14. *Pastoral Constitution on the Church in the Modern World*, nn. 63 ff.; John XXIII, Encyclical, *Mater et magistra;* Encyclical, *Pacem in terris;* Paul VI, Encyclical, *Populorum progressio;* Apostolic Letter, *Octogesima adveniens.*

15. Cf. First Vatican Council, Session III, *Constitution on the Catholic Faith*, chapter 4: Denzinger-Schönmetzer, n. 3016.

16. Cf. *Dogmatic Constitution on Divine Revelation*, n.10.

17. Cf. Pontifical Biblical Commission, Instruction, *Sancta Mater*, on the historical truth of the Gospels, 21 Apr. 1964: AAS 56 (1964) 712 f.

18. John XXIII, Allocution, *Gaudet Mater Ecclesia*, on the occasion of the opening of the Second Vatican Council, 11 Oct. 1962: AAS 54 (1962) 792.

19. Cf. Paul VI, Apostolic Exhortation, *Petrum et Paulum*, 22 Feb. 1967: AAS 59 (1967) 198.

20. Cf. *Dogmatic Constitution on Divine Revelation*, n. 10.

21. Cf. *Dogmatic Constitution on Divine Revelation*, n. 12.

22. Sacred Congregation for Catholic Education, *Circular letter on the teaching of philosophy in Seminaries*, 20 Jan. 1972, Part II, n. 3b: "From the fact that the methods themselves of positive science (exegesis, history, etc.) start their work from various given preliminaries, which implicitly are results of a philosophical choice (today this is especially necessary, for instance, regarding the exegetical method of Rudolf Bultmann), without, however, assuming an absolute, critical function in the face of divine revelation. . . ."

23. *Decree on the Training of Priests*, n. 16.

24. Cf. Leo XIII, Encyclical, *Aeterni Patris*, 4 Aug. 1879: Denzinger-Schönmetzer, n. 3137.

25. Cf. *Dogmatic Constitution on Divine Revelation*, nn. 2-6.

26. *Dogmatic Constitution on Divine Revelation*, n. 10.

27. Ibidem.

28. *Dogmatic Constitution on the Church*, n. 25; Paul VI, Allocution, *Libentissimo sane*, to the International Congress on the Theology of Vatican II, 1 Sept. 1966: AAS 58 (1966) 890 ff.

29. Cf. *Decree on the Ministry and Life of Priests*, n. 4.

30. Cf. *Decree on the Training of Priests*, n. 15.

31. Cf. *Decree on the Training of Priests*, n. 16; *Declaration on Christian Education*, n. 10.

32. Cf. Sacred Congregation for Catholic Education. *Circular letter on the teaching of philosophy in Seminaries*, 20 Jan. 1972, Part III, n. 2.

33. Paul VI, Letter, *Lumen ecclesiae*, on the occasion of the 7th centenary of the death of St. Thomas, 20 Nov. 1974, n. 17: AAS 66 (1974) 690-691; cf. also Allocution, *Nous sommes*, Sixth International Thomistic Congress, 10 Sept. 1965: AAS 57 (1965) 790 ff.

34. *Pastoral Constitution on the Church in the Modern World*, n. 15.

35. With regard to the employment of human sciences, cf. Paul VI, Apostolic Letter, *Octogesima adveniens*, 24 May 1971, nn. 38-41: AAS 63 (1971) 427 ff.; cf. Paul VI, Apostolic Exhortation, *Quinque iam anni*, five years after the conclusion of the Second Vatican Council, 8 Nov. 1970: AAS 63 (1971) 102.

36. Cf. Paul VI, Encyclical, *Ecclesiam suam*, 4 Aug. 1964: AAS 56 (1964) 627-628.

37. Cf. *Pastoral Constitution on the Church in the Modern World*, nn. 35-36, 41-43.

38. Paul VI, Encyclical, *Populorum progressio,* 26 Mar. 1967, nn. 16, 20, 42 and passim: AAS 59 (1967) 265, 267, 278.

39. St. Thomas Aquinas, *Summa theologica,* 1, q. 1, a. 8, ad 2.

40. Cf. *Decree on the Church's Missionary Activity,* nn. 10, 16, 22; *The Basic Plan for Priestly Formation,* n. 64.

Pastoral Constitution on the Church in the Modern World, n. 44: "Thanks to the experience of past ages, the progress of the sciences, and the treasures hidden in the various forms of human culture, the nature of man himself is more clearly revealed and new roads to truth are open. These benefits profit the Church, too. For, from the beginning of her history, she has learned to express the message of Christ with the help of ideas and terminology of various peoples, and has tried to clarify it with the wisdom of philosophers, too. Her purpose has been to adapt the Gospel to the grasp of all as well as to the needs of the learned, insofar as such was appropriate. Indeed, this accommodated preaching of the revealed Word ought to remain the law of all evangelization."

41. With regard to the just limits of theological pluralism, cf. the "proposizioni" of the Pontifical International Theological Commission on "The Unity of Faith and Theological Pluralism" in *La Civilta Cattolica,* 124, 1973, vol. II. 367-369.

Paul VI, Allocution. *We have come,* to the Bishops of Oceania, 1 Dec. 1970, *AAS* 63 (1971) 56; Allocution, *Noi non usciremo,* at the general audience of 28 Aug. 1974; *Insegnamenti di Paolo VI,* XII. 764 ff., Città del Vaticano, 1975.

42. *Decree on the Training of Priests,* n. 14.

43. Ibid.; cf. *The Basic Plan for Priestly Formation,* n. 62.

44. Cf. *The Basic Plan for Priestly Formation,* nn. 77 ff., 80, 81, 90; cf. nn. 60-61.

45. *The Basic Plan for Priestly Formation,* n. 91a.

46. *The Basic Plan for Priestly Formation,* nn. 78-80, 82-84.

47. *The Basic Plan for Priestly Formation,* n. 90.

48. Ibid.

49. Inaugural allocution, *Gaudet Mater Ecclesia,* 11 Oct. 1962: AAS 54 (1962) 792.

50. Cf. *Dogmatic Constitution on Divine Revelation,* n. 24; *The Constitution on the Sacred Liturgy,* n. 16; *Decree on the Training of Priests,* nn. 14, 16; *Decree on the Church's Missionary Activity,* n. 16.

51. *The Basic Plan for Priestly Formation,* nn. 36, 37.

52. *The Basic Plan for Priestly Formation,* n. 71.

53. Paul VI, Allocution, *Nous sommes heureux,* to the International Theological Commission, 11 Oct. 1972: AAS 64 (1972) 683.

54. Cf. *Pastoral Constitution on the Church in the Modern World,* nn. 44, 62.

55. Allocution, *Siamo assai grati,* to the College of Cardinals, 22 June 1973: AAS 65 (1973) 384.

56. *Dogmatic Constitution on Divine Revelation,* n. 24.

57. Cf. Pontifical Biblical Commission, Instruction, *Sancta Mater,* on the historical truth of the Gospels, 21 Apr. 1964: AAS 56 (1964) 713 ff.

58. Cf. *Dogmatic Constitution on Divine Revelation,* n. 12.

59. Cf. Pontifical Biblical Commission, Instruction, *Sancta Mater,* on the historical truth of the Gospels, 21 Apr. 1964, n. 4: AAS 56 (1964) 717-718.

60. Cf. *The Basic Plan for Priestly Formation,* n. 78.

61. Cf. *The Constitution on the Sacred Liturgy,* n. 24.

62. Cf. *Decree on the Training of Priests,* n. 16; and also Sacred Congregation for Catholic Education, Circular, *Synodi Episcopalis,* 22 May 1968, in which, for an adequate theological formation of priests, there is sought, amongst other things, "a united structure of teaching; a very precise idea of what theological work is and of its sources; *a solid historical formation.*"

63. *Decree on the Training of Priests,* n. 16.

64. *Decree on Ecumenism,* n. 11.

65. *Decree on the Training of Priests,* n. 16.

66. Paul VI, Encyclical, *Ecclesiam suam,* 4 Aug. 1964: AAS 56 (1964) 640-641.

67 Cf. Sacred Congregation for the Doctrine of the Faith, Declaration, *Persona humana,* n. 9, 29 Dec. 1975: *L'Osservatore Romano,* 16 Jan. 1976, 1.

68. *Pastoral Constitution on the Church in the Modern World,* n. 46.

69. Cf. *The Basic Plan for Priestly Formation,* n. 94.

70. Cf. *The Basic Plan for Priestly Formation,* n. 79.

71. Cf. *The Basic Plan for Priestly Formation,* n. 84b; *Normae quaedam ad Constitutionem Apostolicam "Deus scientiarum Dominus" de studiis academicis ecclesiasticis recognoscendam,* n. 33.

72. Cf. *The Basic Plan for Priestly Formation,* n. 79.

73. Cf. the documents published: The Secretariat for Promoting Christian Unity, *Directorium,* Pars altera (see above all n. 75: *De oecumenismo ut peculiari disciplina);* Sacred Congregation for the Evangelization of the Peoples, *Circular letter on the missionary dimension of priestly formation,* Pentecost 1970; Secretariat for Non-Believers, the note on the study of atheism, 10 July 1970; Sacred Congregation for Catholic Education. *Circular letter on the teaching of the philosophy in Seminaries,* 20 Jan. 1972; *Circular letter on the study of Canon Law,* 1 Mar. 1975. The same Sacred Congregation for Catholic Education, in these recent years, has been published in the review "Seminarium" series of articles giving an orientation toward the promotion of the conciliar renewal of the various disciplines in the philosophico-theological curriculum.

74. Cf. *The Basic Plan for Priestly Formation,* nn. 32-38.

75. Cf. *The Basic Plan for Priestly Formation*, n. 87.

76. *Decree on Ecumenism*, n. 17.

77. Cf. *The Basic Plan for Priestly Formation*, n. 88.

78. Cf. *The Basic Plan for Priestly Formation*, n. 90.

79. Cf. *The Basic Plan for Priestly Formation*, n. 88.

80. Cf. *The Basic Plan for Priestly Formation*, n. 94.

81. Cf. *Decree on the Training of Priests*, n. 17; *The Basic Plan for Priestly Formation*, nn. 35, 91.

82. *Decree on the Training of Priests*, n. 13; *The Basic Plan for Priestly Formation*, nn. 65 ff.; cf. ibid., nn. 59, 60.

83. Cf. *The Basic Plan for Priestly Formation*, nn. 60, 61, 70, 75; and also Sacred Congregation for Catholic Education, *Circular letter on the teaching of philosophy in Seminaries*, 20 Jan. 1972, Part III, nn. 1, 2.

84. *Decree on the Training of Priests*, n. 13; *The Basic Plan for Priestly Formation*, n. 66.

85. *Decree on the Training of Priests*, n. 13; *The Basic Plan for Priestly Formation*, n. 80.

86. Cf. *The Basic Plan for Priestly Formation*, nn. 35, 38, 91.

87. Cf. *The Basic Plan for Priestly Formation*, n. 61.

88. Cf. *The Basic Plan for Priestly Formation*, n. 2.

The Study of Philosophy in Seminaries

Sacred Congregation for
Catholic Education

1972

The Study of
Philosophy in Seminaries

Rome, January 20, 1972

Prot. N. 137/65

**To the Ordinaries of the World on the
Study of Philosophy in Seminaries**

Your Excellency,

In the present period of various kinds of change in the life of
seminaries, this Sacred Congregation would like to call to Your Excellency's attention a matter which, in our opinion, is of great importance.

As is well known, among the various problems connected with the
conciliar renewal of seminaries, a particular place is held by the philosophical formation of future priests. The Second Vatican Council, with
the intention of creating a solid base for the study of theology, and of
setting down the necessary premises for a fruitful encounter between the
Church and the world, faith and science, and the spiritual patrimony of
Christianity with modern culture, thought it opportune to insist, among
other things, on a profound reform in the teaching of philosophy, offering
for this purpose certain fundamental directives (See the Decree *Optatam
totius [Decree on the Training of Priests]*, n. 15; the Pastoral Constitution
*Gaudium et spes [Pastoral Constitution on the Church in the Modern
World]*, n. 62 passim; and the Decree *Ad gentes [Decree on the Church's
Missionary Activity]*, n. 16).

A vast and demanding program is supposed which, in present circumstances, while assuming a certain urgency on the one hand, is encountering not a few difficulties on the other. As a matter of fact, the Sacred
Congregation for Catholic Education, which has been following matters
in this area with special interest, has been able to note on various occasions not only praiseworthy efforts and progress, but also, unfortunately,
signs of disquiet which are sometimes causing discouragement and lack
of confidence.

Today, at a distance of six years from the Council, it is necessary to take
stock of the situation and draw concrete and precise conclusions for the
future. In fact, the difficulties which the efforts for philosophical renewal
today encounter are undeniable and as such demand a careful examina-

tion together with an attentive study of the proper remedies to overcome them.

I. Current Difficulties in Philosophical Studies

The present reform of philosophical studies in seminaries should be seen in the framework of the spiritual climate of the times, which confronts philosophy with both a favorable and a hostile attitude. While on the one hand our times, with their many social changes and ideological movements, are richly suitable for a serious rethinking of philosophy, on the other a tendency can be seen toward undervaluing philosophy even to the point of declaring, in some extreme cases, that it is useless or to be avoided. There can be no doubt that modern culture, shutting itself off always more and more to the problem of transcendence, is becoming adverse to authentic philosophical thought, particularly to metaphysical speculation which alone is able to reach absolute values.

In this regard, first of all, one must mention the modern spirit of technology which tends to reduce *homo sapiens* to *homo faber*. Technology, while bringing to mankind numerous and undeniable advantages, is not always favorable toward giving man a sense of spiritual values. As is commonly seen today, the mind of man seems predominantly turned toward the material world, toward the concrete, toward the domination of nature by means of scientific and technical progress, reducing knowledge to the level of the methods of the positive sciences. The unilateral accent placed on action looking to the future and optimism nourished by an almost unlimited confidence in progress, while aimed at immediate and fundamental changes in the economic, social, and political fields, has a tendency to overlook the permanent character of certain moral and spiritual values and, above all, to consider as superfluous, or even harmful, authentic philosophical speculation, which rather should be thought of as the indispensable foundation for such changes. In such a climate, serious research in the highest truths is often unappreciated, and the criteria of truth are no longer the sound and indisputable principles of metaphysics, but rather the "present time" and "success." Therefore, it is easy to understand how the spirit of our times shows itself to be ever more anti-metaphysical and consequently open to every kind of relativism.

It is no wonder that in this context many no longer can find a place for a philosophy which is distinct from the positive sciences. Today, as a matter of fact, while there can be noted by almost everyone a clear diminishing of interest in the classical philosophical disciplines, the importance of the natural sciences and anthropology is being rapidly increased. With these an attempt is made to give an exhaustive explanation of reality to the point of completely eliminating philosophy as something archaic and destined to be bypassed. In this way instead of the looked-for encounter which could contribute to the true benefit and progress of both science and philosophy, there is present rather an antagonism with negative consequences for both.

While many scientists are opposed to a philosophy distinct from the positive sciences, even to the point of disputing its existence, there are certain theologians who consider philosophy useless and harmful for priestly formation. These theologians maintain that the purity of the gospel message was compromised in the course of history by the introduction of Greek speculation into the sacred sciences. They think that scholastic philosophy has weighed down speculative theology with a quantity of false problems and they are of the opinion that the theological disciplines must be undertaken exclusively with historical method.

Other difficulties are born from the very field of philosophy itself. In fact, even where philosophy is not opposed, philosophical pluralism makes ever greater advances, due no doubt not only to encountering various cultures of the world and the diversity and complexity of philosophical currents, but also to the almost inexhaustible sources of human experience. This process is growing, notwithstanding the admirable efforts which various modern philosophers are making to give more coherence to their systems and more balance to their positions. The immensity and depth of the questions arising from various new philosophies and from scientific progress is such as to render extremely difficult not only a synthesis, but also an assimilation of these new notions, so necessary for teaching philosophy in a way that is living and efficacious.

It is natural that this situation should have serious repercussions on the study of philosophy in seminaries, and should be reflected both in the professors and in the students. It is commonly noticed how grave and many are the exigencies that impose themselves today on a professor of philosophy: the need to assimilate a great quantity of new ideas deriving from a variety of philosophical mentalities and from the progress of science; problems that are often totally new; the need for a new adaptation of language, teaching method, etc. And, all this has to be addressed often in a relatively restricted period of time, with little means, and with a student body not always adequately interested or prepared.

Not a few difficulties come from the students. Although they frequently show interest in certain problems touching men and society, they are not given any encouragement by the modern cultural climate to study philosophy, being in general much more attuned to images than to reflection. And, above all, their previous training is often of a mainly technical nature and directed to practical matters. There are other circumstances of a more special nature which render the study of philosophy less attractive to students today: the perplexity which many display in front of the multiplicity of contradictory philosophical currents; the over-involved (in their opinion) search for truth, which cannot possibly be unbiased; the aversion to fixed systems, especially if recommended by authority; the deficiencies of a poorly updated teaching, presenting outmoded problems, distant from real life; a certain archaic philosophical way of speaking, little intelligible to modern man; an excessive abstraction which impedes the students' clear view of the connection between philosophy and theology and, most of all, between philosophy and pastoral activity for which they desire most seriously to prepare themselves.

From these things there can be seen in various seminaries a certain sense of discomfort, of uneasiness, and of dissatisfaction regarding philosophy and doubts about the value and practical utility of philosophical studies. From these things also we can see the phenomenon of the partial or complete abandonment of the authentic teaching of philosophy in favor of the sciences, which seem to be more real and directed to the concrete needs of life.

As can be seen, the main difficulties which place the study of philosophy in seminaries into question today seem capable of being reduced to the three following points:

1. Philosophy does not any longer have a proper object. It has been in fact absorbed and substituted for by the positive sciences, natural and humane, which are concerned with true and real problems and which are studied with the help of those methods which are recognized today as uniquely valid. This is the attitude inspired by the currents of positivism, neo-positivism, and structuralism.

2. Philosophy has lost its importance for religion and for theology: theological studies must detach themselves from philosophical speculation as from a useless word-game and must build up in full autonomy on a positive base, furnished by historical criteria and by special methods of exegesis. Theology of the future will, therefore, be the special competence of historians and philologists.

3. Contemporary philosophy has become today an esoteric science, inaccessible to the greater part of the candidates for the priesthood: the modern schools of philosophy (phenomenology, existentialism, structuralism, neo-positivism, etc.) carry on their labors at such a level of technicality of vocabulary, analysis, and demonstrations as to have become a highly specialized field for select students. Therefore neither the suitability nor the possibility of inserting such a difficult and complex study into the ordinary formation of candidates for the priesthood is seen.

It is understandable that these obstacles would seem to many insuperable and as such should cause in certain areas a very real sense of discouragement.

II. The Necessity of
Philosophy for Future Priests

1. Although understanding all that has been mentioned above, we are nevertheless convinced that all the tendencies to abandon philosophy or to diminish its importance can be overcome and, therefore, ought not to be a cause for discouragement. Even though the obstacles which today militate against the teaching of philosophy are many and difficult, it is hard to see how philosophy can be under-valued or simply suppressed in a process of formation toward a true and authentic humanism, and especially in view of the mission of the priesthood. Indeed, a desire to give in to such tendencies would mean ignorance of all that is most genuine and deep in modern thought. There can be no doubt that the most fundamental problems of philosophy are found today more than ever at the center of the anxieties of contemporary men, even to the extent of having invaded the entire field of modern culture: literature (novels, essays, poetry, etc.), the theatre, the cinema, radio and television, and even song. Here are constantly evoked the eternal themes of human thought: the meaning of life and death; the meaning of good and evil; the basis of true values; the dignity and rights of the human person; the confrontation between culture and a spiritual heritage; the scandal of suffering, injustice, oppression, and violence; the nature and the law of love; the order and disorder in nature; the problems of education, authority and freedom; the meaning of history and progress; the mystery of the transcendent; and, finally, at the depth of all these problems, God, His existence, His personal characteristics, and His providence.

2. It is evident that none of these problems can find an adequate solution on the level of the positive sciences, natural or humane, because the specific methods of these sciences do not provide any possibility of confronting them in a satisfactory way. Such questions as these pertain to the specific sphere of philosophy, which, transcending all merely exterior and partial aspects of phenomena, addresses itself to the whole of reality, seeking to comprehend and to explain it in the light of ultimate causes.

Thus philosophy, while needing the support of the empirical sciences, is nevertheless in itself a science that is distinct from the others, autonomous, and of the highest importance for man, who is interested not only in recording, describing, and ordering various phenomena, but above all in understanding their true value and ultimate meaning. It is clear that any other type of knowledge of reality does not bring things to this supreme level of knowledge which is the characteristic prerogative of the human spirit. As long as there is not an answer to these fundamental questions, all culture remains inferior to the speculative capacity of our intellects. If it can be said that philosophy, therefore, has an irreplaceable cultural value, it constitutes the soul of authentic culture, inasmuch as it puts the questions about the meaning of things and about the existence of man in a way that is truly adequate to the deepest human aspirations.

3. Also in many instances, an exclusive recourse to the light of revelation is not even possible. Such an attitude would be fundamentally insufficient for the following reasons:

a) A complete adherence by man to divine revelation cannot be conceived as an act of blind faith, a fideism lacking rational motivation. The act of faith presupposes of its nature "the reasons for believing," the "motives of credibility," which are in great measure philosophical: the knowledge of God; the concept of creation; providence; discernment of the true revealed religion; knowledge of man himself as a free and responsible person. It could be said that every word of the New Testament formally presupposes these fundamental philosophical ideas. Therefore, a priest needs philosophy to secure for his own personal faith the rational basis of scientific worth which will match his intellectual attainments.

b) The problem of *fides quaerens intellectum* has not lost any of its reality. Revealed truth always requires reflection on the part of the believer. It invites a work of analysis, of deeper study, and of synthesis, which work is called speculative theology.

Evidently here must be no repetition of the error of past centuries when theological speculation was often carried on in an exaggerated and unilateral way without sufficient regard for biblical and patristic studies. In this regard, it is necessary to restore the primacy of study to the sources of revelation as well as to the transmission of the gospel message through the centuries, a primacy that is beyond discussion and that can never be diminished in importance. It is proper to condemn any unjustified intrusion of philosophy into an area that is essentially that of revealed knowledge. But today, with a correct equilibrium established and enormous progress accomplished in the biblical sciences and in all the sectors of positive theology, it is both possible and necessary to complete and perfect this historical labor with a labor of rational reflection on the data of revelation. Thus there can be set forth richer and more certain data which in time the speculative theologian must confront with a critical understanding of the concepts and mental categories in which revelation is expressed. In this delicate work, the speculative theologian must not only use the treasures resulting from the discoveries of the natural and especially the humane sciences (psychology, anthropology, sociology, linguistics, pedagogy, etc.), but he must also have recourse in a special way to the help of a sound philosophy so that it can make its contribution to the reflection on the presuppositions and on the conclusions of the knowledge furnished by the positive disciplines. From the fact that the methods themselves of positive science (exegesis, history, etc.) start their work from various given preliminaries, which implicitly are results of a philosophical choice, a sound philosophy can notably contribute, among other things, to a critical evaluation and a clarification of such a choice (today this is especially necessary, for instance, regarding the exegetical method of Rudolf Bultmann), without, however, assuming an absolute critical function in the face of divine revelation.

This reciprocal influence of the two sciences, deeply rooted already in their very natures, has become accentuated in recent times by new situations created in the field of theology; theology, seeking to open up new dimensions (historical, anthropological, existential, personalistic) and to develop new aspects (psychological, socio-political, correct practice, etc.) as well as to deepen its methods (the hermeneutic problem), is facing a new type of problem which sometimes touches the very presuppositions of theological knowledge (as, for instance, the possibility of dogmatic definitions of permanent value) and which, therefore, requires a new clarification and deepening of certain concepts, as, for instance, the truth, the capacity and limits of human understanding; progress, evolution, human nature and the human person; the natural law, the imputability of moral actions, etc.

c) Philosophy is also irreplaceable for the encounter and dialogue between believers and unbelievers. In this regard, philosophy has a very evident pastoral value. It is, therefore, inadmissible that a Catholic priest, called to exercise his ministry in the midst of a pluralistic society where fundamental philosophical problems are being debated through all the means of social communication and on every cultural level, should be unable to engage in an intelligent exchange of views with non-Christians on the fundamental questions which are close to his own personal faith and which are the problems most agitating the world.

d) Finally, it must be pointed out that all pastoral direction, pedagogical choices, juridic norms, social reforms, and many political decisions carry within themselves philosophical presuppositions and consequences which need to be clearly and critically evaluated. There can be no doubt that authentic philosophy can notably contribute to humanizing the world and its culture, supplying a proper hierarchy of values so necessary for any fruitful action.

III. Some Indications for the Teaching of Philosophy

We have tried to make clear why a solid formation in philosophy is today more necessary than ever for future priests. At the same time we have tried to answer some objections brought against philosophy by positive scientists and by some theological circles. It now remains to answer those difficulties which come from the actual situation of philosophy itself, that is, philosophical pluralism, the highly technical level of the vocabulary, etc.

These difficulties are real but they must not be exaggerated. In every case it is a good thing to wish to obtain the highest possible level; but on the other hand, we must be realistic and avoid the fault of "perfectionism." In the difficulties of the present time, each seminary must come to realize what is possible, taking into account the concrete situation and the local resources, without attempting a completely perfect ideal.

1. The first efforts must be directed to the concrete organization of studies in accordance with the following objectives:

a) Provide for a solid professional preparation for the teachers. Given the increased demands of philosophy, it is absolutely necessary that the professors be given a serious and specific preparation, acquired in centers of study which give assurances of being proper from the doctrinal point of view and as institutions of authentic philosophical research.

b) Promote by every means the permanent updating of the professors by courses of study and meeting for the exchange of ideas and for the exchange of teaching experiences. To assist in the accomplishment of their work a contribution could be made by suitable economic remuneration and a correct distribution of the teaching load, giving to each one a chance for serious and systematic personal study.

c) To face up to the difficulties of the students, improve the methods of teaching as set forth in the Decree *Optatam totius,* n. 17 and in the *Ratio Fundamentalis [The Basic Plan . . .],* chap. XV, but always preserving intact the time assigned to the study of philosophy, that is, the two years set out in n. 61c of the *Ratio Fundamentalis.*

For a more secure orientation for the students it would be well to promote, within the autonomy of the single disciplines, a dialogue between the teachers of philosophy and those of theology to create a certain coherence between the two, according to the requirement for an efficacious interdisciplinary collaboration of the *Ratio Fundamentalis,* n. 61b; chap. XI, note 148a.

d) Improve the library of the seminary, making sure that it has enough good publications useful for the research of both the professors and the students.

e) Promote a close collaboration between the seminary and other theological institutes, working toward an exchange of teachers.

Evidently the local authorities must judge the suitability of the adoption of these and other appropriate remedies according to concrete necessity. In every case, however, in all the desirable efforts of renewal, one must never forget the fundamental importance of Higher Schools of Philosophy (Philosophical Faculties) and for the other Centers specializing in philosophical studies. To these pertain the delicate and grave duty either of preparing future teachers or of sustaining this formative activity by periodic courses of renewal. To them also belongs the duty to diffuse scientific data and, most important, to publish suitable textbooks answering the needs of our times. It must be, therefore, one of the main concerns of the competent authorities to see to the organization and the functioning of such institutions.

2. In the same measure with which there is established a sound organization of studies, there must also be provided a solution to the more important and delicate problems of the content of the teaching and of the program of studies. These problems must be faced bearing in mind the purpose of these studies in the framework of priestly formation.

Although the Second Vatican Council drew out with clarity certain fundamental lines for the proper renewal of philosophical teaching, today six years after the Council, we have unfortunately to admit that not all seminaries are following these lines wished by the Church. Various causes, often complex and difficult to define, have brought about a situation in which the teaching of philosophy, instead of going ahead, has lost much of its vigor, presenting uncertainty with regard to its content and with regard to its purpose. In view of this situation, it is necessary to set down the following:

Philosophical formation in seminaries may not be limited to teaching the students to *philosophize*. Certainly it is important that the young seminarians learn to *philosophize,* that is, to search with sincere and continuous love for the truth, developing and improving their critical sense, recognizing the limits of human knowledge and deepening the rational presuppositions of their proper faith. But this is not enough. It is necessary that the teaching of philosophy present the valid principles and materials which the students can attentively consider, seek to weigh, and gradually assimilate.

Nor may the teaching of philosophy be reduced to an inquiry which limits itself to gathering and describing with the help of humane sciences the data of experience. It is necessary that it go on to a truly philosophical reflection in the light of secure metaphysical principles in a way as to come to affirmations that are of an objective and absolute value.

To this end, the history of philosophy is certainly useful, since it presents the main solutions that the great thinkers of humanity sought to give through the centuries to the problems of the world and of life. Also useful is the study of contemporary philosophy and the study of works selected from literature to better comprehend the problems of today. But, the teaching of philosophy may not be reduced to the presentation of what others have said. It is rather necessary to help the young student to directly face reality, to seek to confront and examine the various solutions to its problems and to form proper convictions and to arrive at a coherent vision of reality.

It is clear, furthermore, that this coherent vision of reality to which philosophical studies must bring seminarians, cannot be in contrast with Christian revelation. Certainly there is no difficulty in admitting a healthy philosophical pluralism, due to the diversity of regions, cultures, and mentalities through which different ways to the same truth can be pursued. This truth, of course, can be presented and explained in various ways. However, it is not possible to admit a philosophical pluralism which compromises the fundamental nucleus of affirmations connected with revelation, since a contradiction is not possible between the naturally knowable truths of philosophy and the supernatural truths of faith. With this in view, one can then affirm in general that the very nature of the Judeo-Christian revelation is absolutely incompatible with all relativism, epistemological, moral or metaphysical, with all materialism, pantheism, immanentism, subjectivism, and atheism.

Furthermore the above-mentioned fundamental nucleus of truths contains in a special way the certitude:

a) that human knowledge is capable of gathering from contingent reality objective and necessary truths, and thus of arriving at a critical realism, a point of departure for ontology;

b) that it is possible to construct a realistic ontology which brings to light transcendental values and ends with the affirmation of a personal Absolute and Creator of the Universe;

c) that there is likewise possible an anthropology which safeguards the authentic spirituality of man, leading to a theocentric ethic, transcending earthly life, and at the same time open to the social dimension of man.

This fundamental nucleus of truths which excludes every historical relativism and every idealistic or materialistic immanentism, corresponds to that solid and coherent knowledge of man, of the world, and of God of which the Second Vatican Council spoke (Decree *Optatam totius,* n. 15). The Council wished that the teaching of philosophy in seminaries should be based upon the riches of past thought which have been handed down (*innixi patrimonio philosophico perenniter valido,* ibid.) but should also be open to accepting the riches which modern thought continually brings forth (*ratione habita quoque philosophicarum investigationum progredientis aetatis,* ibid.).

In this sense the repeated recommendations of the Church about the philosophy of Saint Thomas Aquinas remain fully justified and still valid. In this philosophy the first principles of natural truth are clearly and organically enunciated and harmonized with revelation. Within it also is enclosed that creative dynamism which, as the biographers attest, marked the teaching of Saint Thomas and which must also characterize the teaching of those who desire to follow his footsteps in a continual and renewed synthesizing of the valid conclusions received from tradition with new conquests of human thought.

All of this must be done taking into particular account the type of problem and characteristics proper to the various cultures and regions, making it possible for the students to have an adequate grasp of the major philosophical ideas of their own time and own environment so that their studying of philosophy will be a real preparation for the life and ministry which awaits them, and so that they will be in position to dialogue with the men of their own time (Decree *Optatam totius,* ibid.), not only the believers, but also with those who have no faith.

Your Excellency, in calling to your attention the problems in the philosophical formation of future priests, we wish to offer you something to consider and above all some help toward a suitable renewal in this area which the present circumstances show to be so important. Fully conscious of the limits of this letter, restricted only to essentials — given its purpose — we hope nevertheless that it, together with the clear texts of the Second Vatican Council and of the *Ratio Fundamentalis Institutionis Sacerdotalis [The Basic Plan for Priestly Formation],* can furnish at least some useful indications and guidelines to teachers in their work.

Assuring you and all who are dedicating themselves to the formation of your seminarians of our greetings and cordial good wishes, we remain with every sentiment of high esteem,

Fraternally yours in Jesus Christ

Gabriel-Marie Cardinal Garrone

Joseph Schröffer
Secretary

Instruction on Liturgical Formation in Seminaries

Sacred Congregation for
Catholic Education
1979

Instruction on
Liturgical Formation in
Seminaries

In the ecclesiastical formation of future priests, a formation renewed following the prescriptions of the Second Vatican Council, the Sacred Congregation for Catholic Education has been working for many years to provide suitable helps to the Bishops' Conferences. To the various documents and pedagogical assistance already produced with this end in view, this *Instruction on Liturgical Formation in Seminaries* is now added. Its purpose is to offer suitable directives and norms so that the liturgical life and the study of the sacred liturgy in institutions of priestly formation might be better adapted to modern needs. The great importance which the sacred liturgy occupies in the life of the Church demands that the contemporary candidate for the priesthood be given a proper formation both in the area of correct practice and in assiduous study, so that he will be most able to carry out his pastoral ministry in this field.

Introduction

A) The Importance of
the Liturgy in Priestly Formation

1. The importance of the sacred liturgy in priestly formation is clear to all. Priests indeed are consecrated to God by the bishop not only to preach the Gospel and to pasture the faithful, but also so that, constituted in a special way as participants in the priesthood of Christ, they might preside over liturgical actions in the person of Christ the Head, who continually exercises in the liturgy His priestly office for us through the Holy Spirit.[1] Since the liturgy, in which "the work of our Redemption is carried on," is the outstanding means "by which the faithful express in their lives and manifest to others the mystery of Christ and the real nature of the true Church,"[2] its diligent exercise and study will bestow on future priests a more solid knowledge and firmness in their faith as well as opening up for them a living experience of the Church.

2. All genuine liturgical formation involves not only doctrine but also practice. This practice, as a "mystagogical" formation, is obtained first and mainly through the very liturgical life of the students into which they are daily more deeply initiated through liturgical actions celebrated in common. This careful and practical initiation is the foundation of all further liturgical study and it is presupposed that this has already been acquired when liturgical questions are explained.

B) The Opportuneness of This Document in Present Circumstances

3. Formation in the sacred liturgy is especially urgent today. After the publication of new liturgical books according to the liturgical renewal decreed by the Second Vatican Council, there is a need to promote the correct instruction of future priests so they might thus be rendered more apt to understand clearly the character and force of the renewed sacred liturgy, to insert it into their spiritual lives and into their daily conduct, and to communicate it suitably to the faithful.[3]

4. Furthermore, greater emphasis on liturgical formation in seminaries is needed also in order to confront the new pedagogical problematic which comes from the growing secularization of society. This clouds the nature of the sacred liturgy in the minds of people, making it more difficult for them to live and participate in it more deeply. The students themselves notice this difficulty and thus they often express a desire for a deeper and more authentic liturgical life.

5. The compelling need for an updated initiation in the liturgy was already clearly expressed in the Second Vatican Council, both in the Constitution *"Sacrosanctum Concilium"* [*The Constitution on the Sacred Liturgy*][4] and in the Decree *"Optatam totius"* [*Decree on the Training of Priests*],[5] as well as in the document of this Sacred Congregation entitled *"Ratio fundamentalis institutionis sacerdotalis"* [*The Basic Plan for Priestly Formation*].[6] The norms of this latter document, taken from other documents of the Church, supply useful directives for the Bishops' Conferences in their task of determining particular prescriptions in this material, according to their local needs, in their own national or regional *"Rationes institutionis sacerdotalis."*[7]

From various parts of the world, requests have been coming to the Sacred Congregation to issue more complete pedagogical norms, based upon recent experience, which would concern both the correct regulation of liturgical life in seminaries and the teaching of the sacred liturgy.

C) The Nature of This Instruction

6. Moved by these reasons, this Sacred Congregation, after consultation with the Sacred Congregation for the Sacraments and Divine Worship, has decreed the publication of this Instruction. It is complementary to the *"Ratio fundamentalis"* and it enjoys the same obligatory force.[8] It sets out only matters of universal import,[9] leaving to the Bishops' Conferences the duty to direct a further development of this matter or to choose the more suitable way of acting, when a variety of options is presented.[10]

Also, the Congregation wishes that this present Instruction be effective, in the editing and updating of the *"Rationes institutionis sacerdotalis,"* by more clearly illustrating the material pertaining to the study of the sacred liturgy as well as in the liturgical order and life of the seminaries.

7. This Instruction, in the norms it prescribes, considers two aspects of liturgical formation: the practical (mystagogical), which pertains to the correct and orderly celebration of the sacred liturgy, and the theoretical (doctrinal), which places in clearer light the science of the liturgy, as one of the principal theological disciplines to be taught.

Part One
The Liturgical Life of Seminaries

1) General Principles for Promoting the Liturgical Life of Seminaries

a) Special introduction into the liturgical life in a previous spiritual apprenticeship

8. "So that spiritual training can rest upon a firmer basis and students can embrace their vocation with a decision maturely weighed," [11] it belongs to bishops to establish at the beginning of the first year of seminary life an appropriate period of time for a more intense spiritual apprenticeship. For this period of time, it is recommended that those students entering a seminary for the first time be given a suitable, short introduction into the liturgy, which they need to participate fruitfully in the spiritual life of the seminary from the very beginning. This would include some catechetical instruction about the Mass, the liturgical year, the Sacrament of Penance, and the Liturgy of the Hours.

b) Pedagogical principles regarding the introduction into the liturgical life

9. An authentic initiation or "mystagogia" should mainly illustrate those fundamentals on which the liturgical life is established, that is to say, the history of salvation, the paschal mystery of Christ, the genuine nature of the Church, the presence of Christ in liturgical actions, the hearing of the Word of God, the spirit of prayer, adoration, and thanksgiving, and the expectation of the coming of the Lord. [12]

10. § 1: Liturgical celebration, as the prayer of the Church, participates in her very nature. As such, it impels towards a simultaneous union of the voices of all and the heart and soul of each person, belonging therefore, fully to the community and to the individual. Indeed, "spiritual life is not confined to participation in the liturgy." [13] For liturgical and personal piety mutually support and complement each other. Familiar communion in prayer with Christ leads to fuller, knowledgeable, and pious participation in the sacred liturgy. On the other hand, private devotion receives example and nourishment from liturgical life.

It follows that in a seminary both the liturgy and private spiritual exercises are to be fostered and suitably joined together. [14] According to local needs, insistence should be made upon the community and its proper spirituality if this is not adequately understood or else upon personal acts of piety [15] if these are held in less esteem.

§ 2: Devotional exercises recommended by the Church should be so arranged that they are compatible with liturgical seasons and so with the sacred liturgy. Thus, in a certain way, they derive from the liturgy at the same time that they lead the students to the liturgy. [16]

§ 3: From a deeper participation in the liturgical life, the students should learn to foster an interior life and acquire a deep spirit of meditation and of spiritual conversion. Furthermore, liturgical instruction should point out to the students the close connection between the sacred liturgy and the daily life of a priest and lay people. This stimulates the apostolate and requires a true witness of a living faith that works through charity.[17]

11. That understanding of the liturgy which is considered necessary for a priest and which seminarians must acquire demands a diligent familiarity with the Bible, as the conciliar Constitution *"Sacrosanctum Concilium"* [18] recommends, and also some familiarity with the writings of the Fathers of the Church.[19] This disposition of spirit will gradually be acquired by the students as they progress in their studies, in the spiritual life, and in participation in liturgical celebrations, especially in the Liturgy of the Hours and in celebrations of God's Word.[20] Care should be taken to effect this through the above efforts and also to ensure special study so that the seminarists will be introduced into understanding that symbolical, liturgical language by which, through sensible signs, words, and gestures, divine things are signified and, in the case of the sacraments, actually caused.

c) The seminary community gathered for liturgical celebration

12. Liturgical celebration, while making any Christian community so solidly firm that its members become "one in heart and soul" (Acts 4.32), much more ought to unify the community of the seminary and develop a community spirit among the students. The students are to be formed in the seminary in order that, through sacramental ordination, they will participate in the one priesthood, they will acquire a common priestly spirit, they will become cooperators with their bishop and will be closely united to him, and they will exercise a ministry of building up the Church. Thus, the liturgical celebration in a seminary is to be done in such a way that its community and supernatural nature will shine out and thus it will truly be a source and bond of community life which is proper to a seminary and is particularly apt to prepare the students for the unity of the presbyterate.[21]

The Rector and the teachers should take care to celebrate the liturgy together with their students, so that the community nature of the liturgy and its riches will be made more clear. Also the teachers who do not reside in the seminary sometimes should be given the opportunity to join with the priests and students of the seminary and to participate in the sacred actions.

The students ought not only to actively participate in the liturgy but also should be invited to collaborate with the teachers in preparing it.

13. So that the students might experience the mystery of the Church as hierarchical, namely as consisting of a variety of members and distinct ministries, it should be suitably arranged that in the seminary there be deacons, acolytes, and lectors, who must be imbued with the spirituality of their respective offices, and who should exercise their ministries in liturgical actions.[22] Thus the proper office of the ministerial priesthood will be clear to all the students, as well as the offices of deacon, lector, and acolyte.

In each seminary there should be a *"schola cantorum,"* according to the norm of the Instruction *"Musicam sacram,"* n. 19.

14. Although it would be better for the whole community as a general rule to participate in the liturgy, sometimes it will be opportune to celebrate some liturgical actions in small groups. This could be for those students who recently entered the seminary and are in need of liturgical catechesis, as mentioned in n. 8 above, or, in regional seminaries, for the students from the same diocese, or for some other sufficient reason. Caution should be exercised, however, to ensure that such groups do not infringe upon the unity of the whole community and that the prescriptions of the Holy See are observed.[23]

15. Therefore, it should be carefully provided that the authentic, ecclesial nature of a liturgical assembly is clearly pointed out. The community of the seminary, as a part of the Church, is distinct and very different from other communities and groups. Thus, it must be an expression of the Church herself and it must be open to the whole ecclesial community. Sometimes the seminary community should participate in parish liturgical celebrations, principally on special occasions and, above all, on those notable occasions when the seminarians are gathered around the bishop.

While the liturgical life of the diocese centered around the bishop is recommended to all the faithful,[24] this is more necessary for those who are to be the future collaborators of the bishop. Therefore, in the major solemnities and especially in the paschal triduum and other circumstances dictated by diocesan tradition, the seminarians, mainly the deacons, ought to be with their bishop and ought to carry out around him those ministries which are theirs by ordination or installation, either in the cathedral or in another church where the bishop celebrates the liturgy. There could be some difficulty in this practice for those seminaries where the students come from various dioceses. Sometimes opportunities should be provided for them to participate in the life of their own diocese and to be with their own bishop for the sacred liturgy. But, they should also learn to serve the local church where they are and the local bishop according to tradition.

d) The celebration itself

16. The students should remember that liturgical actions are not private but are celebrations of the Church. They belong to the whole body of the Church and show forth and affect that body. That is why these actions are governed by the laws of the Church.[25] Therefore, the celebration of the liturgy in seminaries must be exemplary with regard not only to the ritual, but also to the spiritual and pastoral mentality adopted,[26] the observance of the norms and the liturgical texts, and the laws issued by the Apostolic See and the Bishops' Conferences.

17. So that the students might be introduced with greater spiritual profit into the riches of the liturgy and to prepare them practically for their future ministry, a healthy variety in the way of celebrating and participating in the liturgy should be fostered.[27] This variety concerns the ways of celebrating Mass, the celebrations of the Word, whether penitential or baptismal, and bestowing blessings, whether with greater or lesser solemnity, adapted to various circumstances and exigencies, as these are permitted or recommended in the liturgical books and in the prescriptions of the Apostolic See.

This means the art of making the right choice from among the various possibilities offered in the liturgical books or even of choosing, composing, and using new texts adapted to various occasions (for instance, in the bidding prayers or admonitions). It is the duty of the teachers in the seminary, however, not only to help and lead the students, but also to correct them patiently so that there is formed in them a genuine notion of the liturgy solidly rooted in the doctrine and sense of the Church. Thus the future priests will be educated not only in how to use efficaciously in their pastoral practice the various possibilities offered by the renewed liturgy, but they will also be educated to observe proper limits.

18. The concern for variety mentioned above must never draw attention away from the need to grasp deeply and intimately those elements of the sacred liturgy which belong to its unchangeable part, as this is of divine institution.[28] The structure of the liturgy always remains the same and many gestures and texts of greater importance are often repeated. Therefore, the students are to be helped to penetrate more profoundly these parts of the liturgy and to meditate on them and think about them. They are to learn to draw out and to take from them ever fresh spiritual nourishment.

19. It is most valuable for the students to be familiar with the Latin language and with Gregorian chant. Not only will this provide for the faithful the possibility of singing and praying together in large groups, as the Second Vatican Council prescribes,[29] but it will be especially suitable for future priests, that they might penetrate more deeply into the tradition of the praying Church in order to grasp the genuine sense of the texts and to elucidate the vernacular translations by comparing them with the original texts.

e) Preparing the students for the future office of leader of the liturgy

20. Great care should be exercised in preparing the students to fulfill the office of moderator of the liturgy and president of the liturgical assembly by teaching them all things regarding a correct celebration of the liturgy, most especially holy Mass.[30] However, there is a twofold distortion to be avoided in this: 1) The students should not consider and experience the celebration of the liturgy as mere practice for learning their future pastoral roles. On the contrary, they must participate here and now in the liturgical mysteries taking due account of their present status. Their participation should be full, understanding, and devout. 2) Nor should those liturgical texts be chosen which, it might be presumed, are suitable to be used for the faithful in future pastoral work. Rather it is better that they here and now experience all the riches of ecclesiastical prayer so that, imbued with these, they might afterwards be able to communicate these riches to the faithful.

21. What the students live and learn in the seminary should be put into practice in suitable pastoral activities. The appropriate time for this kind of initiation into liturgical activity and especially that in which the students are instructed in how to carry out different offices in various ways in parochial celebrations would be diverse, apt occasions during the school year. These occasions, however, would be especially offered during vacation periods and also — as a type of a more profound apprenticeship — before the end of their theological studies, when the future priests, generally already ordained deacons, have more possibilities in the ministries of the liturgy. So that this introduction into liturgical work will achieve its ends, however, and contribute to the proper preparation of the students, it is necessary that it be supervised and moderated by the seminary instructors or else by the diocesan liturgical experts.[31]

2) Norms for Individual Liturgical Acts

a) The Mass and the worship of the Holy Eucharist

22. The Eucharistic Sacrifice is to appear to the students as the true source and apex of the whole Christian life through which they share in the love of Christ, drawing from this richest of fonts supernatural strength for their spiritual lives and for their apostolic labor.[32] It will be well to help them grasp this through the homily of the celebrant. Care must be taken to instill into the minds of the seminarists a strong affection for the Mass and for the most Holy Eucharist, which they might not have had before their entry into the seminary. Inculcated into their minds, as future presbyters, must be the idea that celebrating the Eucharistic Sacrifice is the principal office of a priest, an office in which our redemption is continuously exercised. Thus while joined to the action of Christ the Priest, they offer themselves entirely to God each day.[33]

23. It is most fitting that the daily celebration of the Eucharist, completed with the reception of holy communion, always carried out in complete freedom and in a worthy manner, be the center of the seminary's entire life. The students should participate in this celebration in a conscientious way.[54]

With the exceptions noted in n. 14 above, the Mass must be the work of the entire seminary community. In it each and every person is to share according to his status. Thus, the priests who live in the seminary and who are not bound by pastoral obligation to celebrate Mass somewhere else should, as a praiseworthy act, concelebrate. Also the deacons, acolytes, and lectors should do their respective tasks.[35]

It is desirable that some parts of the Mass be always sung.[36]

24. Communion under both species, a fuller form of the sign[37] is recommended in seminaries, always, however, providing that the norms are observed which are in the General Introduction of the Roman Missal and in the decrees of the Bishops.

25. During vacations the students, by regularly and constantly attending weekday Mass, should show their spiritual maturity and love of their priestly vocations.

26. In view of some modern ideas spread about here and there, seminarians should be warned about how strongly the Church advises priests to celebrate Mass daily, even if they are not bound to do so by a pastoral obligation or even if the faithful cannot be present. The celebration of the Eucharistic Sacrifice even then is an action of Christ and the Church offered to God for the salvation of the whole world.[38]

27. Sharing in the Mass with correct piety, spirit of faith, and understanding, the students ought to be led to a more ardent devotion to the Holy Eucharist, according to the mind of Encyclical Letter, *"Mysterium Fidei,"* and the Instruction, *"Eucharisticum mysterium."*[39] There the practice of spending some time in prayer after having received holy communion and visiting the chapel during the day to pray before the Blessed Sacrament is recommended. Indeed, on some days of the year the most Blessed Sacrament could be exposed, according to the norms contained in the same Instruction[40] and according to the dispositions of the local Ordinary.

In arranging seminary chapels, the tabernacle in which the Holy Eucharist is reserved, is to be so placed as to favor private visits, so that the students will not neglect to honor our Lord in the Blessed Sacrament fruitfully and easily even by private adoration.[41]

b) The Liturgy of the Hours

28. The renewed Liturgy of the Hours[42] has opened up great spiritual riches for the praying Church, especially for priests, deacons, and those religious bound to the choir. But, it also includes the whole People of God who are strongly invited to share in it.[43] Therefore, the Liturgy of the Hours is to be held in high honor in seminaries, not only by those bound to recite it, namely the priests and deacons, but also by the entire body of students.

29. The celebration of the Hours, therefore, is to be fostered in the seminary and often, especially on Sundays and feastdays, it should be solemnized with song. In the Liturgy of the Hours it is appropriate that the leader presiding at it should assist the students with short explanations. Thus, they will better taste the daily riches of the office, they will grow accustomed to understand and love it, and they will learn to draw nourishment from it for their personal prayer and contemplation. In this way the Liturgy of the Hours will be harmonized with the exercise of other legitimate devotions and will not operate to their exclusion.

30. Usually it is to be celebrated in common observing the proper time of day: Lauds as morning prayer and Vespers as evening prayer. "By a venerable tradition of the Universal Church, they are the two hinges on which the daily office turns."[44]

Wherever possible, Compline is to be recited before the students retire to their rooms and, when it is not possible to recite it in common, the students should be counselled to say it in private.

Where it is the custom to gather in common for some other prayers during the day, it is useful to celebrate the "middle hour."

Especially on the vigils of Sundays and solemnities it is laudable to celebrate the Office of Reading and to do this, at least sometimes, by means of the rite known as the *"vigilia protracta"* as described in the book containing the Liturgy of the Hours.

Finally, during spiritual retreats it would be proper to celebrate the entire divine office with each of the Hours said at its proper time.

31. Great care must be exercised to form the minds of the students so that at the time of their diaconate they will accept the mandate from the Church of celebrating the whole Liturgy of the Hours each day gladly and with due understanding of what they are doing. For the Church deputes this task to those who share in sacred Orders "so that the office of the whole community might certainly and continuously be carried out at least by these men and so that the prayer of Christ might ceaselessly continue in the Church."[45]

Therefore, seminary superiors ought to recall to their students how necessary it is to be specially prepared for an apt initiation into the recitation of the office, even beyond a lively, liturgical experience in its recitation. Consequently, the students must be taught not only the doctrinal principles set out in the *"Institutio generalis de liturgia horarum,"* but also to understand the psalms, in the light of the New Testament and of Tradition, so as to discern the mystery of Christ in them and to be able to draw from them nourishment for their private prayers.[46]

c) Sunday and the liturgical year

32. For seminarians Sunday should be — whether they participate in the Mass at the seminary or are sent out into parishes — both in the celebration of the liturgy and throughout the course of the whole day, "the original feast day," which must be taught and inculcated into the students as a joyful celebration of the paschal mystery. [47]

The annual cycle of the mysteries of Christ should be celebrated in seminaries with special fervor, according to the idea of the Constitution *"Sacrosanctum Concilium."* [48]

Therefore, besides the Mass and the Liturgy of the Hours, celebrated according to the norms of the liturgical books, care should be taken so that in seminaries Sundays and the main feasts of our Lord, of the Blessed Virgin Mary, and of the saints are given a feastday character making them really become days of joy.

Special importance is to be given to the celebration of the patronal feast of the diocese — or of the region if the seminary is "regional." The life and spirit of the patron saints should be familiar to the students. Also care should be taken to celebrate suitably the feast of the dedication of the cathedral church and the anniversary of the local bishop's ordination.

To prepare for each celebration, the kind of catechetical instruction should be given to the seminarists which is, at the same time, adapted to the minds of present day students and to the needs of future priests.

The pastoral value of popular customs should be explained. The whole liturgical year should be not only a liturgical celebration, but a way of life, in the manner of a spiritual journey, in which the mystery of Christ is communicated.

33. Full and perfect formation of the students requires that, throughout their years of preparation in the seminary, they experience the richer and more developed forms of the liturgical celebrations of the seasons and solemnities of the liturgical year. Since after their ordination to the sacerdotal ministry they will be directing the liturgy and feast day solemnities will increase their apostolic activity, they will be obliged to repeat these celebrations in various places, oftentimes in more simple form, as provided for in the liturgical books. Thus it is clear that the way the students experience the liturgy in the seminary will be an example for them on which their future pastoral ministry will be based as well as the foundation for their meditation on and knowledge of the liturgical year.

34. A correct and adapted pedagogy used in these matters cannot overlook the special nature of our age, which is marked, at least in some places, by a less lively faith. This seems to lead to lesser understanding of the sacred seasons and feasts. One must bear in mind that those students, who before their entry into the seminary did not have a fervent and deep experience of the liturgical year, must be formed to grasp the supernatural meaning of these things, so they will be capable of acquiring a deeper recognition of the salvific nature of these events and will receive the grace that is found in them.

d) The sacrament of penance

35. In the spiritual life of future priests, great importance is to be given to the Sacrament of Penance, which, because it is a sacrament, is among all penitential acts the action most capable of arousing in them those dispositions required by the following of Christ and the spirit of the Gospel.

These are daily conversion, purity of heart, and the virtue of penance coming from love of sacrifice.

36. The students, therefore, should often go to the Sacrament of Reconciliation to acquire the grace they need for their daily spiritual development.[49] Frequent confession "is not a mere ritualistic repetition nor some kind of psychological exercise, but it is the careful work of perfecting the grace of Baptism so that, while we carry in our bodies the death of Jesus Christ, we allow the life of Jesus more and more to be manifested in us."[50]

Access to the Sacrament of Reconciliation is to be a very personal and individual act, while its liturgical character is always to be retained. Generally, it is to be distinct from spiritual direction. The frequency of confession is to be decided by each person with his own confessor, following the traditions of the spiritual masters and the laws of the Church.

Furthermore, to point out more clearly the ecclesial nature of penance[51] it sometimes helps, especially during Lent and during spiritual retreats, to have a liturgical, penitential celebration, according to what is proposed in the Roman Ritual, either without sacramental confession or else with confession and individual absolution. In this latter case, however, everyone's freedom is to be respected.

e) The celebration of ordinations and of the preparatory rites

37. The Church accompanies candidates for the priesthood in their initiation, one that is not merely doctrinal and spiritual in formation, but one that also consists of certain religious ceremonies.

During the course of study and following the norms set down by the Bishops' Conference, the time comes when following the application of the aspirants it is agreed that they have the necessary gifts and show themselves to be sufficiently mature. They are then invited to manifest this proposal publicly. After he receives this proposal in writing, the bishop gives ecclesial force to their selection and receives them through the rite of admission, that is, admission among the candidates aspiring to the diaconate and the priesthood.[52]

Then, observing the time intervals established or to be established by the Holy See or the Bishops' Conference, these same candidates, in the course of their theological curriculum[53] are to receive the ministries of lector and acolyte, unless they have already been installed in them. These they are to exercise for a suitable length of time and in this way they will be prepared to carry out their future duties with regard to the word and the altar in a more fitting manner.[54]

38. The celebration of these rituals together with the instructions that precede them provide a fine occasion to instruct the students in each of them and to help them to understand better the meaning, importance, and duties of the office they receive and to obtain the suitable spiritual enrichment which is demanded for the exercise of each ministry and order. Further elements for this spiritual and doctrinal preparation of the students can be easily deduced from the guidelines set down about the offices of lector and acolyte in the Motu Proprio *"Ad pascendum"* [55] and *"Ministeria quaedam."* [56]

Insofar as possible, these celebrations should involve the participation of the entire seminary community and thus could take place either in the seminary or in the candidates' home parishes.

39. Although much pastoral fruit can be produced when they are held in the home parish of the seminarian or in the parish where he exercised some pastoral ministry, sacred ordinations to the diaconate and to the priesthood are joyful events which involve the entire diocesan community. Therefore, the whole diocese should be informed about them and invited to attend them. The celebration of these events, which should be prepared with great care and dignity, requires that in the course of them the bishop be surrounded by his priests, deacons, seminarians, and faithful laity.

40. Sacred ordinations deeply affect the life of the whole seminary community. Not only the ordinands, but all the seminarians should be given a previous catechetical instruction concerning the rites and texts. This will help them draw from these ceremonies the authentic doctrine of the priesthood and the spiritual character of the apostolic life.

41. Lectors and acolytes ought to exercise their offices. Also the deacons, before they are called to the priesthood, should exercise their ordained ministry for some time either in the seminary or in some parish or, better still, in association with the bishop.

42. Since the Church has made some considerable changes in the rites and steps leading up to the priesthood, it is patently clear that seminary superiors must adapt themselves to these changes and also renew their style of formational work so that this new discipline will bear its desired fruits.

Part Two
The Teaching of the Sacred Liturgy
in Seminaries

a) General principle

43. Besides the first and elementary introduction in the liturgy which is to be imparted, when necessary, when the students first enter the seminary, as mentioned in n. 8 above,[57] the Bishops' Conferences are to arrange that in their national *"Ratio institutionis"* the teaching of the liturgy is given that place in the four-year theology course which satisfies the prescription of the Constitution *"Sacrosanctum Concilium,"* n. 16: "The study of the sacred liturgy is to be ranked among the compulsory and major courses in seminaries and religious houses of studies; in theological Faculties it is to rank among the principal subjects. It is to be taught under its theological, historical, spiritual, pastoral, and juridical aspects." This prescription, which is summed up in n. 79 of the *"Ratio fundamentalis,"* must be understood in its genuine sense and put into effect, as the following paragraphs indicate.

b) The proper object and purpose of this study

44. Liturgical studies are to be imparted in such a way that the needs of modern times are suitably met. These are mainly theological, pastoral, and ecumenical:

a. The strict connection between the liturgy and the doctrine of the faith has a special importance for the correct liturgical formation of future priests. This must be clearly pointed out as the study of the liturgy unfolds. In prayer the Church especially expresses her faith so that *"legem credendi lex statuat supplicandi."* [58] Therefore, the *"lex supplicandi"* is not only to be observed in a way that the *"lex credendi"* is not endangered, but scholars working in the field of sacred liturgy are to investigate carefully the tradition of divine worship, particularly when they study the nature of the Church and the doctrine and discipline of the sacraments.

b. With regard to the pastoral aspect, it is of the highest importance that liturgical renewal promoted by the Second Vatican Council be correctly and fully grasped by future priests in the light of sound doctrine and of tradition, both Western and Eastern. The norms of the renewed liturgy should be explained to the students so they will understand better the reasons for the adjustments and changes decreed by the Church. This will help them to discern the options which can be legitimately selected and to know the serious and difficult questions presently being discussed in this field, thus being able to distinguish the immutable part of the liturgy which comes from divine institution from other parts which can be changed.[59]

c. Also ecumenical dialogue, promoted by the same Second Vatican Council, requires a careful liturgical preparation. As a matter of fact, this dialogue gives rise to many difficult liturgical questions and to evaluate them adequately requires a good preparation by the students.

c) The scope of liturgical studies and teaching procedures

45. It belongs to each Bishops' Conference to determine in its individual *"Ratio institutionis"* the way in which the liturgy is to be taught in the seminaries. In the Appendix to this Instruction there is a list, by way of example, of the main points that seem opportune to treat. Here, meanwhile, the more general norms are simply outlined.

46. Above everything else liturgical acts, both as regards their texts and their ceremonies, must be explained to the students.

The prayers and orations offered by the sacred liturgy are to be explained in a way that sheds light upon the doctrinal treasures and the spiritual values they contain. For this it is not enough to read them in their vernacular translations, but it is necessary to use the original texts and to have them illustrated with the help of Sacred Scripture and of the traditions of the Fathers. Furthermore, the literary form of Christian "euchology" and especially of the psalms is not easily understood without a certain ability in literary appreciation having been acquired.

The teacher should instruct the students with care in the *"Institutiones"* which are found in the foreword of the Missal and the book of the Liturgy of the Hours. This also applies to the *"Praenotanda"* which are found at the beginning of each chapter in the Roman Ritual. In these documents one can find the theological doctrine, the pastoral motivation, and the spiritual aspect not only of the rites in general but also of each of their parts. Then too, since these documents often propose a variety of ways of enacting the same ceremonies, the teacher, in using them, should so develop the judgment of the students as to give them the capacity to know how to evaluate and discern the various ways of doing things which can be legitimately selected according to different circumstances. Also they should be led to understand why the rubrics use such terms as *"de more,"* *"pro opportunitate,"* or *"iis quae laudabiliter fiunt."*

47. Since the historical part of the liturgy has assumed great importance,[60] it is advisable that, in teaching, the history of the rites be carefully described, enabling the students to understand better their meaning and to grasp how they are composed of unchangeable elements coming from God's institution and other elements "which can and ought to be varied in the course of time whenever there are parts of them which seem to respond less than adequately to the very nature of the liturgy or which have become less functional."[61] It should be pointed out how in various circumstances the Church displayed her pastoral art by taking into account the different customs of people and their various cultures. Moreover, especially from studying the historical documents of the rites, sacramental theology can be helped to acquire greater clarity and certitude.

48. In describing the rites from the historical viewpoint, due importance ought to be given also to the traditions of the Oriental Churches: "For, distinguished as they are by their venerable antiquity, they are bright with that tradition which was handed down from the Apostles through the Fathers, a tradition which forms part of the divinely revealed and undivided heritage of the Catholic Church."[62] Indeed, pastoral reasons also draw attention in these days to the value of knowing these Eastern-rite liturgies.

49. However, it is preferable that, beyond the treatment given to single liturgical actions, the very nature of the entire liturgy should be theologically explained, following the mind of the Constitution, *"Sacrosanctum Concilium,"* nn. 5 to 11. For this purpose seminarians are to be brought to a deep understanding of the paschal mystery of Christ "from Whom all sacraments and sacramentals draw their power,"[63] the history of salvation,[64] and the presence of Christ in the sacred liturgy.[65] Also, the idea of signs must be studied since the liturgy uses perceptible things to signify invisible, divine reality[66] so that through these signs, in a way proper to each of them, the sanctification of men and women might be effected.[67] From these signs it must be made clear how the liturgical assembly manifests God's Church insofar as she is the People of God, enjoying unity along with a distinction of various ministries.[68]

50. For a deeper theological treatment of the liturgy as well as to resolve many problems confronting pastors of souls in the ordering and promoting of the liturgy, it is necessary to appreciate certain findings of modern sciences, such as anthropology, sociology, linguistics and the comparative history of religions, etc. These throw more than a little light in certain cases on liturgical studies, but only within the limits established by the supernatural nature of the liturgy. In these matters what must be cultivated in the students is a sense of discernment, giving them the capacity to evaluate soundly the importance of these kinds of disciplines while at the same time teaching them to avoid anything that could lessen the full, supernatural force of Catholic worship.

In the use of these sciences, the following norm should be observed, ". . . care must be taken to avoid multiplying the number of courses. Rather insert new questions or new ways of looking at things into the courses which are already provided, where this is possible."[69]

d) The endowments of a liturgy professor and the relationship of the liturgy with other disciplines taught in seminaries

51. So that all this will be correctly taught, there ought to be in each seminary a special professor suitably prepared to teach liturgy. As far as possible he should have had his preparation in an Institute which has this special purpose.[70] He should have studied theology and history and ought to understand pastoral reality as well as being endowed with a sense of the public prayer of the Church. He should well understand that his work is not simply scientific and technical but rather "mystagogical," so that he may introduce the students into the liturgical life and into its spiritual character.

52. In a special way the professors of Sacred Scripture must remember how much richer is the selection of biblical readings offered to the faithful in the renewed liturgy in these times. Indeed, it should be taught how all liturgical actions and signs derive their meaning from Holy Scripture.[71] Hence it will be necessary that future priests receive a fuller understanding of the sacred texts and of the history of salvation. This means not only the science of exegesis, but also "that warm and living love for Scripture to which the venerable tradition of both Eastern and Western rites gives testimony."[72]

53. To achieve greater progress in liturgical study more than a little help will come from its coordination with other disciplines, as the Second Vatican Council recommends.[73] Thus, for example, in treating especially the doctrine and practice of the sacraments, there ought to be close cooperation between the liturgy professor and the professors of dogma, moral, and canon law. There should be frequent conversations to foster a fruitful common spirit with everyone working together for the same end in order to avoid frequent repetition of the same things and, indeed, to avoid contradicting each other.

54. In arranging the class schedule for the theological courses, it would be desirable, if possible, to treat liturgical questions at the same time that theological questions on similar issues are being taught. For instance, at the time that ecclesiology is taught, the liturgy classes would explain the theological nature of the praying Church, and so forth.

In some seminaries it perhaps might help to have the liturgy professor also teach the whole tract on the sacraments. This would be done of course only if he were as well versed in sacramental theology as in liturgy.

55. Care must be taken that from the study of liturgy those elements and aspects are drawn out that can contribute to the final theological synthesis which, according to the *"Ratio fundamentalis,"* n. 63, should involve the whole theological curriculum. This is especially important at the final stage of the theological studies.

e) Music and sacred art

56. Given the importance of sacred music in liturgical celebrations, the students should be trained in music by experts, including a practical training, in those things necessary for them in their future roles as presidents and moderators of liturgical celebrations. In this training account should be taken not only of the talents of the individual students, but also of new techniques, now generally used in music schools which will make this instruction more profitable for the students. Above all, care must be taken that the students are not simply taught a vocal or instrumental art, but that they are given a true and authentic formation of their minds and their feelings, molding them to know and appreciate the better musical works of the past and also to know how to choose soundly and correctly from among present day experiments. [74]

57. Equally, the seminarians, "during their philosophical and theological studies are to be taught about the history and development of sacred art and about the sound principles underlying the production of its works. As a result they will be able to appreciate and preserve the Church's venerable monuments and be in a position to aid, by good advice, artists who are engaged in producing works of art." [75] Indeed, the archaeological study of Christian antiquities can contribute much toward throwing light on the liturgical life and the faith of the early Church.

58. Finally, it is extremely necessary that the students be taught the art of speaking and of using symbols, as well as how to use communications media. Indeed, in liturgical celebrations it is of the highest importance that the faithful be able to understand the priest, not only in what he says, whether in the homily or in the prayers and orations, but also in what he does by way of gestures and actions. Formation for this purpose is of such high importance in the renewed liturgy that it deserves very special consideration.

f) Practical pastoral apprenticeship in liturgical ministry

59. Practical pastoral apprenticeship in liturgical ministry must be imparted at suitable times throughout the whole course of study in various selected circumstances.[76] It reaches its peak during the final year of study, when future priests, after their seminary liturgical life has given them a taste from the fountain of true Christian spirituality, will receive a more careful preparation specifically adapted to the special circumstances in which they will be exercising their priestly ministry. During this time of practical formation, there must be insistence upon the pastoral norms and cautions which the bishops have decreed in regard to preparation for and administration of the sacraments. In imparting this formation, the seminary professors should consult the diocesan liturgical commission.

This adaptation to local conditions and prescriptions requires that the student also must learn and appreciate the various forms of popular devotion which are approved and recommended by Church authorities.[77]

g) More thorough liturgical preparation for some students

60. In order that dioceses might have at their disposition some priests who are well qualified and able to teach liturgy and to direct diocesan liturgical commissions, it is necessary that some candidates who are gifted in this line be prepared for such work. Therefore, after such priests have finished their normal seminary course and have spent some time in pastoral work they should be sent by their bishops to attend one of these specialized Institutes established by the Holy See or by the Bishops' Conferences.[78] This is especially urgent for those places where, in the judgment of competent Church authorities, a more thorough liturgical adaptation is needed.

h) Liturgical formation in the continuing education of priests

61. In the field of continuing or permanent education of priests who have already finished their seminary course, according to the norm of the Second Vatican Council,[79] there ought to be a place for studying sacred liturgy. This is quite important because in the course of normal seminary training it is not possible to exhaust the treasury of the sacred liturgy and because modern circumstances make this advisable. As a matter of fact, human and societal customs change so rapidly now that it is not possible to foresee, during the seminary training period, what new difficulties will show up in pastoral work nor what kind of liturgical confusion might arise. Neither is it possible to overlook the wide and swift diffusion of periodicals, meetings, use of the media, and the pressure of public opinion, which also affect the sacred liturgy, posing for it difficult questions, which nevertheless must be answered by priests since it involves their daily activity.

Conclusion

62. Ever greater fruit is being daily produced by the renewed liturgy. This is not surprising since the liturgy is the outstanding means by which the faithful can express in their lives and manifest to others the mystery of Christ and the real nature of the true Church. Priests and seminarians must recognize more than the other faithful these benefits, since in the liturgy they acquire a deeper and fuller experience of the priesthood and its requirements. They are invited to "imitate what they handle."

In this way, therefore, the assiduous study and exercise of the sacred liturgy ceaselessly recalls to their minds the goal toward which all their apostolic labors tend. At the same time all their study efforts, their pastoral work, and their interior lives become more mature and more deeply unified.

Given at Rome from the offices of the Sacred Congregation for Catholic Education on the Solemnity of Pentecost Sunday, the third day of June in the year of our Lord 1979.

Gabriel-Marie Cardinal Garrone
Prefect

Antonio-María Javierre-Ortas
Titular Archbishop of Meta
Secretary

Appendix

A List of Questions Which Seem Important to Treat in the Liturgical Instruction Imparted in Seminaries

The modern need for a deeper liturgical formation

1. According to the norm laid down in the Constitution, *"Sacrosanctum Concilium,"* "the study of the sacred liturgy is to be ranked among the compulsory and major courses in seminaries and religious houses of study; in Faculties of sacred theology it is to rank among the principal subjects. It is to be taught under its theological, historical, spiritual, pastoral, and juridical aspects." [1]

Thus, the discipline of the liturgy is to be taught in such a way as to satisfy modern day needs:

a) the renewal of the liturgy, begun by the Second Vatican Council and now being put into effect, ought to be grasped in the light of liturgical tradition, not only of the West but also of the Eastern-rite churches; [2]

b) since the Second Vatican Council promoted liturgical renewal according to the spirit and traditions of various peoples, [3] a more careful and detailed study of the liturgy, both historically and theologically, is needed so as to avoid harming the authentic and true spirit of liturgical reform;

c) in ecumenical dialogue there are many questions of a difficult nature that arise from the liturgy, both doctrinally, such as the sacrificial nature of the Mass, Holy Orders, and the other sacraments, and pastorally, as described in the Ecumenical Directory and in other documents issued by the Apostolic See;

d) finally and in a very special way, since the *"legem credendi lex statuat supplicandi,"* liturgical tradition should be so studied as to shed light upon doctrinal and disciplinary questions which are being discussed today concerning the mystery of Christ and the sacraments. Indeed, the sacred liturgy through prayer opens up for the students the source of the Christian mystery and thus it nourishes their spiritual lives and fosters unity among the various disciplines of the theological course to a high degree.

The nature of this list

2. The items on this list which are proposed here are not intended as a rigid framework for setting up the curriculum for liturgical formation. Rather this is to be done according to the requirements of local circumstances.

According to the norm laid down by the *"Ratio fundamentalis institutionis sacerdotalis,"* the seminarians are to begin their studies with an introductory course in which they are initiated into the mystery of Christ and the history of salvation, a course which is "designed to enable the students to appreciate the idea which lies behind their ecclesiastical studies, their general plan, and their connection with the apostolate. At the same time it should help them to deepen their own faith, to understand at greater depth their priestly vocation, and consequently to commit themselves with greater awareness." [4] This cannot be done unless at the same time they are given a suitable introduction to the liturgy, which could be either a part of this introductory course or else a course apart, especially imparted at the beginning of the philosophy-theology curriculum. In this introduction there should be some treatment of the role of the sacred liturgy in the economy of salvation, in the life of the Church, and in the spiritual life of each Christian. It would be most useful at the beginning of the course to give the students a brief explanation of the Mass and of the major Hours of the Divine Office.

3. The order of the liturgical matters presented above could be changed around so that liturgical formation harmonizes more closely with the other theological disciplines and with the life of the seminary itself. For instance, a deeper study of the first chapter of the Second Vatican Council's Constitution on the liturgy will be most profitably received by the students who already have been instructed in some of the first, elementary notions of sacred theology. Also it is sometimes useful to treat the liturgical year and the various celebrations of the liturgy while they are actually being celebrated. Similarly, to associate the liturgical study of the sacraments with the theological study of them is most opportune.

4. All the material presented on this list is not intended to be what the liturgy professor must impart with fullness in his lectures. He should make a selection of the topics which will succeed in giving his students an essential, global view of the liturgy, at least by touching upon the main points and by avoiding omissions which would be harmful to the preparation of future priests. The more detailed questions, not dealt with in the lectures, should be proposed to the seminarians for their private study or for study in small groups, as has already proved useful for obtaining fine results in other disciplines.

5. The liturgy teacher must not forget that his main job is to lead the students to study the liturgical texts which the seminarists must understand. This is so that, when they become celebrants of the liturgy, they will be capable of leading the people to a knowledgeable and fruitful participation in the mystery of Christ.

6. When it is pointed out, as often is done in this list, that the ancient sources be approached and studied, this should be understood as an exhortation to an ideal which, of course, can only be reached by taking account of the particular resources and limitations of the individual seminaries.

The suitability of harmonizing this discipline with other seminary studies

7. Great care should be exercised to join together harmoniously liturgical studies with other disciplines being taught, as the Instruction states in nn. 52-56. There are many questions which are interconnected, especially regarding the doctrine of the sacraments and their pastoral administration. These questions should be treated either by the liturgy professor or by other professors, but care should be taken to be certain to avoid omissions as well as useless repetition. Indeed there should be interdisciplinary cooperation so that at the same time matters will be treated from the liturgical, dogmatic, canonical, historical, and pastoral points of view, providing the students with special advantages.

Part One
Norms and Principles

Article I: The nature of the sacred liturgy and its importance in the Church's life

8. It is helpful to begin with an introduction into the idea of worship presented from the anthropological and psychological viewpoint, inasmuch as it influences the human mind and may be found, albeit in a deformed way, even in secularized societies.

9. The Christian liturgy, however, completes and goes far beyond the simple idea of cult. This will be made clear by explaining and commenting on the doctrine in nn. 5-13 of the Constitution *Sacrosanctum Concilium;*

a) the nature of the liturgy which "rightly is considered as an exercise of the priestly office of Jesus Christ. In the liturgy the sanctification of man is manifested by signs perceptible to the senses and is effected in a way which is proper to each of these signs; in the liturgy full public worship is performed by the Mystical Body of Christ Jesus, that is by the Head and His members."[5]

b) the paschal mystery of Christ, His passion, resurrection from the dead, and His ascension, celebrated in the liturgy of Church[6] "whence all sacraments and sacramentals draw their power."[7]

c) the place the liturgy has in the economy of salvation. That is to say, that "the wonders wrought by God among the people of the Old Testament were but a prelude"[8] to the salvific work of Christ because "all of this happened to them as a presage."[9] Indeed the work of Christ was done when He was born of a woman, made subject to the law, suffered under Pontius Pilate, and rose on the third day; the Church preaches the Good News until the end of the world, celebrates the Eucharist, and administers the other sacraments, recognizing the presence of Christ in the sacred liturgy[10] and she anticipates in the earthly liturgy that of heaven[11] when God shall be all in all.

Furthermore one must explain:

d) how the liturgy uses perceptible sacred signs to signify invisible divine things and how through these signs, each in its own way, the sanctification of mankind is effected.[12]

e) how the liturgy, as an exercise of the priestly office of Christ consists of a twofold movement: from God to mankind to bring about sanctification and from mankind to God to give Him adoration in spirit and in truth.[13]

f) although the sacred liturgy does not exhaust the entire activity of the Church, it is, nevertheless, "the summit toward which all the action of the Church is directed and at the same time the fountain from which all her power flows." It should prove helpful to explain this thoroughly according to the mind of the Constitution.[14]

Article II: The nature of the liturgy as properly hierarchical and communitarian. Liturgical law

10. According to the norms of nn. 26-32 and 41-42 of the Constitution, the principles should be explained concerning the liturgical assembly, namely the holy people convoked and ordered under the leadership of the bishop (or of the priest who stands in his place). This should be suitably explained from the doctrine of Sacred Scripture, from the examples of the early Church, and from the texts of the Fathers.

Furthermore, it is fitting to include an explanation of the conditions under which it is legitimate to celebrate the liturgy even quasi-privately.

11. There must be insistence upon the different status of members and the variety of offices which is demanded by a liturgical assembly. Therefore, there must be a description of the parts of the celebrant, of the ministers, of the choir, and of the people. The part of the faithful laity and their active participation should be explained according to the mind of the Second Vatican Council. At the same time, the distinction must be explained between the common priesthood of all baptized people and the ministerial priesthood by virtue of which the presiding priest leads the liturgical assembly "in the person of Christ." [15]

12. The pre-eminent office of the bishop is to be set out according to the mind of the dogmatic Constitution *"Lumen Gentium"* [*Dogmatic Constitution on the Church*].

13. With a short historical exposition, the professor should demonstrate how liturgical laws are under the control of the sacred hierarchy and how this belongs to the hierarchy by divine right. Also it should be explained how, in the course of time, there has been, obviously, some variety in the way this right has been exercised.

Thus the instruction comes up to the present day, setting out what is decreed about the liturgy in the Constitution n. 22, namely the parts to be exercised by the Apostolic See, the Bishops' Conferences, and the local bishops.

14. Likewise by an historical exposition, it should be set out why the Church, little by little even from the most ancient times, has forbidden improvisation in the composition and offering of made-up prayers in the liturgy and how, at the present time, she has imposed limits upon flexibility, variety, and experiments.

Article III: The instructive and pastoral nature of the liturgy

15. "In the liturgy God speaks to His people and Christ is still proclaiming His Gospel and the people reply to God in song and prayer." [16] The first part of the liturgy is, therefore, given over to Sacred Scripture, that is to say the word of God both read and listened to by all, or else sung by the assembly. The teacher should treat more widely the use of Sacred Scripture both in the readings and in the songs taken from them. Nor should the instructor neglect to lecture about non-biblical readings and about the hymns composed by the Church. General principles should be put forward about Bible celebrations, the homily, and catechetics, emphasizing the great importance of Sacred Scripture for understanding the signs, actions, and prayers of the liturgy. [17]

16. Great care should be shown in pointing out the specific usefulness of sacred song and its place in the liturgy. Thus, there should be pointed out the diverse kinds of songs: psalmody by which the psalms and biblical hymns are sung; hymn singing; doxologies; acclamations, etc. With various examples one should point out the dialogue that takes place between the celebrant and the assembled faithful.

17. The different kinds of prayers should be explained: both the priest's prayer (for instance, orations, thanksgivings, blessings, exorcisms, indicative formulas, private prayers), and the prayer of the assembled faithful (such as Sunday prayers, silent prayer, litanies, etc.).

18. If possible, a brief history of sacred song, should be given including its origins, its early development, and the nature of Gregorian chant. One should also recall other forms of approved tradition and should finally point out the principles in the Instruction of the Sacred Congregation of Rites of March 5, 1967, about sacred music in the liturgy.

19. Something should also be said about liturgical language, setting out a brief history of the discipline in this matter both of the West and of the East. If the teacher has the skill and training, it could be shown how the translation of the sacred books, especially from Greek into Latin, brought about the formation of a Christian language and it could be shown how certain principles are to regulate translations into the vernacular today.

20. Since the liturgy does not only use words but also signs "chosen by Christ or by the Church to signify invisible divine reality," [18] one should speak, in the lessons given, both about gestures and physical bearing as well as about the material things used in liturgical worship. When teaching about the gestures and bearing and their meaning and their power to move souls, one should draw instruction from Sacred Scripture and from the works of the Church Fathers. With care, efforts must be made not to allow this teaching to remain abstract, but insure that it filters down to liturgical practice. Even if done briefly, it is helpful to explain singly the meaning, especially the biblical meaning, of the various natural elements used in the liturgy, such as light, water, bread, wine, oil, incense, etc., in particular, those elements which serve as the material of the sacramental signs.

21. Since today there are some "who try to divest liturgical worship of its sacred character and therefore believe falsely that one is not to use things and garments which are sacred but substitute for them things which are common and vulgar," it will be necessary to refute these opinions just as one must do with those who "pervert the genuine nature of the sacred liturgy." [19]

22. There should be a theological explanation about the places dedicated to worship and to their meaning. The rite for the dedication of a church should be explained. Also the purpose of the altar, the place destined for the reservation of the Blessed Sacrament, the chair of the celebrant, the ambo (pulpit), and the baptistry should be studied.

23. Efforts should be made so that the seminarians are trained to draw from the ideas of their other studies a better understanding of the history and laws of sacred art. Something appropriate should be said about Christian iconography and about the principles of modern sacred art which need to be respected as they are useful for Christian people.

24. From all this the teaching role of the liturgy is quite clear and it is also clear how, "although the sacred liturgy is above all the worship of the divine Majesty, it also contains abundant instruction for the faithful." [20] Account must be taken of the proposition that *"legem credendi lex statuat supplicandi"* (the law of prayer establishes the law of belief) and thus the norms should be taught for distinguishing the matters which the Church proposes in her liturgy for the faithful to believe from others over which the Magisterium does not exercise its authority because of their nature.

25. In all these things account must be taken of the difficulties faced by modern man, and apt means for confronting them should be proposed to future pastors of souls. For this it is useful to have in mind some of the sciences of man, such as psychology and sociology, taking account, however, of what is stated in the Instruction above in n. 50.

Article IV: The notion of the history of the sacred liturgy

26. When giving an orderly exposition of the individual liturgical actions and of the sacraments, the history of each rite must be dwelt upon both to effect understanding of modern liturgical usage and to make sacramental theology more clear and precise.

To allow everything in the course of the liturgical lectures to proceed better, it will be useful to give some short emphasis to each phase and to all periods in the whole history of the liturgy and to point out the reciprocal connection between the liturgy and Christian spirituality.

This, insofar as possible, should begin with a description of Jewish prayer used in the time of Christ, especially that of the synagogue, that used in private homes and that of the passover celebration, so that the seminarians can recognize the similarities to Christian prayer while also noting what is "original" about Christian prayer.

Then there should be a description of the liturgical assembly in the age of the Apostles. It is also desirable that the students be exposed to the liturgical sources of the first centuries (for instance, the Didache, Saint Clement of Rome, Saint Justin, Saint Irenaeus, Tertullian, Hippolytus of Rome, Saint Cyprian, the Didascalia and the Apostolic Constitutions, the Pilgrimage of Egeria) and texts selected from the early anaphoras and from the catecheses of the Fathers.

27. As the laws and texts of the liturgy gradually evolve in the churches in various regions, it would be suitable at this point to delineate the diverse liturgical families, both of the East and of the West, with a brief explanation of their origin, their history, and their characteristics. This is of the highest importance especially for those areas where many faithful of the Eastern-rite churches live.

It is advisable to make clear the affinities among the rites. In explaining the individual liturgical actions, especially the sacraments, a special place should be given to the texts and rites of the different liturgies which serve to enrich doctrine and nourish devotion.

28. The work of the Council of Trent should be set out, showing how it corrected liturgical abuses and promoted liturgical unity. The decrees of this Council about the sacred liturgy should be presented. Likewise, it should be explained how, through the disposition of this Council, and according to its mind, the Roman Pontiffs amended the liturgical books, which were widely disseminated and remained in use until our own time. Then, it would be opportune to narrate briefly how from the 17th to the 19th century, notwithstanding all sorts of difficulties, the liturgy made progress, thanks especially to the quality of historical study: thus we could mention devotion to the Eucharist, the conscientious observance of the rubrics, pastoral work promoted in various places so that the faithful might understand and participate in the liturgy. This led the way to the renewal begun by Pope Saint Pius X in our century and greatly promoted by the Second Vatican Ecumenical Council.

29. To understand better modern liturgical renewal, it would be most useful to outline for the students the series of documents by means of which liturgical renewal was gradually accomplished.

Part Two
The Mass and Eucharistic Worship

Article I: The general notions of the Mass to be explained to the students

30. Before all else, there must be an explanation of the New Testament texts about the institution of the Eucharist. They should be compared with the texts of Jewish prayers used in daily life and in the passover supper as well as with other testimony which surrounds the Eucharistic institution.

31. There should follow a short history of the Mass so as to make clear the common elements of the Mass as they appear in all the liturgies, so these might be better understood in the present day Eucharistic celebration and be more easily presented to the Christian people.

It is desirable that the students, where possible, actually read some of the early Mass texts, either selected from works of the Fathers or taken from the ancient liturgies. These can be found today in many good anthologies.

Especially in areas where there are faithful of the Eastern rites, the seminarists should receive some idea about the Mass in those rites, particularly about their spiritual aspect.

32. The various ways of celebrating the Mass should be described: stational Masses, Mass with the people present, Mass without people present. According to the *"Institutio generalis missalis Romani,"* published in 1970, the parts should be set out: of the celebrant, the concelebrants, the ministers, the choir, and the faithful.

33. Concelebration should be treated more completely along with an explanation of its present discipline in the tradition of the West and the East.

34. According to the mind of the *"Institutio generalis"* (chapters 5-6) mentioned above the requisites for celebrating Mass ought to be explained. These derive not only from force of tradition and law but also from the necessities of the human mind and human nature itself: these include the church building, the altar, the altar's ornamentation, the sacred vessels, the vestments of the priests and ministers, etc.

Article II: Norms for explaining correctly to the students the individual parts of the Mass and of the rites

35. The instructors are to explain the two parts that, in a certain sense, constitute the Mass, namely the liturgy of the word and that of the Eucharist, both so closely joined together as to form one single act of worship.[21]

36. The teacher then should explain fully the individual rites in the Mass, giving to each its proper importance: thus, for instance, an explanation should be given of the entrance rite, the stages of the readings in the liturgy of the word, up to the Gospel, the homily and the prayer of the faithful, the role of the offertory, the nature and format of the entire Eucharistic prayer, the rite of preparation for communion, and the final and concluding rites.

As far as possible, the individual rites should be explained under their historical aspect and also by comparing them to the rites of other liturgies.

37. In the same way other constituent parts of the Eucharistic prayer should be defined and explained.[22]

38. The distribution of Holy Communion under both species should be presented under its historical, theological, and pastoral aspects.

39. According to the mind of the Instruction *"Eucharisticum mysterium"* of May 25, 1967, some indication should be given of how the faithful are to be instructed to participate in the Mass so as to obtain greater fruits from this participation and also how the Eucharist is to be seen as the center of the entire sacramental system.

40. When the instructor speaks about the liturgy of the word, he should also speak about the celebrations of the word as indicated in the Constitution in article 35, 4.[23]

Article III: Eucharistic worship outside of Mass

41. Since the worship of the Holy Eucharist outside of Mass has greatly developed through the centuries, care must be taken to explain this, taking account of the Holy Sacrifice of the Mass itself and the mind of the above-mentioned Instruction of May 25, 1967. Also there should be a lecture on the part of the Roman Ritual entitled *"De sacra communione et de cultu mysterii eucharistici extra missam,"* issued on June 21, 1973.

The reception of Holy Communion outside of Mass and also the custody of the Blessed Sacrament, including the theological and pastoral reason for these practices and the juridical conditions that regulate them, should be spoken about.

Then, there should be lectures about other devotions connected with the Holy Eucharist and their principal forms, which are: processions, exposition of the most Blessed Sacrament, Eucharistic Congresses. These are recommended, and they are regulated by these same documents to be sure that they derive from Holy Mass and stimulate the faithful toward participation in the Sacrifice and in Holy Communion.

Part Three
The Other Sacraments and the Sacramentals

42. The commentary imparted on the renewed Pontifical and the Ritual should be mainly taken from the texts themselves and their *"Praenotanda"* so that the doctrine contained there might be drawn out. It helps, in explaining and understanding this, to take account of the history of the rites. Each part of this study should include pastoral instruction by which the candidates for the priesthood will be prepared for their future sacred ministry.

Article I: Christian initiation

43. Christian initiation, that is, the rite of the catechumenate, the sacraments of Baptism and Confirmation along with first Communion, must be diligently explained since it is the foundation of the catechetical instruction that is given to children and also since, in many parts of the world, a large number of adults are led through the same stages in their Christian initiation.

44. It is, therefore, desirable that a thorough explanation be given of the history of the baptismal liturgy and of the liturgical catechumenate so that the arrangement of conferring Baptism on adults by stages might be rightly understood and shown. The baptismal rites should be explained in connection with the liturgy of Lent, the text of the Mass for the blessing of the oils, and the rites and texts of the Easter vigil and the octave of Easter.

45. The students should be asked and encouraged to read the baptismal catecheses of the Fathers of the Church, easily accessible today, since there are editions printed in the original languages as well as in the vernacular.

46. It is suitable to give a short explanation of the baptismal anniversary celebrations both the older and the newer forms, using this occasion for a careful pastoral instruction on their importance and on the fruits that can be legitimately expected from these celebrations in the spiritual life of the parish and of the faithful.

47. In the same way and along similar lines, the rite of Confirmation should be explained as set out in the Apostolic Constitution *"Divinae consortium,"* of Pope Paul VI, issued on August 15, 1971. This should be done in such a way that light is thrown on the force of this sacrament and its close connection with Baptism.

In a special way either the liturgy professor or the professor of pastoral theology must explain the spiritual resources provided by a good preparation and celebration of Confirmation. They also must, at the same time, explain the regulations about this matter laid down by Bishops' Conferences and the local Ordinary.

48. It is appropriate also to speak briefly about the Eucharist as the "crowning" of the sacraments of initiation and about the admission of youngsters to first Holy Communion.

Article II: The sacrament of Holy Orders and the various ministries

49. The rite and discipline of the sacrament of Holy Orders and of the various other ministries of the Church must be presented and explained with a fullness that corresponds to the dispositions for their renewal as set down by the Second Vatican Council. There is some question as to whether this matter should be treated in its normal place during the course of the liturgy lectures or left to a gradual treatment to be done at the times the seminarians are admitted to the ministries and to Sacred Orders.

As a minimum, however, the liturgy teacher has the task of explaining the texts of the new Roman Pontifical and illustrating through a study of historical tradition the Apostolic Constitution *"Pontificalis Romani,"* issued on June 18, 1968, and the Motu Proprio *"Sacrum diaconatus ordinem,"* issued on June 18, 1967, as well as both *"Ad pascendum"* and *"Ministeria quaedam,"* issued on August 15, 1972.

Insofar as possible, something should be said about the ritual of ordination used in the churches of the Eastern-rites, especially in those areas where many of the faithful of these rites reside.

50. Efforts should be made to explain well the rite of episcopal consecration so that it will be clear that all the Orders and ministries have reference to the bishop and especially that it is clear that priests are collaborators with the bishop and have received *"secundi meriti munus."*

Article III: Matrimony and virginity

51. The rite of marriage is to be presented historically, illustrating its variety and its proper use adapted to different places. It should be shown that the rite has been always adapted to the religious and civil customs of diverse peoples. The texts and the readings, which the new Ritual abundantly offers, should be described.

Since, according to the doctrine of the New Testament and of the Church Fathers, Christian matrimony and sacred virginity are closely associated and understood together, it is fitting to harmonize the presentation of the liturgy of marriage with the ligurgy of the consecration of virgins, described in the restored Roman Pontifical.

Article IV: The liturgy of religious consecration

52. The rite of the consecration of virgins and the rite of religious profession, when they are briefly described, show how religious life constitutes a special state of life in the Church, as taught by the Second Vatican Council, in the dogmatic Constitution, *"Lumen gentium."* [24]

Article V: The penitential liturgy

53. Highly desirable for the students is a short and succinct history of the liturgy and the discipline of penance so they might more easily grasp the meaning of the sacrament of Penance and of other penitential acts.

With the help of the new Roman Ritual and of the Pastoral Norms issued by the Sacred Congregation for the Doctrine of the Faith on June 16, 1972, the rite of the sacrament of Penance should be explained and there should be an instruction about the conditions under which it is permitted to impart general absolution.

Also there should be a description of the penitential nature of the Lenten liturgy, of the importance of the penitential act at the beginning of Mass, and of the norms in the above cited documents for the celebration of the penitential rites.

Article VI: The liturgy of the sick

54. Explanation should be given of the Apostolic Constitution *"Sacram unctionem,"* issued on November 30, 1972, and of the *"Ordo unctionis infirmorum eorumque pastoralis curae"* as found in the new Roman Ritual. This reform, set up by the Second Vatican Council,[25] might be opportunely presented in connection with the study of the history of the liturgy.

Article VII: The liturgy of Christian death

55. The liturgy course should also treat the liturgy of the dying and of the dead. This should indeed include treatment of Holy Viaticum, and then the rite of the recommendation of a dying person's soul, and, finally, the funeral rites. Due light should be thrown upon all the aspects of these rites in which the paschal mystery is relived. The students should indeed be exhorted to make good choices from among the great riches offered in the texts of the new Ritual. They should be instructed about the pastoral care of the dying and about the pastoral importance of funeral celebrations.

Article VIII: The sacramentals

56. There must be some treatment of processions in general and their religious importance. Also it should be shown how pilgrimages are really a certain form of procession and it should be explained how they have pastoral value.

57. From the historical and theological point of view there should be an explanation, even if brief, of blessings, with insistence upon their useful-ness and value in sanctifying everyday life. An attitude of respect for the various legitimate ways in which a Christian practices his faith in the course of his life must be inculcated into the students. At the same time, the seminarians should be warned to be cautious and to avoid abuses and superstitions.

Part Four
The Sanctification of Time

58. A study of Sunday as the day which is "the foundation and the nucleus of the whole liturgical year"[26] should be given priority.

Article I: Sunday

59. The highest importance must be given to Sunday. Its definition and elements should be explained according to the Constitution on the sacred liturgy of the Second Vatican Council.[27] With historical demonstration it should be shown that Sunday is the weekly Easter, closely joined to the original situation of the early Church, through apostolic tradition, since it takes its origin from the very day of the Lord's resurrection.[28]

60. Pastoral reasons should be carefully put forth which can lead to a true sanctification of this day as all the faithful are duty bound to observe.

61. The Sundays "during the ordinary time of the year" offer to the Christian people great riches from God's word. Therefore, students must be taught how to promote these riches through the faithful and diligent observance of the laws regarding liturgical celebrations.

Article II: The liturgical year

62. Even though the students are taught by their superiors and teachers wisely and carefully to celebrate the seasons and feasts as they occur throughout the year, it is still fitting to treat in the lectures in an ordered and harmonious manner a summary of the main aspects of the liturgical year. This should be done in the light of history and according to the mind of the Motu Proprio entitled *"Mysterii paschalis,"* issued by Pope Paul VI on February 14, 1969.

63. Above all else, there should be a treatment of the history and spiritual character of Easter and the Easter season, namely, the fifty days after Easter which close with the Solemnity of Pentecost, the Easter triduum, and the preparation for Easter, that is, Lent. Most of all the seminarians should be trained to live the paschal mystery in the depths of their souls and to prepare themselves for their future paschal ministry.

64. Then there should be an explanation of the Christmas and the Epiphany cycle of feasts along with their history and their spiritual meaning.

65. There should be a brief explanation of the more recent Solemnities of our Lord inserted into the liturgical year: the Holy Trinity, Corpus Christi, the Sacred Heart, Christ the King, etc.

66. There should also be an historical instruction about the veneration paid to the Blessed Virgin Mary in the Church.[29] There should follow a special study of her feasts as they occur throughout the year.

67. With regard to the veneration paid to the saints whose "Memorials" have been introduced into the liturgical year, account should be taken of the doctrine contained in the Constitution on the sacred liturgy of the Second Vatican Council.[30] There should be a short description of historic origin and development of the cult of the martyrs and of the other saints, the devotion owed to their tombs and their relics, and the importance of the veneration of the saints for a Christian life.

Article III: The sanctification of the hours of the day and the Divine Office

68. So that the souls of the students will be prepared to solemnize in a pious and fruitful way the Divine Office, it is important for the liturgy teacher to go over with them the *"Institutio generalis"* which is a preface to the book of the Liturgy of the Hours, promulgated by Pope Paul VI on November 1, 1970.

69. There must be insistence upon the doctrinal part of this *"Institutio"* (Chapter 1). Above all it must be shown how Christ entrusts to His Church the duty of praising God, which is done not only through the Holy Eucharist but also in other ways, including especially the Divine Office.[31]

70. From the testimony given by the Acts of the Apostles and by Church Tradition, one can show the great importance of the Hours of the Office for the sanctification of the whole day and of each part of the day, and how suitably this satisfies the divine precept to pray always. The symbolic force of each of the Hours can be clearly deduced from the early spiritual writers and from the prayers found in the new book of the Liturgy of the Hours.

71. Arguments should be presented to support the special spiritual and pastoral weight given to Lauds and Vespers which the Second Vatican Council calls the hinges of the whole Office.[32]

72. An explanation should be given of how the Church recites as her own this daily prayer as truly "the voice of the bride addressing her bridegroom, the very prayer which Christ Himself together with His Body addresses to His Father."[33]

73. The devotion of the students to the psalms should be fostered through the lectures in exegesis given by the professor of Sacred Scripture and also by the titles and descriptive prayers contained in the book of the Liturgy of the Hours.[34]

74. From the decrees of the Second Vatican Council[35] there should be an explanation of the communitarian nature of the Divine Office, the general invitation of all the faithful to join in its recitation, and also the special mandate by which priests and others are deputed to this work of celebrating this marvelous song of praise.

75. It would be useful to mention something about the traditions of the different churches regarding the structure and celebration of the Office and also to give a brief historical description of the Roman Office and the changes effected in it from the sixteenth century to the present day.

Notes

1. Cf. Vatican Council II, *Decree on the Ministry and Life of Priests*, nn. 2, 5, 9, 12.
2. Cf. Vat. Coun. II, *The Constitution on the Sacred Liturgy*, n. 2.
3. Cf. ibid., n. 14.
4. Cf. nn. 15-17.
5. Cf. nn. 4, 8, 16, 19.
6. Cf. nn. 14, 52, 53, 79, 94, 98.
7. Cf. Vat. Coun. II, *Decree on the Training of Priests*, n. 1.
8. Cf. *The Basic Plan for Priestly Formation*, Preliminary Remarks, n. 2.
9. Cf. ibid., n. 7.
10. Cf. ibid., n. 3.
11. Cf. *Decree on the Training of Priests*, n. 12.
12. Cf. *The Constitution on the Sacred Liturgy*, nn. 5-8.
13. *The Constitution on the Sacred Liturgy*, n. 12.
14. Cf. *Decree on the Training of Priests*, n. 8.
15. Cf. *The Basic Plan for Priestly Formation*, n. 54.
16. Cf. *The Constitution on the Sacred Liturgy*, n. 13.
17. Cf. ibid., nn. 10-11; *The Basic Plan for Priestly Formation*, n. 53.
18. Cf. nn. 24, 90.
19. Cf. *The Basic Plan for Priestly Formation*, n. 54 f.
20. Cf. ibid., n. 53.
21. Cf. ibid., nn. 46 and 47.
22. Cf. *The Constitution on the Sacred Liturgy*, n. 28.
23. Cf. Sacred Congregation for Divine Worship, Instruction, *De missis pro coetibus particularibus*, 15 May 1969: AAS 61 (1969) 806 ff.
24. Cf. *The Constitution on the Liturgy*, n. 41.
25. Cf. *The Constitution on the Sacred Liturgy*, nn. 23 and 26.
26. Cf. n. 46 below.
27. Cf. *The Basic Plan for Priestly Formation*, n. 52.
28. Cf. *The Constitution on the Sacred Liturgy*, n. 21.
29. Cf. *The Constitution on the Sacred Liturgy*, n. 54.
30. Cf. Sacred Congregation of Rites, Instruction, *Eucharisticum mysterium*, 25 May 1967: AAS 59 (1967) 552-553, n. 20.
31. Cf. *The Basic Plan for Priestly Formation*, nn. 94, 97-99.
32. Cf. *Dogmatic Constitution on the Church*, n. 11; *Decree on the Up-to-date Renewal of Religious Life*, n. 6; *The Basic Plan for Priestly Formation*, n. 52; John Paul II, Encyclical, *Redemptor hominis*, 4 Mar. 1979: AAS 71 (1979) 310 ff.
33. Cf. *Degree on the Ministry and Life of Priests*, n. 13.
34. Cf. *The Basic Plan for Priestly Formation*, n. 52.
35. Cf. n. 10 above and n. 41 below.
36. Cf. Sacred Congregation of Rites, Instruction, *Musicam sacram*, published on 5 Mar. 1967: AAS 59 (1967) 300 ff. and also the *Institutiones generales Missalis Romani*.
37. Cf. Sacred Congregation of Rites, Instruction, *Eucharisticum mysterium*, published on 25 May 1967, n. 32: AAS 59 (1967) 558: "In ea enim forma signum eucharistici convivii perfectius elucet et clarius exprimitur voluntas qua novum et aeternum testamentum in sanguine Domini ratum habetur, necnon ratio inter convivium eucharisticum et convivium eschatologicum in regno Patris."
38. Cf. *Decree on the Ministry and Life of Priests*, n. 13; Paul VI, Encyclical, *Mysterium fidei*, 3 Sept. 1965: AAS 57 (1965) 761.
39. Cf. Paul VI, Encyclical, *Mysterium fidei*, 3 Sept. 1965: AAS 57 (1965) 770-773; and Sacred Congregation of Rites, Instruction, *Eucharisticum mysterium*, op. cit. mainly nn. 38 and 50. Also cf. the Roman Ritual, *De sacra communione et de cultu mysterii eucharistici extra Missam*, published in 1973 by the Vatican Polyglot Press. Also see the *Decree on the Ministry and Life of Priests*, n. 18.
40. Cf. Sacred Congregation of Rites, Instruction, *Eucharisticum mysterium*, nn. 62-66.
41. Cf. ibid., n. 53.
42. Cf. Paul VI, Apostolic Constitution, *Laudis canticum*, 1 Nov. 1970: AAS 63 (1971) 527 ff.
43. Cf. *Institutio generalis de liturgia horarum*, nn. 20, 22, 26-27.
44. *The Constitution on the Sacred Liturgy*, n. 89.
45. *Institutio generalis de liturgia horarum*, n. 28; cf. *Decree on the Ministry and Life of Priests*, n. 13.
46. Cf. *The Basic Plan for Priestly Formation*, n. 53.
47. Cf. *The Constitution on the Sacred Liturgy*, n. 106.
48. Cf. nn. 102-105, 108-111.
49. Cf. *The Basic Plan for Priestly Formation*, n. 55.
50. Roman Ritual . . ., *Rite of Penance*, Introduction, n. 7; John Paul II, Encyclical, *Redemptor hominis*, 4 Mar. 1979: AAS 71 (1979) 314 ff.
51. Cf. Roman Ritual . . ., *The Rite of Penance*, Introduction, n. 22.

52. Cf. Paul VI, Motu Proprio, *Ad pascendum*, 15 Aug. 1972, I and III: AAS 64 (1972) 538-539.
53. Cf. ibid., IV: AAS 64 (1972) 539.
54. Cf. ibid., II: AAS 64 (1972) 539.
55. Cf. ibid., Ic: AAS 64 (1972) 539.
56. Cf. *Ministeria quaedam*, V and VI: AAS 64 (1972) 532-533.
57. This first liturgical apprenticeship can be made a part of the "Introductory Course in the Mystery of Christ and the History of Salvation" which the *Decree on the Training of Priests*, n. 14, and *The Basic Plan for Priestly Formation*, n. 62, speak about.
58. Cf. Saint Prosper of Aquitane, *Indiculus*, ch. 8: Denzinger-Schönmetzer, n. 246.
59. Cf. *The Basic Plan for Priestly Formation*, n. 79; cf. *The Constitution on the Sacred Liturgy*, n. 21.
60. Cf. n. 44 above.
61. *The Constitution on the Sacred Liturgy*, n. 21.
62. Vat. Coun. II, *Decree on the Catholic Eastern Churches*, n. 1.
63. *The Constitution on the Sacred Liturgy*, n. 61.
64. Cf. ibid., n. 5.
65. Cf. ibid., nn. 6-7.
66. Cf. ibid., n. 33.
67. Cf. ibid., n. 7.
68. Cf. ibid., nn. 26-32, 41-42.
69. *The Basic Plan for Priestly Formation*, n. 80.
70. Cf. *The Constitution on the Sacred Liturgy*, n. 15; Sacred Congregation of Rites, *Instructio ad exsecutionem Constitutionis de sacra Liturgia recte ordinandam*, issued on 26 Sept. 1964, n. 11: AAS 66 (1964) 879.
71. Cf. *The Constitution on the Sacred Liturgy*, n. 24.
72. Ibid.
73. *The Constitution on the Sacred Liturgy*, n. 16: "Moreover, other professors while striving to expound the mystery of Christ and the history of salvation from the angle proper to each of their own subjects must nevertheless do so in a way which will clearly bring out the connection between their subjects and the liturgy, as also the unity which underlies all priestly training." Cf. *Decree on the Training of Priests*, n. 16; *The Basic Plan for Priestly Formation*, n. 90.
74. Cf. *The Constitution on the Sacred Liturgy*, nn. 112-121; Sacred Congregation of Rites, Instruction, *Musicam sacram*, 5 Mar. 1967: AAS 59 (1967) 300 ff.
75. *The Constitution on the Sacred Liturgy*, n. 129.
76. Cf. nn. 20-21 above.
77. Cf. *The Constitution on the Sacred Liturgy*, n. 13.
78. Cf. *The Basic Plan for Priestly Formation*, n. 85.
79. Cf. *Decree on the Training of Priests*, n. 22; *The Basic Plan for Priestly Formation*, nn. 100-101.

Appendix

1. N. 16; and also the *Decree on the Training of Priests*, n. 16.
2. Cf. *The Basic Plan for Priestly Formation*, n. 79.
3. Cf. *The Constitution on the Sacred Liturgy*, nn. 37-40.
4. N. 62.
5. Cf. *The Constitution on the Sacred Liturgy*, n. 7.
6. Cf. ibid., n. 6.
7. Cf. ibid., n. 61.
8. Cf. ibid., n. 5.
9. 1 Cor. 10.11.
10. Cf. *The Constitution on the Sacred Liturgy*, nn. 6-7.
11. Cf. ibid., n. 8.
12. Cf. ibid., nn. 7 and 33.
13. Cf. ibid., nn. 5-7.
14. Cf. ibid., nn. 9-13.
15. Cf. John Paul II, Encyclical, *Redemptor hominis*, 4 Mar. 1979: AAS 71 (1979) 311; Letter, to all the Priests of the Church, 8 Apr. 1979, in *L'Osservatore Romano*, 9-10 Apr. 1979.
16. Cf. *The Constitution on the Sacred Liturgy*, n. 33.
17. Cf. ibid., n. 24.
18. Ibid., n. 33.
19. Cf. Paul VI, Allocution, to the Liturgical Consilium, 14 Oct. 1968.
20. *The Constitution on the Sacred Liturgy*, n. 33.
21. Cf. *The Constitution on the Sacred Liturgy*, n. 56.
22. Cf. *Institutio generalis*, n. 55; Sacred Congregation for Divine Worship, Circular Letter on the Eucharistic prayers, 27 Apr. 1973.
23. Cf. Sacred Congregation of Rites, Instruction, 26 Sept. 1964, nn. 37-39.
24. Cf. Chapter VI.
25. Cf. *The Constitution on the Sacred Liturgy*, nn. 73-75.
26. Ibid., n. 106.
27. Cf. ibid.

28. Cf. ibid.

29. Cf. *The Constitution on the Sacred Liturgy*, n. 103.

30. Cf. ibid., n. 104.

31. Cf. ibid., n. 83.

32. Ibid., n. 89; *Institutio generalis*, nn. 37-54.

33. Cf. *The Constitution on the Sacred Liturgy*, n. 84; *Institutio generalis*, nn. 15-16.

34. Cf. *Institutio generalis*, nn. 100-135.

35. Cf. *The Constitution on the Sacred Liturgy*, nn. 84-100; *Decree on the Ministry and Life of Priests*, nn. 6 and 13; *Dogmatic Constitution on the Church*, n. 41; *Institutio generalis*, nn. 20-37.

On the Teaching of Canon Law to Those Preparing to Be Priests

Sacred Congregation for
Catholic Education

1975

On the Teaching of
Canon Law
to Those Preparing to Be Priests

Rome, April 2, 1975

Prot. N. 194/74

To local Ordinaries [including Hierarchs of the Eastern rites], to Major Religious Superiors, and to the Rectors of Major Seminaries and Scholasticates:

In recent years the study of Church Law has undergone, for various reasons, a lessening of interest, especially among ecclesiastical students. This has had a certain disorienting effect upon the Church.

The Sacred Congregation for Catholic Education, having been asked about this situation from many different sources and conscious as well of its responsibilities in the field of theological and priestly formation, feels that it has the duty to call the attention first of all of local Ordinaries [including Oriental rite Hierarchs] and Major Religious Superiors to the necessity for the study of Canon Law. Study of Church Law is needed in the preparation of all future shepherds of soul as well as to provide men for the Church who will be particularly qualified in the canonical-legal field, competent in interpreting and diligent in defending and enforcing both the Law as it now stands and the future Code.

It does not seem superfluous here to have a look at the difficulties that are commonly met today concerning this study, even among those students aspiring to be priests. These can be basically reduced to two problems: a) the supposed disuse of the present Code of Canon Law along with the lack of a new Code; and b) an imperfect and sometimes false interpretation of the ecclesiology of the Second Vatican Council.

The *first difficulty* vanishes when one remembers that the Code of Canon Law is not abrogated. Futhermore, it will be impossible to have prudent pastors of souls, teachers, ecclesiastical tribunal officials, scholars, and executives of Church Law if the men in these roles have not previously mastered juridico-historical skills in Canon Law and have not a firm grasp of the Law that is now in force. Also, consideration must be given to the fact that, after the recent Council, a great number of official documents have been issued touching upon the application of conciliar dispositions. Many of these documents have a profoundly juridical character. They need to be thoroughly taught and learned. It is clear that this large amount of material must be studied not only by canonical specialists, but also by all who are preparing to be priests and by students in Faculties of Theology and Canon Law.

The *second difficulty* is somewhat more subtle inasmuch as it touches on the basic reason for disinterest in canonical disciplines. It requires some reflection in order to comprehend how the ecclesiology of the

Second Vatican Council actually solicits the promotion of the "Law" in the Church.

I. The Function and the Role of Canon Law in the Church

The Ecumenical Council recently concluded, especially in the Dogmatic Constitution, *Lumen gentium [Dogmatic Constitution on the Church]*, sets forth a deeper understanding of the Church in her twofold aspect: charismatic and institutional. The outlook here is, above all, Christocentric, that is, the Church is seen as the continuation of the Incarnation and of the Easter Mystery. Among the co-essential elements of the Church, first place is given to the ontology of grace, the communication of the Divine Life. The sacramental and hierarchical structure of the Church serves as means to this end, namely to the communication of the Divine Life.

The Council, after emphasizing the sacramental structure of the Church, has underlined the fact that both the Society which is constituted by an organic hierarchy and the Mystical Body of Christ, the visible community and the supernatural entity, form only one complex reality, an element that is twofold, human and divine. The Church is compared by analogy to the mystery of the Incarnate Word: "Just as the assumed nature inseparably united to the Divine Word serves Him as a living instrument of salvation, so, in a similar way, does the communal structure of the Church serve Christ's Spirit, Who vivifies her by building up her Body" (*Lumen gentium*, n. 8); "(The Church) united on behalf of heavenly values and enriched by them . . . has been constituted and organized in the world as a Society by Christ and is equipped with those means which befit her as a visible and social unity. Thus the Church, at one and the same time a visible community and a spiritual community, goes forward together with humanity . . ." (*Gaudium et spes [Pastoral Constitution on the Church in the Modern World]*, n. 40).

This view of the Church makes it easy to see how, in her totality and in her unity, the Church is inseparably, although under different aspects, a community of grace and a hierarchical Society. One can also see that her structures are and must ever be profoundly determined in their nature by a supernatural point of view. Between the divine and human elements in the Church the kind of relationship must be maintained which was established by Christ Himself.

In the light of the conciliar ecclesiology, therefore, the place and the necessity of Canon Law appear more clearly. The "Law" acquires greater value because its function in the Church's life is better understood.

Certainly, a primacy must always be accorded to charity, "but love without a justice that is expressed in law cannot exist. Both of these (charity and justice) must go together and complete each other conjointly, coming forth as they do from one source which is God. For the rest, Saint Paul says, the kingdom of God is justice, peace, and joy in the Holy Spirit (Rom. 14.17)" (Pope Paul VI to the participants in the "Cursus renovationis canonicae pro iudicibus aliisque tribunalium administris" held at the Pontifical Gregorian University: AAS 66 [1974] 12).

While first place is assigned to the spirit and to the interior life, nevertheless belonging organically to the Body of the Church, the presence of Church authority, and submission to this authority always remain as irreplaceably necessary elements willed by the Divine Founder of the Catholic Church. In the Church "freedom and authority are not terms of opposition, but rather values complementing one another. Their mutual cooperation promotes the growth of the community and at the same time the capacity for initiative and enrichment of its single members. In calling attention to the principle of authority and to the necessity for a juridic order, nothing is being taken away from the value of freedom or from the esteem in which it ought to be held. This recalling to authority rather serves to stress the need for a secure and efficacious safeguarding of the goods which all have a right to possess, including the basic one of exercising freedom itself. Only a social system that is well ordered can guarantee liberty adequately. As a matter of fact, what would freedom be worth to an individual if it were not protected by wise and suitable norms?" (Pope Paul VI to the Judges of the Sacred Roman Rota, 29 Jan. 1970: AAS 62 [1970] 115).

Furthermore, the Second Vatican Council, particularly in the Dogmatic Constitution, *Lumen gentium,* provides for a better understanding of the role and function of Canon Law also in the local Church. The principle of subsidiarity demonstrates that, beyond the norms that are valid for the Universal Church, there could be norms particular to the local Churches as well.

II. The Need for
Studying Canon Law

The above considerations can help to shed more light upon the necessity of promoting canonical learning not only in a universal context, but also on every organizational level of the Church. Competent canonists are needed in teaching theology, in the structures of diocesan curial offices, in regional Church tribunals, in the governmental structure of Religious Families, etc. The Bishops' Conferences, various Synods, diocesan Ordinaries and Religious Superiors need to have people to rely on who are juridically prepared. Such men not only can help in canonically forming future priests and in correctly interpreting general laws, but they also can be useful in formulating, with appropriate competence, local laws, that is, they can help to draft these laws in the best way from the point of view of content and form. They can also assist in the application of these particular laws.

It is not useless to mention here that, following a period of experimentation as set out in the Motu Proprio *Ecclesiae Sanctae* of 1966, work is presently going on to revise particular laws (constitutions) and to study new structures in Religious Institutes.

What is being touched upon, consequently, as irreplaceable is the collaboration of canonists with the authorities of the Church in their function of governing her (which cannot be separated from their function of giving her "pastoral care"). The purposes of this collaboration are an orderly and peaceful development of the social life of the whole Christian Community, the promotion of the Church's apostolate, and the correct protection of the rights of everyone.

It flows from this that there is severe need for the proper preparation of canonists. Nobody can deny that even a priest who is directly occupied with the care of souls needs an adequate training in law to carry out suitably his pastoral ministry in the way a good shepherd should.

From all that has been asserted here, it follows that Bishops and Major Religious Superiors must become more conscious of their obligation to promote and encourage the study of Canon Law. Thus, it is to local Ordinaries [including Eastern rite Hierarchs] as well as to Superiors of Religious Families that the Sacred Congregation for Catholic Education, in accord with the Sacred Congregations for the Oriental Churches, for the Evangelization of Peoples, and for Religious and Secular Institutes, confides these reflections, certain that they, fully conscious of this problem in the Church and filled with their usual careful and customary pastoral attention, will make a decisive contribution to the hoped-for solution.

III. Practical Directives

In order to facilitate the concrete realization of what has been stated above, the following dispositions are enacted:

1. No Major Seminary or Scholasticate (and, *a fortiori* no Faculty, School, Institute, or Department of Theology) may be without a professorship of Canon Law (cf. *Ratio Fundamentalis Institutionis Sacerdotalis [The Basic Plan for Priestly Formation]*, n. 34). The teaching of Church Law must be ranked with the necessary disciplines.

2. In the lessons imparted to the students, they should be taught the general theological foundation of all Canon Law and also the theological basis of each particular juridical institute. In this general way, the spirit that animates the Law of the Church, a Law that is different from other laws, should be shown to the seminarians. They should also be taught to see the pastoral function of Canon Law.

3. Instruction in Church Law must be given in such a way that future priests will grasp the principles and norms of the Code, comprehending these principles and norms as ordered to the pastoral life. In the course of the canonical formation given, if and when needed, there should be no hesitation in teaching the history of various laws, linking them up with the theology of historical periods. Seminarians should also receive a sufficient amount of information about the civil laws of their proper country insofar as these might touch upon Canon Law. They should be taught especially those areas of competence where the jurisdiction of Church and State overlap. (Of course, this is even beyond Concordat Law which naturally should be taught to seminarians in those places where it exists.)

4. Given the exigencies of ecumenism and the obedience which is due to ecclesiastical legislation in this matter, instruction in Canon Law must treat the questions touching upon ecumenism which have juridical implications, especially those things involving the liturgical and sacramental fields.

5. So that their formation in Canon Law will not be only theoretical, seminarians should be introduced to canonical practices, both administrative and judicial, by learning and using appropriate and precise formularies, by viewing juridical procedures (with analysis of their various phases of development), etc. To accomplish this practical end, it would be very useful to organize visits of the seminarists to chancery offices and to diocesan and regional tribunals as well as to invite to the seminary judges, defenders of the bond, etc., to give some lectures.

6. More particularly, with regard to the method of teaching: a) The way that Canon Law is taught in seminaries ought to be different from the way it is done in Faculties or Schools of Canon Law, since there is a diversity of finality involved in these two different kinds of institutions. Left aside in seminaries, then, should be disputed questions and the deep study of monographic research, unless it is seen that some of this kind of material has an importance for the pastoral formation of the students; b) In the *Ratio institutionis sacerdotalis* for each single country (See the Decree *Optatum totius [Decree on the Training of Priests]*, n. 1) or for each Religious Family, there must be listed specifically the matters that are to be taught. With even more specific character the study program for each Major Seminary and Religious House of Studies must set out these canonical matters along with a list of the precise number of hours assigned to the study of Canon Law.

7. Those who teach Canon Law must keep in close contact with those teaching other theological disciplines so that, in a spirit of fraternal collaboration, they might make their contribution both to the planning and the implementation of the seminary's study program (which, in its turn, ought to be a carrying out of the "Ratio" of the National Episcopal Conference or Religious Family).

8. Local Ordinaries [including Eastern rite Hierarchs] and Major Religious Superiors should be certain that those who teach Canon Law themselves regularly take updating courses. Such courses for this purpose should be organized and offered not only by Canon Law Faculties or similar entities but also by the very Conference of Bishops and Major Religious Superiors.

9. In promoting the continuing education of the clergy, care should be taken to arrange that in the courses (even in various kinds of pastoral institutes) some treatment be imparted of canonical and legal questions.

10. Finally, local Ordinaries [including the Hierarchs of the Oriental rites] as well as Major Religious Superiors should not neglect to send some of their priests to study at the various Faculties of Canon Law so as to have available for their needs a suitable number of Canon Law teachers. Some other priests might be sent to specialize in aspects of law that need to be known in a particular Diocese or Religious Family. Also Latin rite Ordinaries in whose Dioceses there are faithful belonging to the Eastern Churches, whether Catholic or Orthodox, should take care that some of their priests attend specialized courses in Oriental Church Law or even attend the Faculty of Oriental Canon Law which exists at the Pontifical Oriental Institute in Rome.

Certain that your gracious and generous collaboration in these matters will make a contribution toward solving a troublesome problem in the Church, we assure you of our sentiments of respect and esteem. We are

Very truly yours in Christ Jesus,

Gabriel-Marie Cardinal Garrone

J. Schröffer,
Secretary

A Guide to
Formation in Priestly Celibacy

Sacred Congregation for Catholic
Education
1974

A Guide to Formation in Priestly Celibacy

A Presentation

The Holy Father in his Encyclical Letter *Sacerdotalis caelibatus* (n. 16) found an "opportunity for setting forth anew and in a way more suited to the men of our time the fundamental reasons for sacred celibacy." At the same time he was concerned that those who decide to become priests be suitably trained in this matter and, therefore, His Holiness willed that "apposite instructions be drawn up with the help of truly qualified men treating with all necessary detail the theme of chastity. They should be sent out as soon as possible to provide those who, within the Church, have the great responsibility of preparing future priests, with timely and competent assistance" (n. 61).

This present document is to be understood as an answer to this order of the Pope.

The late hour for this publication can be explained above all by the concern that — following the instructions of the Encyclical —many experts be consulted. Furthermore, given the seriousness of this matter, it was necessary to go through several editings of the text so that the observations that were received from many quarters might be taken into account. Also this lateness can be explained by a concern to submit the text to the Episcopal Conferences and then to look at it again in the light of their suggestions.

The up-to-date character and suitability of this document, given the fact that it does not enter into the theoretical discussion of celibacy, was not spoiled by this delay.

The spirit of this "orientation" is sufficiently emphasized in the text itself, in the title, and in the foreword. Education for celibacy is motivated and regulated, before everything else, by the love of Christ which is at the bottom of this commitment. Without a deep love of Christ, sacerdotal celibacy loses all meaning.

Still, the meaning and exercise of celibacy are conditioned by human elements which must absolutely be looked at. Indeed, it would be a serious mistake, today more than ever, not to take them into account.

The Sacred Congregation for Catholic Education, which, for reasons of competence, has undertaken the preparation of this document, is happy to offer it to Bishops and to those in charge of the formation of candidates for the priesthood. It is our hope that this contribution to their difficult work — in an area that is extremely delicate yet fundamental — will be favorably received, responsibly studied, and, with the help of God's grace, put to practical use for the good of the Church.

Rome, from the offices of the Sacred Congregation, Holy Thursday, April 11, 1974.

G.-M. Cardinal Garrone
Prefect
J. Schröffer
Secretary

Foreword

1. Nature and purposes of these guidelines

This document does not present "directives" so much as a general orientation about formation for priestly celibacy, perennially valid no matter what the social conditions might be, but which needs an educator's skill to be put into practice. This is a response to the desire expressed in the Encyclical Letter *On Priestly Celibacy* that appropriate instructions be issued to help those who have the serious responsibility of preparing future priests for a life of sacerdotal celibacy.[1]

These guidelines arise from the present-day conditions of the Church and have as their purpose the forming of candidates for the priesthood in sacred celibacy, freely accepted as a gift from the Holy Spirit. This, however, is not intended to derogate in any way from the different situation in the life and educational approach of the Eastern rites of the Church.

Holy celibacy is a "precious gift" which God freely gives to those whom He calls. Those so called, however, have the duty to foster the most favorable conditions so that this gift might bear its fruit.[2] It is the educator's task, therefore, to cultivate in his students an appreciation for the gift of celibacy, a disposition for its acceptance, a recognition of its presence, and its practice.

2. The specific reason for these guidelines

Sex education, whether as a preparation for marriage or for celibacy, is a difficult and delicate matter, especially in the social and cultural climate of today. This is particularly the case regarding complete formation of those who are preparing for a life consecrated to God. As the recent document of the 1971 Synod of Bishops emphasizes, "in today's world celibacy is threatened from all sides by special difficulties, which, nonetheless, priests have experienced in various other times through the centuries." Indeed, "it must be recognized that celibacy, as a gift from God, cannot be kept unless the candidate is properly prepared for it."[3]

Training men for a consecrated single life is an inescapable duty which falls upon all educators: the community of the family, of the parish, and of the seminary. In large measure, these bear the responsibility to form candidates for the priestly life.

The problem of formation for a celibate life is considered here mainly from the natural aspect in accordance with the principles of education. It must be constantly borne in mind, however, that such a problem cannot be resolved simply on the natural level, even with the best dispositions on the part of the candidates and the greatest care on the part of educators. Grace is a fundamental and necessary element in this formation — as Sacred Scripture emphatically states (Ps. 126; Mk. 4.26-29; 10.27; Lk. 1.37; Jn. 15.5; I Cor. 3.6; Gal. 5.22-23; Phil. 4.13). It is, moreover, equally essential to maintain the faithful observance of "the ascetical norms which have been tested by the experience of the Church and which are by no means less necessary in today's world."[4]

Young students must be convinced of the necessity of a very special asceticism in their lives, one that is far more demanding than what is required of the ordinary faithful and which is special to those aspiring to the priesthood.[5]

From their seminary days they must learn to recognize above everything the need to cultivate with all their hearts the grace which binds them to Christ, and seek to deepen their understanding of this mystery of sanctification. They must acquire an ever-increasing sense of the mystery of the Church and realize that otherwise their state of life will almost certainly begin to appear, even to them, inconsistent and absurd.[6]

3. Reasons for up-dating

The problem under discussion has always existed. But it has acquired a special urgency and a greater importance in our day on account of a number of factors and causes among which the following deserve special mention:

—in the unfolding of salvation history, priestly celibacy is lived in accordance with new ways of thinking. It must be a witness to salvation offered to men according to their present-day spiritual needs;

—the human sciences—education, psychology and sociology—are in a continual state of development; they are ever searching for new methods, theoretical and practical;[7]

—seminarians themselves manifest a new psychological sensitivity, tending to reject the bonds of convention and wanting to walk in the human order like other men. They extol freedom of choice and open-ended commitment to the ideal of the Gospel.

In the face of this, it is the duty of educators to be always up-to-date themselves. They must also read the signs of the times in the secular and Christian world of today.

All human institutions which proclaim lasting values and which are not merely expressions of some relative truth must undergo periodical up-dating. Priestly values, precisely because they are permanent and imperishable, must be considered in the context of a pilgrim Church moving towards the Risen Lord. These values must be expressed in a way that is suited to the present age. Indeed educators must proclaim a love for the eternal meaning of the priesthood, but in a manner adapted to our times.

4. Adaptation to the situation of the local Churches

Formation in celibacy must be adapted not only to differing civilizations and historical periods, but also to the conditions of the local Churches. Since these can differ considerably from one to another, their members' psychological and sociological outlooks will differ accordingly and they will bear witness to the Gospel in different ways. Seminary training must, therefore, reflect the kind of education which is suited to local Church life, always, of course, in accordance with the norms established by the Bishops' Conferences. Priestly celibacy, like the priesthood itself, is a consecration to God on behalf of the people whom priests are sent to serve.[8]

These guidelines, which apply to today, are not intended to usurp the responsibility of the local Church to educate its priests. On the contrary, local Churches have a duty to re-examine their spiritual needs, their ecclesiastical life-style and the efficiency of the local seminaries to provide a solid education and a witness in the world of today. Indeed, each single presbyterate ought to discover God's plan by studying present-day problems in the light of God's Word.[9]

5. Adaptation to the individual

This document presents a number of suggestions for training to a life of celibacy. Although it is divided into sections, it would be a mistake to suppose that they can be taken separately without reference to the development of the single theme of the whole work. It is also important to remember that despite great bio-psychological and socio-cultural differences among individual seminarians, the fact remains that problems about sex are substantially identical for all human beings, regardless of their state of life.

The universal character of this matter indicates that there can be some general guidelines for it. It is necessary, of course, that these guidelines be put into practice and when doing so that effort be made to find the best way to apply them to the needs of the individuals being trained. It is the individual who is to be directed towards and selected for the priesthood, and a constant search needs to be made for the best means of doing so even when one is dealing with a variety of persons with characteristics in the normal range of human behavior, but particularly when one also has the duty to recognize those who are truly atypical or possess deviant personalities.

These guidelines are written with the training of normal men in mind, since candidates for the priesthood ought to be normal. In cases of more or less abnormal persons, a more specialized kind of work has to be undertaken, but, of course, that kind of student must be clearly told that the prestly life is not for him.

Part I
The Meaning of Celibacy
in Contemporary Priestly Life

6. States of authentic Christian life

Matrimony and celibacy are two states of life which are authentically Christian. Both are ways of following the Christian vocation, a vocation that is expressed in its fulness in the totality of the Church.[10]

Celibacy for the kingdom of heaven (Mt. 19.12) is a gift that Jesus Christ gave to His Church. It is not a charism that belongs essentially or exclusively to the priesthood. It is not the unique vocation of a priest. It can be seen in the Church lived in a variety of ways by groups of persons called to the practice of the evangelical counsels.

Celibacy constitutes a sign which completes the total picture of the other evangelical counsels. Insofar as it is chosen for the kingdom of heaven, it implies fundamentally the Gospel virtues of poverty and obedience. In fact, these are intimately connected with one another, and complementary to each other, and they signify a life which is perfectly evangelical in nature.

I. Celibacy in the Life of the Church

7. Meaning of the sacrament of Holy Orders

The sacraments of Baptism and Holy Orders enable Christians to share, through the paschal mystery of our Lord, in the priesthood of Christ. Holy Orders is a participation in the "capital" function of Christ the Priest. It confers the ministerial priesthood which is different, not only in degree, but *in essence* from the common priesthood bestowed by Baptism.[11] It makes priests to be "ministers," that is, representatives of Christ as Head of the Church and partakers of the authority by which Christ Himself causes His Body to grow and sanctifies and governs It.[12]

Presbyters "by virtue of the unction of the Holy Spirit, are marked with a special character by which they resemble Christ the Priest."[13] As other Christs and with the love of Christ, they are sent to save the People of God; they are called to direct men, through the ecclesial community founded on God's Word and the Eucharist, to an ever deeper and larger life in the Spirit of Christ, which brings them progressively closer to living like those who have risen in the Lord, always witnessing to His resurrection.

8. The priesthood and the evangelical virtues

The evangelical virtues are at the same time both imperatives and graces of priestly consecration. A candidate for the priesthood, by his consecration to Christ the Priest, assumes also the Gospel's commitment connected with it, prolonging the very mission of Christ and bearing witness to Him by an evangelical life.

The ministerial priesthood demands a special kind of love, which is called pastoral charity, by which a priest endeavors to give his entire life for the salvation of others. The ministerial priesthood requires this so that love can be offered to others. The evangelical counsels are precisely to be of service in this pastoral charity.

If it is true that every Christian is consecrated to God in Christ and to the service of his brothers, it is no less true that consecration to God in the priesthood demands an even more generous and complete dedication. It is precisely in the practice of the evangelical virtues that one finds an adequate response to the ideal of priestly perfection.

9. Specific nature of celibacy

Celibacy has a clearly positive value in that it makes one totally available for the exercise of the priestly ministry. It means consecration to God with an undivided heart. It is a sign which testifies to an almost paradoxical love for the kingdom of heaven.

Speaking of celibacy, the Synod cited above states: "priestly celibacy harmonizes fully with the calling to follow Christ and also with the unconditioned response of the called, who assumes the duty of pastoral service." The same document underlines the fact that "if celibacy is lived in the spirit of the Gospel, in prayer, vigilance, poverty, joy, the shunning of honors and in fraternal love, it becomes a sign which cannot long remain hidden; on the contrary, it will effectively proclaim Christ to the human race, even in our time." [14]

Celibacy transcends the natural order. It involves a total personal commitment. It cannot be maintained except with God's grace. More than a mere law of the Church, celibacy must be understood as a "qualification" which receives added value because it is publicly offered in the presence of the whole Church. Celibacy is an offering, an oblation, a real and true sacrifice publicly given, not merely the giving up of the sacrament of Marriage, for the sake of the kingdom of heaven. "The seminarian must understand this form of life not as something imposed from without, but rather as an expression of his own free giving, which, in turn, is accepted and ratified by the Church in the person of the Bishop." [15]

10. Celibacy and the apostolate

It is a fact that Jesus Christ placed before all His disciples very strict requirements in order that they might be His followers. But He demanded even more from those whom He called to follow Him as His apostles. Peter, Andrew, James, and John left everything to follow Christ (Mk. 1.16-20). Jesus Himself praised celibacy embraced for the kingdom of heaven (Mt. 19.12). The Apostle Paul, who personally lived this evangelical radicalism, considered celibacy a divine gift through which, with an undivided heart, one could better dedicate oneself to the Lord.

Through celibacy, the availability of the ministers of the Church is reinforced, their power to bear witness is increased, and they preserve the freedom to oppose every oppression. The celibate shares wondrously in the "kenosis," which was the chosen way of Christ in His paschal mystery.

Implanted in priestly life, even though not absolutely necessary either for the priesthood or the exercise of the priesthood, celibacy is most fitting because it sheds luster on the nature of the priesthood and it enhances the work of the priesthood itself. It eminently actualizes that consecration to God, conformity to Christ, and dedication to the Church which are the characteristics proper to the priesthood. It expresses the ideal which the priestly character is supposed to convey.

11. Celibacy viewed eschatologically

Celibacy brings into focus and gives impetus to priestly love. It enables a priest to perfect this love and, in a very real way, to anticipate the future life of love with the Risen Christ to which the eyes of a priest must be turned.[16]

By celibacy, embraced and lived for the sake of the kingdom of heaven, a priest answers the call to imitate Christ. He anticipates the world to come, already present through faith and charity. Consecrated celibacy constitutes a sign of eschatological hope, a prophetic sign of that future reality when all men, united in Jesus by His Spirit, will live only to glorify the Father.

Every Christian has a duty to be united with the love of Christ and to bear witness to this love. Thus, every Christian life is permeated with an eschatological character, from martyrdom to the religious life, from the priesthood to the married state. Strictly speaking, celibacy does not, therefore, confer an eschatological character on the priesthood. The priest already has this in himself, just as Christians in all other states and vocations possess it in themselves, in their own special way.[17] But, priestly celibacy harmonizes with the eschatological aspect of the priesthood, and in certain ways, reinforces this aspect and enables the priest to be very fully immersed in the perfect love of the Risen Christ.[18]

II. Priestly Celibacy in Modern Life

12. Problems of priestly celibacy

Today the question is asked whether a priest could not remain a good priest without remaining celibate. However one looks at it — whether from the natural or the Christian point of view — the choice of priestly celibacy seems to imply the sacrifice of something good. For instance, it is possible to suppose that marriage, in certain places, might facilitate an interest in priestly vocations and even, for some priests, might mean a better balanced emotional life. However, such reasoning would not be able to take away the fact that celibacy, in itself, is more appropriate to the mission of the priest and that this sacrifice can be transformed into redemptive love.

There is no state of life or vocation that does not imply the sacrifice of something good. This is not only because vocations are lived by created human beings, but also because they come from an outpouring of the grace of the Easter mystery of our Lord.

Whether it is appropriate to link celibacy with the priestly office or to allow the two to be separated in some limited way is not simply a matter of

161

disciplinary choice. It is a pastoral decision of the Church's government based not solely on reasons of faith, nor on the results of sociological research, but on a mixture of both.[19] In any analysis of the values of the priesthood, these two elements are codetermining factors, that is, a living faith and a studied reflection on the experience of priests.

13. Reasons for celibacy

The Church has deep reasons for demanding celibacy of her priests. They are founded on the priest's imitation of Christ, on his role as representative of Christ, Head and Leader of the community, on his availability for service which is indispensable for the constant building up of the Church.[20] The Church is not prompted by reasons of "ritualistic purity" nor by the concept that only through celibacy is holiness possible.

Among the historical reasons adduced to justify a priest's celibacy there may be some which are no longer valid with the passing of time, but this should not cause the rejection of the connection between celibacy and the priesthood. This connection is a living reality in the Church. It is experience that is linked not so much to this or that argument as to the fundamental fact and reality of Christianity itself, which is the Person of Jesus Christ, at the same time Virgin and Priest.[21]

The Church has never set out celibacy as simply an external, impersonal element, but as an integral part of a priest's life and ministry. It always originates as a gift given from above, a gift which pervades a priestly vocation, becoming an essential and qualifying component of it.

14. Relationship between celibacy and the priesthood

The relationship between celibacy and the priesthood appears all the more clear as one considers the christological, ecclesiological, and eschatological aspects of celibacy. This is why the Second Vatican Council speaks of a manifold fitness (*multimodam convenientiam*) when referring to the consecration and mission of the priest within the framework of the mystery of Christ and the Church.[22] The 1971 Synod of Bishops reaffirmed the existing law of celibacy "by reason of the intimate and manifold fitness between the office of pastor and the celibate life."[23]

A priest is a representative of the Person of Christ. By his ordination he is deputed to build up the People of God through his ministry of Word and Eucharist and to show forth brotherly love in a unique and sacramental manner. Equally in both these ways he contributes to the cause of the building of the kingdom.

The invitation of Jesus to the apostles to leave everything enabled them to be more available for the coming of the kingdom. But it did more. It also offered them the opportunity of entering the apostolic communion where they could experience deep and enriching interpersonal relationships.

Priestly celibacy is a communion in the celibacy of Christ. The newness of the Catholic priesthood is an intimate sharing in the very newness of Christ.[24] It is a vision of faith that has consequently governed the development of arguments in favor of sacred celibacy in its christological, ecclesiological and eschatological meaning.[25]

A priest, who really shares in the one and only priesthood of our Redeemer, finds in Him "an immediate model and a supreme ideal."

Such a high ideal is obviously capable of inspiring heroism and even the most difficult undertakings.[26] Hence, there arises a desire in those exercising the priesthood to reproduce the same conditions and outlook of life as Christ experienced, in order to effect the closest possible imitation of Him.[27]

15. Modern difficulties with clerical celibacy

Priestly celibacy does not enjoy the esteem of modern society.[28] Ideas today are in a process of radical revision. Society does not stress the stability of vocation, but rather the opposite. This situation is especially responsible for producing a celibacy crisis. According to one opinion, celibacy interferes to some degree with the priest's mission to the poor and downtrodden. The priest should want to be part of the human struggle, without privileges, exemptions, or limitations. He should want to share in the basic human experiences (work, insecurity, housing, love, culture, recreation, etc.). Most of all he should feel strongly drawn to human love.

Apart from the fact that today it is not easily understood, priestly celibacy is especially difficult for those who feel their autonomy is restricted or their rights are being ignored. In these situations, a person instinctively seeks, as a form of compensation, a supplemental dose of affection, even though it is forbidden.

Indeed, a search for compensatory affection may be made easy by the simple fact that women, with whom a priest establishes a relationship by reason of his ministry, are inclined to confide in him precisely because his celibate state encourages trust. At times women might seek in him masculine support. Furthermore, in today's widely promiscuous environment, the problem is made more acute because of provocative fashions and the widespread use of the means of social communication (press, cinema, radio, television),[29] dangers to which the chastity of candidates for the priesthood is also exposed.

16. Presuppositions for training for celibacy

Looked at from today's point of view, the celibate must obviously be a person who is allowed to develop to human emotional maturity while preserving a life of continence as an expression of apostolic love.[30] Continence, when it is not inspired interiorly by apostolic love, is not the continence of the Gospel. For the consecrated person who has chosen celibacy in order to live and communicate ecclesial charity in the most heartfelt and unique way possible, continence without apostolic love is a contradiction.

A celibate person who is emotionally and spiritually mature does not feel himself hemmed in by canonical legislation extrinsic to his life. Nor does such a celibate see the necessary precautions, which he must always take, as something imposed on him from outside.

Celibate chastity is not some kind of taxation that has to be paid to the Lord, but rather a gift that one receives from His mercy. A person entering this state of life must not see himself so much taking on a burden as rather receiving a liberating grace.

The purpose of seminary formation is to form a responsible and mature man into a faithful and perfect priest. Modern conditions in the world, socially negative as they are, do not make becoming mature and responsible an easy task. This places an increasing personal burden on the candidates for the priesthood themselves, since the duty of fully bringing their vocations to realization rests basically on them.

Part II
Goals of Seminary Training

17. Threefold structure of seminary training

An enlightened training for priestly celibacy will take into account all the aims of seminary formation. Woven into this general pattern of formation will be the specific elements necessary for a training in priestly celibacy. It is precisely these elements which are the object of these guidelines.

Seminary training must have as its aim the forming of men into shepherds of souls, after the example of Our Lord Jesus Christ, Teacher, Priest, and Pastor.[31] Such an educational purpose presupposes and implies that the students will be at the same time formed as men, as Christians, and as priests.[32] Therefore, plans for priestly formation should have three aims, answering the need to form personalities which are integrally human, Christian, and priestly.

Educational planning must always show a full and balanced regard for the relationships among these three levels of formation, never giving more attention to one than to another, neither separating Christian formation from the human, nor priestly formation from Christian.

Essential distinctions, to be harmonized in unity, must be kept clear in this threefold structure of training — human, Christian, priestly. So too their complementarity and interaction: indeed, if training for manhood is a pre-condition for living a Christian life, grace is the dynamic force for the realization of a full humanity.

I. Formation in Human Maturity

18. Concept of human maturity

The specific matter of priestly celibacy is associated with the basic problem of the emotional maturity of the candidate. It is part of the wider and essential problem of psychological and moral maturity. Human maturity, as shown by a mature personality, is a harmony of elements and an integration of tendencies and values.

As modern psychologists correctly observe, maturity is not one single quality; it has many facets, each of which can be developed in various ways, and must be carefully considered when determining the criteria by which maturity is judged. Maturity, then, is a global condition qualified by a typical mode of being, and by a style which, while it escapes objective measurement, manifests itself in its own special way.

Maturity is a complex reality which cannot be easily or fully defined. In general, however, one can judge as mature a man who has brought to reality his vocation as a man; in other words, a person who has acquired a ready and habitual capacity to act freely; a man who has integrated his developed human potential with habits of virtue; a man who has acquired an easy and habitual emotional self-control by integrating his emotional drives and placing them at the service of his reason; a man who enjoys community living because of his willingness to give himself to serve others; one who devotes himself to his profession steadily and calmly; one whose conduct obviously follows his conscience; a man who uses freedom to explore, investigate, and develop; who can mold events and bring them to future fruition; finally, a man who has succeeded in bringing all his specifically human possibilities and potentialities to their due development.

19. Human maturity in education

Educating a man means promoting his "growth" in various primary areas (physical, intellectual, moral, social, religious) and in certain secondary areas (artistic training, vocational training — in the sense of professional education, training for a certain role in human society), but in such a way that the whole complex work of education be so coordinated as to result in a unified whole of the biopsycho-social personality of each person in his own proper and particular individuality.

What makes a man educated is his ability freely, consciously, and responsibly to will "the good" with the fullness of his psychological and spiritual personality. This is the kind of human maturity which the Council presented as the purpose of education. To be educated to this degree is the inalienable right of every man.[33] This is all the more applicable when one is dealing with the formation of students in a seminary. This is because God calls real men and if there are no men, there can be no call.[34]

Seminary formation must allow the candidates to develop as men in such a way that their religious training will not replace their human formation, but rather will gradually penetrate and purify it.

20. Human emotional maturity

Maturity must be acquired in all its aspects, including, naturally and above all, emotional maturity. Indeed the role of the emotions must be considered a fundamental element in the building of the personality. For this element is one of the major contributory processes in personality-integration, in the unfolding of emotional and sexual relationships, finding responsible fulfillment in work or a profession, and in cultivating friendly social contacts. Precisely because the emotions are looked at as basic to a person, emotional maturity can be held to be an indispensable requirement for the best functioning of a personality.

Considered as a part of psychic life, the emotions are variously understood: either as the complex of internal and external reactions to satisfaction, or as the ability to show feelings, or as the ability to love, or as the potential for a man to form attachments.

A well-integrated person knows how to make his reason rule his emotional nature, while the less adjusted a person is, the more his emotions will dominate his rational nature. Therefore, an educational program that aims to form a well-developed personality must above all help the students to acquire the ability to balance their emotions.

Deeply connected with the emotional factor is the problem of adaptation, which consists in facing one's problems calmly, accepting responsibility for them, and working out solutions for the difficulties encountered. Inability to adapt, on the other hand, carries with it a domination by negative emotions, hostility factors, a feeling of dependence, social inadequacy, and, at the same time, the pressure of unresolved problems.

21. Man's sexual maturity

When referring to emotions, the "sexual dimension" is especially important. The existence of a close link between emotions and sexuality and their interdependence in the wholeness of a personality cannot be denied, even though these two things are diversely understood. In order to talk about a person as mature, his sexual instinct must have overcome two immature tendencies, narcissism and homosexuality, and must have arrived at heterosexuality. This is the first step in sexual development, but a second step is also necessary, namely "love" must be seen as gift and not a form of selfishness.

The consequence of this development is sexual conduct on a level that can be properly called "human," whereby a person gains self-knowledge with self-esteem, and acquires a new concept of himself.

Sexuality must be considered as a determining factor in the maturing of the personality. Sexual maturity represents a vital step in the attainment of psychological adulthood. Hence, it is necessary to give a proper place to sex in the total picture of a personality in the process of formation.

A mature sexuality, with the characteristics here underlined, cannot be attained without conflict or without sacrifice and difficulty. A maturing person must always struggle because at every moment he has to make a choice: what need, that is, should he satisfy along one or other line of his potentialities.

22. Integrated sexuality

To adequately judge what is "well-adjusted sexuality" remains a most difficult problem. Sex should be looked on as one of the human values, not as something negative or frustrating for an individual's development. The intrinsic worth of sex must be seen and accepted as having a proper place in the scale of values, a place that is important as an "element of expression" and as "an integrating factor."

Sexual maturity entails not only accepting sex as part of the totality of human values, but also seeing it as giving a possibility for "offering," that is, a capacity for giving pure love, altruistic love. When such a capacity is sufficiently acquired, an individual becomes capable of spontaneous contacts, emotional self-control and commitment of his free will. This giving aspect of sex involves a feeling of being "one for another." Therefore, self-giving is not entirely separate from receiving. Sex introduces into life an aspect of relationship and, therefore, the capability of both giving and receiving, a disposition to accept love that is offered in order to let oneself be fully possessed.

23. Human self-control

In order to make full use of his potential, an individual must gain self-control. What he must control are the continuing changes that go on within him, as they go on in everyone, that is, his desires, impulses, thoughts and habits. Self-control really means self-discipline: imposing order on mental activity and external behavior in such a way as to produce joy, happiness, and well-being.

The dynamic structuring of a person is marked by conflicts and tensions. He only reaches his full maturity by a gradual and progressive combination of contrasting forces. There is tension between a person's ideals and his drives, and it is exactly in this area that self-control is required if one wants to attain stability, adaptation, and success.

Self-control does not mean a static quality or a colorless stability in one's social and personal behavior. One can note rather in the human psyche an impulse toward self-improvement. It is a tendency which, through conscious action and personal effort, goes beyond merely spontaneous development or simple biological growth. Men do not only grow and develop but, since they think and are free, they also make progress. This interior drive that generates progress is nothing other than the actualization of man's ever-fresh potentialities. The process of making a personality whole is done by repeatedly satisfying some drives and not satisfying others. In other words, it is brought about by channelling both the drives and activated potentialities of an individual. In man's very dynamism there is implicit a practice of asceticism — but one of an eminently positive kind.

II. Formation in Christian Maturity

24. The Christian dimension in education

Christian education — to which a Christian as a child of God through Baptism has a right — ought to help a person become mature not only in a human way, but principally in a Christian sense. Christian maturity comes about by a gradual growth in the faith, by the adoration of God as Father — especially through participation in the Liturgy — by growing more perfect in Christ, and by contributing to the building up of His Mystical Body.

A Christian, even though he is already living in Christ, can never feel adequately transformed in His Spirit. He has continually to complete the work of creation-redemption within himself as well as in other men and in all earthly things. Nevertheless, one can affirm that there does exist something called Christian maturity.

Seminary training, then, must bring maturity to the Christian personality of the students.[35] The education given in seminaries must primarily envisage unity, that is, what is common, and only after that, differentiation.[36] Following this line, the training in seminaries should not be completely different from the normal education of the Christian. In fact there are not two types of education, but one basic type. This is the education of a Christian man, which in a later stage is differentiated between the distinct vocation of the lay person and that of the priest.

25. Maturity as a requirement of the Christian life

Even prior to its requirement for the priestly state, human maturity is an elementary requirement for a Christian life. The history of priests who have defected is often that of men somehow lacking: of personalities without unity or integration where one would look in vain for maturity and balance.

Christianity certainly should be seen in its transcendental dimension, but it can also be viewed in its capacity for human advancement. This is especially true today when there is a particular sensitivity about everything that concerns that development of mankind.

Psychological and emotional maturity is the goal of the many social and personal efforts being made for the complete development of man. It can be viewed as the premise of a rich supernatural development. This is the kind of maturity that Saint Paul exhorted the Ephesians to acquire so that they might arrive at the dimension of "the perfect Man, fully mature with the fulness of Christ Himself" (Eph. 4.13).

The invitation to develop a fully human personality, although always present in the documents of the Magisterium, has recently taken on a particular urgency because of the progress of human science.[37]

26. Emotional maturity of the Christian

Emotional maturity receives enormous help from a Christian education. Indeed, insofar as the conditioning of the emotions is concerned, attention should not only be paid to natural factors, but also to the emotional repercussions resulting from sharing through Baptism in the very life of Jesus Christ, being under the influence of the gifts of the Holy Spirit, and hearing the Word of the Lord.

A Christian lives in the Catholic Church, which is essentially a "brotherhood and a union of love," "a communion of life, charity, and truth."[38] So sharing in the extensive social life of the Church, he finds ways wide open to love in his encounter with God and with his brothers.

Living in union with God and his neighbor, a Christian will find the kind of peace and security that endures, despite possible disturbances that come from struggling with his lower nature. The fact is that a Christian life does not eliminate the spontaneous reactions of nature, nor does it destroy neurotic inclinations acquired in childhood or deriving from a mistaken or an incomplete type of religious upbringing.

In this connection, it is good to mention that Christian training can help a great deal towards a man's positive acceptance of himself for what he really is, with his complex make-up, capacities, weaknesses, and lack of talent. Accepting oneself is an essential prerequisite for the personal maturing process at all levels. When, instead of such positive self-acceptance, there is the phenomenon called regression, one frequently sees abnormal behavior with compensatory overtones.

27. The sexual maturity of a Christian

Christian pedagogy, in accordance with God's revelation, has its own proper perspective and evaluation of sex. Christianity sees sex as part of God's creation, a reality which does not have the body alone as its object, but involves the entire human being, a reality which has a determining role in the way a man matures, both physically and morally and, therefore, in the way a man develops in his resemblance to God. It sees sex as a reality which is actualized in personal encounter. Precisely because of this mutual person to person encounter, human sexual relationships are fundamentally different from animal mating.

In Christian education, love means the ability to open one's self to the needs of one's neighbor. It means conquering every form of selfishness. It means self-giving to others for the sake of others. Finally, it means active participation in the life of the community. Christian education holds that this kind of authentic love, which is the vocation of all men, can be lived both in matrimony and in celibacy.

Sexual fulfillment achieved in marriage is not necessary for the emotional formation of the human personality; nor will marriage in itself bring about harmonious development of the emotions. On the other hand, man is capable of sublimating his sexuality and finding fulfillment in non-sexual emotional relationships.

The virtue that governs the use of sex is chastity. This is a natural virtue; but in a Christian it acquires a supernatural dimension. Christian chastity leads to sanctity inasmuch as it is part of the supernatural order. The workings of the theological virtues give a new and higher significance to chastity and even change its very nature.[39] It becomes a gift from God with a power that enables the will not so much to supress sexual desires as to integrate the sex drive into the entirety of the Christian personality.

28. Christian self-control

Dominating control over sensual passion is demanded for a real spiritual life in Christ (I Cor. 1.23). To suffer together with Jesus means to mortify one's passions for the purpose of being mystically united to Christ crucified. It is impossible to yield to concupiscence and at the same time lead the life of the Spirit (Rom. 8.13; I Cor. 6.9; Eph. 5.5).

The Easter mystery, which, through Baptism, is at the root of Christian life, expresses in the truest and most vital way the basic dynamism of Christian existence. This mystery effectively brings together the basic requirements of a person both as human and as Christian, namely a self-affirmation in the very act of giving oneself to God and to neighbor.

In the present plan of salvation, the paschal mystery offers a theological and psychological basis for the kind of asceticism which alone seems capable of re-establishing the original harmony in man. The way of life revealed to us by the Easter mystery inseparably unites "renunciation" of some kinds of conduct with genuine "offering" of self, just as the death and resurrection of Jesus are theologically inseparable.

Urged on by love, which grows stronger not weaker with effort, a Christian practices asceticism without even adverting to its existence, and renounces things often without realizing it, because he feels the powerful attraction of a higher ideal.

III. Formation in Priestly Maturity

29. Formation from a pastoral viewpoint

The fundamental feature of a priestly personality, according to the Second Vatican Council, is that of a shepherd of souls, on the model of Jesus Christ, Teacher, Priest, and Pastor.[40] As a pastor, the priest must possess the charism of supporting and guiding the Christian community; he must build up the Catholic Church.

The principal purpose of seminary formation is to train true pastors of souls.[41] Pastoral formation is not to be only a separate aspect or part of formation; it should characterize priestly formation as such; should inspire and penetrate everything that has to do with the personal formation of candidates for the priesthood.

Everything in seminary formation ought to converge with complete harmony towards the goal of forming priest-pastors.[42] This means that all the elements that make up the structure and function of a seminary have to be thought out and effectively geared toward the attainment of this goal. Educators have to keep before their eyes, besides their specialized activity and its aim, the pastoral formation of the seminarians.

30. Human and Christian maturity in priests

A priestly vocation demands human and Christian maturity so that the answer to this divine call may be an answer based on faith, and so that the seminarian may be able to understand the sense of a vocation from God, and realize what it demands.

The specific maturity of the priest must be sought in what differentiates him from the ordinary Christian, that is to say, in his unique relationship with the Body of Christ present in the Holy Eucharist as the principle and source of the ecclesial community of salvation and its saving mission. The priest is a "man of God taken from among men." His spirituality oscillates between these two poles, God and mankind. The relation between these two terms of reference is not one of alternatives, either God or men, but rather one of unity, both God and men. To be closely united to mankind a priest has to be deeply united with God first.

During his time of formation, a seminarist must pass from preadolescent immaturity to adult maturity, from an ordinary Christian life to a mature Christian life. In other words, he must learn to live, in a profoundly intense way, a life of faith, hope, and charity in Christ. Finally, he must advance to the level of priestly maturity, a more intimate sharing in the teaching, sanctifying, and ruling mission of Christ the Priest. Sacerdotal maturity includes and strengthens human and Christian maturity, but at the same time, it goes beyond these, permeating all the human and Christian elements in him, including, therefore, his emotional, sexual and active life.

31. Emotional maturity in the priest

The choice of priestly celibacy does not interfere with the normal development of a person's emotional life, but, on the contrary, it presupposes it. A celibate is called to express his ability to love in a special way. Having grown up in human and divine love, a priest can responsibly decide the manner in which he will, for his whole life, form his emotional relationships.

Celibacy chosen "for the sake of the kingdom of heaven" is the celibacy proper to the priest. It is falling in love. It is possible only for someone who has integrated it into his spiritual life. It is a matter of choosing exclusively, perpetually, and completely the unique and supreme love of Christ for the purpose of more deeply sharing His lot by the resplendent and heroic logic of a singular and unlimited love for Christ the Lord and for His Church.[43]

By virtue of his celibacy, a priest becomes more totally a man of God. He lets himself be more completely taken over by Christ, and lives only for Him. Virginal love invites him to possess God in a fuller way, to reflect Him and give Him to others in His fullness.

The love that a priest has for others must be essentially pastoral in aim. Externally it should be shown by a warmheartedness which is indispensable in disposing people to accept the spiritual support a priest offers them.

A priest can form true and profound friendships. These are particularly useful to his emotional development when they are fostered within the priestly fraternity.[44]

32. Sexual maturity in the priest

Celibacy, as a personal option made for a higher good, even one completely on the natural level, can result in a fully mature and integrated personality. This can be even more true when celibacy is chosen for the kingdom of heaven, as can be seen in the lives of many saints and faithful, who dedicate themselves in a celibate life to the service of God and man, promoting human and Christian progress.[45]

The exclusive nature of a candidate's choice of priestly celibacy, when he becomes a special possession of God, determines also his duties and particular dedication to the love of God in Christ. One who chooses virginity in virtue of his determination to give himself exclusively to sharing in the priesthood of Christ is obliged to grow in love of God and his neighbor. If he does not progress in his love, he is not following his vocation.

There is something sublime in the qualities roused in a man's heart by natural fatherhood: an altruistic spirit, the assumption of heavy responsibilities, a capacity for love and a dedication enough to make any sacrifice, daily bearing of life's burdens and difficulties, prudent care for the future, etc. However, all this is equally true of spiritual paternity. Moreover, spiritual fatherhood, not being confined to the natural order, is even more responsible and heroic.

For this reason, celibacy is not for everyone. Celibacy requires a special vocation from the Lord. Throughout the whole of life, it is never without risk and danger, since something can always occur to take the heart out of a man's universal and pastoral fatherhood and his exclusive dedication to Christ.

33. Self-control of the priest

Continuous self-control implies constant effort. This is necessary not only to acquire emotional maturity, but also for persevering in it. Ongoing self-control impedes regression from emotional adulthood once this is attained. It is an irreplaceable factor in the practice of human, Christian, and priestly chastity, which should always be able to check any new or unforeseen resurgence of emotional stimulation.[46]

In the Christian view of continuous and progressive self-control, priestly celibacy appears as a lifelong offering to our Lord. To be consecrated in holy celibacy is not simply a single action made once at ordination. It is rather something that has to be renewed again and again, in the constant vigilance a priest must exercise when faced with human attraction and the emotions and passion of affection and love.

Just as with natural human love, the fullness of love which is involved in celibacy requires the daily practice of glad self-renunciation. This is the only way to conquer the difficulties that, with the passage of time, can come from boredom or from the weakness of the flesh.

A priest should always find an incentive for self-control in the thought that the personal sacrifice demanded by his celibacy is serving the whole Church. His sacrifice underlines the spiritual dimension that must mark all love worthy of the name and it merits grace for Christian families. [47]

Part III
Guidelines for Seminary Formation

34. Difficulties in formation

Training for a chaste life touches directly the sensitivity and feelings of the young and could disturb them psychologically. They can be extremely vivid and unruly. This is not unusual, considering the age we are dealing with, and one can expect the most surprising reactions. For example, in trying to forestall future deviation one could easily provoke it; exaggerating the importance of light developmental aberrations could give rise to obsessive complications and thus interfere with the elimination of these aberrations altogether.

What is being dealt with here is the training of an instinct which, more than any other, is subject to difficulty because of the intrusion of many psychological factors. Difficulty also comes simply from the range of differences that exist among individuals of the same sex. If sex education is hard when one is undertaking normal marriage preparation, how much more difficult it is when one undertakes to educate someone for a life of priestly celibacy, which is a supernatural mystery and the fruit of divine grace!

There is really no adequate or definitive solution to a problem of this sort which remains always open-ended. There cannot be a final solution because every solution has to depend upon the psychological and physical development of human life, on the rapid environmental and sociological changes in society, and on frequently unforeseeable circumstances. Among these latter, one would have to include supernatural aid which is not under human control and which depends upon God's generosity, even though He is disposed to grant even more than one might request.

I. Criteria to Be Followed by the Educator

35. Awareness of the complexity of the problem

The educator must be aware of the fact that the psychic, moral, and religious life of the future adult and future priest he is dealing with will greatly depend on his understanding and his manner of dealing with and solving the problems of forming the student in chastity. Hence, he must use the greatest tact in treating sexual and emotional problems in students' formative years.

The educator must thoroughly understand the physiological, psychological, pedagogical, moral, and ascetical complexity of celibacy and chastity. The aim of priestly celibacy is the attainment of a chastity which is valued, loved, guarded, solidly possessed and thoroughly tested, a chastity that not only resists the blows which can ever increase in intensity, but which is an inspiration for the apostolate.

Therefore, the kind of training in chastity that is given in seminaries must be enlightened, that is, based on clear teaching, avoiding any reticence or insincerity. It must be positive, which is to say, it must be directed towards the acquisition of a mature attitude to sex as a correct and happy manner of loving, and not simply as something which is to be avoided as sinful. At the same time, it must also be complete, organic, and personalized, that is, adapted to each individual in his concrete yet different personal development. [48]

Candidates for the priesthood will be able to overcome the difficulties that are peculiar to celibacy provided the proper conditions are maintained. This means they must achieve a natural equilibrium through the effect of an ordered network of human relationships. They must grow in the spiritual life through prayer, self-denial, burning love for God and neighbor, and the other normal aids to the spiritual life. They should have warm and brotherly contacts with their Bishop and other priests, and pastoral structures should be adapted to accomplish this. They should, finally, experience a sense of confidence through the spirit of cooperation which permeates the whole ecclesial community. [49]

36. Normal and abnormal situations

In general, the approach to sex must be based on simplicity, normality, and realism. The general character of a person should be borne in mind and not only his isolated or unusual actions. In this area, as in others, repressive methods often have the effect of reinforcing, rather than lessening, bad habits and sexual mistakes.

The educator should remember that the way to train young men in matters of sex is to appeal to their noblest sentiments, leading them to understand that to reach maturity they have to acquire a strong character, a well-integrated personality, and a knowledge of how to practice self-control. It is even proper to appeal to their pride, showing them that some kinds of sexual misbehavior are an indication of faulty personality development and a residual infantilism. They should be instructed that such activity is inconsistent in a person who intends to live a life marked by high ideals and true human dignity.

An educator, however, cannot remain indifferent to sexual misbehavior in the formative years of a student. He must intervene to solve the problem in a positive way and not simply dismiss the matter as an isolated incident. He must assist the student to raise his whole personality to a higher and more integrated outlook, using the means that naturally arise in the circumstances.

There are many people today who suffer from real forms of sexual neurosis. These neuroses have their basis in natural predispositions, but they raise their troubled heads because of the stimulation given them by conditions in modern life. It is the modern environment, in fact, that provides men with ample opportunities to act out their fantasies. This kind of problem arises especially during puberty. However, it is a well-known fact that enlightened direction can notably facilitate the overcoming of this kind of crisis and securely assure the integral development of the personality of the young.

37. Human and spiritual direction

A young person at the beginning of his life cannot be left alone; he needs direction, stability of judgment, and firmness of will. The problem, however, is that this same young man is often unstable and resists help.

The counsellor must be extremely careful and discreet because any suggestion that is given which does not respond to a real need could be rejected as an intrusion or a violation of personal privacy. He must be like a friend who simply stands by to offer comfort in difficult moments, counsel in times of doubt or indecision, help in moments of moral danger, without ever being too heavy with either words or presence.

A young man wants to know about sex because he considers it part of his life. Reticence on the matter will simply have the effect of further arousing his curiosity. What must be done is to guide him to regard sexual questions as a serious matter and to have a deep respect for the human person and its incomparable value, both in himself and in others.

In dealing with misconduct and with all sexual problems, educators should take the precautions of not frightening him since fear foments anxiety; not employing coercion since this leads to false or abnormal conduct; never showing ridicule when treating of anything that has been confided by a young man or else the embarrassment will cause him to retire permanently into his shell; and never dramatizing the issue in such a way as to discourage.

38. Testing vocations

An important element in training for a life of celibacy is to help the individual himself to evaluate his own inclinations and to judge his own ability to overcome possible difficulties connected with celibate living. If he becomes aware that he is not endowed with the necessary qualities, he should be helped to make a different vocational choice with a good conscience, with courage, and with conviction.[50]

Errors in discerning vocations are not rare, and in all too many cases psychological defects, sometimes of a pathological kind, reveal themselves only after ordination to the priesthood. Detecting defects earlier would help avoid many tragic experiences.

Selecting candidates for the priestly life is a very difficult task. All those engaged in training students for the priesthood need to take this office very seriously and prepare themselves accordingly.[51] Selection should be done in accordance with modern, psychological diagnosis without losing sight of supernatural factors and of the complexities of human influences on an individual.

Educators, who themselves are well-prepared for their work, should be able to verify the authenticity of vocations in normal individuals by using the usual criteria for vocational discernment. However, when in doubt or when seminary superiors feel that a student needs particular help to decide his vocation, special remedies may be employed, such as a psychological testing before the candidate begins his theological course. Maybe even a specialized psychotherapeutic examination will be found advisable or he may be advised to interrupt his ecclesiastical studies in order to work for a time in some other profession.

39. Sex education as a problem for educators

The purpose of sex education is to bring a person's knowledge of sexual matters up to a par with his knowledge of other matters, and to integrate it into the whole process of education. However, even when confronted with ignorance or mistaken notions about sex, one has to avoid an over-emphasis in which sex is made to appear the sole, or the most important, element of human motivation.

Sex education needs to follow the line of personal development. It should therefore be adapted to the age, sex, and environment of the subject by means of formation "which is both positive and prudent."[52]

Among all the areas in the field of education, sex education today seems to be the one fraught with most problems. It is not simply a question of uncertainties and difficulties over method, but the personality of the educator and his own past emotions about the subject enter the picture as well. The educator has to try to understand the inner workings of his own sexual nature, often operating at an unconscious level, without erroneously assuming that this aspect of his life is simply a matter of irrational impulse.

Without careful preparation anyone who undertakes this task, one of the most difficult in the educational field, cannot possibly produce any positive results. This preparation entails a knowledge of juvenile development and an awareness of the family conditions and relationships of the students. He must also acquire a vocabulary that is appropriate to the subject, and adhere to a correct standard of values.

Above all, those who are entrusted with sex education have to be themselves persons who are sexually mature and balanced. Even more than a knowledge of method and subject matter, in sex education it is the personality of the educator that really counts. It is the way he practices what he preaches and the style of life he adopts and lives that matter. Knowledge, correct advice, and solicitude for the student are important in the teacher, but even more important is the educator's own personal conduct.

II. Guidelines for Sex Education

40. Sex education as a formative process

Teachers should remember that sex education cannot be treated apart from the whole process of moral formation and training. Sex education must be actively directed to the individual, imparted in an environment that is protective and formative, and it must be based on mutual trust between student and teacher.

From the standpoint of an educator's responsibility, it is just as wrong to ignore sex as it is to treat it in isolation. Human sexuality is a fact that has to be recognised, and it has to be understood in relation to the needs of the whole person. Similarly the only method of imparting sex education is to integrate it into the general program of education of the whole person. It is part of the continuing process of the development of the total human personality.

Sex education therefore must be integrated into the general formation of the seminarian. A chaste life is a work of art and implies a parallel development of the whole person. Purity cannot be mastered by concentrating on it as a fixed and isolated idea, but only by including it in a wider view of life that includes justice and charity, elements absolutely necessary to give any life meaning and value. Purity, then, must be seen as a part of what a complete human being is.

41. Personalized sex education

The educator should lead candidates for the priesthood to the "discovery" of making a fundamental option in their lives, guiding and helping them to see chastity as something good, to see it as something good *for them,* helping them to transform this option into action, and finally, assisting them to persevere in its practice in such a way that its maintenance becomes second nature and a normal characteristic of their lives.

It is the good more than the evil, the virtue rather than the vice, which should be put before the seminarian in an effort to strengthen his emotions and will. It is the positive strengths and values that will help him in time of disturbance. Besides ethical and religious considerations, it is right to teach that sex provides a reservoir of virile qualities for the body, spirit, and heart.

To accomplish its essential moral purpose, which is so intimately linked to the human personality, sex education should be imparted individually. It should aim to help each individual person resolve his own problems. To carry out such a personalized type of education fruitfully, the educator has to be able to detect the needs and resources of each individual student so that he might apportion, according to the capacity and the necessity of each individual, the required natural and supernatural means of aid.

42. The environmental factor in sex education

A personal relationship between teacher and pupil and individualized direction are not enough. For purposes of formation the whole living environment requires wise organization. This means both the elimination, as far as possible, of harmful influences and training students to react properly to any adverse influences which the environment might provoke.[53]

The environment should be lively, full of activity, yet serene, with a high moral tone and full of healthy friendship. It ought to be such as to facilitate the transfer of the seminarians' emotional energies and interests to what is good so as to avoid focusing them on dangerous things.

An important element in the creation of good environment is the community spirit of the students. It is impossible to create the ideal environment for the practice of purity without forming an uplifting community spirit based on mutual respect between students and the cultivation in them of a deep appreciation of virtue.

However, life in a seminary is temporary and intermittent. Therefore, seminarians have to be prepared to live, with fidelity and fulfillment, a life outside the seminary "in a world which tends to exile man from himself and compromise both his spiritual unity and his union with God."[54]

43. Formational dialogue and sex education

A young person needs a friend in whom he can confide and trust. Without the help of a wise and friendly guide, normal anxieties will become increasingly complicated, leading to discouragement and failure. Nevertheless, the teacher-friend cannot give guidance unless he knows the student well, which means the student must confide in him with candor. This kind of mutual and confidential relationship can only come about if the educator places himself at the disposal of the students and patiently waits for time, good will, and grace to work.

While respecting the freedom that has to exist in the area of spiritual direction, every seminary educator should exhort and seek to convince the students about the need to have a spiritual guide in whom they can confide with frankness and trust. Above all, the educator should endeavor to make himself the sort of person who deserves their esteem and confidence.

When an educator has created an atmosphere of mutual trust, he will be in a position to conduct a work of discreet, progressive, and personalized instruction which is an important part of training in chastity. Done skillfully, this will also have the effect of consolidating the students' trust and affection for the educator himself.

44. Personal and progressive sex education

Sex education includes not only intellectual instruction but also moral training. As such it is a necessary duty, not only because it provides for the solution of sexual difficulties, but also because it offers defensive tools to those who would otherwise be defenseless in the face of personal failures or harmful experiences which must be avoided.[55]

The educator's task is not only to teach, but, above all, to help form consciences. He has to train the students to make decisions that are free yet correct, because these alone are what should govern their affective lives.

Nevertheless, sex education must be gradual. One has to measure the approach by the age of the person one is dealing with, by the degree of positive intervention required, by the character and state of life of each individual. The first and natural setting for this kind of education is the family. Hence the primary role belongs to parents. The role of the teacher is merely to supplement family deficiency.[56]

45. Modesty and sex education

An essential concomitant of human sensitiveness—no matter how this is expressed—should be modesty. This may be described as a spontaneous reaction against anything that would unmask our unadorned instincts. When someone acts with conscious modesty, he tries to avoid undesirable circumstances and those thoughts and deeds which demean the spiritual dignity of his personality. It is the means to insure that love is present in a person's sex life and that sex does not upset that balance of character which chastity promotes.

Modesty and a higher moral life go together. From the sexual point of view, modesty is the voice of conscience, an interior recoiling from any unnatural behavior. As such, a sense of modesty is a protection of one's personality and has a particular pedagogical value. It is impossible to train someone in chastity without at the same time developing in him a sense of modesty.

However, excessively rigid training in this field could multiply problems and increase anxiety in the young. The aim should be to free one from unwarranted and foolish exaggeration which only serves to increase the influence of temptation and distracts one from living a calm and normal life.

Education in modesty should be indirect and yet at the same time positive. Young people tend to be hero-worshippers and particularly attractive models of virtue should be presented to them. Their aesthetic sense must be developed too, an appreciation of beauty in nature, art, and the moral life. In addition they need to be helped to formulate for themselves a code of spiritual values capable of attainment with faith and drive.

46. Sex education and love

Sexual maturity goes hand in hand with emotional maturity. Education for chastity means, in large part, educating the heart. It is a problem of love.

Human love is not perfect from the start. It has to develop and become perfect through a long process of growth and purification. In a child, it is sense-orientated, egoistic, and self-indulgent. In an adult, it should become spiritual, unselfish, altruistic, self-sacrificing, an image of the kind of love God has for us. A seminarian needs help to walk, not run, on this path of development uninterruptedly.

Particular mention needs to be made at this juncture of the necessity to develop the students' own enormous reserves of affection. Ideals ought to be urged upon them — ideals of truth, beauty, justice, goodness, purity, generosity, self-giving and heroism. They also should be helped to form real and uplifting friendships.

They should not only be made aware of any ambiguous elements present in some of their friendships, but also be reminded of their duty to show the love they have for their friends to everyone. The unsubstantial sentimentality of youth has to be sobered down, purified, and regulated. They need to anchor their affections in both reason and faith so that, in full awareness, they will demonstrate their love with uprightness and set their sights on the true goals, both natural and supernatural, of love.[57]

III. Guidelines for Training in Celibacy

47. Truth and authenticity of celibacy

Celibacy, which is a value, a grace, a charism, has to be presented in its true light if it is to be appreciated, chosen, and genuinely lived. Its presentation, therefore, must be calm and serene, confronting the prejudices and objections currently brought against it. This is one of the first tasks of the educator.

In his seminary training a candidate for the priesthood must be helped to realize the role of sex in marriage. Being consecrated in a celibate life presupposes that one knows what conjugal love entails. But also seminary formation must help a student discover the meaning and role that sex plays in a state of celibacy consecrated to God in Christ.[58] It is not a question of suppressing, but of sublimating, love and sexuality. In this area of formation more than simple instruction is needed. Rather, real training will form the candidates into men who love with charity all human beings "with the tenderness of Christ."[59]

Priestly celibacy is not simply to be identified with remaining unmarried or with sexual continence. It is a renunciation of three natural tendencies: genital function, conjugal love, and natural fatherhood, made "for the love of the kingdom of heaven." To be a genuine and sincere witness to religious values, it can never be a negation of, or a flight from, sex, but rather it must be the sublimation of sexuality.

48. Interior working of the life of celibacy

While the motives for choosing celibacy are particularly personal to each candidate, through his developing relationship with God and others these motives are subject to a process of growth. It is here that attention should be paid more than in trying to evaluate the initial motivation.

The importance of growth in the right psychological attitude towards celibacy on the part of the seminary student has to be kept in mind. An ideally balanced life is not reached all at once, neither in marriage nor in celibacy.[60]

An inclination towards marriage and family life, which makes their renunciation painful, ought not to be regarded necessarily as a contradiction to a celibate vocation. Even if the pain is lifelong, this does not prejudice the genuineness of the call to virginity, provided one can live exclusively for God with full and free assent of the will. Celibacy is a call from God that can well include the continuing sacrifice of a strong propensity for marriage.

49. Relationships and solitude

Voluntary celibacy makes sense when it is viewed in a context of relationships with others lived in a fraternal community where one can "reach" others without "having" them, that is, when it is an exercise in non-possessiveness. It is a sign of celibacy rightly assumed when one can create and maintain worthwhile interpersonal relationships while experiencing the presence of friends even in their absence, refusing to impose oneself on them, and showing that need of them is limited. Hence, it can be said that celibacy is also an acceptance of "solitude."[61]

There is a mysterious kind of solitude that forms an essential element of the human condition. It is always in solitude that a person discovers his own identity and potential. It is there that the great decisions of life are made. The solitude of priestly celibacy is charged with such values.

The priest, who is destined to lead men to God through Christ, will accomplish this only if he radiates the goodness and love of God in himself. In harmony, therefore, with his state of life, a priest must always be ready to put his own interests in second place and subordinate the satisfying of his own tendencies, to the love of his neighbor to which he is dedicated by reason of his priesthood.

50. Training conditions for a celibate life

In accordance with the principle already established that sex education must be part of the total formation of the person, it is essential to seminarists to grow in all the natural and supernatural virtues.[62] Students should be shown how all virtues are organically linked together through charity, which is at the root of all virtuous living. They must be convinced of the need to give themselves constantly and totally to the attainment of perfect charity, "the bond of perfection" (Col. 3.14).

As they gradually deepen their convictions and grow in their sense of responsibility towards their vocation, seminarists must be guided towards the acquisition of an active zeal for the goal of living in perfect chastity without compromise or concession, in the full realization that, even from a human point of view, they are not inferior to others.

Every candidate for the priesthood must know himself thoroughly, his physical, psychological, moral, religious, and emotional dispositions, so that he can answer the call of God with a mature, responsible, and considered decision.[63] He must give himself completely and continuously to Christ, the Eternal High Priest, and to His Church with full freedom of will.[64] Every seminarian must be able and willing to keep the commandments of God and to observe the discipline of the Church.[65]

51. Training for true love in celibacy

Far from implying lack of concern for sexual relationship, a mature acceptance of celibacy demands that students be trained to take cognizance of its importance and place among the rest of the qualities which make for a fully integrated personality. This involves training the heart, affections, and sentiments. It means being open to others. In a word, it means a progressive and controlled development of one's sexual and emotional powers. It is not sufficient to live a material celibacy. One must love others in a priestly fashion. It would be a serious contradiction of an ecclesiastical vocation if a candidate for the priesthood were to be selfish, closed to affection, and worried only about himself and his own well-being. On the other hand, an excessively affectionate nature, an over-sympathetic temperament, and an inclination to emotional attachments are not suitable for a celibate life either.

Celibacy is a vocation to a special kind of love. It must be lived in a climate of friendship and, above all else, in friendship with God in Christ.[66] The priest must live a life of love which can only be found in God as its highest source. He must exercise this life in imitation of Christ, extending it to all without exception and with that sense of responsibility which is an indication of a mature personality.

52. Relationship between religious fervor and chastity

A student's fidelity to his chosen state in life demands day-to-day renewal. Unless he is guided to base himself on well-grounded motives and to will to live a life of genuine chastity, he will inevitably wallow in a sort of no-man's land without either human or God-given joy.

In view of the profound relationship between religious fervour and chastity and because celibacy has a specifically sacred and Christian meaning, it is essential that the devotional formation imparted in the seminary should be improved and deepened.[67] Students must be in close touch with the sources of a genuine spiritual life, which is the only thing capable of giving a solid foundation to the observance of sacred virginity.[66]

Celibacy is a lifelong offering, in which one makes the sacrifices which changing situations in life demand and enjoys a life enriched by dimensions as wide as the Church. One must always measure the sincerity and generosity of one's first self-offering, becoming slowly and surely more like to Jesus Christ in the depths of one's being. It is a permanent state of abandonment of trust in the help of the Holy Spirit. It symbolizes and witnesses to the "eternal priesthood" of Jesus Christ before all the People of God.

IV. Training in Priestly Asceticism

53. The need for asceticism

Formation for the priesthood, and more precisely a celibate priesthood, requires an asceticism which is superior to that required by the rest of the faithful and which is special to those aspiring to be priests. Although severe, it must not overwhelm, and is actually the considered and assiduous practice of all those special virtues which make a man a priest.[69] It should be an asceticism which is both "interiorly and exteriorly manly"[70] enabling the priest to stay faithful to his priestly commitments[71] and to have a guarantee of success in his work.[72]

The attainment of Christian sanctity demands an ascesis of self-denial, which is an ascesis of liberation. According to the teaching of the Second Vatican Council, self-denial is the exercise of a kingly power and is necessary to effect the reign of love.[73] Love and self-denial complement each other, since self-denial frees man and makes room for love; love, in turn, induces one to self-denial.

A candidate for the priesthood is the recipient of the "grace of vocation" which brings him the precious gift of a chaste life.[74] As he becomes more conscious of this gift, he should be prompted to respond to it with enormous gratitude to God and to correspond to this grace with the utmost freedom and generosity.[75] Asceticism is the decisive answer to this gift, an answer which a seminarist should want to make with the whole of his life.

54. Characteristics of priestly asceticism

Mortification which is a part of every Christian and of every human life is even more relevant to the priestly life. In fact, the priestly activity of Christ, in its full biblical meaning, makes no sense at all unless one remembers that Christ is "Priest and Victim," and that He sacrificed Himself upon the altar of the Cross for the love of mankind, a sacrifice that anticipated the Mass, where He renews this self-immolation in an unbloody manner on our altars.

Since this constitutes the apex of the priestly mission of Jesus, one cannot imagine it could be otherwise in the lives and mission of those called to participate in His priesthood, to assume the very Person of Christ, and to continue His work. The holiness of the priest, and consequently his spirituality, must clearly be centered on the fact that he, too, must be priest and victim, in union with Christ, High Priest and Spotless Victim.

While it underscores the necessity of a strong practice of asceticism and is directed at removing every obstacle to the priestly ministry, this truth is a positive invitation to follow the royal road of the cross. It is an invitation to "bear in our bodies the suffering of Christ, in order that the life of Christ might be made manifest in us" (2 Cor. 4.10). It is a positive invitation to accept, from the bottom of one's heart, the implications of what it means to be consecrated as a priest. [76]

This is the meaning of the connection, clearly emphasized by the Council, between the main function of the priest and his obligation to imitate what he handles. [77]

This emphasis given to priestly asceticism should by no means neglect the fact that marriage also is a state of life that is sacrificial and which can involve both mortification and the sacrifice of worldly desires.

55. Ascetic commitment in seminary life

In the light of today's climate of general rejection of mortification, one cannot too strongly insist that seminarians be thoroughly convinced that without a committed asceticism any maturity, be it human, Christian, or priestly is impossible. They must appreciate that it is an indispensable condition for growing in participation in the paschal mystery of Christ.

One who has reached spiritual maturity is faithful to commitments once made. This is also the highest type of freedom. But maturity and freedom can only be attained by means of a long and uninterrupted practice of self-control and self-giving throughout the years of formation. "An aspirant to the priesthood will thus acquire, with the help of divine grace, a balanced, strong, and mature personality which is a synthesis of what is natural and acquired, a harmonious combination of all his faculties illumined by faith and union with Christ Who has chosen him for Himself and for the ministry of the world's salvation." [78]

56. The fundamental option demands faith

It is not without reason that the Magisterium of the Church insists on the prophetic function of those who follow the evangelical counsels. A prophet is not only one who predicts the future, but also one who bears witness to the reality and the nearness of God. [79]

Falling in love with the Invisible God cannot but imply a vision of the supernatural and a knowledge which transcends the senses. Priestly and religious celibacy is an offering made to the Lord. It surpasses all human reckoning in terms of fruitfulness or return. It is a sacrifice that can only be understood by faith.

Deep spirituality is required in one who progresses towards union with God — a searching self-discipline because he, like every man, must discover and accept the limits revealed in the depths of his being. Nothing is possible without a generous acceptance of these limits. It is something like Jacob's wrestling with the angel (Gen. 32.24-32). He too must accept the disappointment of frustrated hopes and dreams.

V. The Problem of Emotional Integrity

57. A delicate and strongly debated problem

A seminary student is no different from any other young person in recognizing a need for emotional integrity; in other words he feels the need to have a balanced and serene attitude with regard to sex in general and with regard to women in particular. It is a question of attaining the right equilibrium, self-control, or, as often expressed, a state of maturity in which the emotions are so well integrated that a young person will conduct himself perfectly normally in whatever situation he might find himself.

It is clear that such maturity can be reached only through contacts with other persons, in friendships, conversation, working together, recreation and sharing similar interests. These things have great importance in the lives of the young. In the give and take that they involve, a man soon learns his own limitations and realizes that he is not self-sufficient. This can be the basis for rich spiritual experience.

However, when persons of the opposite sex are involved, it can become very difficult to live maturing relationships. One needs ability and responsibility to be aware of the ambiguities that can creep into such relationships and the will to order one's desires and emotions accordingly. A prudent "discernment of spirits" which is sensitive to the movements of both nature and grace is also necessary.

With regard to seminarians' relationships with women, there has been a notable change in these past few years. Until a short while ago there prevailed an attitude of caution and reserve — even to the point, in some extreme cases, of an exaggerated isolation of the students. Today on the other hand, a giddy optimism is gaining ground, which is based upon rash overconfidence and which, not content with the usual and ordinary kind of contacts which life provides, is deliberately promoting the cultivation of frequent meetings with girls for the purpose of "more easily gaining emotional maturity."

58. The theology of chastity

Seminarians should be carefully instructed in the theology of chastity. They should be shown how the practice of this virtue is one of the great dogmas of Christianity, and the apostolic fruitfulness of consecrated virginity. Every experience of good and evil affects our inmost being, our personality, and, consequently our apostolic efficiency—for good or ill.

Our religion places a great value on the virtue of purity. It points out the means that must be used to preserve and defend it: jealous care, reserve, interior control over imagination and desires, and external discipline of the senses.

Training in purity would be incomplete if it did not also include instruction concerning the nature of temptations against purity, their sources and causes, their various forms and the spiritual remedies and methods to be used to fight them.

59. Towards a positive solution of the problem

As in all human relationships, so too in the relations between seminarists and women, the correct course to follow is that of truth and sincerity. Genuineness in behavior automatically excludes everything that is fake and artificial. It is obvious that such a course will exclude every relationship that is intended to have an advantage for only one of the parties, the other being "used" to accomplish some goal.

Therefore, all these relationships are obviously excluded for a future priest. There are still the normal and ordinary human contacts that come in the course of life which require that women be treated in accordance with the principles of healthy human behavior: with courtesy, respect, and, most important of all, charity, which is due to everyone.

This level of female relationship will give seminarians sufficient occasions to develop, to acquire self-knowledge, to refine their characters, to test their strengths and weaknesses, and to learn what in them needs strength and encouragement. They should eventually be sufficiently in command of themselves to be able to terminate or suspend any such relationships without feeling upset. This supposes a healthy spiritual life, imbued with a spirit of vigilant mortification and continual self-control.

Since self-control is so necessary, seminarists should be encouraged to face up to their emotions, prudently yet honestly: "They should expose love openly and with confidence to their spiritual directors and superiors, and learn to judge it in the Lord with their help. They should, however, avoid individual relationships, particularly any of a solitary or protracted nature, with people of the opposite sex. They ought rather to endeavor to practice a love open to all and therefore truly chaste. This they should habitually ask for as a gift from God."[80]

The importance given to spiritual direction presupposes, naturally, that the spiritual director has all the necessary qualities. Evidently, he will not be able to solve these problems by a one-system-for-all method, but will have to treat them case by case. He will have to take into account the differences between individuals and the character and emotions of each candidate. He will have to help each one individually to face the possible crises that can disturb or destroy his vocation.

60. Formation demanded by the pastoral life

The problem of the relationship between seminarists and women is not simply a question of the student's present personal life, but also of his future pastoral activity. It is precisely because of his future pastoral commitment that "particular attention should be paid to the preparation of students for a correct and healthy relationship with women. This will involve instruction in the character and psychology of women as it is affected by the sort of life they lead and by their age. The purpose of this is to enable them, as priests engaged in the pastoral ministry, to undertake a more effective spiritual care of women and behave towards them with the normality and prudence which befit ministers of Christ."[81]

From this it is clear that a good and healthy relationship towards women cannot be a matter of improvisation. It has to be achieved through a slow and delicate training process. Seminaries have the task of preparing students for contact with women, assisting them in the acquisition of dominion over their emotional reactions in the presence of women, and opening them to a realization of woman's place in the spiritual order. Such a preparation will also help seminarians deepen their humanity, delicacy, and tact, which must be a mark of every pastoral relationship.

61. A word about friendships

In these modern days something has to be said about the possibility of friendship between a seminarian (or a priest) and a woman. This is a relation that requires careful attention and a balance which is far from common.

It is an admitted fact that normal human relations can, under certain conditions, contribute to the natural and spiritual maturing of the seminarist. But, at the same time, one must be on one's guard against particular friendships which are dangerous and incompatible with a priestly vocation since they interfere with freedom of heart and universality of love. The nature of the mission for which a seminarian is preparing requires that his spirit remain open to all mankind with a universal love that is "sincere, human, fraternal, personal, and offered to God after the example of Christ, a love for all men, but above all for the poor and the distressed and for their fellows."[82]

This implies that superiors and spiritual directors know how to give positive help to the young men confided to their care. It is often difficult to know at the beginning of relationships what they are or will become. It is easy for someone to think that something is "spiritual" when it is no such thing. Even when intentions are apparently most correct, one has to remember how powerful emotional relationships can be, leading to a blindness towards or an underestimating of the real dangers that such friendships can entail. In fact, love, when it involves the senses, is ambivalent in nature. It can easily veer towards concupiscence and impede development instead of assuring, as it should do, the full flowering of personal maturity. The result is that the alleged spiritual advantages that a seminarian would like to think he receives from friendships of this nature remain hypothetical and uncertain, while the dangers and difficulties are both significant and real.

One must be realistic and accept the fact that human nature can so easily deceive. It is often easy to believe that certain kinds of relationships are necessary when they are not, and to paint with false supernatural motives something which is merely an inclination of fallen nature.[83]

VI. Difficulties in the Process of Formation

62. The task of education during adolescence

An educator must be familiar with the personality of the student as he goes through the various phases of growth. Insofar as this concerns adolescents, in particular, it should be noted that this period of life is characterized by a process of physiological maturing, emerging sexual desires, and a great deal of imaginative fantasizing about sexual matters.

An adolescent needs help to form a healthy idea of what sex is all about and to come to realize its place in the order of values. He needs to learn how to react when facing temptations to impurity or when confronting situations involving sex. He must learn to control his instincts, not in fear, but in the serenity which only a knowledge of the truth can bring.

With this in mind, education has to develop within the group situation the emotional potential of the adolescent, assisting him to objectivize his sexual drive and channel it in the direction of total self-giving. This is an arduous task. It should not be a cause of surprise if an adolescent withdraws within himself and feels that he is misunderstood by everyone around him. Moreover, it is understandable in this situation that he might be driven to center his erotic attention upon himself and make the task of sexual integration yet more difficult.

63. The phenomenon of self-abuse in adolescents

One of the causes of masturbation is sexual imbalance. The other causes are generally of an occasional and secondary nature, albeit contributing to its appearance and continuation. In education, efforts should be directed rather towards the causes than to attacking the problem directly. Only in this way can one promote the effective development of boyish instincts — which means an interior growing up towards domination of instinct. This is the growth that the causes mentioned above tend to obstruct.

Fear, threats, physical or spiritual intimidation are best avoided. These could encourage the formation of obsessions and compromise the possibility of a balanced sexual attitude, making him turn further in on himself instead of opening himself to others. Success as always will depend on the degree of awareness of the real causes of the problem. This is what formation needs to be particularly concerned with.

Self-abuse upsets the kind of life which is the educator's aim. He cannot remain indifferent to the closed-up attitude which results from this. Nevertheless, he should not over-dramatize the fact of masturbation nor lessen his esteem and goodwill for the individual afflicted. As he comes into deeper contact with the supernatural and self-sacrificing love of the educator, the youth is bound to be aware of his place in the communion of charity and will begin to feel himself drawn out of his isolation.

In trying to meet each difficulty, it is better not to offer a ready-made take-it-or-leave-it solution. Rather, using the occasion for real interior growth, help and encourage the sufferer in such a way that he finds his own remedy. Not only will he then solve this one problem, but will learn the art of resolving all the other problems which eventually he will have to face.

64. Seminary formation of adolescents

Given that seminary training aims to impart an integrated human, Christian, and priestly formation to its students, the most difficult aspect during adolescence is to decide how much of this training should be Christian and how much of it should be priestly formation. Adolescents should only gradually be introduced to a specifically priestly formation. Great wisdom lies behind this.

For the majority of the candidates the motives in their vocation are initially very vague. They want to be of service to mankind, to the Church, to Christ, but their ideas about Christ and the Church are often unclear. Frequently their attitude is simply one of availability in a purely humanitarian sense which bears little reference to God, Christ, or the Church. In fact, for many adolescents their view of life is still very general. Philanthropy and religion are not very distinct as yet.

This is the reason why there are many adolescents who feel inclined to the priesthood. But as soon as their humanitarian interests begin to take clearer shape, they give up their vocation and leave the seminary unless their attitude has been enriched with religious motivation. One must help these young men to grasp at the right time what a life consecrated to God is all about. It is no use imposing on them right from the start a way of life which is already fully priestly.

65. The task of education during the post-adolescent years

In youth, love tends to express itself in highly varied sexual manifestations, entailing a combination of psycho-sexual and psycho-emotional factors. Despite appearances and often promiscuous attitudes among youth, young men have little knowledge of true feminine psychology. Women fascinate them, but they do not know why and this bothers them. They often surrender to counterfeit love, instead of discovering that chastity and love are actually the same virtue and that both are active, fruitful, and forgetful of self.

An educator should pay close attention to the fact that youth is the time for a decisive and definitive choice of a state of life. They must be given a clear view of all the possibilities open to them to enable them to make a free choice. This is the time when they must be guided to understand the true theology of matrimony and of consecrated celibacy.[84] This is also the time when prejudices and "the false theories that maintain that perfect continence is impossible or harmful to man"[85] must be definitely eliminated.

66. Perseverance in vocations

The real problem today is not merely that young men have little inclination towards a priestly vocation. It is also the problem of perseverance in their vocation and their adherence to all the demands that a vocation entails. Objective causes for this lack of perseverance derive from the culture and the environment of today in which the young live. But, without a doubt, there is also an important subjective cause which deserves the attention of educators. This is the unwarranted devaluation of a state of consecration to God in the priesthood.

The youth of today are no less generous than those of yesterday, but they need guidance on the path to commitment. Youth need high ideals to challenge them to heroism. It is a bad mistake, therefore, to reduce the priestly vocation to the dimensions of an ordinary life, without sacrifice or commitment. Young people will not respond generously unless the recruiting appeal is based on those qualities which ring true to the spirit of youth: a taste for hardship, the need for dedication, and the joy of sacrifice.

Young people have to be brought to feel deeply "how gratefully this state (of celibacy) deserves to be undertaken, not only as a requisite of Church law, but as a precious gift which should be humbly sought of God and to which they should freely and generously hasten to respond through the energizing and fortifying grace of the Holy Spirit."[86]

67. Particular difficulties of adulthood

It is only realistic to suppose that a priest, like any other human being, will be subject to the crises of the human condition and the difficulties that mark a man's development: emotional crises, sex, relationship with authority, finding his true place in the world and the Church, crises of the spiritual order. For this reason, candidates for the priesthood must be prepared to face such problems in a spirit of sacrifice, with courage and constancy.

It is an important stage when a man passes the mid-way point in life. The basic problems will have already been solved between the ages of 20 and 30, problems such as vocation, profession, and life-direction. The chances of going back are slim.

At this age youth is gone with its outlook and its prerogatives: enthusiasm, hopes, dreams of sanctity, and great works done for the Church. Instead a wiser, more calm and balanced life sets in; but also more vulnerable. Perhaps one has already at this age achieved recognition, a position of responsibility, success. But, maybe the individual has failed both from a human and from an apostolic standpoint. He can simply be resigned to a state of obscurity.

This can bring torment to some priests, an interior restlessness, a crisis "of emptiness," filled only with dissatisfaction and frustration over ideals no longer attainable. In such circumstances a need for human companionship can make itself felt very strongly indeed.

68. Reason for crises in priestly lives

From the point of view of family life, a priest will find himself alone. Usually the family in which he grew up as a boy is gone and he has no family of his own. The apostolic enthusiasm that sustained him in his younger days has waned and he feels himself shunned by the younger generation. So at about the age of 40 interior and exterior loneliness generally awaits him. It is then that he may feel more consciously the loss of what he has renounced and the burden of celibacy.

Add to this a measure of monotony in a ministry that seems always the same and maybe include a feeling of dissatisfaction with one's environment and mistrust of the hierarchy of the Church. When things never change, nor is there hope of change, there often can be dissatisfaction.

He withdraws sadly into himself, is irritable and bad-tempered. At this point the danger is that he will begin to rediscover and overestimate the pleasurable things in life from which he separated himself when he consecrated himself to God. He will undergo the spiritual crisis of distaste for his regular work and his prayers coupled with a skepticism over his spiritual progress and a conviction that all his efforts are futile.

69. Preventing and solving these difficulties

A priest who finds himself in this situation must first of all be patient with himself and accept himself for what he is without being upset at the onslaught of desire. These impulses are part of human nature, and a priestly vocation does not take away nature. Impatience in the face of these urgings and a failure to understand them are causes for defections or for tediousness in a vocation.

However, a patient and calm acceptance of what the years are bringing will not suffice, nor be possible, without a living faith and a humble and active union with God. One needs to repeat frequently the words of Saint Paul (2 Tim. 1.12): "I know Whom I have believed and I am sure." This humble and lively union with God, forged out of a knowledge of self, trust, abandonment to His Will, and prayer will bring constant freshness to a priest's spiritual life and will keep him young as the years speed by. Union with God and the eyes of faith will enable difficulties to be put in their true perspective. Even if difficulties remain, their weight will be lightened, and the experience of emptiness and solitude will be transformed into a precious offering to God.

If the crisis is so deep that a priest asks to be allowed to suspend his ecclesiastical obligations in order to live and think things out as a layman for a while, it is preferable that he be admitted to a community environment in which love and charity prevail and where he can be assisted to recapture an outlook of faith by some spiritual and pastoral activity.

Part IV
The Seminary as a Center of Education

70. Conditions for seminary formation

Far from being an isolated component in the spiritual structure of a priest's personality, chastity constitutes the culmination of a balanced life strong in faith and solidly built on an ardent charity.

This is why nothing in the life or climate of a seminary can be indifferent to the building up of this virtue. Indeed, the whole seminary atmosphere must be regarded as a principal and fundamental factor in the work of formation. It is, therefore, necessary to recall the essential features of seminary life which, directly or indirectly, have a bearing on formation in chastity.

Every seminary must be such as to "intensify in each student the joy of his calling." [87] Celibacy lived for the kingdom of God must be shown to be a wonderful grace ever since men first heard the joyful tidings of the resurrection of Christ.

In order to impart this spirit of joy, students should be given a taste for the practice of ecclesial and apostolic charity, which is equally a love of Christ, a communion in friendship with superiors and fellow students, an evangelical spirit, and a desire to be cooperative. This aspect of the program cannot so much be taught as caught—by the example of life as it is lived in the seminary.

There follow some further suggestions aimed at creating an atmosphere in the seminary which will further the formation of the students. These suggestions are based on a wise use of interpersonal relationships, an intense spiritual life, an ardent ecclesial charity, the use of appropriate contacts with the outside world, and an adequate use of the means of social communication.

I. The Atmosphere of the Seminary

71. The seminary as a fraternal community

The climate in which human relationships are exercised in a seminary is an important factor in pastoral formation. Before he takes out of the seminary the riches that are to be found there, a student has first to give something. He has to give to the environment in which he lives a spirit of mutual service which consists in each contributing his share to the creation of conditions of life which favor the development of his companions.

There are certain trends which characterize this seminary atmosphere. First of all, one would hope that in a seminary community, every student will *freely* examine his vocation, and not simply take it for granted merely because he finds himself in a seminary. [88] Due account should be taken of the variety of dispositions with regard to the students' vocations and the changeableness of the minds of the young. Educators should respect each and every student and should not establish degrees of worthiness. At no time should it even be hinted that someone who changes his mind *in the seminary* is a traitor. All the students should be regularly reminded that they have a personal right and obligation to deeply study their vocation and to choose with complete freedom.

A successful seminary community also depends on the establishment of interpersonal relationships characterized by a *family-like trust* and *brotherly type friendships*. [89] It should be remembered that trust is not imposed by authority, but has to be won and inspired. And friendship can be encouraged or destroyed. It can be encouraged when the seminary is in itself a school of friendship, where the spirit of brotherhood is promoted even on the purely human level and where the seminary positively believes in it. Nothing destroys it so much as a spirit of malicious insinuation or sourness. True formation for celibacy must be rooted in a spirit of fraternity. [90]

A life filled with brotherly love and harmony, which is industrious and replete with a human and supernatural warmth, irradiates over all a sense of restful calm, equanimity, and deep satisfaction. In this sort of atmosphere students will be, as it were, immunized from the need to seek emotional compensations outside the community. It will be more difficult for them to regret the renunciation which their choice of celibacy has involved.

72. The seminary as a community which forms

In the last analysis, maturity means adherence to and love for reality, one's own, that of others, God's. Hence, the most formative instrument is an atmosphere of *truth;* or, in other words, a spirit of openness and loyalty, affection, respect, and communication. In this climate the discovery of one's vocation will be gradually achieved as the result of a mature choice rather than an effect of external conditioning. The atmosphere of a seminary will contribute to the mature development of the candidates in the measure in which it will be warm with truly human relationships, capable of stimulating personal responsibility and initiative while gradually leading to a convinced and reasonable obedience which is proper to the children of God.

It is hard to imagine how seminary life can fulfill its function without close collaboration between staff and students in which the personality, abilities and competence of each student can be evaluated. Solidarity and social intercourse must be adopted as program and method for the entire seminary. "Under their Rector's lead superiors and professors shall be united in spirit and action, forming one family with the students to fulfill the Lord's prayer 'that they all may be one' (Jn. 17.11), thus fostering in the students joy in their vocations." [91]

73. The group dynamic in seminary formation

To promote personal formation one must place students in an environment which is favorable to the development of all their qualities and potential. To help achieve this, while always protecting the *unity of the seminary,* circumstances may encourage the division of students into smaller groups. [92] This system is helpful in activating the bonds which bind each to the other, in ensuring a fair division of tasks between members of the group in accordance with each one's abilities and directing them to the common good.

Moreover, one cannot afford to overlook the fact that the way priests frequently have to live and act is pluralistic. It is right that this attitude be imparted in the seminary and made part of seminary life itself.

The group system could serve this purpose, particularly if the groups can be organized in relation to actual diocesan needs, and, therefore, to the future fields of the students' ministry. They could serve a positively dynamic and pastoral purpose. Surrounding them, other circles with an apostolic or purely human interest can help form bonds of friendship and cooperation. This could add to the richness and vitality of the students' formation.

74. The function of discipline and rule

The atmosphere of freedom, respect for the individual, and the value placed on personal initiative should not be interpreted as freedom from every kind of discipline. A seminarian who *freely* chooses to enter a seminary must also *freely* accept and respect its terms. Discipline is part of the spiritual structure of the whole life of a student and priest. When it is "interiorized" it becomes an indispensable component of his spiritual life.[93] This does not mean that discipline is only interior; it is "personal and communitarian,"[94] and exterior.[95]

While the discipline set out by the Rule of Life of the seminary retains its vital importance, the heart of seminary formation is to be found in the influence of the human and Christian relationship which exists between seminarist and educator. This implies that the students are not left to themselves and that educators cannot dispense themselves from their duty of being present with, indeed very close to, the students. Iron discipline, a minutely drawn rulebook, or rigid surveillance are no substitute for the educator himself being present to guide and strengthen the students with friendship, intimate conversation, and watchful care over their way of life.[96]

General principles of formation need an individual approach in their application. There is no such thing as one kind of formation that is suited to all. Sometimes a superior will allow a particular student of whom he has personal knowledge to follow a course of action involving risks, being convinced that ultimately he will find out for himself what is good and what is not, instead of having a mode of conduct rigidly imposed on him. At other times a responsible superior will intervene decisively to save someone who is presuming too much on himself or who, without sufficient reason, is placing himself in grave danger.

II. The Seminary and the Spiritual Life

75. The life of prayer in formation

The choice of celibacy must be made with magnanimity. It must be made with the full realization that it is no small thing to dedicate one's entire life to one gigantic love which embraces at the same time God, Christ, and souls. It must be made with the full realization that while celibacy is a great gift of God to be asked for with humility,[97] it is also a gift that a man gives to God. This generosity will open the heart of the seminarist increasingly to prayer, adoration, and contemplation of Him Who is the recipient of this gift and Who will be for him a source of constant joy and youthful spirit.[98]

A seminary must introduce its students to the practice of habitual and spontaneous meeting and dialogue with God in Christ by the manifold ways of prayer, Liturgy, meditation on the Word of God and study of the Person of Christ, the center of every reflection in faith and theology.

A life centered on God in prayer is absolutely essential for a life of consecration. A seminarian and a priest must have the gift of piety to a high degree; it is nothing less than a tremendous love of God. They are, and must always remain, the privileged witnesses of the beauty and happiness that come from intimacy with the God of revelation.

The man who is celibate by calling and abandons prayer is on the verge of ruin as far as his celibacy is concerned. The whole basis of his life consists in his relationship with God, and this relationship is kept alive by prayer—the prayer of the Church herself, and the personal prayer of the priest in his daily personal devotions. It is impossible for a priest to be good in giving spiritual direction unless he prays. Without a rich, spiritual relationship with God in his life, no priest can give effective help to anyone.

76. Criteria for the revision of forms of piety

Before one sets about revising forms of piety, it is important to establish what reason lies behind them. Forms correspond to needs. The psychological and pastoral needs of today will suggest what adaptations are necessary in the forms of piety. Today a certain spontaneity is recommended in devotion in which one opens one's heart to the loving friendship of Christ in an encounter with the Heavenly Father.[99] Personal piety based on the mystery of salvation should not be considered an "extra" to one's daily life, but rather as life's constant living inspiration.

Spontaneous prayer has its place. However, it would be an illusion and a fundamental error to believe that praying only when one feels an inclination to do so is more fruitful than praying at the times set down by rule. It is equally erroneous to maintain that praying at set times causes disaffection towards prayer. Promote spontaneous prayer, but, above all, promote the interiorizing of all prayer.

Religious education should endeavor to highlight the value of practices of piety as expressions of the life of the Gospel in which we share in the intimacy of the Father through Christ in the Holy Spirit.[100]

77. Liturgical formation of seminarists

Seminarists must be formed, not simply to assist at sacred functions, but to share in and to live an intensely sacramental and liturgical life. For a man who is not disposed to seek to follow Christ, the Liturgy can appear to be simply a tiresome performance. However, every effort must be made to prepare devotional services and liturgical ceremonies in a manner which will appeal to young people and enable them to participate in them gladly and willingly.[101] It is important that they acquire a sense of the Liturgy as a community living of the life of Christ.

The ministry of the priest is primarily not human work, but the work of Christ in Person. The priest, therefore, has to fulfill his ministry according to the Spirit of Christ, High Priest and Eternal Shepherd. How close should be the intimacy between Christ and the priest! Seminary training must be geared to the acquisition of this perfection: to prepare the students to live interiorly the life of Christ and to prepare them to perform their ministerial functions in His Spirit. [102]

78. Meditation on the Word of God

In the presence of God in Christ, a seminarian should love to meditate, whether alone or in a group, on the words of revelation. [103] He should try to apply them to his daily life. He should develop the habit of seeing the whole of Christian life (its traditions, institutions, persons, and doctrines) in the light of the Gospel, in the realization that it is the Word of God which judges and converts the Church. This should inspire his personal and apostolic activity.

Communion with Christ, moreover, is not only communion with His thinking. Above all it is communion with His life of love, of which His Easter mystery is the central act and the most authentic and powerful expression (Rom. 6.2-11). No baptized Christian, and certainly no priest, can remain a simple spectator to this mystery, but must participate in it, imitating Christ, Who died for sins and rose for the glory of His Father, and thus manifest Christ to the world (Phil. 3.8-11; 2 Cor. 4.10; 3.18).

This baptismal and priestly participation, however, cannot be brought about except through the working of the Holy Spirit, since the paschal mystery becomes ours only because of its Author, the Holy Spirit. Such a spirituality must guide from within the life of anyone called to the ministerial priesthood.

79. Formation through theological study

The modern seminarian has a very special need: what is termed "a living synthesis of faith." This is a faith which has to be discovered for oneself and sheds light on one's daily life, not merely a faith limited to adherence to a number of determined truths, but also the practical exercise of Christian choice and the source of Christian trust in Christ and His Church. A serious emotional crisis in a priest is almost always preceded by a weakening or a dimming of faith.

The study of theology should deepen the spirit of faith in seminarians. The "Introduction to the Mystery of Christ" and the "History of Salvation" are to be taught, not only for the students' spiritual benefit, but also to give them a single organic vision of all their priestly studies. [104]

The seminary should give the students a systematic and organic presentation of all theology and, in addition, an introduction to biblical, patristic, historical, and sociological research with a view to assisting them to acquire a personal, critical ability to evaluate modern thought. All of this should serve to cultivate in the students a profound faith which is sensitive to the needs of our times, yet always nourished by the love of Christ working in the Catholic Church. [105]

These exhortations concerning the general spiritual climate of the seminary cannot be considered extrinsic to the main concern of this document, formation in chastity. If a seminary cannot produce this atmosphere and the future priest is consequently uninfluenced by it, there is little hope that chastity, without such nourishment, will survive.

III. The Seminary and Ecclesial Charity

80. Relationship between superiors and seminarians

A seminarian needs to be immersed in an atmosphere of apostolic charity. The aim of a seminary is to enable him to experience that to live as a Christian in the spirit of Christ and as a priest in celibacy one thing is needed: to practice and give witness to ecclesial charity in the Lord. Living charity, which is a gift of the Holy Spirit, is an instrument for the education, conversion, and sanctification of oneself and others. [106]

Seminary superiors must appear to the students not simply as those who give orders, directives, warnings, and punishments, but also as those who arouse love among their subjects and witness to this love in their own personal lives. The higher the authority, the more profound the obligation to be the source of unity in charity. [107] It is precisely by means of the love and charity displayed by a superior that a student is enabled to acquire the same love of God.

When a seminarian has tasted the charity of the Lord through the person of his priest-educator he will know what it means when he comes to express it tomorrow in the context of the presbyterium gathered around the Bishop and to communicate it to his flock. [108]

The charity he experiences in the seminary and in his diocese will help a priest to live his celibate life in serenity without any nostalgia for a lay life. [109]

81. Formation in apostolic charity

The spiritual formation of candidates for the priesthood must be pastorally orientated and be programmed with a view to their future ministry. Priests are the official builders of the community of the Church. Not only are they given spiritual power for this ministry (2 Cor. 10.8; 13.10), but they are expected to "treat all with outstanding humanity in imitation of the Lord." [110]

Community life in the seminary, animated by sincere charity and radiating apostolic zeal, is a preparation for — even a prelude to — fraternal cooperation among the clergy in apostolic work. [111] Students should, therefore, feel themselves bound to their diocese and interested in its problems. Thus they should gain a diocesan spirituality which has its roots, in other words, in their future sphere of work. [112]

Union with God in prayer and the love of silence and spiritual things are no obstacles to, but rather requirements of an apostolic concern for the vicissitudes of man and the "signs of the times." They are a response from the future priest's loving solicitude and his sincere, selfless devotion. [113]

A seminarist should grasp the meaning of the connection between his celibacy and apostolic concern. Voluntary celibacy is a witness of love, "an answer of love to the love" of Christ. In Him loving in human fashion receives, through grace, a new and incomparable strength. [114]

Perfect chastity is lived by a priest "not out of contempt for the gift of life, but for a higher love of that new kind of life which flows from the paschal mystery." [115] For a priest human love is sacrificed for the love of Christ and, therefore, for the love of the Church and of all mankind. For this love a priest gives up other attachments and legitimate affections. [116]

82. Growing in the imitation of Christ

The example of the Supreme Shepherd shows clearly how supernatural is the priest's mission of redemption. The primary and fundamental source of his pastorate and what it means to be a pastor is his living, total consecration to Christ, given to the world by the Father.[117]

The sacrament which deputes a baptized person a pastor makes him an "elect of Christ" for the salvation of his brothers, contracted out to Jesus Christ in fraternal love (Phil. 3.12; Gal. 1.10; 5.13). It is a life of complete submission to the demands of the love of God, of disposability to the action of grace, a living less and less for oneself and more and more for Him Who brings all things to their fruition (2 Cor. 5.14-15).

Shepherds of souls must continue to be formed in that love which is, of its nature, exclusive. They must realize that the "yes" they once said to the Bishop who ordained them committed them permanently and completely to God's saving love. In the priestly prayer of Jesus it is impossible to separate the "for them" from the "I give myself." So also in the formation of priests, consecration to God cannot be separated from service of the brethren. Rather the one must be completely grounded in the other.

IV. Necessity and Means of Contact with the World

83. New requirements in priestly formation

Seminaries have sought rightly to preserve their students from too much worldly influence in order to establish a climate better adapted to the interior life. Alongside this concern, which is still required and valid even today, the need has arisen to establish some contact between the student and the world and with the situation in which the family of man in reality lives. When all is said and done about seminary formation, one has to face the fact that it is not possible to pretend to maintain a kind of segregation from the world which can only be pure fancy today.

It is impossible to abstract oneself from the subtle, often critical, state of the unbelieving contemporary world. Young students cannot afford to be ignorant of the realities of the world in which they are going to be called to work. Nor must they be allowed to be because the presentation of the faith demands that it be presented relevantly to the people addressed. Therefore, the formation of priests today must be undertaken with eyes wide-open, with honesty, courage, and in ways which were not perhaps required in the past.[118]

This means that the student should be helped by a formation which is both positive and grounded in theology to face risks and overcome mistakes and ambiguities surrounding the final choice he will make definitively at his ordination. His basic decision to embrace the priesthood must be prompted not by fear or ignorance of the world or a repudiation of the realities of life, but by his clear vision of his true meaning in the world and of his relationship to others.

84. The purpose of interpersonal relationships

Complete isolation in a seminary could prevent a seminarist from appreciating the problems of his own generation. He might become inclined to assume conventional and depersonalized forms of relationships with others. It could deprive him of the opportunity to make a responsible decision about his vocation in relation to the world outside. It could make understanding of men and life, where he is going to have to carry out his apostolate, more difficult.[119] Without an appreciation for the trials which beset human beings outside, he could be insensitive as a priest to the problems of others. Finally, there is the danger of creating in seminarians a spirit of privileged caste.

Human relations are not only an instrument in the apostolate; they are, in their theological aspect, a value in their own right. The Christian, as an image of God in Christ, is called to live in the world as a new creature. It is the priest, through his mission of living in charity and friendship, in intimate and fraternal affection and family-like unity, who expresses in himself the true meaning of the new creature in Christ.

It is precisely because of the need for the education of students not to be divorced from contact with modern man that the Magisterium of the Church has called for a formation of students for the priesthood with emphasis on such virtues as friendship, loyalty, reliance on one's word, and the capacity to give to others generously and faithfully.[120]

85. Seminarians and their families

Home life plays an important role in training a candidate for the priesthood. It is there, for example, that he can discover meaning, value, and difficulties in human love. The family teaches him the importance and value of an affective relationship and the possibility also of appreciating particular aspects of feminine psychology.

The time he spends with his family is very important for the formation of a seminarist, not only during summer vacations, but also during the academic year. It presents the opportunity for engaging in a number of social contacts in the course of his recreation, employment, or pastoral activity, and can test the usefulness and relevance of the counsels he has received in the seminary. Taken seriously, this aspect of the students' formation can awaken the sense of responsibility and the spiritual lives of the members of the family and the parish clergy.

The family should be the "garden" in which vocations are born and grow. It ought to be the "first seminary" and thereafter the primary cooperator with the seminary.[121] Nevertheless, in view of the numerous serious shortcomings in many families today, care has to be taken that the family does not destroy what the seminary is trying to build.

If families are to carry out a complementing and sustaining role in the formation and perseverance of the future priest, a good deal of pastoral formation of the family needs to be undertaken. One of the main objects of the work for vocations consists precisely in eliciting the cooperation of families, bringing parents to a knowledge of what they can and must do in regard to the discovery and growth of sacred vocations.

The tasks of parents with regard to Church vocations are manifold because they are called to prepare, cultivate, and support the vocations God gives to their children. They have to acquire for themselves and their families profound moral and religious values, a deep and convinced spirit of religious practice, exemplary Christian moral conduct, a concern for the Church and its apostolate, a decent education for their children, and a correct concept of what a vocation is.

86. Relationship with the local parish

A Christian lives out his experience of faith and welcomes the invitation to help extend the faith to others in an ecclesial community. Such a community, where the various roles of priests and lay people are correctly lived and where the Lord is the center of every activity, helps each one in the community to understand the ecclesial dimension of his own vocation.

Therefore, the parish has a necessary part to play in the emergence of priestly vocations, and in the seminarian's perseverance. The parish must do all in its power to involve its Church students in the apostolic activity of the community.[122]

This goal can be reached by a parish if it is a genuine community living a life of faith and duly concerned for the realization of the kingdom of God; if the priests of the parish influence the young by the example of their holy lives and their pastoral zeal; if the faithful are interested in promoting vocations, pray for vocations and the sanctification of priests; if the laity collaborate in carrying out the community's pastoral obligations.

87. Contact with the world

A seminary today has to be a community open to the life of today. It has to maintain contacts of all sorts, contacts with the families of the students, contacts with the world of youth, contacts with the life of the Church both on a local and a universal level, and contacts with the problems of mankind.[123]

But when one says that it should be "open" and not "closed," this is far from meaning in some unplanned or mindless fashion. It means rather that it must be designed to produce students who will be capable of a truly human and priestly relationship with others, an openness of spirit to their problems and an ability to engage in dialogue.[124]

A priest is called to be in the world, to understand the world, and to accept the world, but, at the same time, to undertake a mission which distinguishes him from the world. He can never be in all things "like them." The true priest is a solitary, living in solidarity with the world around him. His work keeps him in simultaneous contact with the community of men and the communion of saints. He lives among men, but keeps in his sight God.[125]

A seminarian must be formed to live in a worldly environment with the soul of a priest. He must be taught to assume a proper bearing in the company of others and to let his interior, spiritual strength dictate his personal reactions in conversation. Seminary training must form him to be able to stand up spiritually on his own feet in the face of the pressures that will come from his surroundings.

88. Training to be an apostolic presence in the world

Seminary students have to learn to adopt an apostolic outlook in their outside contacts. It was for this reason that the Second Vatican Council expressed the desire that students be introduced to the apostolate—not so much to make a contribution to parochial work — as to create in them a pastoral attitude in their dealings with others, to arouse in them a taste for the apostolate of charity which could inspire their daily round of duty, as well as spurring them on to discover a means of exercising the apostolate in accordance with modern needs.[126]

It is of fundamental importance to send seminarists into the apostolate, and to do so not just to help the clergy but to acquire a missionary spirit and apostolic charity and, futhermore, to enable them to learn up-to-date techniques and evaluate the results afterwards.[127] Their celibacy must also, then, be integrated into their personal apostolic mission.

To accomplish the high ideals of the pastoral formation of future priests requires a highly qualified staff. They must be skilled men, true animators, who are capable of assisting the students and are responsible for the necessary pastoral evaluation of their work and for pastoral supervision. It is a waste of time to talk about the seminary rule or the need for the seminary to be open to the world unless the seminary is under the direction of priests who have the talent and ability to be true educators.[128]

89. Instruments of social communication

Communications media play an important role in forming men today, and so, too, in forming priests. These media are not unrelated to the problem of forming men in perfect chastity since so often they have become too involved in sex. They are, for better or worse, problems that touch the personal life of a priest who will be using them and will be subject to their influence. They also touch the pastoral work of the priest because these media both form, inform, and transform his people and shape their social consciousness. He has to help his people use them properly and guard against their harmful effects.[129]

It is not, therefore, simply and solely for their personal formation but also to prepare them for the apostolate that aspirants for the priesthood should be introduced to the correct use of these instruments of social communication (press, radio, television, cinema, etc.) and should, in general, be equipped to communicate their thoughts by the spoken and written word to the men of our time in a manner adapted to the mind of today.

Evidently this is a serious problem of enormous proportions, particularly if one takes into account the real situation of the press and the wide use and influence of radio and television. The fact is that the internal and external environment of the seminary community depends greatly on the media which, therefore, have it within their power to form or de-form candidates for the priesthood.

The formational problem presented by the media cannot be reduced merely to a disciplinary regulation of their use. It is above all a question of positive education, of reflection on the social phenomena in which we are immersed. It is the problem of seminary personnel being prepared and specialized enough to look after this aspect of training. It is not only a question of trying to limit the damage that dangerous instruments can do, but of forming future priests who will be capable of living responsibly in the hard world of reality.

Conclusion

90. Formation as a synthesis of nature and grace

It is hoped that the guidelines and suggestions presented here will be of some service to seminary staffs. They have been inspired by a study of the elements of nature and grace which go into seminary and priestly formation. Aware of their high calling and responsibility, educators in seminaries should endeavor at all times to combine the resources offered by nature and grace in their work.

Effective training for priestly celibacy must begin with the individual as he is and help him develop and reach perfection. He has, therefore, to be known and understood in himself. As one finds him so one adapts the means of training to his individual mentality—a mentality formed by his personal background, a conflation of individual and social influences.

The natural conditions which favor the spiritual life can be summed up in the concept of maturity. To use every effort in order to reach maturity in oneself, and to assist others to reach theirs, signifies cooperation with divine grace to construct the spiritual edifice which is a man and, *a fortiori,* which is a priest.

While it is true that the spiritual life depends essentially on grace in its mysteriousness and, as such, transcends the psychic mechanisms of man, it is nonetheless true that these mechanisms affect the action of grace. It is important, therefore, that the personality of the seminarian becomes more richly human in order to serve better as a sign and instrument of the call of the Holy Spirit.

It is the task of formation to enhance the humanity of the individual, to direct him towards, and to bring him if possible to, perfection in such a way as to enable the action of grace to be more effective. The training process will be effective in proportion to the degree of attention paid to the individual conditions, be they normal or otherwise, of the candidate. Only then can one make a human person into a valid instrument for the work of divine grace.

Notes

1. Paul VI, Encyclical, *Sacerdotalis caelibatus*, 24 June 1967: AAS 59 (1967) 682, n. 61.
2. Cf. Vat. Coun. II, *Decree on the Training of Priests*, n. 10; *Decree on the Ministry and Life of Priests*, n. 16; *Decree on the Up-to-date Renewal of Religious Life*, n. 12; Paul VI, Apostolic Exhortation, *Evangelica testificatio*, 29 June 1971: AAS 63 (1971) 505, n. 15; Synod Document, *The Ministerial Priesthood*, part a, I, n. 4, d: AAS 63 (1971) 917.
3. Synod Document, *The Ministerial Priesthood*, 30 Nov. 1971, loc. cit., 917.
4. Cf. Vat. Coun. II, *Decree on the Ministry and Life of Priests*, n. 16.
5. Cf. Paul VI, Encyclical, *Sacerdotalis caelibatus*, 684 ff., n. 70.
6. Cf. Paul VI, Encyclical, *Sacerdotalis caelibatus*, 687, n. 75.
7. Cf. Vat. Coun. II, *Pastoral Constitution on the Church in the Modern World*, n. 1; *Declaration on Christian Education*, n. 1; Paul VI, Encyclical, *Sacerdotalis caelibatus*, loc. cit., 681, n. 61.
8. Cf. Vat. Coun. II, *Decree on the Training of Priests*, n. 1.
9. Cf. Vat. Coun. II, *Decree on the Ministry and Life of Priests*, n. 16.
10. Cf. Paul VI, Encyclical, *Sacerdotalis caelibatus*, loc. cit., 665, n. 20.
11. Cf. Vat. Coun. II, *Dogmatic Constitution on the Church*, n. 10.
12. Cf. Vat. Coun. II, *Decree on the Ministry and Life of Priests*, n. 2.
13. Vat. Coun. II, *Decree on the Ministry and Life of Priests*, n. 2. Cf. *Dogmatic Constitution on the Church*, n. 28; Paul VI, Encyclical, *Sacerdotalis caelibatus*, loc. cit., 664, n. 19 ff.
14. Synod Document, *The Ministerial Priesthood*, 30 Nov. 1971, loc. cit., 915.
15. Synod Document, *The Ministerial Priesthood*, 30 Nov. 1971, loc. cit., 916.
16. Cf. Vat. Coun. II, *Decree on the Training of Priests*, n. 10; *Decree on the Ministry and Life of Priests*, n. 16.
17. Cf. Vat. Coun. II, *Decree on the Ministry and Life of Priests*, n. 16; Paul VI, Encyclical, *Sacerdotalis caelibatus*, loc. cit., 663, n. 17.
18. Cf. Vat. Coun. II, *Decree on the Training of Priests*, n. 10; Paul VI, Encyclical, *Sacerdotalis caelibatus*, loc. cit., 670 ff., nn. 33-34.
19. Cf. Vat. Coun. II, *Dogmatic Constitution on the Church*, n. 29; Paul VI, Encyclical, *Sacerdotalis caelibatus*, loc. cit., 674, n. 42.
20. Cf. Vat. Coun. II, *Decree on the Ministry and Life of Priests*, n. 16; Synod Document, *The Ministerial Priesthood*, 30 Nov. 1971, loc. cit., 915.
21. Cf. Vat. Coun. II, *Dogmatic Constitution on the Church*, nn. 43, 46.
22. Cf. Vat. Coun. II, *Decree on the Ministry and Life of Priests*, n. 16.
23. Synod Document, *The Ministerial Priesthood*, 30 Nov. 1971, loc. cit., 916.
24. Cf. Paul VI, Encyclical, *Sacerdotalis caelibatus*, loc. cit., 664, n. 19.
25. Cf. Paul VI, Encyclical, *Sacerdotalis caelibatus*, loc. cit., 663-670, nn. 17-34.
26. Cf. Paul VI, Encyclical, *Sacerdotalis caelibatus*, loc. cit., 664, n. 19, 666, n. 31.
27. Cf. Paul VI, Encyclical, *Sacerdotalis caelibatus*, loc. cit., 665, n. 21.
28. Cf. Paul VI, Encyclical, *Sacerdotalis caelibatus*, loc. cit., 657, n. 1.
29. Cf. Vat. Coun. II, *Decree on the Training of Priests*, n. 10.
30. Cf. Vat. Coun. II, *Decree on the Training of Priests*, nn. 10-11.
31. Cf. Vat. Coun. II, *Decree on the Training of Priests*, n. 4; *Dogmatic Constitution on the Church*, n. 28.
32. Paul VI, in the Encyclical, *Summi Dei Verbum*, 4 Nov. 1963: AAS 55 (1963) 984 ff. calls attention to "the necessity of the simultaneous formation of the man, the Christian and the priest" and affirms that "the formation of the man must go hand in hand with that of the Christian and the future priest."
33. Cf. Vat. Coun. II, *Declaration on Christian Education*, n. 1.
34. Cf. Vat. Coun. II, *Decree on the Training of Priests*, n. 11.
35. Cf. Vat. Coun. II, *Decree on the Training of Priests*, nn. 3, 8, 11; Sacred Congregation for Catholic Education, *The Basic Plan for Priestly Formation*, Rome, 1970, nn. 48-58.
36. Cf. Vat. Coun. II, *Dogmatic Constitution on the Church*, Chapters II, III,IV.
37. Cf. Vat. Coun. II, *Declaration on Christian Education*, nn. 1-2; *Decree on the Training of Priests*, nn. 10-11; *Decree on the Apostolate of Lay People*, n. 29; *Decree on the Up-to-date Renewal of Religious Life*, n. 12; Paul VI, Encyclical, *Populorum progressio*, 26 Mar. 1967: AAS 59 (1967) 265, n. 16; Sacred Congregation for Catholic Education, *The Basic Plan . . .*, n. 51.
38. Vat. Coun. II, *Dogmatic Constitution of the Church*, n. 9.
39. Cf. *Summa theologica*, I-II, q. 63, a. 4.
40. Cf. Vat. Coun. II, *Dogmatic Constitution on the Church*, n. 28; *Decree on the Ministry and Life of Priests*, nn. 4-9.
41. Cf. Vat. Coun. II, *Decree on the Training of Priests*, n. 4.
42. Cf. Vat. Coun. II, *Decree on the Training of Priests*, nn. 8-20; Sacred Congregation for Catholic Education, *The Basic Plan . . .*, nn. 44-49.
43. Cf. Paul VI, Encyclical, *Sacerdotalis caelibatus*, loc. cit., 666 ff., nn. 24 ff.
44. Cf. Vat. Coun. II, *Decree on the Ministry and Life of Priests*, nn. 8, 14; Paul VI, Encyclical, *Sacerdotalis caelibatus*, loc. cit., 688-689, nn. 79-81.
45. Cf. Synod Document, *The Ministerial Priesthood*, 30 Nov. 1971, loc. cit., 915.

46. Cf. Vat. Coun. II, *Decree on the Ministry and Life of Priests*, n. 16; Paul VI, Encyclical, *Sacerdotalis caelibatus*, loc. cit., 686-688, nn. 73, 77.

47. Cf. Paul VI, Encyclical, *Sacerdotalis caelibatus*, loc. cit., 679, n. 57.

48. Cf. Sacred Congregation for Catholic Education, *The Basic Plan . . .*, n. 48.

49. Cf. Vat. Coun. II, *Decree on the Up-to-date Renewal of Religious Life*, n. 12; Synod Document, *The Ministerial Priesthood*, 30 Nov. 1971, loc. cit., 917.

50. Cf. Vat. Coun. II, *Decree on the Training of Priests*, n. 6; Sacred Congregation for Catholic Education, *The Basic Plan . . .*, nn. 39-41.

51. Cf. Paul VI, Encyclical, *Sacerdotalis caelibatus*, loc. cit., 683, n. 64; Vat. Coun. II, *Decree on the Training of Priests*, n. 6.

52. Vat. Coun. II, *Declaration on Christian Education*, n. 1.

53. Cf. Pius XII, Encyclical, *Sacra virginitas*, 25 Mar. 1954: AAS 46 (1954) 183-186.

54. Paul VI, Apostolic Exhortation, *Evangelica testificatio*, 29 June 1971: AAS 63 (1971) 515, n. 33.

55. Cf. Vat. Coun. II, *Declaration on Christian Education*, n. 1; Pius XII, Allocution, *Magis quam*, to the Carmelite Order, 23 Sept. 1951: Discourses and Radio Broadcasts, XIII, 256; Encyclical, *Sacra virginitas*, loc. cit., 183-186.

56. Cf. Vat. Coun. II, *Declaration on Christian Education*, nn. 3, 8; *Pastoral Constitution on the Church in the Modern World*, n. 49.

57. Cf. Vat. Coun. II, *Decree on the Training of Priests*, n. 10; Pius XII, Apostolic Exhortation, *Menti nostrae*, 23 Sept. 1950: AAS 42 (1950) 687.

58. Cf. Vat. Coun. II, *Decree on the Training of Priests*, n. 10; Sacred Congregation for Catholic Education, *The Basic Plan . . .*, n. 48.

59. Cf. Paul VI, Encyclical, *Sacerdotalis caelibatus*, loc. cit., 682, n. 63; Sacred Congregation for Catholic Education, *The Basic Plan . . .*, n. 48.

60. Cf. Paul VI, Encyclical, *Sacerdotalis caelibatus*, loc. cit., 686, n. 73.

61. Cf. Paul VI, Encyclical, *Sacerdotalis caelibatus*, loc. cit. 680, nn. 58-59; Vat. Coun. II, *Decree on the Ministry and Life of Priests*, n. 3.

62. Cf. Vat. Coun. II, *Decree on the Training of Priests*, n. 11; Sacred Congregation for Catholic Education, *The Basic Plan . . .*, nn. 48, 51, 54.

63. Cf. Paul VI, Encyclical, *Sacerdotalis caelibatus*, loc. cit., 684, n. 67.

64. Cf. Paul VI, Encyclical, *Sacerdotalis caelibatus*, loc. cit., 684, n. 69; 686, n. 72.

65. Cf. Paul VI, Encyclical, *Sacerdotalis caelibatus*, loc. cit., 684, n. 70.

66. Cf. Paul VI, Encyclical, *Sacerdotalis caelibatus*, loc. cit., 664-670, nn. 19-34.

67. Cf. Vat. Coun. II, *Decree on the Ministry and Life of Priests*, n. 18.

68. Cf. Paul VI, Encyclical, *Sacerdotalis caelibatus*, loc. cit., 687, n. 75.

69. Paul VI, Encyclical, *Sacerdotalis caelibatus*, loc. cit., 684, n. 70.

70. Paul VI, Encyclical, *Sacerdotalis caelibatus*, loc. cit., 688, n. 78.

71. Cf. Paul VI, Encyclical, *Sacerdotalis caelibatus*, loc. cit., 691, n. 86.

72. Cf. Paul VI, Encyclical, *Sacerdotalis caelibatus*, loc. cit., 692, n. 90.

73. Cf. Vat. Coun. II, *Dogmatic Constitution on the Church*, n. 36.

74. Cf. Vat. Coun. II, *Decree on the Training of Priests*, n. 10.

75. Cf. Vat. Coun. II, *Decree on the Training of Priests*, n. 10.

76. Cf. Paul VI, Encyclical, *Sacerdotalis caelibatus*, loc. cit., 684, n. 70; 688, n. 78; Vat. Coun. II, *Decree on the Ministry and Life of Priests*, n. 16.

77. Cf. Vat. Coun. II, *Decree on the Ministry and Life of Priests*, nn. 13, 14; Paul VI, Encyclical, *Sacerdotalis caelibatus*, loc. cit., 688, n. 78.

78. Paul VI, Encyclical, *Sacerdotalis caelibatus*, loc. cit., 685, n. 70.

79. Cf. Vat. Coun. II, *Dogmatic Constitution on the Church*, n. 44.

80. Sacred Congregation for Catholic Education, *The Basic Plan . . .*, n. 48.

81. Sacred Congregation for Catholic Education, *The Basic Plan . . .*, n. 95.

82. Sacred Congregation for Catholic Education, *The Basic Plan . . .*, n. 48.

83. Cf. Paul VI, Encyclical, *Sacerdotalis caelibatus*, loc. cit., 688, n. 77.

84. Cf. Vat. Coun. II, *Decree on the Training of Priests*, n. 10.

85. Vat. Coun. II, *Decree on the Up-to-date Renewal of Religious Life*, n. 12.

86. Vat. Coun. II, *Decree on the Training of Priests*, n. 10.

87. Vat. Coun. II, *Decree on the Training of Priests*, n. 5.

88. Cf. Sacred Congregation for Catholic Education, *The Basic Plan . . .*, n. 13.

89. Cf. Sacred Congregation for Catholic Education, *The Basic Plan . . .*, nn. 13, 14, 46, 48.

90. Cf. Vat. Coun. II, *Decree on the Up-to-date Renewal of Religious Life*, n. 12.

91. Vat. Coun. II, *Decree on the Training of Priests*, n. 5.

92. Cf. Vat. Coun. II, *Decree on the Training of Priests*, n. 7; Sacred Congregation for Catholic Education, *The Basic Plan . . .*, n. 23.

93. Paul VI, Encyclical, *Sacerdotalis caelibatus*, loc. cit., 683, n. 66.

94. Paul VI, Encyclical, *Sacerdotalis caelibatus*, loc. cit., 683, n. 66.

95. Cf. Paul VI, Encyclical, *Sacerdotalis caelibatus*, loc. cit., 688, n. 78.

96. Cf. Paul VI, Encyclical, *Sacerdotalis caelibatus*, loc. cit., 684, n. 68; Vat. Coun. II, *Decree on the Training of Priests*, n. 11.

97. Cf. Vat. Coun. II, *Decree on the Training of Priests*, n. 10.

98. Cf. Sacred Congregation for Catholic Education, *The Basic Plan . . .*, n. 54.

99. Cf. Vat. Coun. II, *Decree on the Training of Priests*, nn. 4, 16; *Decree on the Ministry and Life of Priests*, n. 13.

100. Cf. Vat. Coun. II, *Decree on the Training of Priests*, n. 8; *Decree on the Ministry and Life of Priests*, n. 18.

101. Cf. Sacred Congregation for Catholic Education, *The Basic Plan . . .*, n. 14.

102. Cf. Sacred Congregation for Catholic Education, *The Basic Plan . . .*, nn. 44-45.

103. Cf. Vat. Coun. II, *Decree on the Training of Priests*, n. 8.

104. Cf. Vat. Coun. II, *Decree on the Training of Priests*, n. 14; Sacred Congregation for Catholic Education, *The Basic Plan . . .*, n. 62.

105. Cf. Vat. Coun. II, *Decree on the Training of Priests*, nn. 16-17; Sacred Congregation for Catholic Education, *The Basic Plan . . .*, nn. 76-80.

106. Cf. Vat. Coun. II, *Decree on the Ministry and Life of Priests*, n. 11; *Decree on the Up-to-date Renewal of Religious Life*, n. 12.

107. Cf. Vat. Coun. II, *Decree on the Ministry and Life of Priests*, n. 11; *Decree on the Up-to-date Renewal of Religious Life*, n. 24.

108. Cf. Vat. Coun. II, *Decree on the Training of Priests*, n. 8.

109. Cf. Vat. Coun. II, *Decree on the Up-to-date Renewal of Religious Life*, n. 12; Paul VI, Encyclical, *Sacerdotalis caelibatus*, loc. cit., 688-689, nn. 79-80.

110. Vat. Coun. II, *Decree on the Ministry and Life of Priests*, n. 6.

111. Cf. Sacred Congregation for Catholic Education, *The Basic Plan . . .*, n. 46.

112. Cf. Sacred Congregation for Catholic Education, *The Basic Plan . . .*, n. 47.

113. Cf. Sacred Congregation for Catholic Education, *The Basic Plan . . .*, n. 47.

114. Cf. Paul VI, Encyclical, *Sacerdotalis caelibatus*, loc. cit., 666, n. 24.

115. Paul VI, Encyclical, *Sacerdotalis caelibatus*, loc. cit., 661, n. 13.

116. Cf. Paul VI, Encyclical, *Sacerdotalis caelibatus*, loc. cit., 661, 667, 668, 669, nn. 13, 20, 26, 30.

117. Cf. Vat. Coun. II, *Decree on the Ministry and Life of Priests*, n. 14.

118. Cf. Sacred Congregation for Catholic Education, *The Basic Plan . . .*, n. 69.

119. Cf. Vat. Coun. II, *Decree on the Training of Priests*, nn. 3, 19.

120. Cf. Vat. Coun. II, *Decree on the Training of Priests*, n. 11; Sacred Congregation for Catholic Education, *The Basic Plan . . .*, 51, 69.

121. Cf. Pius XI, Encyclical, *Ad catholici sacerdotii*, 20 Dec. 1935: AAS 28 (1936) 5 ff.; Vat. Coun. II, *Decree on the Training of Priests*, n. 2.

122. Cf. Vat. Coun II, *Decree on the Training of Priests*, n. 2; Sacred Congregation for Catholic Education, *The Basic Plan . . .*, n. 11; Vat. Coun. II, *Decree on the Ministry and Life of Priests*, n. 11; *Decree on the Church's Missionary Activity*, n. 19.

123. Cf. Sacred Congregation for Catholic Education, *The Basic Plan . . .*, n. 12.

124. Cf. Sacred Congregation for Catholic Education, *The Basic Plan . . .*, nn. 12, 20, 47, 51, 58, 69, 95.

125. Cf. Vat. Coun. II, *Decree on the Ministry and Life of Priests*, n. 17.

126. Cf. Vat. Coun. II, *Decree on the Training of Priests*, nn. 12, 19.

127. Cf. Vat. Coun. II, *Decree on the Training of Priests*, nn. 19-21.

128. Cf. Sacred Congregation for Catholic Education, *The Basic Plan . . .*, nn. 30-31.

129. Cf. Vat. Coun. II, *Decree on the Means of Social Communication*, passim; Pontifical Commission for Social Communication, Pastoral Instruction, *Communio et progressio*, 23 May 1971; AAS 63 (1971) 593 ff. passim.

Circular Letter Concerning Some of the More Urgent Aspects of Spiritual Formation in Seminaries

Sacred Congregation for
Catholic Education
1980

Circular Letter Concerning Some of the More Urgent Aspects of Spiritual Formation in Seminaries

To All Local Ordinaries

The document entitled *Ratio fundamentalis institutionis sacerdotalis [The Basic Plan for Priestly Formation]* and, following this, the various national "Rationes" produced by Bishops' Conferences have given to *spiritual formation* its deserved place, namely, the most important of all.

However, there are many signs today which indicate that it might be opportune and useful to reflect further and deeper on this matter. We presume that people today are ready to accept such further reflection and, with the help of God's grace, we expect rich fruit from it.

After pointing out encouraging signs in this field, the present circular letter aims not at producing a complete and systematic study, but at calling the attention of seminary authorities to certain, selected areas where immediate effort seems to be needed. At the conclusion, a suggestion will be proposed that could be quite important for the future of the priesthood in the Catholic Church.

I. Introduction

Providential signs

The sign which we would like to point out first, since it has made the greatest impression on us in this Sacred Congregation, is the truly exceptional quality of the *"Plans of Action for Vocations,"* which we ventured to ask the bishops to prepare and which are arriving here at a rate that we had never dared to expect. The climate of courageous faith shown by the spiritual aspects of these "Plans" indicates that the time might have arrived for some initiatives in the spiritual field that will not be undertaken in vain. If these "Plans" put forward by the dioceses were concerned only or mainly with clever vocational techniques, they would not justify this present circular letter. However, the position that prayer occupies in them — always in the forefront of every initiative and the animating force behind it — brings evidence of the presence of a grace. We are living in one of the "favorable times" when generous commitments can be demanded.

Resurgence of vocations

Moreover, projects and hopes are not the only things involved. The widespread increase in the *number of vocations* throughout the world confirms the presence of a providential activity which is bearing fruit. Of course, many dioceses and even entire countries — although these are in the minority — are still behind in this trend and are a source of worry. But, it is remarkable that in those places where the upward trend is the strongest, and especially where it is most unexpectedly vigorous, one often comes across the following interpretation of the facts by the bishops: it is, first of all, to the spiritual renewal of seminaries that the increase must be attributed. This renewal has been sought and produced in different forms, but there are certain common points to which we must return if we are to gather any profit from these experiences and find our way forward.

The urge to pray

Another consideration cannot be ignored. Everyone today agrees that recognition must be given to a real *"urge to pray"* more or less everywhere in the Church and even outside of her. The number of "centers" is almost beyond counting where people come to learn about prayer, where they gather to pray and where they hope to find a "teacher of prayer." People sometimes go to great lengths in order to find such a person and run the almost certain risk of losing their way and being disappointed. A new method needs only to be suggested somewhere and immediately students are found who arrive ready to try it out. But, whatever may be the spiritual qualities involved, whatever may be the setbacks and errors, it is undeniable that there exists a general and profound inclination to pray. In many ways this invitation to prayer is receiving a worthy answer. But, do we realize sufficiently the extent of this quest or the extraordinary opportunity that is being offered to the Church for the progress of the faith? We do, so long as we are able to find in our priests real "teachers of prayer" with a firm knowledge of tradition, priests who experience God in a deep and fervent way, who are capable of being wise and prudent "directors of souls" following the paths of the great masters, and who are also responsive to the needs of the time. This is quite a different matter from judging various prayer movements, often confused in their origins. Rather it means helping priests to be able to reply effectively to the call God gives to His chosen ones, so that they can become "teachers of prayer."

Spiritual resurgence in the Church

Furthermore, the *general context of the life of the Church* must be taken into consideration here. Can one avoid the feeling that the Church has just lived through an impressive series of events, the spiritual richness of which has disconcerted the usual opinion makers and left them confounded, as if they were faced with evidence of the intervention of something that goes beyond human factors? Who was not struck and even dumbfounded by the surprising dignity of the funeral of Pope Paul VI? The whole world was able to witness this through our advanced means of social communication. Who did not suspect that there was at least something other than a prominent "news story" in the astonishingly rapid and unanimous conclaves which followed and in the eventual arrival of the Pope "from afar," whose simplicity and radiant faith immediately captured the hearts of the faithful? One can suppose that the presence of such a leader—emerging from the storms of the post-conciliar period—is an exceptional opportunity for encouraging priests to arm themselves with that same faith, a faith that springs from sources of prayer.

The young generation

We must note here the extent to which the younger generation have in their own way responded to the situation which we have been describing. Young people are waiting for Christ. They are awaiting someone to point Him out to them and to make them love Him. They are ready to welcome priests who are able to do this. Many of them would give themselves enthusiastically for this very mission. Therefore, our seminaries must be prepared to meet their expectations. The future of the Church at the present moment depends most of all on the spiritual formation of future priests.

In the soul of a young person today spiritual hunger naturally and generally takes the form of an anxious search for a *reason for living,* which the world about him does not provide. It leaves him to face life while being deprived of what would give sense or purpose to life. We ourselves know, through faith, that this reason for living is none other than Christ. The young man who aspires to the priesthood usually has already begun to understand this. He also knows that other young people already have some intuition about Christ and that, more or less distinctly, they have already begun to call on His name. He would like to make Him known to them in fullness of truth. He expects the seminary to make him capable of rendering this service to them.

Christ the ideal of the seminarian

No other group than the young is more aware of the spiritual vacuum that needs to be filled. However, because of this there is no other group in which solutions born of despair are more to be feared: the attraction of false ideologies, the mindless promise of destructive experiences such as drugtaking, the rejection of all constraint whether moral, familial, or social, and, in extreme cases, the renunciation of life itself. One who brings to this generation the Person of Jesus Christ, Who is the only true response, will himself have to be solidly prepared for his task and *to have found in Christ not only light but strength,* the true reason for living, the authentic model for humanity to follow, the Saviour to Whom we must submit and with Whom we must "cooperate" to use a well-known phrase of Saint Theresa of Avila.

It is from this starting point that the essential task of a seminary must begin, the task that belongs to all who are responsible for forming future priests.

It is towards Christ in fact that grace has attracted the gaze of the young men who aspire to His priesthood. They have already given Him their hearts in an outburst of generosity which is still ignorant of the demands of formation, but which already instinctively consents to all the sacrifices involved. The future priest knows that he will have to give everything and, in the depths of his soul, he already has done so.

Jesus Christ: life in a seminary must be designed solely to allow this initial grace to come to full maturity, according to the measure in which it is given to each. The heart of the future priest will have to free itself from everything which, by nature or habit, could constitute an obstacle to the development in him of the love of Christ. All the resources of his being must be employed so that they become instruments to the accomplishment of this one end. It must be Christ Who is known, sought, loved evermore fully through study, through personal sacrifice, victory over self and in the slow conquest of the virtues of justice, temperance, fortitude, and prudence. It must be Christ Who is contemplated with enough fervent and patient persistence so that, little by little, according to the admirable idea of Saint Paul (cf. 2 Cor. 3.18) the very face of Christ is imprinted on that of believers. It must be Christ Who is ceaselessly offered to the Father for the salvation of the world in the mystery of which the future priest will be fully the minister. It is Christ Whom a future priest cannot fail to proclaim and Whose kingdom, by the power of the Holy Spirit and to the glory of the Father, must be the permanent concern and the only reason for a seminarian's existence.

II. Guidelines

Four directives

We believe it is our duty to point out *four of the most urgent guidelines* which the work of spiritual formation for future priests ought to follow:
1. Priests need to be formed in such a way that the *Word of God* is welcomed by them and loved in depth. This Word is none other than Christ Himself. For this end we must begin with the cultivation of *a sense of genuine interior silence.* To acquire such a sense is difficult. As Saint Ignatius of Loyola says, "To find Christ" is not possible without long and well-directed, patient effort. It is the way of prayer which is esteemed, loved, desired here despite all the distractions and all the obstacles. The future priest, through his own real experience, must be able to be a "teacher of prayer" for all those who will come to him or whom he will seek out, and for all whom so many false prophets today easily lead astray.
2. Priests need to be formed today who recognize in the *Paschal Mystery,* of which they will be the ministers, the supreme expression of God's Word. To this end they must be taught the way *to communion in the mystery of Christ Who died and rose from the dead.* It is there that Christ is truly the "Saviour." If the image we have of Christ is not that of the "Crucified One," we have an image of someone else. Saint Paul recalled this with singular vigor (cf. 1 Cor. 1.23; 2.2) Now it is the priest who in the Eucharistic Mystery makes present the sacrifice of Christ and gathers the Christian People around him to participate in it. One can say, without hesitation or exaggeration, therefore, that the life of a seminary can be judged by the understanding it is able to impart to future priests about this Mystery and about the inalienable responsibility which priests have to make the faithful communicate worthily in it.
3. Priests need to be formed who are fearless in accepting the fact that real communion with Christ entails self-denial, and, in particular, in understanding that following Christ entails genuine obedience. Thus the seminary will have to impart *a sense of penance.* This means, of course, the

Sacrament of Penance, but also and above all, it means teaching seminarians that penance which is indispensable for anyone who wants to live in Christ, not participating falsely in His Mystery, not refusing a share in His passion, but carrying one's cross in His footsteps, acquiring those virtues which support a Christian soul and enable it to prevail, that is to say, "stand firm" against the enemy in the combat, which Saint Paul compares to the contests in a stadium (1 Cor. 9.24). A seminary which allows a future priest to leave unaware of the struggles which await him and of self-denial, without which his fidelity is impossible, just as for the ordinary faithful, would have gravely failed in its mission.

4. Finally, a seminary ought to be a school of filial love towards her who is the *"Mother of Jesus"* and whom Christ on the cross gave us as our mother. This must not be merely a pietistic and sentimental note attached to spiritual formation in seminaries. Rather the taste for prayer to the Blessed Virgin, confidence in her intercession, and sound habits in this area are to be an integral part of the formation program of a seminary.

Now we shall discuss each of these points more thoroughly.

1. Christ the Word of God

Interior silence

A candidate for the priesthood must become capable of listening to and understanding the Word, the *"Verbum Dei."*

It is not necessary to insist here on the manifest quest for *interior silence,* both among Christians and non-Christians alike. One could cite the groups being formed, the "centers" being created, the often frantic search for those who are deemed able to unlock a "secret" in regard to this matter, the interest shown in various formulas which more or less take their inspiration from certain areas of Asia, etc.

Let us leave aside all detailed description of these searches for silence and all attempts at judgment. Let us here simply recognize the quest and go on to draw conclusions in regard to our future priests. They must receive an experience of interior silence. They must acquire a genuine sense of it. They must become capable of communicating it to others.

First of all, it is important that priests should have a precise idea about this silence. They must know in what it consists. Surely nobody will confuse it with a simple external silence, from which, however, it is in a certain way inseparable, which we shall mention later. There are other, more serious, ambiguities in this field, and many people become exposed to them when they get involved in oriental mysticism or other similar activities. Christian mysticism has no other aim than to bring about a meeting with Christ, to foster an interior intimacy and a real dialogue with Him. Genuine interior silence, about which someone like Saint John of the Cross speaks so well, has in Christ its source and its goal. It is the fruit of living faith and of charity. It is abandonment to God and dependence upon Him and is, in itself, "distinct from one's feelings and from the extraordinary" (Saint Louis Marie Grignion de Montfort). It is a profound attitude of soul which seeks everything from God and is entirely turned towards Him. It is not linked essentially to any bodily position and even less does it concern a sensible manifestation of the Holy Spirit. This is what the seminarian will have to be made to discover and accept. This will be done by training him in the school of sound spiritual masters and in that of the Church herself in her official prayers.

The art of prayer

To attain interior silence proper steps must be taken. Training in this field is slow and difficult because it involves liberating a man from certain internal inclinations and from the constant distractions of the world. Without pretending to make quick and superficial judgments about some methods proposed here and there, we must beware of "short cuts" which promise too much too soon, throw us off the right track, and create false quests with an illusion of almost automatic and deceptive results. What results? A certain human warmth is taken for spiritual well-being; violence is done to the body in a way that harms the soul; beguiling music is taken for prayer, etc. The school of faith is arduous and it is this that we are speaking about here. The true instruments in this area are: contact with authentic teachers, prayer that is patiently cultivated, and, above all, a perfect and deep participation and sharing in the official prayer of the Church. We must add to this the presence of a guide, the sort of director which the future priest himself will become tomorrow. Furthermore, we must not separate this aspect of the life of faith, which is truly fundamental, from the other aspects of formation, making the rule a faith which is exercised through love.

Spiritual masters

The Church, thank God, has never lacked "spiritual teachers." Their recognized personal sanctity and the extraordinary fecundity of their activity are there to invite us and encourage us. They are the "saints" who have formed generations of saints. Everyone remembers their names, but how many future priests will come into real contact with them before leaving the seminary? How many will, through such contact, acquire a genuine spiritual climate for themselves, a taste for the things of God, and a desire for interior silence, which is not deceptive and which allows them to discern falsehood in these areas? Every seminary must have a policy about this and each seminary must give its students a habit and a taste for the great spiritual writers, the real "classics." Reading these classics does not exclude other spiritual reading, but reading these writers must be a preeminent activity and must remain indispensable.

Learning how to pray

In this context, the students *must be taught to pray.* They must accept the fact that at first this will be arduous and sometimes disappointing. There should be no fear of issuing rules, of humbly adopting a method, and of putting the method into practice. If in a given context ample prayer in common is not thought possible, then at least the times for private prayer must be firmly stipulated and the seminary must make certain that personal prayer is conscientiously carried out. Abstract preparation should be avoided. Instead, one must turn to the Gospel and constantly recall the goal: "to search for Christ," "to wait on Him alone," "not thinking a beautiful idea is necessarily a good result," "learning the limits of one's knowledge," "deepening rather then widening one's experience," etc. This then effects a development; from simply listening one passes to asking, from wordless adoration one passes to praise, etc. This is what the guide or director must continually call to the seminarian's mind so that he will not go astray and may evaluate his progress correctly.

Prayer of the Church

Nothing, however, is more important and decisive than a deeper and more complete participation in the *official prayer of the Church*. This is to say, first of all, the Mass and the Liturgy of the Word which constitutes the first part of it. (We shall return to this later.) But, it also means the Liturgy of the Hours. The prayer of the Church is nourished by the prayer of the psalms. The Church receives from God Himself these "inspired" words. They are like the "mold" into which she pours human thoughts and feelings. It is the Holy Spirit Who through the psalms suggests words and forms the heart. It was thus that Jesus prayed. His passion bears witness to this. It was thus that Mary prayed, if one accepts the evidence of her "Magnificat." There is no prayer more able gradually to create the inner silence that men seek, the silence which is true, the silence which comes from God, than the Divine Office when it is simply, intelligently, and perfectly sung, either inwardly or, better still, in community.

External silence

In all of this, *material silence* is not useless nor a matter of indifference. When inner silence exists it calls forth external silence. It demands this and it fosters it. In its turn external silence serves the purposes of interior silence. In a seminary, which is preparing future teachers of prayer, there must be external silence. The seminary Rule of Life must provide for this as a priority. However, if the students do not understand the origin of such silence and what it is meant for, it can only be received by them as meaningless and be badly accepted. On the other hand, where internal silence has been deepened, the demand for material silence is all the stronger and more vigorous. There can be no doubt that in a seminary where external silence does not exist interior silence is also absent.

General seminary climate

It is immediately obvious that such initiation into prayer requires certain conditions and if such conditions are not provided, seminaries are failing in their duty. We have already stated that formation for prayer is inseparable from *general education*. It cannot remain isolated. It must be linked to a life of neighborly love and to a search for Christ through study and to service in the kingdom of God which is present and will be present in the future in the Church. However, training in prayer also demands specific and particular methods. Above all, the main task of those responsible for the running of seminary is the formation of the students in interior silence. They must make continual and concerted efforts in this undertaking. Each has a special part to play in this, from the Rector to the Spiritual Director, to each member of the staff. If this chain is broken, there is no real formation. If each seminary authority is not aware of his responsibility for this formation in his conscience and in fact or if he does not allow this to be the object of mutual and continuous reflection, the best methods will lose their value because the right general climate does not exist.

2. The Word of the Cross: The Redemptive Sacrifice

Sacrament and sacrifice

The prayer of the Church reaches its "apex" in the Liturgy of the Eucharist. In the words of the Constitution on the Liturgy of the Second Vatican Council (n. 10) it is "the summit and the source." In fact, the Eucharist is nothing other than the sacrifice of the Lord which is offered and shared within the community of the baptized. The providential renewal begun by Pope Saint Pius X has born great fruit and the Second Vatican Council has given new thrust to this effort. Future priests must be able to exploit this movement in depth and at the same time maintain its proper direction. Today this requires a firm hand, a solid and sure theological sense, an absolute fidelity to the discipline of the Church, and deep and well-nourished personal experience.

The Eucharist is the "Sacrament of the Redemptive Sacrifice." Theology has never ceased explaining this mystery from which the Church permanently draws life. The fullness of this mystery is such that human thought can scarcely grasp it. At times there is a risk of reducing it in order to make it fit within the categories of human reason. At other times there is risk of exploiting one aspect of it to the detriment of others, which is to say there is a risk of disturbing the structure of our faith. That is why in a seminary the doctrine about this matter must be taught with extreme care and must be constantly recalled. No single aspect should be sacrificed to another. The teaching of the Council of Trent on the reality of the sacrifice must be professed in all its force as must the teaching on the "real presence." The aspect of brotherly communion, however deeply understood, cannot overshadow the fundamental aspect of the sacrifice of Christ, outside of which the Eucharistic Banquet loses its meaning. The deviations which are occurring today on these points cannot be ignored and future priests must be carefully warned about them. Pastoral work which does not have its basis in doctrine cannot be considered beneficial.

Eucharistic adoration

Euchartistic faith has undergone an inevitable and gradual development through the centuries in the matter of worship outside of the liturgical sacrifice. This has opened up a certain space for Eucharistic prayer, offered with grateful fervor, to Christ given for us in the host and sacramentally present, beyond the confines of the Mass, especially reserved as "Viaticum" for the dying. The continuous development of the cult of Eucharistic adoration is one of the most marvelous experiences of the Church. The extraordinary sanctity which has developed from it and the number of whole communities specifically consecrated to this adoration are a guarantee of the authenticity of its inspiration. Someone like Brother Charles de Foucauld, alone in the desert with the Eucharist, yet shining out in the Church through his "Little Brothers" and "Little Sisters," is a most striking example of this in our own time. A priest who does not have his fervor, who does not acquire a taste for this adoration and is unable to communicate this to others is betraying the Eucharist itself and is blocking the way of the faithful to an incomparable treasure.

The priesthood

The doctrine of the *priesthood* is grafted onto this. The encouragement given to the theological consideration of ministries in the Church should not cast doubt on the doctrine of priestly ministry as this was happily and solidly defined in the Church, especially in the Council of Trent. Clerics and laypeople have a complementary mission in the Church. The development of lay ministries does not alter the specific nature of the ministerial priesthood. Far from compromising the sense and importance of God's Word, the Eucharistic Action consecrates it. Two aspects are welded and bound together in the person of the priest, the two aspects by which people are given food from heaven. These are the two aspects which are stressed so strongly as radically united in the sixth chapter of the Gospel according to Saint John, speaking about the preaching of Jesus at Capharnaum. The priest is ordained to prepare and distribute under two sacramental forms—that of the sign of the word and that under the sign of bread—the eternal bread which is Christ.

Even in these, his own fields, in missionary areas, the ministerial priest might need some assistance. However, whatever aids the Church recognizes as legitimate and on occasion necessary from the laity, a priest cannot lose nor abandon his own essential responsibility. When a layman is asked to preach, the priest remains responsible for the choice of a collaborator, whose appointment cannot be taken lightly, and for the contents of what he preaches. It is exactly the same way when the priest chooses extraordinary ministers of Holy Communion. This is why the seminary must attach extreme importance to the means which the Church has instituted for preparing future priests to become conscious of the charge laid upon them and its special significance. The two liturgical ministries, which formerly were called minor orders, namely lectorate and acolytate, are no less indispensable or serious today in the rather modest garb they now wear. To underrate their value, for example by conferring them both at the same time, is to go against a good of the first order and to deprive oneself of a supernatural, pedagogical resource in a serious area. One ought to reread the moving letter of Saint Cyprian (Epistle XXXVIII, in the edition of Can. Bayard, Paris, 1925, pp. 96-97) in which he called to the office of lector a young Christian who rendered himself worthy of it by risking martyrdom. Saint Cyprian presents this office as necessary and desired preparation for higher responsibility, that of the priesthood.

The discipline of the Church

Understanding the Eucharist leads one to understand and to respect meticulously the discipline of the Church in this matter. People often speak today about "creativity." However, this can only be understood correctly within the framework of the rules formulated by the Church. The rules which order prayer must be accepted with the same obedience as those which concern faith, according to the classical formula "lex orandi est lex credendi." These are inseparable. The rules formulated by the Church are deeply linked to the essential values which individuals might lose sight of, even inspired, as they might be, by real pastoral concerns. Thus it is possible for the faith to become disordered. Furthermore, this produces difficult problems and painful divisions. The essential point of reference here is the Ecumenical Council. It has been abundantly proved that the general orientations of the Council, if they are faithfully observed, do not irritate the People of God. They rebel only against novelties and excesses. For instance, the Council is far from having banned the use of the Latin language. Indeed, it did the contrary. Thus the systematic exclusion of Latin is an abuse no less to be condemned than the systematic desire of some people to use it exclusively. Its sudden and total disappearance will not be without serious pastoral consequences. Only in a gradual way can the "Word of God" take on, for the general good, the apparel of everyday language. Otherwise it will be confused with the "words of men" in the consciences of the faithful (cf. 1 Tm. 2.13). This is why the seminary must ensure that future priests understand the seriousness of what is at stake and help them not only to practice but also to love obedience. There is quite enough room for new initiatives in the liturgy within the framework of the official directives.

Christ the bread of life; Word and Eucharist

The disciples on the road to Emmaus felt their hearts burn within them (cf. Lk. 24.32) while Scripture was being explained to them by the mysterious traveller. But, they recognized Him only in "the breaking of the bread." At each Mass the Church retraces the same road. Through His Holy Spirit Christ comments on the Scriptures for His people so that they may be ready to take part in the Banquet prepared by His hands. The deep unity of the mystery of the Divine Word, now offered so liberally in the liturgy, with the Eucharist itself is something that must be evermore deeply experienced by future priests. There are in fact not two separate "tables" since the one leads to the other, just as the revelation in the sixth chapter of the Gospel according to Saint John goes from the bread of the Word to the bread of the Eucharist. The whole of this Gospel is slanted towards the "hour" of Christ which He spends so much time explaining. The whole teaching of the Word was designed to bring people to an understanding of the Paschal Mystery. In fact, it was "for this that He had come." The Liturgy of the Word prepares one for the sacrifice. It is in this Liturgy of the Word which precedes the Eucharist that the Word acquires its full meaning. It lives fully only through formal contact with the Eucharist. The "celebrations of the Word" provided for by the Ecumenical Council cannot avoid making reference to the Eucharist. And, it is here that the prayer life of a future priest must realize its full promise, find its full significance, and locate its true value.

Clerical dress

It can be truly said that one can *judge the spiritual climate of a seminary* by its participation in the Eucharist. Is this not the place perhaps to note that at the Eucharist people see the need and the meaning of clerical dress, which has been too easily abandoned, to the harm of the very pastoral work this was supposed to foster?

Pope John Paul II has already recalled on several occasions the need for a priest to appear before men for what he is, one of them, certainly, but marked by a deep sign which sets him apart and which sends him out in the name of God to God's followers and to all the world. Now how is it possible to deny the evidence? In the eyes of the faithful and in the very conscience of the priest the significance of the "sacraments of faith" is steadily degraded when a priest is habitually negligent about his clothing or even fully secularized when he is the minister of them. These sacraments include Penance, Anointing the Sick, and, above all, the Holy Eucharist. Often the situation ends with the priest not even using the prescribed liturgical vestments. If this trend is thought to be inevitable the end is disastrous and fatal. The seminary has no right to be lax when faced with such possible consequences. It must have the courage to speak, to explain, and to make demands upon its students.

3. The Word of the Cross: Spiritual Sacrifices

Alongside the Eucharist *Penance* must be assigned an important place. This word has been used as the name of a sacrament, but when used in the context of priestly life one must obviously extend its meaning to one which involves an effort tending to unite one with Christ the Redeemer and to participate personally in His passion in an effective way. The priest must become a "teacher of penance" to others in the same way he must be a "teacher of prayer."

Preparation for penance

The Second Vatican Council did not relegate the Sacrament of Penance to the shadows. If it seems to have become less important when compared to the practice of the recent past, one can state that this is a real abuse. *"Penitential celebrations"* were not designed to gradually eliminate individual confession and to substitute for it "general absolution," which some falsely claim is a return to early Christian practice. Public penance in the early Church involved a small number of specific sinners who were well known from private contact over a period of time with the bishop. The so-called "public" penance involved bringing to public notice a penitent whose penitential journey had up to that time been private. What has this ancient rite got in common with an absolution given to an indeterminate group about whom nothing is known? Even if the Church allows "general absolution" in cases of necessity and under certain conditions, it is in private penance, in the way in which theology has progressively defined and explained it, that one finds a resemblance to the public penance of the past ages. Having said this, it must now be asserted that penitential services are a very fine initiative which in a timely way bring people's consciences to a state where they feel able to go *individually* to a priest. Some find these devotional services provide a suitable spiritual atmosphere, which they did not have in the past, enabling them to gain a clear idea about the will of God and His specific demands and allowing them to put things right which had been long amiss. One can see what kind of rich training the seminary must give to future priests if they are to succeed in this area, following the Instruction on Liturgical Formation in Seminaries, issued by the Sacred Congregation for Catholic Education recently (n. 35). Through authentic contact with the Word of God, seminarians must be trained to have a right idea about *the structure of a Christian conscience,* which is certainly based on charity, but which is also well aware of how charity has to be translated into action, in justice, temperance, fortitude, and prudence, to use the classical expressions. At the same time they must be trained to put all this reflection and investigation *in the context of the love of God* from which genuine and calm contrition can spring.

Private penance

From all this, *personal contact with a priest* becomes a natural consequence. Nothing can take the place of that meeting with a priest when a mind that has been informed and a heart that has been stirred asks him whom God has given the power to forgive sins to utter those irreplaceable words which we hear so often in the Gospels and which touch the heart of each repentant sinner: "Your sins are forgiven." If possible and when it is thought useful this pardon is matched with appropriate advice. While the preparation may have been communal and has permitted each penitent to benefit from the prayers of all, the pardon is, of itself, personal and incommunicable. The seminary must impart to its students a taste for this private absolution along with one for communal celebrations of penance where these are possible. The future priest who has grasped this well will find the courage to impose on himself the hard regime that made the Cure of Ars a saint and of which someone like Saint John Bosco has given a magnificent example in more recent times.

Spiritual directors

It is important to note that, in the context of the Sacrament of Penance which is worthily and authentically received, the light of the Lord passes freely and goes beyond pardon. A priest who hears confessions becomes in many cases a "spiritual director." He helps people to discern the ways of the Lord. How many vocations have never been discovered through a lack of this unique supernatural contact in the course of which a priest could have at least asked a question? One can probably attribute the striking slackening off in the number of vocations at least partially to the gradual decline in the practice of private confession. A seminary must realize that it is preparing future "spiritual directors."

Self-denial and the rule of life

The Sacrament of Penance is never anything other than the intervention of God Who comes to bring to fruition an individual's work, in which the penitenial service was a preliminary and fortunate stage. God comes to meet the penitent who must continue as a Christian to carry his cross in the footsteps of Christ. The expression "self-denial" is rarely heard today. Self-denial itself is accepted very unwillingly. However, it is indispensable for everyone according to his state in life. A priest cannot be faithful to the charge laid upon him and to all his priestly commitments, especially celibacy, if he has not been prepared to accept and impose upon himself real discipline. Seminaries do not always have the courage to say this or to demand it, especially in relationship to a *"Rule of Life,"* a set of rules which are wise, modest, and yet firm and which will prepare the students to impose on themselves in the future a Rule of Life. The absence of precise rules to be obeyed is a source of many problems for a priest. He is left open to wasting time, to losing all idea of his mission and of the restraints it imposes on him, to a progressive vulnerability to all attacks of his feelings, etc. It should be remembered what sacrifices conjugal fidelity involves. Surely priestly fidelity can demand no less. This would be quite paradoxical. A priest simply is not permitted to see, hear, say, or experience everything he feels inclined toward. A seminary must train future priests to enable them, in their inner liberty, to bear sacrifices and to accept personal discipline both intelligently and loyally.

Obedience

One cannot avoid pausing a moment to consider the problem of *obedience*. The word "obedience" must stop being a forbidden word. One cannot be a disciple of Christ and still deny a title which Saint Paul uses for Christ as one of His claims to glory (cf. Phil. 2.8-9). Not only is personal freedom uncompromised by obedience but, when it is well understood, it is the highest expression of freedom.

Obviously then, obedience must be well understood.

One certainly cannot claim to be obedient to God when he refuses to obey those to whom God has confided His mission. Indeed, the exercise of authority and obedience cannot be understood unless on both sides there is expressly involved a notion of obedience to God. In this matter both the Rector and the seminarian must have their attention fixed constantly on the will of God. This will of God is made explicit in the "common good" of the seminary. It is the Rector's job to clearly define this "common good," to help people to see it and accept it, to help them understand it and love it, to stimulate people to put their initiatives and good will at its service, to interest his students in grasping this "common good" in those points where they might find it unclear, and to dialogue about it. Finally, he must judge with authority and without hesitation. It is the duty of a future priest to listen to and understand the Rector whom the Lord has given the mission of governing in His name. It is also his job to cooperate, according to his capacity, in bringing about the fulfillment of the common good. This always consists in creating and maintaining an atmosphere in which the priesthood of Christ can be discerned and recommended to all, in which the grace of God can do its work in everyone, and in which not more or less is demanded than people are capable of giving.

Obedience will always be a sacrifice. It must at the same time be a joy for it is a way of loving God. In the future, a young priest will have to practice obedience in many ways. He must in the seminary be enabled to understand it in the person of Christ and to love it. In this context one can authentically experience a real brotherly, Christian community in the seminary in which all are bound together by the will to cooperate with each other for the good of the kingdom of God.

4. The Word Made Flesh in the Womb of the Virgin Mary

The Marian Mystery an object of faith

A point of major importance would be omitted in the present circumstances if there was neglect in remembering briefly and firmly the place that should be occupied in seminary life by *devotion to the Blessed Virgin Mary.*

The word "devotion" today is rather equivocal. It might seem that what is being dealt with here is a personal and entirely optional matter. In fact, it is a question quite simply of accepting the faith of the Church and living out what our creed requires us to believe. The Word of God became incarnate in the womb of the Virgin Mary. The words of Christ on the cross would serve to show, were it needful, that it is not some simple, ephemeral contribution made by Mary to the economy of salvation that we are concerned with here. The annunciation is another name for the incarnation. The Church gradually has become more aware of the marian mystery. Far from adding her own conjectures to what she found in Sacred Scripture about Mary, she has met the Virgin at every stage of her journey towards the discovery of Christ.

Christology is also mariology. The fervor with which our Supreme Pontiff, Pope John Paul II, lives the marian mystery is nothing other than fidelity. This is the way in which love of the Blessed Virgin must be taught in a seminary. The problems which christology face today could find their main solution in a fidelity of this kind. In particular, devotion to the Blessed Virgin Mary can and must be a guarantee against everything which would tend to eradicate the historicity of the mystery of Christ. One cannot help but wonder whether the decline in devotion to the Blessed Virgin Mary does not often mask a certain hesitation to profess frankly and openly the mystery of Christ and the incarnation.

Marian attitude

Obviously, the mystery of the Virgin cannot be *lived out* except in an inner climate of simplicity and abandonment, which has nothing to do with sweet sentimentality and superficial outpouring of feelings. Contact with the Blessed Virgin can only lead to greater contact with Christ and His cross. Nothing better introduces one, in the spirit of the Second Vatican Council and of the Apostolic Exhortation *"Marialis cultus"* of Pope Paul VI, to the joy of believing. "Blessed are you who have believed" (Lk. 1.45). A seminary must give its students, without shrinking from this task, a sense of the authentic mystery of Mary. This should be done through the means traditionally used by the Church to arrive at a real interior devotion, such as the saints possessed as, in the expression of Saint Louis Marie Grignion de Montfort, the "secret" of salvation.

III. Conclusion

In conclusion we wish to offer a suggestion. In fact, we would like this suggestion to be followed and gradually to become part of the normal seminary practice in a solid and lasting way.

The ideal which we have in part described is not easy to attain. The generous young men who offer themselves for the priesthood come from a world in which inner recollection is almost impossible because of continuous overexcitement of the senses and of overabundance of concepts. Experience shows that a *period of preparation* for the seminary, given over exclusively to spiritual formation, is not only not superfluous but can bring surprising results. There is evidence from seminaries in which the number of candidates has suddenly gone up. In these the people responsible attribute this to such a brave initiative. This period of spiritual apprenticeship is welcomed by the students. It appears that it is the diocesan authorities who are rather opposed to this spiritual propaedeutic period. This seems to come from a lack of priests and a view that it would be foolish to institute such a practice. In reality, were it tried they would soon become convinced of its benefits. Permit us to insist, in conclusion, that this suggestion be tried.

This period of preparation would benefit from being conducted somewhere other than the seminary itself. It should be of sufficient duration. Thus something could be achieved at the beginning which might be very difficult or impossible to achieve later on when seminary training is taken up with a great deal of intellectual work. Then the students often do not have the leisure and the freedom of mind to accomplish a real spiritual apprenticeship.

If this suggestion is followed, the things indicated in this circular would have a good chance of success and one could expect they would bear rich fruit.

Evidently, this will not always be possible. But, other possibilities might open themselves up to generous imaginations who will try to understand and put into practice the matters mentioned in this circular letter and who are prepared to give themselves trustfully to Christ so that their labors may be helped and sustained by His grace.

Given at Rome, from the offices of the Sacred Congregation for Catholic Education, the 6th of January in the year of our Lord 1980, the Solemnity of the Epiphany.

Gabriel-Marie Cardinal Garrone
Prefect

Antonio M. Javierre-Ortas
Titular Archbishop of Meta
Secretary

Pope John Paul II
Apostolic Constitution,
Sapientia Christiana,
on Ecclesiastical Universities
and Faculties
and
Norms of Application
of the
Sacred Congregation for
Catholic Education for the
Correct Implementation
of the Above

1979

Apostolic Constitution, *Sapientia Christiana,* on Ecclesiastical Universities and Faculties

John Paul, Bishop
Servant of the Servants of God
for Perpetual Remembrance

Foreword

I

Christian wisdom, which the Church teaches by divine authority, continuously inspires the faithful of Christ zealously to endeavor to relate human affairs and activities with religious values in a single living synthesis. Under the direction of these values all things are mutually connected for the glory of God and the integral development of the human person, a development that includes both corporal and spiritual well-being.[1]

Indeed, the Church's mission of spreading the Gospel not only demands that the Good News be preached ever more widely and to ever greater numbers of men and women, but the very power of the Gospel should permeate thought patterns, standards of judgment, and norms of behavior; in a word, it is necessary that the whole of human culture be steeped in the Gospel.[2]

The cultural atmosphere in which a human being lives has a great influence upon his or her way of thinking and, thus, of acting. Therefore, a division between faith and culture is more than a small impediment to evangelization, while a culture penetrated with the Christian spirit is an instrument that favors the spreading of the Good News.

Furthermore, the Gospel is intended for all peoples of every age and land and is not bound exclusively to any particular culture. It is valid for pervading all cultures so as to illumine them with the light of divine revelation and to purify human conduct, renewing them in Christ.

For this reason, the Church of Christ strives to bring the Good News to every sector of humanity so as to be able to convert the consciences of human beings, both individually and collectively, and to fill with the light of the Gospel their works and undertakings, their entire lives, and, indeed, the whole of the social environment in which they are engaged. In this way the Church carries out her mission of evangelizing also by advancing human culture.[3]

II

In this activity of the Church with regard to culture, Catholic universities have had and still have special importance. By their nature they aim to secure that "the Christian outlook should acquire a public, stable, and universal influence in the whole process of the promotion of higher culture."[4]

In fact, as my predecessor Pope Pius XI recalled in the preface to the Apostolic Constitution *Deus Scientiarum Dominus,*[5] there arose within the Church, from her earliest period, *didascaleia* for imparting instruction in Christian wisdom so that people's lives and conduct might be formed. From these houses of Christian wisdom the most illustrious Fathers and Doctors of the Church, teachers and ecclesiastical writers drew their knowledge.

With the passing of centuries schools were established in the neighborhood of cathedrals and monasteries, thanks especially to the zealous initiatives of bishops and monks. These schools imparted both ecclesiastical doctrine and secular culture, forming them into one whole. From these schools arose the universitites, those glorious institutions of the Middle Ages which, from their beginning, had the Church as their most bountiful mother and patroness.

Subsequently, when civil authorities, to promote the common good, began and developed their own universities, the Church, loyal to her very nature, did not desist from founding and favoring such kinds of centers of learning and institutions of instruction. This is shown by the considerable number of Catholic universities established in recent times in nearly all parts of the world. Conscious of her worldwide salvific mission, the Church wishes to be especially joined to these centers of higher learning and she desires that they flourish everywhere and work effectively to make Christ's true message present in the field of human culture and to make it advance in that field.

In order that Catholic universities might better achieve this goal, my predecessor Pope Pius XII, sought to stimulate their united activity when, by his Apostolic Brief of 27 July 1949 he formally established the International Federation of Catholic Universities. It was "to include all Athenaea which the Holy See either has canonically erected or will in the future erect in the world, or will have explicitly recognized as following the norms of Catholic teaching and as completely in conformity with that teaching."[6]

The Second Vatican Council, for this reason, did not hesitate to affirm that "the Church devotes considerable care to schools of higher learning," and it strongly recommended that Catholic universities should "be established in suitable locations throughout the world" and that "the students of these institutions should be truly outstanding in learning, ready to shoulder duties of major responsibility in society and to witness to the faith before the world."[7] As the Church well knows, "the future of society and of the Church herself is closely bound up with the development of young people engaged in higher studies."[8]

III

It is not surprising, however, that among Catholic universities the Church has always promoted with special care *Ecclesiastical Faculties and Universities,* which is to say those concerned particularly with Christian revelation and questions connected therewith and which are therefore more closely connected with her mission of evangelization.

In the first place, the Church has entrusted to these Faculties the task of preparing with special care students for the priestly ministry, for teaching the sacred sciences, and for the more arduous tasks of the apostolate. It is also the task of these Faculites "to explore more profoundly the various areas of the sacred disciplines so that day by day a deeper understanding of sacred revelation will be developed, the heritage of Christian wisdom handed down by our ancestors will be more plainly brought into view, dialogue will be fostered with our separated brothers and sisters and with non-Christians, and solutions will be found for problems raised by doctrinal progress."[9]

In fact, new sciences and new discoveries pose new problems that involve the sacred disciplines and demand an answer. While carrying out their primary duty of attaining through theological research a deeper grasp of revealed truth, those engaged in the sacred sciences should therefore maintain contact with scholars of other diciplines, whether these are believers or not, and should try to evaluate and interpret the latters' affirmations and judge them in the light of revealed truth.[10]

From this assiduous contact with reality, theologians are also encouraged to seek a more suitable way of communicating doctrine to their contemporaries working in other various fields of knowledge, for "the deposit of faith, or the truths contained in our venerable doctrine, is one thing; quite another is the way in which these truths are formulated, while preserving the same sense and meaning."[11] This will be very useful so that among the People of God religious practice and uprightness of soul may proceed at an equal pace with the progress of science and technology, and so that, in pastoral work, the faithful may be gradually led to a purer and more mature life of faith.

The possibility of a connection with the mission of evangelization also exists in Faculties of other sciences which, although lacking a special link with Christian revelation, can still help considerably in the work of evangelizing. These are looked at by the Church precisely under this aspect when they are erected as Ecclesiastical Faculties. They therefore have a particular relationship with the Church's Hierarchy.

Thus, the Apostolic See, in carrying out its mission, is clearly aware of its right and duty to erect and promote Ecclesiastical Faculties dependent on itself, either with a separate existence or as parts of universities, Faculties destined for the education of both ecclesiastical and lay students. This See is very desirous that the whole People of God, under the guidance of their Shepherds, should cooperate to ensure that these centers of learning contribute effectively to the growth of the faith and of Christian life.

IV

Ecclesiastical Faculties — which are ordered to the common good of the Church and have a valuable relationship with the whole ecclesial community—ought to be conscious of their importance in the Church and of their participation in the ministry of the Church. Indeed, those Faculties which treat of matters that are close to Christian revelation should also be mindful of the orders which Christ, the Supreme Teacher, gave to his Church regarding this ministry: "Go therefore and make disciples of all nations, baptizing them in the name of the Father and of the Son and of the Holy Spirit, teaching them to observe all that I have commanded you" (Mt. 28.19-20). From this it follows that there must be in these Faculties that adherence by which they are joined to the full doctrine of Christ, whose authentic guardian and interpreter has always been through the ages the Magisterium of the Church.

Bishops' Conferences in the individual nations and regions where these Faculties exist must diligently see to their care and progress, at the same time that they ceaselessly promote their fidelity to the Church's doctrine, so that these Faculties may bear witness before the whole community of the faithful to their wholehearted following of the above-mentioned command of Christ. This witness must always be borne both by the Faculty as such and by each and every member of the Faculty. Ecclesiastical Universities and Faculties have been constituted in the Church for the building up and perfecting of Christ's faithful, and they must always bear this in mind as a criterion in the carrying out of their work.

Teachers are invested with very weighty responsibility in fulfilling a special ministry of the word of God and in being instructors of the faith for the young. Let them, above all, therefore be for their students, and for the rest of the faithful, witnesses of the living truth of the Gospel and examples of fidelity to the Church. It is fitting to recall the serious words of Pope Paul VI: "The task of the theologian is carried out with a view to building up ecclesial communion so that the People of God may grow in the experience of faith." [12]

V

To attain these purposes, Ecclesiastical Faculties should be organized in such a way as to respond to the new demands of the present day. For this reason, the Second Vatican Council stated that their laws should be subjected to revision. [13]

In fact, the Apostolic Constitution *Deus Scientiarum Dominus*, promulgated by my predecessor Pope Pius XI on 24 May 1931, did much in its time to renew higher ecclesiastical studies. However, as a result of changed circumstances, it now needs to be suitably adapted and altered.

In the course of nearly fifty years great changes have taken place not only in civil society but also in the Church herself. Important events, especially the Second Vatican Council, have occurred, events which have affected both the internal life of the Church and her external relationships with Christians of other churches, with non-Christians, and with non-believers, as well as with all those in favor of a more human civilization.

In addition, there is a steadily growing interest being shown in the theological sciences, not only among the clergy but also by lay people, who are attending theological schools in increasing numbers. These schools, have, as a consequence, greatly multiplied in recent times.

Finally, a new attitude has arisen about the structure of universities and Faculties, both civil and ecclesiastical. This is a result of the justified desire for a university life open to greater participation, a desire felt by all those in any way involved in university life.

Nor can one ignore the great *evolution* that has taken place in pedagogical and didactic methods, which call for new ways of organizing studies. Then too there is the closer connection that is being felt more and more between various sciences and disciplines, as well as the desire for greater cooperation in the whole university environment.

To meet these new demands, the Sacred Congregation for Catholic Education, responding to the mandate received from the Council, already in 1967 began to study the question of renewal along the lines indicated by the Council. On 20 May 1968, it promulgated the *Normae quaedam ad Constitutionem Apostolicam "Deus Scientiarum Dominus" de studiis academicis ecclesiasticis recognoscendam,* which has exercised a beneficial influence during recent years.

VI

Now, however, this work needs to be completed and perfected with a new law. This law, abrogating the Apostolic Constitution *Deus Scientiarum Dominus* and the Norms of Application attached to it, as well as the *Normae quaedam* published on 20 May 1968 by the Sacred Congregation for Catholic Education, includes some still valid elements from these documents, while laying down new norms whereby the renewal that has already successfully begun can be developed and completed.

Nobody is unaware of the difficulties that appear to impede the promulgation of a new Apostolic Constitution. In the first place, there is the "passage of time" which brings changes so rapidly that it seems impossible to lay down anything stable and permanent. Then there is the "diversity of places" which seems to call for a *pluralism* which would make it appear almost impossible to issue common norms, valid for for all parts of the world.

Since however there exist Ecclesiastical Faculties throughout the world, which are erected and approved by the Holy See and which grant academic degrees in its name, it is necessary that a certain substantial unity be respected and that the requisites for gaining academic degrees be clearly laid down and have universal value. Things which are necessary and which are foreseen as being relatively stable must be set down by law, while at the same time a proper freedom must be left for introducing into the Statutes of the individual Faculties further specifications, taking into account varying local conditions and the university customs obtaining in each region. In this way, legitimate progress in academic studies is neither hindered nor restricted, but rather is directed through right channels towards obtaining better results. Moreover, together with the legitimate differentiation of the Faculties, the unity of the Catholic Church in these centers of education will also be clear to everyone.

Therefore, the Sacred Congregation for Catholic Education, by command of my predecessor Pope Paul VI, has consulted, first of all, the Ecclesiastical Universities and Faculties themselves, then, the departments of the Roman Curia and the other bodies interested. After this, it established a commission of experts who, under the direction of the same Congregation, have carefully reviewed the legislation covering ecclesiastical academic studies.

This work has now been successfully completed, and Pope Paul VI was about to promulgate this Constitution, as he so ardently desired to do, when he died; likewise Pope John Paul I was prevented by sudden death from doing so. After long and careful consideration of the matter, I decree and lay down, by my apostolic authority, the following laws and norms.

Part One
General Norms

Section I
Nature and Purpose of Ecclesiastical Universities and Faculties

Article 1. To carry out the ministry of evangelization given to the Church by Christ, the Church has the right and duty to erect and promote Universities and Faculties which depend upon herself.

Article 2. In this Constitution the terms Ecclesiastical Universities and Faculties mean those which have been canonically erected or approved by the Apostolic See, which foster and teach sacred doctrine and the sciences connected therewith, and which have the right to confer academic degrees by the authority of the Holy See.

Article 3. The purpose of Ecclesiastical Faculties are:

§ 1. through scientific research to cultivate and promote their own disciplines, and especially to deepen knowledge of Christian revelation and of matters connected with it, to enunciate systematically the truths contained therein, to consider in the light of revelation the most recent progress of the sciences, and to present them to the people of the present day in a manner adapted to various cultures;

§ 2. to train the students to a level of high qualification in their own disciplines, according to Catholic doctrine, to prepare them properly to face their tasks, and to promote the continuing permanent education of the ministers of the Church;

§ 3. to collaborate intensely, in accordance with their own nature and in close communion with the Hierarchy, with the local and the universal Church, in the whole work of evangelization.

Article 4. It is the duty of Bishops' Conferences to follow carefully the life and progress of Ecclesiastical Universities and Faculties, because of their special ecclesial importance.

Article 5. The canonical erection or approval of Ecclesiastical Universities and Faculties is reserved to the Sacred Congregation for Catholic Education, which governs them according to law.[14]

Article 6. Only Universities and Faculties canonically erected or approved by the Holy See and ordered according to the norms of this present Constitution have the right to confer academic degrees which have canonical value, with the exception of the special right of the Pontifical Biblical Commission.[15]

Article 7. The Statutes of each University or Faculty, which must be drawn up in accordance with the present Constitution, require approval by the Sacred Congregation for Catholic Education.

Article 8. Ecclesiastical Faculties erected or approved by the Holy See in non-ecclesiastical universities, which confer both canonical and civil academic degrees, must observe the prescriptions of the present Constitution, account being taken of the conventions signed by the Holy See with various nations or with the universities themselves.

Article 9. § 1. Faculties which have not been canonically erected or

233

approved by the Holy See may not confer academic degrees having canonical value.

§ 2. Academic degrees conferred by such Faculties, if they are to have value for some canonical effects only, require the recognition of the Sacred Congregation for Catholic Education.

§ 3. For this recognition, to be given for individual degrees for a special reason, the conditions laid down by the Sacred Congregation must be fulfilled.

Article 10. For the correct carrying out of the present Constitution, the Norms of application issued by the Sacred Congregation for Catholic Education must be observed.

Section II
The Academic Community
and Its Government

Article 11. § 1. Since the University or Faculty forms a sort of community, all the people in it, either as individuals or as members of councils, must feel, each according to his or her own status, coresponsible for the common good and must strive to work for the institution's goals.

§ 2. Therefore, their rights and duties within the academic community must be accurately set down in the Statutes, to ensure that they are properly exercised with correctly established limits.

Article 12. The Chancellor represents the Holy See to the University or Faculty and equally the University or Faculty to the Holy See. He promotes the continuation and progress of the University or Faculty and he fosters its communion with the local and universal Church.

Article 13. § 1. The Chancellor is the Prelate Ordinary on whom the University or Faculty legally depends, unless the Holy See established otherwise.

§ 2. Where conditions favor such a post, it is also possible to have a Vice-Chancellor, whose authority is determined in the Statutes.

Article 14. If the Chancellor is someone other than the local Ordinary, the statutory norms are to establish how the Ordinary and the Chancellor carry out their respective offices in mutual accord.

Article 15. The academic authorities are personal and collegial. Personal authorities are, in the first place, the Rector or President and the Dean. The collegial authorities are the various directive organisms or councils of the University or Faculty.

Article 16. The Statutes of the University or Faculty must very carefully set out the names and offices of the academic authorities, determining the way they are designated and their term of office, taking into account both the canonical nature of the individual University or Faculty and the university practice in the local area.

Article 17. Those designated as academic authorities are to be people who are truly knowledgeable about university life and, usually, who come from among the teachers of some Faculty.

Article 18. The Rector and the President are named, or at least confirmed, by the Sacred Congregation for Catholic Education.

Article 19. § 1. The Statutes determine how the personal and the collegial authorities are to collaborate with each other, so that, carefully observing the principle of collegiality, especially in more serious matters and above all in those of an academic nature, the persons in authority will enjoy that exercise of power which really corresponds to their office.

§ 2. This applies, in the first place, to the Rector, who has the duty to govern the entire University and to promote, in a suitable way, its unity, cooperation, and progress.

Article 20. § 1. When Faculties are parts of an Ecclesiastical University, their governance must be coordinated through the Statutes with the governance of the entire University in such a way that the good of the single Faculties is assured, at the same time that the good of the whole University is promoted and the cooperation of all the Faculties with each other is favored.

§ 2. The canonical exigencies of Ecclesiastical Faculties must be safeguarded even when such Faculties are inserted into non-ecclesiastical universities.

Article 21. When a Faculty is joined to a seminary or college, the Statutes, while always having due concern for cooperation in everything pertaining to the students' good, must clearly and effectively provide that the academic direction and administration of the Faculty is correctly distinct from the governance and administration of the seminary or college.

Section III
Teachers

Article 22. In each Faculty there must be a number of teachers, especially permanent ones, which corresponds to the importance and development of the individual disciplines as well as to the proper care and profit of the students.

Article 23. There must be various ranks of teachers, determined in the Statutes, according to their measure of preparation, their insertion into the Faculty, their permanence, and their responsibility to the Faculty, taking into account the university practice of the local area.

Article 24. The Statutes are to define which authorities are responsible for hiring, naming, and promoting teachers, especially when it is a question of giving them a permanent position.

Article 25. § 1. To be legitimately hired as a permanent teacher in a Faculty, a person must:

1) be distinguished by wealth of knowledge, witness of life, and a sense of responsibility;

2) have a suitable doctorate or equivalent title or exceptional and singular scientific accomplishment;

3) show documentary proof of suitability for doing scientific research, especially by a published dissertation;

4) demonstrate teaching ability.

§ 2. These requirements for taking on permanent teachers must be applied also, in proportionate measure, for hiring nonpermanent ones.

§ 3. In hiring teachers, the scientific requirements in current force in the university practice of the local area should be taken into account.

Article 26. § 1. All teachers of every rank must be marked by an upright life, integrity of doctrine, and devotion to duty, so that they can effectively contribute to the proper goals of an Ecclesiastical Faculty.

§ 2. Those who teach matters touching on faith and morals are to be conscious of their duty to carry out their work in full communion with the authentic Magisterium of the Church, above all, with that of the Roman Pontiff.[16]

Article 27. § 1. Those who teach disciplines concerning faith or morals must receive, after making their profession of faith, a canonical mission from the Chancellor or his delegate, for they do not teach on their own authority but by virtue of the mission they have received from the Church. The other teachers must receive permission to teach from the Chancellor or his delegate.

§ 2. All teachers, before they are given a permanent post or before they are promoted to the highest category of teacher, or else in both cases, as the Statutes are to state, must receive a declaration of *nihil obstat* from the Holy See.

Article 28. Promotion to the higher ranks of teachers is to take place only after a suitable interval of time and with due reference to teaching skill, to research accomplished, to the publication of scientific works, to the spirit of cooperation in teaching and in research, and to commitment to the Faculty.

Article 29. The teachers, in order to carry out their tasks satisfactorily, must be free from other employment which cannot be reconciled with their duty to do research and to instruct, according to what the Statutes require for each rank of teacher.

Article 30. The Statutes must state:

a) when and under which conditions a teaching post ends;

b) for what reasons and in which ways a teacher can be suspended, or even deprived of his post, so as to safeguard suitably the rights of the teachers, of the Faculty or University, and, above all, of the students and also of the ecclesial community.

Section IV
Students

Article 31. Ecclesiastical Faculties are open to all, whether ecclesiastics or laity, who can legally give testimony to leading a moral life and to having completed the previous studies appropriate to enrolling in the Faculty.

Article 32. § 1. To enroll in a Faculty in order to obtain an academic degree, one must present that kind of study title which would be necessary to permit enrollment in a civil university of one's own country or of the country where the Faculty is located.

§ 2. The Faculty, in its own Statutes, should determine what, besides what is contained in § 1 above, is needed for entrance into its course of study, including ancient and modern language requirements.

Article 33. Students must faithfully observe the laws of the Faculty about the general program and about discipline—in the first place about the study program, class attendance, and examinations—as well as all that pertains to the life of the Faculty.

Article 34. The Statutes should define how the students, either individually or collectively, take part in the university community life in those aspects which can contribute to the common good of the Faculty or University.

Article 35. The Statutes should equally determine how the students can for serious reasons be suspended from certain rights or be deprived of them or even be expelled from the Faculty, in such a way that the rights of the students, of the Faculty or University, and also of the ecclesial community are appropriately protected.

Section V
Officials and Staff Assistants

Article 36. § 1. In governing and administering a University or Faculty, the authorities are to be assisted by officials trained for various tasks.

§ 2. The officials are, first of all, the Secretary, the Librarian, and the Financial Procurator.

Article 37. There should also be other staff assistants who have the task of vigilance, order, and other duties, according to the needs of the University or Faculty.

Section VI
Study Program

Article 38. § 1. In arranging the studies, the principles and norms which for different matters are contained in ecclesiastical documents, especially those of the Second Vatican Council, must be carefully observed. At the same time account must be taken of sound advances coming from scientific progress which can contribute to answering the questions being currently asked.

§ 2. In the single Faculties let that scientific method be used which corresponds to the needs of the individual sciences. Up-to-date didactic and teaching methods should be applied in an appropriate way, in order to bring about the personal involvement of the students and their suitable, active participation in their studies.

Article 39. § 1. Following the norm of the Second Vatican Council, according to the nature of each Faculty:

1) just freedom[17] should be acknowledged in research and teaching so that true progress can be obtained in learning and understanding divine truth;

2) at the same time it is clear that:

a) true freedom in teaching is necessarily contained within the limits of God's Word, as this is constantly taught by the Church's Magisterium;

b) likewise, true freedom in research is necessarily based upon firm adherence to God's Word and deference to the Church's Magisterium, whose duty it is to interpret authentically the Word of God.

§ 2. Therefore, in such a weighty matter one must proceed with prudence, with trust, and without suspicion, at the same time with judgment and without rashness, especially in teaching, while working to harmonize studiously the necessities of science with the pastoral needs of the People of God.

Article 40. In each Faculty the curriculum of studies is to be suitably organized in steps or cycles, adapted to the material. These are usually as follows:

a) first, a general instruction is imparted, covering a coordinated presentation of all the disciplines, along with an introduction into scientific methodology;

b) next, one section of the disciplines is studied more profoundly, at the same time that the students practice scientific research more fully;

c) finally, there is progress toward scientific maturity, especially through a written work which truly makes a contribution to the advance of the science.

Article 41. § 1. The disciplines which are absolutely necessary for the Faculty to achieve its purposes should be determined. Those also should be set out which in a different way are helpful to these purposes and, therefore, how these are suitably distinguished one from another.

§ 2. In each Faculty the disciplines should be arranged in such a way that they form an organic body, so as to serve the solid and coherent formation of the students and to facilitate collaboration by the teachers.

Article 42. Lectures, especially in the basic cycle, must be given, and the students must attend them, according to the norms to be determined in the Statutes.

Article 43. Practical exercises and seminars, mainly in the specialization cycle, must be assiduously carried on under the direction of the teachers. These ought to be constantly complemented by private study and frequent discussions with the teachers.

Article 44. The Statutes of the Faculty are to define which examinations or which equivalent tests the students are to take, whether written or oral, at the end of the semester, of the year, and especially of the cycle, so that their ability can be verified in regard to continuing in the Faculty and in regard to receiving academic degrees.

Article 45. Likewise the Statutes are to determine what value is to be given for studies taken elsewhere, especially in regard to being dispensed from some disciplines or examinations or even in regard to reducing the curriculum, always, however, respecting the prescriptions of the Sacred Congregation for Catholic Education.

Section VII
Academic Degrees

Article 46. § 1. After each cycle of the curriculum of studies, the suitable academic degree can be conferred, which must be established for each Faculty, with attention given to the duration of the cycle and to the disciplines taught in it.

§ 2. Therefore, according to the general and special norms of this Constitution, all degrees conferred are to be determined in the Statutes of the individual Faculties.

Article 47. § 1. The academic degrees conferred by an Ecclesiastical Faculty are: Baccalaureate, Licentiate, and Doctorate.

§ 2. Special qualifications can be added to the names of these degrees according to the diversity of Faculties and the order of studies in the individual Faculties.

Article 48. Academic degrees can be given different names in the Statutes of the individual Faculties, taking account of the university practice in the local area, indicating, however, with clarity the equivalence these have with the names of the academic degrees above and maintaining uniformity among the Ecclesiastical Faculties of the same area.

Article 49. § 1. Nobody can obtain an academic degree unless properly enrolled in a Faculty, completing the course of studies prescribed by the Statutes, and successfully passing the examinations or tests.

§ 2. Nobody can be admitted to the doctorate unless first having obtained the licentiate.

§ 3. A requisite for obtaining a doctorate, furthermore, is a doctoral dissertation that makes a real contribution to the progress of science, written under the direction of a teacher, publicly defended and collegially approved; the principal part, at least, must be published.

Article 50. § 1. The doctorate is the academic degree which enables one to teach in a Faculty and which is therefore required for this purpose; the licentiate is the academic degree which enables one to teach in a major seminary or equivalent school and which is therefore required for this purpose.

§ 2. The academic degrees which are required for filling various ecclesiastical posts are to be stated by the competent ecclesiastical authority.

Article 51. An honorary doctorate can be conferred for special scientific merit or cultural accomplishment in promoting the ecclesiastical sciences.

Section VIII
Matters Relating to Teaching

Article 52. In order to achieve its proper purposes, especially in regard to scientific research, each University or Faculty must have an adequate library, in keeping with the needs of the staff and students. It must be correctly organized and equipped with an appropriate catalogue.

Article 53. Through an annual allotment of money, the library must continually acquire books, old and new, as well as the principal reviews, so as to be able effectively to serve research, teaching of the disciplines, instructional needs, and the practical exercises and seminars.

Article 54. The library must be headed by a trained librarian, assisted by a suitable council. The librarian participates opportunely in the Council of the University or Faculty.

Article 55. § 1. The Faculty must also have technical equipment, audio-visual materials, etc., to assist its didactic work.

§ 2. In relationship to the special nature and purpose of a University or Faculty, research institutions and scientific laboratories should also be available, as well as other apparatus needed for the accomplishment of its ends.

Section IX
Economic Matters

Article 56. A University or Faculty must have enough money to achieve its purposes properly. Its financial endowments and its property rights are to be carefully described.

Article 57. The Statutes are to determine the duty of the Financial Procurator as well as the part the Rector or President and the University or Faculty Council play in money matters, according to the norms of good economics and so as to preserve healthy administration.

Article 58. Teachers, officials, and staff assistants are to be paid a suitable remuneration, taking account of the customs of the local area, and also taking into consideration social security and insurance protection.

Article 59. Likewise, the Statutes are to determinate the general norms that will indicate the ways the students are to contribute to the expenses of the University or Faculty, by paying admission fees, yearly tuition, examination fees, and diploma fees.

Section X
Planning and Cooperation of Faculties

Article 60. § 1. Great care must be given to the distribution, or as it is called, the planning of Universities and Faculties, so as to provide for their conservation, their progress, and their suitable distribution in different parts of the world.

§ 2. To accomplish this end, the Sacred Congregation for Catholic Education is to be helped by advice from the Bishops' Conferences and from a commission of experts.

Article 61. The erection or approval of a new University or Faculty is decided upon by the Sacred Congregation for Catholic Education when all the requirements are fulfilled. In this the Congregation listens to the local Ordinaries, the Bishops' Conference, and experts, especially from neighboring Faculties.

Article 62. § 1. Affiliation of some institution with a Faculty for the purpose of being able to grant the bachelor's degree is approved by the Sacred Congregation for Catholic Education, after the conditions established by that same Sacred Congregation are fulfilled.

§ 2. It is highly desirable that theological study centers, whether diocesan or religious, be affiliated to a Faculty of Sacred Theology.

Article 63. Aggregation to a Faculty and incorporation into a Faculty by an institution for the purposes of also granting higher academic degrees is decided upon by the Sacred Congregation for Catholic Education, after the conditions established by that same Sacred Congregation are fulfilled.

Article 64. Cooperation between Faculties, whether of the same University or of the same region or of a wider territorial area, is to be diligently striven for. For this cooperation is of great help to the scientific research of the teachers and to the better formation of the students. It also fosters the advance of interdisciplinary collaboration, which appears ever more necessary in current times, as well as contributing to the development of complementarity among Faculties. It also helps to bring about the penetration by Christian wisdom of all culture.

Part Two
Special Norms

Article 65. Besides the norms common to all Ecclesiastical Faculties, which are established in the first part of this Constitution, special norms are given hereunder for certain of those Faculties, because of their particular nature and importance for the Church.

Section I
Faculty of Sacred Theology

Article 66. A Faculty of Sacred Theology has the aim of profoundly studying and systematically explaining, according to the scientific method proper to it, Catholic doctrine, derived with the greatest care from divine revelation. It has the further aim of carefully seeking the solution to human problems in the light of that same revelation.

Article 67. § 1. The study of Sacred Scripture is, as it were, the soul of Sacred Theology, which rests upon the written Word of God together with living Tradition, as its perpetual foundation.[18]

§ 2. The individual theological disciplines are to be taught in such a way that, from their internal structure and from the proper object of each as well as from their connection with other disciplines, including philosophical ones and the sciences of man, the basic unity of theological instruction is quite clear, and in such a way that all the disciplines converge in a profound understanding of the mystery of Christ, so that this can be announced with greater effectiveness to the People of God and to all nations.

Article 68. § 1. Revealed truth must be considered also in connection with contemporary, evolving, scientific accomplishments, so that it can be seen "how faith and reason give harmonious witness to the unity of all truth."[19] Also, its exposition is to be such that, without any change of the truth, there is adaptation to the nature and character of every culture, taking special account of the philosophy and the wisdom of various peoples. However, all syncretism and every kind of false particularism are to be excluded.[20]

§ 2. The positive values in the various cultures and philosophies are to be sought out, carefully examined, and taken up. However, systems and methods incompatible with Christian faith must not be accepted.

Article 69. Ecumenical questions are to be carefully treated, according to the norms of competent Church authorities.[21] Also to be carefully considered are relationships with non-Christian religions; and problems arising from contemporary atheism are to be scrupulously studied.

Article 70. In studying and teaching Catholic doctrine, fidelity to the Magisterium of the Church is always to be emphasized. In the carrying out of teaching duties, especially in the basic cycle, those things are, above all, to be imparted which belong to the received patrimony of the Church. Hypothetical or personal opinions which come from new research are to be modestly presented as such.

Article 71. In presenting doctrine, those norms are to be followed which are in the documents of the Second Vatican Council,[22] as well as those found in more recent documents of the Holy See[23] insofar as these pertain to academic studies.

Article 72. The curriculum of studies of a Faculty of Sacred Theology comprises:

a) the first cycle, fundamentals, which lasts for five years or ten semesters, or else, when a previous two-year philosophy course is an entrance requirement, for three years. Besides a solid philosophical formation, which is a necessary propaedeutic for theological studies, the theological discipline must be taught in such a way that what is presented is an organic exposition of the whole of Catholic doctrine, together with an introduction to theological scientific methodology.

The cycle ends with the academic degree of Baccalaureate or some other suitable degree as the Statutes of the Faculty determine.

b) the second cycle, specialization, which lasts for two years or four semesters. In this cycle the special disciplines are taught corresponding to the nature of the diverse specializations being undertaken. Also seminars and practical exercises are conducted for the acquisition of the ability to do scientific research.

The cycle concludes with the academic degree of a specialized Licentiate.

c) the third cycle, in which for a suitable period of time scientific formation is brought to completion, especially through the writing of a doctrinal dissertation.

The cycle concludes with the academic degree of Doctorate.

Article 73. § 1. To enroll in a Faculty of Sacred Theology, the student must have done the previous studies called for in accordance with article 32 of this Constitution.

§ 2. Where the first cycle of the Faculty lasts for only three years, the student must submit proof of having properly completed a two-year course in philosophy at a Faculty of Philosophy or at an approved institution.

Article 74. § 1. A Faculty of Sacred Theology has the special duty of taking care of the scientific theological formation of those preparing for the priesthood or preparing to hold some ecclesiastical office.

§ 2. For this purpose, special courses suitable for seminarians should be offered. It is also appropriate for the Faculty itself to offer the "pastoral year" required for the priesthood, in addition to the five-year basic cycle. At the end of this year, a special Diploma may be conferred.

Section II
Faculty of Canon Law

Article 75. A Faculty of Canon Law, whether Latin or Oriental, has the aim of cultivating and promoting the juridical disciplines in the light of the law of the Gospel and of deeply instructing the students in these, so as to form researchers, teachers, and others who will be trained to hold special ecclesiastical posts.

Article 76. The curriculum of studies of a Faculty of Canon Law comprises:

a) the first cycle, lasting at least one year or two semesters, in which are studied the general fundamentals of Canon Law and those disciplines which are required for higher juridical formation;

b) the second cycle, lasting two years or four semesters, during which the entire Code of Canon Law is studied in depth, along with other disciplines having an affinity with it;

c) the third cycle, lasting at least a year or two semesters, in which juridical formation is completed and a doctoral dissertation is written.

Article 77. § 1. With regard to the studies prescribed for the first cycle, the Faculty may make use of the studies done in another Faculty and which it can acknowledge as responding to its needs.

§ 2. The second cycle concludes with the Licentiate and the third with the Doctorate.

§ 3. The Statutes of the Faculty are to define the special requirements for the conferring of the academic degrees, observing the Norms of Application of the Sacred Congregation for Catholic Education.

Article 78. To enroll in a Faculty of Canon Law, the student must have done the previous studies called for in accordance with Article 32 of this Constitution.

Section III
Faculty of Philosophy

Article 79. § 1. An Ecclesiastical Faculty of Philosophy has the aim of investigating philosophical problems according to scientific methodology, basing itself on a heritage of perennially valid philosophy.[24] It has to search for solutions in the light of natural reason and, furthermore, it has to demonstrate their consistency with the Christian view of the world, of man, and of God, placing in a proper light the relationship between philosophy and theology.

§ 2. Then, the students are to be instructed so as to make them ready to teach and to fill other suitable intellectual posts as well as to prepare them to promote Christian culture and to undertake a fruitful dialogue with the people of our time.

Article 80. In the teaching of philosophy, the relevant norms should be observed which are contained in the documents of the Second Vatican Council[25] and in other recent documents of the Holy See concerning academic studies.[26]

Article 81. The curriculum of studies of a Faculty of Philosophy comprises:

a) the first cycle, basics, in which for two years or four semesters an organic exposition of the various parts of philosophy is imparted, which includes treating the world, man, and God. It also includes the history of philosophy, together with an introduction into the method of scientific research;

b) the second cycle, the beginning of specialization, in which for two years or four semesters through special disciplines and seminars a more profound consideration is imparted in some sector of philosophy;

c) the third cycle, in which for a suitable period of time philosophical maturity is promoted, especially by means of writing a doctoral dissertation.

Article 82. The first cycle ends with the degree of Baccalaureate, the second with the specialized Licentiate, and the third with the Doctorate.

Article 83. To enroll in a Faculty of Philosophy, the student must have done the previous studies called for in accordance with Article 32 of the Constitution.

Section IV
Other Faculties

Article 84. Besides the Faculties of Sacred Theology, Canon Law, and Philosophy, other Faculties have been or can be canonically erected, according to the needs of the Church and with a view to attaining certain goals, as for instance:

a) a more profound study of certain sciences which are of greater importance to the theological, juridical, and philosophical disciplines;

b) the promotion of other sciences, first of all the humanities, which have a close connection with the theological disciplines or with the work of evangelization;

c) the cultivation of letters which provide a special help either to a better understanding of Christian revelation or else in carrying on the work of evangelizing;

d) finally, the more exacting preparation both of the clergy and laity for properly carrying out specialized apostolic tasks.

Article 85. In order to achieve the goals set down in the preceding article, the following Faculties or institutions "ad instar Facultatis" have already been erected and authorized to grant degrees by the Holy See itself:

—Christian archaeology,
—Biblical studies and ancient Eastern studies,
—Church history,
—Christian and classical literature,
—Liturgy,
—Missiology,
—Sacred Music,
—Psychology,
—Educational science or Pedagogy,
—Religious science,
—Social sciences,
—Arabic studies and Islamology,
—Mediaeval studies,
—Oriental Ecclesiastical studies,
—"Utriusque Iuris" (both canon and civil law).

Article 86. It belongs to the Sacred Congregation for Catholic Education to set out, in accordance with circumstances, special norms for these Faculties, just as has been done in the above sections for the Faculties of Sacred Theology, Canon Law, and Philosophy.

Article 87. The Faculties and Institutes for which special norms have not yet been set out must also draw up their own Statutes. These must conform to the General Norms established in the first part of this Constitution, and they must take into account the special nature and purpose proper to each of these Faculties or Institutes.

Transitional Norms

Article 88. This present Constitution comes into effect on the first day of the 1980-1981 academic year or of the 1981 academic year, according to the scholastic calendar in use in various places.

Article 89. Each University or Faculty must, before 1 January 1981, present its proper Statutes, revised according to this Constitution, to the Sacred Congregation for Catholic Education. If this is not done, its power to give academic degrees is, by this very fact, suspended.

Article 90. In each Faculty the studies must be arranged so that the students can acquire academic degrees according to the norms of this Constitution, immediately upon this Constitution coming into effect, preserving the students' previously acquired rights.

Article 91. The Statutes are to be approved experimentally for three years so that, when this period is completed, they may be perfected and approved definitively.

Article 92. Those Faculties which have a juridical connection with civil authorities may be given a longer period of time to revise their Statutes, provided that this is approved by the Sacred Congregation for Catholic Education.

Article 93. It is the task of the Sacred Congregation for Catholic Education, when, with the passage of time, circumstances shall require it, to propose changes to be introduced into this Constitution, so that this same Constitution may be continuously adapted to the needs of Ecclesiastical Faculties.

Article 94. All laws and customs presently obtaining which are in contradiction to this Constitution are abrogated, whether these are universal or local, even if they are worthy of special or individual mention. Likewise completely abrogated are all privileges hitherto granted by the Holy See to any person, whether physical or moral, if these are contrary to the prescriptions of this Constitution.

It is my will, finally, that this Constitution be established, be valid, and be efficacious always and everywhere, fully and integrally in all its effects, that it be religiously observed by all to whom it pertains, anything to the contrary notwithstanding. If anyone, knowingly or unknowingly, acts otherwise than I have decreed, I order that this action is to be considered null and void.

Given at Saint Peter's in Rome, the fifteenth day of April, the Solemnity of the Resurrection of our Lord Jesus Christ, in the year 1979, the first of my Pontificate.

Norms of Application
of the Sacred Congregation
for Catholic Education
for the Correct Implementation
of the Apostolic Constitution
Sapientia Christiana

The Sacred Congregation for Catholic Education, according to article 10 of the Apostolic Constitution *Sapientia Christiana,* presents to the Ecclesiastical Universities and Faculties the following Norms of Application and orders that they be faithfully observed.

Part One
General Norms

Section I
Nature and Purpose
of Ecclesiastical Universities
and Faculties
(Apostolic Constitution, articles 1-10)

Article 1. By the term University or Faculty is understood also those Athenaea, Institutes, or Academic Centers which have been canonically erected or approved by the Holy See with the right to confer academic degrees by the authority of the same See.

Article 2. With a view to promoting scientific research, a strong recommendation is given for specialized research centers, scientific periodicals and collections, and meetings of learned societies.

Article 3. The tasks for which students can be prepared can be either strictly scientific, such as research or teaching, or else pastoral. Account must be taken of this diversity in the ordering of the studies and in the determining of the academic degrees, while always preserving the scientific nature of the studies for both.

Article 4. Active participation in the ministry of evangelization concerns the action of the Church in pastoral work, in ecumenism, and in missionary undertakings. It also extends to the understanding, defense, and diffusion of the faith. At the same time it extends to the whole context of culture and human society.

Article 5. Bishops' Conferences, joined to the Apostolic See in these matters also, are thus to follow carefully the Universities and Faculties:

1. together with the Chancellor they are to foster their progress and, while of course respecting the autonomy of science according to the mind of the Second Vatican Council, they are to be solicitous for their scientific and ecclesial condition;

2. with regard to common problems which occur within the boundaries of their own region, they are to help, inspire, and harmonize the activity of the Faculties;

3. bearing in mind the needs of the Church and the cultural progress of their own area, they are to take care that there exist an adequate number of such Faculties;

4. to do all this, they are to constitute among themselves a commission for this purpose, which could be helped by a committee of experts.

Article 6. In preparing the Statutes and Study Program, the norms in Appendix I of these directives must be kept in mind.

Article 7. § 1. The canonical value of an academic degree means that such a degree enables one to assume an office in the Church for which a degree is required. This is, first of all, for teaching sacred sciences in Faculties, major seminaries, or equivalent schools.

§ 2. The conditions to be fulfilled for the recognition of individual degrees mentioned in article 9 of the Apostolic Constitution, concern, first of all, besides the consent of the local or regional ecclesiastical authorities, the college of teachers, the study program, and the scientific helps used.

§ 3. Degrees thus recognized, for certain canonical effects only, may never be considered simply as equal to canonical degrees.

Section II
The Academic Community and Its Government
(Apostolic Constitution, articles 11-21)

Article 8. The duty of the Chancellor is:

1. to promote continually the progress of the University or Faculty, to advance scientific progress, to ensure that Catholic doctrine is integrally followed, and to enforce the faithful implementation of the Statutes and the prescriptions of the Holy See;

2. to help ensure close relationships between all the different ranks and members of the community;

3. to propose to the Sacred Congregation for Catholic Education the names of those who are to be nominated or confirmed as Rector and President, as well as the names of the teachers for whom a *nihil obstat* is to be requested;

4. to receive the profession of faith of the Rector and President;

5. to give to or take away from the teachers the canonical mission or permission to teach, according to the norms of the Constitution;

6. to inform the Sacred Congregation for Catholic Education about

more important matters and to send to that Congregation every three years a detailed report on the academic, moral, and economic condition of the University or Faculty.

Article 9. If the University or Faculty depends upon a collegial entity (for instance, on an Episcopal Conference), one designated member of the group is to exercise the office of Chancellor.

Article 10. The local Ordinary, if he is not the Chancellor, since he has the pastoral responsibility for his Diocese, is, whenever something in the University or Faculty is known to be contrary to doctrine, morals, or ecclesiastical discipline, to take the matter to the Chancellor so that the latter may take action. In case the Chancellor does nothing, the Ordinary may have recourse to the Holy See, without prejudice to his own obligation to provide personally for action in those cases which are more serious or urgent and which carry danger for his Diocese.

Article 11. What is contained in article 19 of the Constitution must be explained further in the proper Statutes of the individual Faculties, giving more weight, as the case may require, either to collegial or else to personal government, while always preserving both forms. Account should be taken of the university practice of the region where the Faculty is located or of the Religious Institute on which the Faculty may depend.

Article 12. Besides the University Council (Academic Senate) and the Faculty Council, both of which must everywhere exist even if under different names, the Statutes can suitably establish other special councils or commissions for scientific learning, teaching, discipline, finances, etc.

Article 13. § 1. According to the Constitution, a Rector is one who presides over a University; a President is one who presides over an Institute or a Faculty which exists separately; a Dean is one who presides over a Faculty which is a part of a University.

§ 2. The Statutes are to fix a term of office for these persons (for instance, three years) and are to determine how and how many times their term can be renewed.

Article 14. The office of the Rector or President is:

1. to direct, promote, and coordinate all the activity of the academic community;

2. to be the representative of the University or of the Institute or Faculty existing separately;

3. to convoke the Council of the University or of the Institute or Faculty existing separately and preside over the same according to the norms of the Statutes;

4. to watch over the administration of temporalities;

5. to refer more important matters to the Chancellor;

6. to send, every year, a statistical summary to the Sacred Congregation for Catholic Education, according to the outline provided by the same Congregation.

Article 15. The Dean of the Faculty is:

1. to promote and coordinate all the activity of the Faculty, especially matters regarding studies, and to see to providing with due speed for their needs;

2. to convoke the Faculty Council and preside over it;

3. to admit or exclude students in the name of the Rector according to the norms of the Statutes;

4. to refer to the Rector what is done or proposed by the Faculty;

5. to see that the instructions of higher authorities are carried out.

Section III
Teachers
(Apostolic Constitution, articles 22-30)

Article 16. § 1. Teachers who are permanently attached to a Faculty are, in the first place, those who are assumed in full and firm right and who are called Ordinary Professors; next come Extraordinary Professors. It can also be useful to have others according to university practice.

§ 2. Besides permanent teachers, there are other teachers who are designated by various titles, in the first place, those invited from other Faculties.

§ 3. Finally, it is also opportune to have Teaching Assistants to carry out certain academic functions.

Article 17. By a suitable doctorate is meant one that corresponds to the discipline that is being taught. If the discipline is sacred or connected with the sacred, the doctorate must be canonical. In the event that the doctorate is not canonical, the teacher will usually be required to have at least a canonical licentiate.

Article 18. Non-Catholic teachers, co-opted according to the norms of competent ecclesiastical authority,[1] require permission to teach from the Chancellor.

Article 19. § 1. The Statutes must establish when a permanent status is conferred in relationship with the obtaining of the *nihil obstat* that must be procured in accordance with article 27 of the Constitution.

§ 2. The *nihil obstat* of the Holy See is the declaration that, in accordance with the Constitution and the special Statutes, there is nothing to impede a nomination which is proposed. If some impediment should exist, this will be communicated to the Chancellor who will listen to the teacher in regard to the matter.

§ 3. If particular circumstances of time or place impede the requesting of the *nihil obstat* from the Holy See, the Chancellor is to take counsel with the Sacred Congregation for Catholic Education to find a suitable solution.

§ 4. In Faculties which are under special concordat law the established norms are to be followed.

Article 20. The time interval between promotions, which must be at least three years, is to be set down in the Statutes.

Article 21. § 1. Teachers, first of all the permanent ones, are to seek to collaborate with each other. It is also recommended that there be collaboration with the teachers of other Faculties, especially those with subjects that have an affinity or some connection with those of the Faculty.

§ 2. One cannot be at one and the same time a permanent teacher in more than one Faculty.

Article 22. § 1. The Statutes are to set out with care the procedure in regard to the suspension or dismissal of a teacher, especially in matters concerning doctrine.

§ 2. Care must be taken that, first of all, these matters be settled between the Rector or President or Dean and the teacher himself. If they are not settled there, the matters should be dealt with by an appropriate Council or committee, so that the first examination of the facts be carried out within the University or Faculty itself. If this is not sufficient, the matters are to be referred to the Chancellor, who, with the help of experts, either of the University or the Faculty or from other places, must consider the matter and provide for a solution. The possibility remains open for recourse to the Holy See for a definitive solution, always allowing the teacher to explain and defend himself.

§ 3. However, in more grave or urgent cases for the good of the students and the faithful, the Chancellor can suspend the teacher for the duration of the regular procedure.

Article 23. Diocesan priests and Religious or those equivalent to Religious from whatever Institute, in order to be teachers in a Faculty or to remain as such, must have the consent of their proper Ordinary or Religious Superior, following the norms established in these matters by competent Church authority.

Section IV
Students
(Apostolic Constitution, articles 31-35)

Article 24. § 1. Legal testimony, according to the norm of article 31 of the Constitution:

1) about a moral life is to be given, for clergy and seminarians, by their own Ordinary or his delegate; for all other persons by some ecclesiastic;

2) about previous studies is the study title required in accordance with article 32 of the Constitution.

§ 2. Since the studies required before entry into a University differ from one country to another, the Faculty has the right and duty to investigate whether all the disciplines have been studied which the Faculty itself considers necessary.

§ 3. A suitable knowledge of the Latin language is required for the Faculties of the sacred sciences, so that the students can understand and use the sources and the documents of the Church.[2]

§ 4. If one of the disciplines has been found not to have been studied or to have been studied in an insufficient way, the Faculty is to require that this be made up at a suitable time and verified by an examination.

Article 25. § 1. Besides ordinary students, that is, those studying for academic degrees, extraordinary students can be admitted according to the norms determined in the Statutes.

§ 2. A person can be enrolled as an ordinary student in only one Faculty at a time.

Article 26. The transfer of a student from one Faculty to another can take place only at the beginning of the academic year or semester, after a careful examination of his academic and disciplinary situation. But in any event nobody can be given an academic degree unless all the requirements for the degree are fulfilled as the Statutes of the Faculty demand.

Article 27. In the norms which determine the suspension or the expulsion of a student from a Faculty, the student's right to defend himself must be safeguarded.

Section V
Officials and Staff Assistants
(Apostolic Constitution, articles 36-37)

Article 28. In the Statutes or in some other suitable document of the University or Faculty, the right and duties of the Officials and Staff Assistants should be determined, as well as their participation in the community life of the University.

Section VI
Study Program
(Apostolic Constitution, articles 38-45)

Article 29. The Statutes of each Faculty must define which disciplines (principal and auxiliary) are obligatory and must be followed by all, and which are free or optional.

Article 30. Equally, the Statutes are to determine the practical exercises and seminars in which the students must not only be present but also actively work together with their colleagues and produce their own expositions.

Article 31. The lectures and practical exercises are to be suitably distributed so as to foster private study and personal work under the guidance of the teachers.

Article 32. § 1. The Statutes are also to determine in what way the examiners are to make their judgments about candidates.

§ 2. In the final judgment about the candidates for the individual academic degrees, account is to be taken of all the marks received in the various tests in the same cycle, whether written or oral.

§ 3. In the examinations for the giving of degrees, especially the doctorate, it is also useful to invite examiners from outside the Faculty.

Article 33. The Statutes are to indicate the permanent curricula of studies which are to be instituted in a Faculty for special purposes and indicate the diplomas which are conferred at their conclusion.

Section VII
Academic Degrees
(Apostolic Constitution, articles 46-51)

Article 34. In Ecclesiastical Universities or Faculties which are canonically erected or approved, the academic degrees are given in the name of the Supreme Pontiff.

Article 35. The Statutes are to establish the necessary requisites for the preparation of the doctoral dissertations and the norms for their public defense and publication.

Article 36. A copy of the published dissertation must be sent to the Sacred Congregation for Catholic Education. It is recommended that copies also be sent to other Ecclesiastical Faculties, at least those of the same region, which deal with the same science.

Article 37. Authentic documents regarding the conferring of degrees are to be signed by the Academic Authorities, according to the Statutes, and then are to be countersigned by the Secretary of the University or Faculty and have the appropriate seal affixed.

Article 38. Honorary doctorates are not to be conferred except with the consent of the Chancellor, who, having listened to the opinion of the University or Faculty Council, has obtained the *nihil obstat* of the Holy See.

Section VIII
Matters Relating to Teaching
(Apostolic Constitution, articles 52-55)

Article 39. The University or Faculty must have lecture halls which are truly functional and worthy and suited to the teaching of the disciplines and to the number of students.

Article 40. There must be a library open for consultation, in which the principal works for the scientific work of the teachers and students are available.

Article 41. Library norms are to be established in such a way that access and use is made easy for the students and teachers.

Article 42. Cooperation and coordination between libraries of the same city and region should be fostered.

Section IX
Economic Matters
(Apostolic Constitution, articles 56-59)

Article 43. To provide for continuous good administration, the authorities must inform themselves at set times about the financial situation and they must provide for careful, periodic audits.

Article 44. § 1. Suitable ways should be found so that tuition fees do not keep from academic degrees gifted students who give good hope of one day being useful to the Church.

§ 2. Therefore care must be taken to set up forms of assistance for scholars, whatever their various names (scholarships, study burses, student subsidies, etc.), to be given to needy students.

Section X
Planning and Cooperation of Faculties
(Apostolic Constitution, articles 60-64)

Article 45. § 1. In order to undertake the erection of a new University or Faculty, it is necessary that:

a) a true need or usefulness can be demonstrated, which cannot be satisfied either by affiliation, aggregation, or incorporation;

b) the necessary prerequisites are present, which are mainly:

1) permanently engaged teachers who in number and quality respond to the nature and demands of a Faculty;

2) a suitable number of students;

3) a library with scientific apparatus and suitable buildings;

4) economic means really sufficient for a University or Faculty;

c) the Statutes, together with the Study Program, be exhibited, which are in conformity to the Constitution and to these Norms of Application. cation.

§ 2. The Sacred Congregation for Catholic Education—after listening to the advice first of the Bishops' Conference, mainly from the pastoral viewpoint, and next of experts, principally from nearby Faculties, mainly from the scientific viewpoint—will decide about the suitability of a new erection. This is commonly conceded at first experimentally for a period of time before being definitively confirmed.

Article 46. When, on the other hand, the approval of a University or Faculty is undertaken, this is to be done:

a) after the consent of both the Episcopal Conference and the local diocesan authority is obtained;

b) after the conditions stated in article 45, § 1, under *b)* and *c)* are fulfilled.

Article 47. The conditions for affiliation regard, above all, the number and qualification of teachers, the study program, the library, and the duty of the affiliating Faculty to help the institution being affiliated. Therefore, this is usually granted only when the affiliating Faculty and the affiliated institution are in the same country or cultural region.

Article 48. § 1. Aggregation is the linking with a Faculty of some Institute which embraces only the first and second cycle, for the purpose of granting the degrees corresponding to those cycles through the Faculty.

§ 2. Incorporation is the insertion into a Faculty of some Institute which embraces either the second or third cycle or both, for the purpose of granting the corresponding degrees through the Faculty.

§ 3. Aggregation and incorporation cannot be granted unless the Institute is specially equipped to grant degrees in such a way that there is a well-founded hope that, through the connection with the Faculty, the desired ends will be achieved.

Article 49. § 1. Cooperation is to be fostered among the Ecclesiastical Faculties themselves by means of teachers exhanges, mutual communication of scientific work, and the promoting of common research for the benefit of the People of God.

§ 2. Cooperation with other Faculties, even those of non-Catholics, should be promoted, care always however being taken to preserve one's own identity.

Part Two
Special Norms

Section I
Faculty of Sacred Theology
(Apostolic Constitution, articles 66-74)

Article 50. The theological disciplines are to be taught in such a way that their organic connection is made clear and that light is shed upon the various aspects or dimensions that pertain intrinsically to the nature of sacred doctrine. The chief ones are the biblical, patristic, historical, liturgical, and pastoral dimensions. The students are to be led to a deep grasp of the material, at the same time as they are led to form a personal synthesis, to acquire a mastery of the method of scientific research, and thus to become able to explain sacred doctrine appropriately.

Article 51. The obligatory disciplines are:

1. in the first cycle:

a) the philosophical disciplines needed for theology, which are above all systematic philosophy together with its main parts and its historical evolution;

b) the theological disciplines, namely:

—Sacred Scripture, introduction and exegesis;

—fundamental theology, which also includes reference to ecumenism, non-Christian religions, and atheism;

—dogmatic theology;

—moral and spiritual theology;

—pastoral theology;

—liturgy;

—Church history, patrology, archaeology;

—Canon law.

c) the auxiliary disciplines, namely, some of the sciences of man and, besides Latin, the biblical languages insofar as they are required for the following cycles.

2. in the second cycle: the special disciplines established in various sections, according to the diverse specializations offered, along with the practical exercises and seminars, including written work.

3. in the third cycle: the Statutes are to determine if special disciplines are to be taught and which ones, together with practical exercises and seminars.

Article 52. In the five-year basic cycle, diligent care must be exercised that all the disciplines are taught with order, fullness, and with correct method, so that the student receives harmoniously and effectively a solid, organic, and complete basic instruction in theology, which will enable him either to go on to the next cycle's higher studies or to exercise some office in the Church.

Article 53. Besides examinations or equivalent tests for each discipline, at the end of the first and of the second cycle there is to be a comprehensive examination or equivalent test, so that the student proves that he has received the full and scientific formation demanded by the respective cycle.

Article 54. It belongs to the Faculty to determine under which conditions students who have completed a normal six-year philosophy-theology course in an ordinary seminary or in some other approved institution of higher learning may be admitted into the second cycle, taking account of their previous studies and, where necessary, prescribing special courses and examinations.

Section II
Faculty of Canon Law
(Apostolic Constitution, articles 76-79)

Article 55. In a Faculty of Canon Law, whether Latin or Oriental, there must be a careful setting forth both of the history and texts of ecclesiastical laws and of their disposition and connection.

Article 56. The obligatory disciplines are:

1. in the first cycle:

a) the general fundamentals of canon law;

b) the elements of Sacred Theology (especially of ecclesiology and sacramental theology) and of philosophy (especially ethics and natural law) which by their very nature are prerequisites for the study of canon law. It is useful to add elements from the sciences of man which are connected with the juridical sciences.

2. in the second cycle:

a) the Code of Canon Law with all its various parts and the other canonical laws;

b) the connected disciplines, which are: the philosophy of law, the public law of the Church, fundamentals of Roman law, elements of civil law, the history of canon law. The student must also write a special dissertation.

3. in the third cycle: the Statutes are to determine which special disciplines and which practical exercises are to be prescribed, according to the nature of the Faculty and the needs of the students.

Article 57. § 1. Whoever successfully completes the philosophy-theology curriculum in an ordinary seminary or in some other approved institution of higher learning, or who has already successfully completed the studies of the first cycle, may be admitted directly into the second cycle.

§ 2. A person who has already earned a doctorate of civil law, may be allowed, according to the judgment of the Faculty, to abbreviate the course, always maintaining however the obligation to pass all the examinations and tests required for receiving academic degrees.

Article 58. Besides examinations or equivalent tests for each discipline, at the end of the second cycle there is to be a comprehensive examination or equivalent test, whereby the student proves that he has received the full and scientific formation demanded by the cycle.

Section III
Faculty of Philosophy
(Apostolic Constitution, articles 79-83)

Article 59. § 1. Philosophy is to be taught in such a way that the students in the basic cycle will come to a solid and coherent synthesis of doctrine, will learn to examine and judge the different systems of philosophy, and will also gradually become accustomed to personal philosophical reflection.

§ 2. All of the above is to be perfected in the second cycle, which begins specialization. In this cycle there is to be a deeper grasp of the determined object of philosophy and of the proper philosophical method.

Article 60. The obligatory disciplines are:

1. in the first cycle:

a) systematic philosophy (preceded by a general introduction) with its principal parts: philosophy of knowledge, natural philosophy, philosophy of man, philosophy of being (including natural theology) and moral philosophy;

b) history of philosophy, especially of modern philosophy, with a careful study of the systems which are exercising a major influence;

c) the auxiliary disciplines, namely selected natural and human sciences.

2. in the second cycle: the special disciplines established in various sections, according to the diverse specializations offered, along with practical exercises and seminars, including written work.

3. in the third cycle: the Statutes are to determine if special disciplines are to be taught and which ones, together with the practical exercises and seminars.

Article 61. Besides examinations or equivalent tests for each discipline, at the end of the first and second cycle there is to be a comprehensive examination or equivalent test whereby the student proves that he has received the full and scientific formation demanded by the respective cycle.

Article 62. It belongs to the Faculty to determine under what conditions students who have done a biennium of philosophy in an approved institution, or who have done a six-year philosophy-theology course in an ordinary seminary or equivalent school, may be admitted to the second cycle, taking account of their previous studies and, where necessary, prescribing special courses and examinations.

Section IV
Other Faculties
(Apostolic Constitution, articles 84-87)

Article 63. In accordance with article 86 of the Constitution, the Sacred Congregation for Catholic Education will gradually give special norms for the other Faculties, taking account of the experience already gained in these Faculties and Institutes.

Article 64. In the meantime, in Appendix II there is a list of the areas or divisions of ecclesiastical studies — besides the theological, canonical, and philosophical ones treated of in the three previous sections of these Norms of Application — which at the present time in the Church are ordered academically and are in existence as Faculties, Institutes *ad instar,* or Specialization Sections. The Sacred Congregation for Catholic Education will add to the list of these Sections when appropriate, indicating for these Sections their special purposes and the more important disciplines to be taught and researched.

His Holiness John Paul II, by divine Providence Pope, has ratified, confirmed, and ordered to be published each and every one of these Norms of Application, anything to the contrary notwithstanding.

Given from the offices of the Sacred Congregation for Catholic Education in Rome, 29 April, the Memorial of Saint Catherine of Siena, Virgin and Doctor of the Church, in the year of our Lord 1979.

Gabriel-Marie Cardinal Garrone
Prefect

Antonio-María Javierre-Ortas
Secretary

Appendix I

According to article 6
of Norms of Application

Norms for Drawing up Statutes

Taking into account what is contained in the Apostolic Constitution and in the Norms of Application — and leaving to their own internal regulations what is of a particular or changeable nature — the Universities or Faculties must mainly deal with the following points in drawing up their Statutes:

1. *The name, nature, and purpose* of the University or Faculty (with a brief history in the foreword).

2. *The government* — the Chancellor, the personal and collegial academic authorities: what their exact functions are; how the personal authorities are chosen and how long their term of office is; how the collegial authorities or the members of the Councils are chosen and how long their term is.

3. *The teachers* — what the minimum number of teachers is in each Faculty; into which ranks the permanent and non-permanent are divided; what requisites they must have; how they are hired, named, promoted, and how they cease functioning; their duties and rights.

4. *The students*—requisites for enrollment and their duties and rights.

5. *The officials and staff assistants* — their duties and rights.

6. *The study program* — what the order of studies is in each Faculty; how many cycles it has; what disciplines are taught; which are obligatory; attendance at them; which seminars and practical exercises; which examinations and tests are to be given.

7. *The academic degrees* — which degrees are given in each Faculty and under what conditions.

8. *Matters relating to teaching* — the library; how its conservation and growth are provided for; other didactic helps and scientific laboratories, if required.

9. *Economic matters* — the financial endowment of the University or Faculty and its economic administration; norms for paying the staff assistants, teachers and officials; student fees and payments, burses and scholarships.

10. *Relationships with other Faculties and Institutes, etc.*

Appendix II

According to article 64
of the Norms of Application

Divisions of Ecclesiastical Studies as Now (1979) Existing in the Church

List

Note: These individual study Sectors are listed alphabetically (according to their *Latin* names) and in parenthesis is noted the academic organizational form (whether a Faculty or an Institute *ad instar* or a Sector of specialization) in which it now exists in some ecclesiastical academic center. Not listed are the studies of a theological, philosophical, or canonical kind which are treated in articles 51, 56, and 60 of the Norms of Application.

1. *Arabic-Islamic* studies (an Institute *ad instar,* a specialized Sector in a Theology Faculty).

2. *Christian Archaeology* studies (an Institute *ad instar*).

3. Studies in *Atheism* (a specialized Sector in a Theology and/or Philosophy Faculty).

4. *Biblical* studies (a Faculty of Biblical Science, a specialized Sector in a Theology Faculty).

5. *Catechetical* studies (a specialized Sector in a Theology or Education Faculty).

6. *Ecclesiastical Oriental* studies (a Faculty of Ecclesiastical Oriental Studies).

7. *Education* studies (a Faculty of Education).

8. *Church History* studies (a Faculty of Church History, a specialized Sector in a Theology Faculty).

9. *Comparative Canonical-Civil Juridical* studies (a Faculty of comparative civil law).

10. *Classical and Christian Literary* studies (a Faculty of Christian and Classical Letters).

11. *Liturgical* studies (a Faculty, a specialized Sector in a Theology Faculty).

12. *Mariological* studies (a specialized Sector in a Theology Faculty).

13. *Mediaeval* studies (an Institute *ad instar,* a specialized Sector in a Faculty of Theology or Canon Law or Philosophy).

14. *Missiological* studies (a Faculty of Missiology, a specialized Sector in a Theology Faculty).

15. *Moral* studies (a specialized Sector in a Theology Faculty).

16. Studies in *Sacred Music* (an Institute *ad instar,* a specialized Sector in a Theology Faculty).

17. *Ecumenical* studies (a specialized Sector in a Theology Faculty).

18. *Ancient Oriental* studies (a Faculty of Eastern Antiquity, a specialized Sector in a Theology or Philosophy Faculty).

19. *Pedagogical* studies (a Faculty of Pedagogy, a specialized Sector in a Philosophy or Education Faculty).

20. *Pastoral* studies (a specialized Sector in a Theology Faculty).

21. *Patristic* studies (a specialized Sector in a Theology Faculty).

22. Studies in *Psychology* (an Institute *ad instar,* a specialized Sector in a Faculty of Philosophy, or Pedagogy, or Education).

23. Studies in *Religion and Religious Phenomenology* (a specialized Sector in a Theology or Philosophy Faculty).

24. Catholic *Religious* studies (a Higher Institute of Religious Science).

25. *Sociological* studies (a Faculty of Social Science, a specialized Sector in a Faculty of Education).

26. *Spirituality* studies (a specialized Sector in a Theology Faculty).

27. Studies in the *Theology of Religious life* (a specialized Sector in a Theology Faculty).

Notes

1. Cf. Vatican Ecumenical Council II, *Pastoral Constitution on the Church in the Modern World,* nn. 43 ff.: AAS 58 (1966) 1061 ff.
2. Cf. Apostolic Exhortation, *Evangelii nuntiandi,* nn. 19-20: AAS 68 (1976) 18 f.
3. Cf. ibid., n. 18: AAS 68 (1976) 17 f. and also *Pastoral Constitution on the Church in the Modern World,* n. 58: AAS 58 (1966) 1079.
4. Cf. Vat. Coun. II, *Declaration on Christian Education,* n. 10: AAS 58 (1966) 737.
5. AAS 23 (1931) 241.
6. AAS 42 (1950) 387.
7. *Declaration on Christian Education,* n. 10: AAS 58 (1966) 737.
8. Ibid.
9. Ibid., n. 11: AAS 58 (1966) 738.
10. *Pastoral Constitution on the Church in the Modern World,* n. 62: AAS 58 (1966) 1083.
11. Cf. Pope John XXIII, Allocution, at the opening of the Second Vatican Ecumenical Council: AAS 54 (1962) 792 and also the *Pastoral Constitution on the Church in the Modern World,* n. 62: AAS 58 (1966) 1083.
12. Pope Paul VI, Letter, *Le transfert à Louvain-la-Neuve,* to the Rector of the Catholic University of Louvain, 13 Sept. 1975 (cf. *L'Osservatore Romano,* 22-23 Sept. 1975). Also cf. Pope John Paul II, Encyclical, *Redemptor hominis,* n. 19: AAS 71 (1979) 305 ff.
13. *Declaration on Christian Education,* n. 11: AAS 58 (1966) 738.
14. Cf. Apostolic Constitution, *Regimini ecclesiae universae,* n. 78: AAS 59 (1967) 914.
15. Cf. Motu Proprio, *Sedula cura:* AAS 63 (1971) 665 ff. and also the Decree of the Pontifical Biblical Commission, *Ratio periclitandae doctrinae:* AAS 67 (1975) 153 ff.
16. Cf. Vat. Coun. II, *Dogmatic Constitution on the Church,* n. 25: AAS 57 (1965) 29-31.
17. Vat. Coun. II, *Pastoral Constitution on the Church in the Modern World,* n. 59: AAS 58 (1966) 1080.
18. Vat. Coun. II, *Dogmatic Constitution on Divine Revelation,* n. 24: AAS 58 (1966) 827.
19. Vat. Coun. II, *Declaration on Christian Education,* n. 10: AAS 58 (1966) 737.
20. Vat. Coun. II, *Decree on the Church's Missionary Activity,* n. 22: AAS 58 (1966) 973 ff.
21. See the Ecumenical Directory, Second Part: AAS 62 (1970) 705-724.
22. See especially Vat. Coun. II, *Dogmatic Constitution on Divine Revelation;* AAS 58 (1966) 713 ff.
23. See especially Pope Paul VI, Letter, *Lumen ecclesiae,* about Saint Thomas Aquinas, 20 Nov. 1974: AAS 66 (1974) 673 ff. Also see the circular letters on Catholic Education on the theological formation of future priests, 22 Feb. 1976; on Canon Law studies in Seminaries, 1 Mar. 1975; and on philosophical studies, 20 Jan. 1972.
24. See Vat. Coun. II, *Decree on the Training of Priests,* n. 15: AAS 58 (1966) 722.
25. Especially see the Vat. Coun. II, *Decree on the Training of Priests;* AAS 58 (1966) 713 ff. and the *Declaration on Christian Education:* AAS 58 (1966) 728 ff.
26. See especially Pope Paul VI, Letter, *Lumen ecclesiae,* on Saint Thomas Aquinas, 20 Nov. 1974: AAS 66 (1974) 673 ff. and the circular letter of the Sacred Congregation for Catholic Education on the study of philosophy in Seminaries, 20 Jan. 1972.

1. See the Ecumenical Directory, Second Part: AAS 62 (1970) 705 ff.
2. Vat. Coun. II, *Decree on the Training of Priests,* n. 13: AAS 58 (1966) 721 and Pope Paul VI, Chirograph, *Romani Sermonis:* AAS 68 (1976) 481 ff.

Decree on the Ministry and Life of Priests

Second Vatican Council
1965

Paul, Bishop, Servant of the Servants of God,
together with the Council Fathers,
for a permanent record

Decree on the Ministry and Life of Priests [a]

(Presbyterorum Ordinis)

Introduction

1. This sacred Council has already on several occasions drawn the attention of the world to the excellence of the order of priesthood in the Church.[1] Since however a most important and increasingly difficult role is being assigned to this order in the renewal of Christ's Church it has been thought that it would be extremely useful to treat of the priesthood at greater length and depth. What is said here applies to all priests. It refers in a special way to those who are engaged in the care of souls. It is to be applied to regular clergy insofar as its provisions suit their circumstances.

Through the sacred ordination and mission which they receive from the bishops, priests are promoted to the service of Christ the Teacher, Priest and King; they are given a share in his ministry, through which the Church here on earth is being ceaselessly built up into the People of God, Christ's Body and the temple of the Spirit. For that reason the Council has made the following Decree with the aim of giving more effective support to the ministry of priests and making better provision for their life in the often vastly changed circumstances of the pastoral and human scene.

I. The Priesthood in the Church's Mission

Nature of the priesthood[a]

2. The Lord Jesus "whom the Father consecrated and sent into the world" (Jn. 10.36) makes his whole Mystical Body sharer in the anointing of the Spirit wherewith he has been anointed:[1] for in that Body all the faithful are made a holy and kingly priesthood, they offer spiritual sacrifices to God through Jesus Christ, and they proclaim the virtues of him who has called them out of darkness into his admirable light.[2] Therefore there is no such thing as a member that has not a share in the mission of the whole Body. Rather, every single member ought to reverence Jesus in his heart[3] and by the spirit of prophecy give testimony of Jesus.[4]

However, the Lord also appointed certain men as ministers, in order that they might be united in one body in which "all the members have not the same function" (Rom. 12.4). These men were to hold in the community of the faithful the sacred power of Order, that of offering sacrifice and forgiving sins,[5] and were to exercise the priestly office publicly on behalf of men in the name of Christ. Thus Christ sent the apostles as he himself had been sent by the Father,[6] and then through the apostles made their successors, the bishops,[7] sharers in his consecration and mission.

The function of the bishops' ministry was handed over in a subordinate degree to priests[8] so that they might be appointed in the order of the priesthood and be co-workers of the episcopal order[9] for the proper fulfillment of the apostolic mission that had been entrusted to it by Christ.

Because it is joined with the episcopal order the office of priests shares in the authority by which Christ himself builds up and sanctifies and rules his Body. Hence the priesthood of priests, while presupposing the sacraments of initiation, is nevertheless conferred by its own particular sacrament. Through that sacrament priests by the anointing of the Holy Spirit are signed with a special character and so are configured to Christ the priest in such a way that they are able to act in the person of Christ the head.[10]

Since they share in the function of the apostles in their own degree, priests are given the grace by God to be the ministers of Jesus Christ among the nations, fulfilling the sacred task of the Gospel, that the oblation of the gentiles may be made acceptable and sanctified in the Holy Spirit.[11] For it is by the apostolic herald of the Gospel that the People of God are called together and gathered so that all who belong to this people, sanctified as they are by the Holy Spirit, may offer themselves "a living sacrifice, holy and acceptable to God" (Rom. 12.1). Through the ministry of priests the spiritual sacrifice of the faithful is completed in union with the sacrifice of Christ the only mediator, which in the Eucharist is offered through the priests' hands in the name of the whole Church in an unbloody and sacramental manner until the Lord himself come.[12] The ministry of priests is directed to this and finds its consummation in it. For their ministration, which begins with the announcement of the Gospel, draws its force and power from the sacrifice of Christ and tends to this, that "the whole redeemed city, that is, the whole assembly and community of the saints should be offered as a universal sacrifice to God through the High Priest who offered himself in his passion for us that we might be the body of so great a Head." [13]

Therefore the object that priests strive for by their ministry and life is the procuring of the glory of God the Father in Christ. That glory consists in men's conscious, free and grateful acceptance of God's plan as completed in Christ and their manifestation of it in their whole life. Thus priests, whether they devote themselves to prayer and adoration, or preach the Word, or offer the eucharistic sacrifice and administer the other sacraments, or exercise other services for the benefit of men, are contributing at once to the increase of God's glory and men's growth in the divine life. And all these activities, since they flow from the Pasch of Christ, will find their consummation in the glorious coming of the same Lord, when he shall have delivered up the kingdom to God and the Father. [14]

Place of priests in the world

3. Priests, while being taken from amongst men and appointed for men in the things that appertain to God that they may offer gifts and sacrifices for sin, [15] live with the rest of men as with brothers. So also the Lord Jesus the Son of God, a man sent by the Father to men, dwelt amongst us and willed to be made like to his brothers in all things save only sin. [16] The apostles in their turn imitated him, and St. Paul the teacher of the gentiles, the man "set apart for the Gospel of God" (Rom. 1.1), declares that he became all things to all men that he might save all. [17]

The priests of the New Testament are, it is true, by their vocation to ordination, set apart in some way in the midst of the People of God, but this is not in order that they should be separated from that people or from any man, but that they should be completely consecrated to the task for which God chooses them. [18] They could not be the servants of Christ unless they were witnesses and dispensers of a life other than that of this earth. On the other hand they would be powerless to serve men if they remained aloof from their life and circumstances. [19] Their very ministry makes a special claim on them not to conform themselves to this world; [20] still it requires at the same time that they should live among men in this world and that as good shepherds they should know their sheep and should also seek to lead back those who do not belong to this fold, so that they too may hear the voice of Christ and there may be one fold and one Shepherd. [21]

In the pursuit of this aim priests will be helped by cultivating those virtues which are rightly held in high esteem in human relations. Such qualities are goodness of heart, sincerity, strength and constancy of mind, careful attention to justice, courtesy and others which the apostle Paul recommends when he says: "Whatever is true, whatever is honorable, whatever is just, whatever is pure, whatever is lovely, whatever is gracious, if there is any excellence, if there is anything worthy of praise, think about these things" (Phil. 4.8). [22]

II. The Ministry of Priests

1. Functions of Priests

Priests as Ministers of God's Word

4. The People of God are formed into one in the first place by the Word of the living God,[1] which is quite rightly sought from the mouth of priests.[2] For since nobody can be saved who has not first believed,[3] it is the first task of priests as co-workers of the bishops to preach the Gospel of God to all men.[4] In this way they carry out the Lord's command "Go into all the world and preach the Gospel to every creature" (Mk. 16.15)[5] and thus set up and increase the People of God. For by the saving Word of God faith is aroused in the heart of unbelievers and is nourished in the heart of believers. By this faith then the congregation of the faithful begins and grows, according to the saying of the apostle: "Faith comes from what is heard, and what is heard comes by the preaching of Christ" (Rom. 10.17).

Priests then owe it to everybody to share with them the truth of the Gospel[6] in which they rejoice in the Lord. Therefore, whether by having their conversation heard among the gentiles they lead people to glorify God;[7] or by openly preaching proclaim the mystery of Christ to unbelievers; or teach the Christian message or explain the Church's doctrine; or endeavor to treat of contemporary problems in the light of Christ's teaching — in every case their role is to teach not their own wisdom but the Word of God and to issue an urgent invitation to all men to conversion and to holiness.[8] Moreover, the priest's preaching, often very difficult in present-day conditions, if it is to become more effective in moving the minds of his hearers, must expound the Word of God not merely in a general and abstract way but by an application of the eternal truth of the Gospel to the concrete circumstances of life.

Thus the ministry of the Word is exercised in many different ways according to the needs of the hearers and the spiritual gifts of preachers. In non-Christian territories or societies people are led by the proclamation of the Gospel to faith and by the saving sacraments.[9] In the Christian community itself on the other hand, especially for those who seem to have little understanding or belief underlying their practice, the preaching of the Word is required for the sacramental ministry itself, since the sacraments are sacraments of faith, drawing their origin and nourishment from the Word.[10] This is of paramount importance in the case of the liturgy of the Word within the celebration of Mass where there is an inseparable union of the proclamation of the Lord's death and resurrection, the response of its hearers and the offering itself by which Christ confirmed the new covenant in his blood. In this offering the faithful share both by their sacrificial sentiments and by the reception of the sacrament.[11]

Priests as Ministers of the Sacraments and the Eucharist

5. God, who alone is the holy one and sanctifier, has willed to take men as allies and helpers to become humble servants in his work of sanctification.

The purpose then for which priests are consecrated by God through the ministry of the bishop is that they should be made sharers in a special way in Christ's priesthood and, by carrying out sacred functions, act as his ministers who through his Spirit continually exercises his priestly function for our benefit in the liturgy. [12] By Baptism priests introduce men into the People of God; by the sacrament of Penance they reconcile sinners with God and the Church; by the Anointing of the Sick they relieve those who are ill; and especially by the celebration of Mass they offer Christ's sacrifice sacramentally. But in the celebration of all the sacraments — as St. Ignatius Martyr already asserted in the early Church [13] — priests are hierarchically united with the bishop in various ways and so make him present in a certain sense in individual assemblies of the faithful. [14]

But the other sacraments, and indeed all ecclesiastical ministries and works of the apostolate are bound up with the Eucharist and are directed towards it. [15] For in the most blessed Eucharist is contained the whole spiritual good of the Church, [16] namely Christ himself our Pasch and the living bread which gives life to men through his flesh—that flesh which is given life and gives life through the Holy Spirit. Thus men are invited and led to offer themselves, their works and all creation with Christ. For this reason the Eucharist appears as the source and the summit of all preaching of the Gospel: catechumens are gradually led up to participation in the Eucharist, while the faithful who have already been consecrated in baptism and confirmation are fully incorporated in the Body of Christ by the reception of the Eucharist.

Therefore the eucharistic celebration is the center of the assembly of the faithful over which the priest presides. Hence priests teach the faithful to offer the divine victim to God the Father in the sacrifice of the Mass and with the victim to make an offering of their whole life. In the spirit of Christ the pastor, they instruct them to submit their sins to the Church with a contrite heart in the sacrament of Penance, so that they may be daily more and more converted to the Lord, remembering his words: "Repent, for the kingdom of heaven is at hand" (Mt. 4.17). They teach them to take part in the celebrations of the sacred liturgy in such a way as to achieve sincere prayer in them also. They guide them to the exercise of an ever more perfect spirit of prayer throughout their lives in proportion to each one's graces and needs. They lead all the faithful on to the observance of the duties of their particular state in life, and those who are more advanced to the carrying out of the evangelical counsels in the way suited to their individual cases. Finally they train the faithful so that they will be able to sing in their hearts to the Lord with psalms and hymns and spiritual canticles, giving thanks always for all things in the name of our Lord Jesus Christ to God the Father. [17]

By their fulfillment of the Divine Office priests themselves should extend to the different hours of the day the praise and thanksgiving they offer in the celebration of the Eucharist. By the Office they pray to God in the name of the Church for the whole people entrusted to them and in fact for the whole world.

The house of prayer in which the most holy Eucharist is celebrated and reserved, where the faithful assemble, and where is worshipped the presence of the Son of God our Saviour, offered for us on the sacrificial altar for the help and consolation of the faithful — this house ought to be in good taste and a worthy place for prayer and sacred ceremonial. [18] In it pastors and faithful are called upon to respond with grateful hearts to the gifts of him who through his humanity is unceasingly pouring the divine life into the members of his Body. [19] Priests ought to go to the trouble of properly cultivating liturgical knowledge and art so that by means of their liturgical ministry God the Father, Son, and Holy Spirit may be daily more perfectly praised by the Christian communities entrusted to their care.

Priests as Rulers of God's People

6. Priests exercise the function of Christ as Pastor and Head in proportion to their share of authority. In the name of the bishop they gather the family of God as a brotherhood endowed with the spirit of unity and lead it in Christ through the Spirit to God the Father.[20] For the exercise of this ministry, as for the rest of the priests' functions, a spiritual power is given them, a power whose purpose is to build up.[21] And in building up the Church priests ought to treat everybody with the greatest kindness after the model of our Lord. They should act towards people not according to what may please men,[22] but according to the demands of Christian doctrine and life. They should teach them and warn them as their dearest children,[23] according to the words of the apostle: "Be urgent in season and out of season, convince, rebuke, and exhort, be unfailing in patience and in teaching" (2 Tm. 4.2).[24]

For this reason it is the priests' part as instructors of the people in the faith to see to it either personally or through others that each member of the faithful shall be led in the Holy Spirit to the full development of his own vocation in accordance with the Gospel teaching, and to sincere and active charity and the liberty with which Christ has set us free.[25] Very little good will be achieved by ceremonies however beautiful, or societies however flourishing, if they are not directed towards educating people to reach Christian maturity.[26] To encourage this maturity priests will make their help available to people to enable them to determine the solution to their problems and the will of God in the crises of life, great or small. Christians must also be trained so as not to live only for themselves. Rather, according to the demands of the new law of charity every man as he has received grace ought to minister it one to another,[27] and in this way all should carry out their duties in a Christian way in the community of their fellow men.

Although priests owe service to everybody, the poor and the weaker ones have been committed to their care in a special way. It was with these that the Lord himself associated,[28] and the preaching of the Gospel to them is given as a sign of his messianic mission.[29] Priests will look after young people with special diligence. This applies also to married couples and parents. It is desirable that these should meet in friendly groups to help each other in the task of more easily and more fully living in a Christian way of life that is often difficult. Priests should keep in mind that all religious, men and women, being a particularly eminent group in the Lord's house, are deserving of having special care directed to their spiritual progress for the good of the whole Church. Finally, priests ought to be especially devoted to the sick and the dying, visiting them and comforting them in the Lord.[30]

The pastor's task is not limited to individual care of the faithful. It extends by right also to the formation of a genuine Christian community. But if a community spirit is to be properly cultivated it must embrace not only the local church but the universal Church. A local community ought not merely to promote the care of the faithful within itself, but should be imbued with the missionary spirit and smooth the path to Christ for all men. But it must regard as its special charge those under instruction and the newly converted who are gradually educated in knowing and living the Christian life.

However, no Christian community is built up which does not grow from and hinge on the celebration of the most holy Eucharist. From this all education for community spirit must begin.[31] This eucharistic celebration, to be full and sincere, ought to lead on the one hand to the various works of charity and mutual help, and on the other hand to missionary activity and the various forms of Christian witness.

In addition the ecclesial community exercises a truly motherly function in leading souls to Christ by its charity, its prayer, its example and its penitential works. For it constitutes an effective instrument for showing or smoothing the path towards Christ and his Church for those who have not yet found faith; while also encouraging, supporting and strengthening believers for their spiritual struggles.

In building up a community of Christians, priests can never be the servants of any human ideology or party. Rather their task as heralds of the Gospel and pastors of the Church is the attainment of the spiritual growth of the Body of Christ.

II. Priests' Relation with Others

Relation between Bishops and the Priestly Body

7. All priests share with the bishops the one identical priesthood and ministry of Christ. Consequently the very unity of their consecration and mission requires their hierarchical union with the order of bishops.[32] This unity is best shown on some occasions by liturgical concelebration, and priests also affirm their union with the bishops in the eucharistic celebration.[33] Bishops, therefore, because of the gift of the Holy Spirit that has been given to priests at their ordination, will regard them as their indispensable helpers and advisers in the ministry and in the task of teaching, sanctifying and shepherding the People of God.[34] This has been forcefully emphasized from the earliest ages of the Church by the liturgical documents. These solemnly pray God for the pouring out upon the priest to be ordained of "the spirit of grace and counsel, that he may help and govern the people in a pure heart,"[35] just as in the desert the spirit of Moses was made grow into the minds of the seventy wise men[36] "whom he employed as helpers and easily governed countless multitudes among the people."[37]

On account of this common sharing in the same priesthood and ministry then, bishops are to regard their priests as brothers and friends[38] and are to take the greatest interest they are capable of in their welfare both temporal and spiritual. For on their shoulders particularly falls the burden of sanctifying their priests:[39] therefore they are to exercise the greatest care in the progressive formation of their diocesan body of priests.[40] They should be glad to listen to their priests' views and even consult them and hold conference with them about matters that concern the needs of pastoral work and the good of the diocese. But for this to be reduced to practice a group or senate of priests[41] should be set up in a way suited to present-day needs,[42] and in a form and with rules to be determined by law. This group would represent the body of priests and by their advice could effectively help the bishop in the management of the diocese.

Priests for their part should keep in mind the fullness of the sacrament of Order which bishops enjoy and should reverence in their persons the authority of Christ the supreme Pastor. They should therefore be attached to their bishop with sincere charity and obedience.[43] That priestly obedience, inspired through and through by the spirit of cooperation, is based on that sharing of the episcopal ministry which is conferred on priests by the sacrament of Order and the canonical mission.[44]

There is all the more need in our day for union of priests with bishops because in this age of ours apostolic enterprises must necessarily for various reasons take on many different forms. And not only that, but they must often overstep the bounds of one parish or diocese. Hence no priest is sufficiently equipped to carry out his own mission alone and as it were single-handed. He can only do so by joining forces with other priests, under the leadership of those who are rulers of the Church.

Brotherly Bond and Cooperation among Priests

8. All priests, who are constituted in the order of priesthood by the sacrament of Order, are bound together by an intimate sacramental brotherhood; but in a special way they form one priestly body in the diocese to which they are attached under their own bishop. For even though they may be assigned different duties, yet they fulfill the one priestly service for people. Indeed all priests are sent to cooperate in the same work. This is true whether the ministry they exercise be parochial or supra-parochial; whether their task be research or teaching, or even if they engage in manual labor and share the lot of the workers, where that appears to be of advantage and has the approval of the competent authority; or finally if they carry out other apostolic works or those directed towards the apostolate. They all contribute to the same purpose, namely the building up of the body of Christ, and this, especially in our times, demands many kinds of duties and fresh adaptations.

For this reason it is of great importance that all priests, whether diocesan or regular, should help each other, so that they may be fellow-helpers of the truth.[45] Each is joined to the rest of the members of this priestly body by special ties of apostolic charity of ministry and of brotherhood. This is signified liturgically from ancient times by the fact that the priests present at an ordination are invited to impose hands, along with the ordaining bishop, on the chosen candidate, and when priests concelebrate the sacred Eucharist in a spirit of harmony. So priests are all united with their brother-priests by the bond of charity, prayer, and total cooperation. In this way is shown forth that unity with which Christ willed his own to be perfected in one, that the world might know that the Son had been sent by the Father.[46]

From this it follows that older priests should sincerely accept the younger ones as brothers and be a help to them in facing the first tasks and responsibilities of their ministry. They should make an effort also to understand their outlook even though it may be different from their own, and should give kindly encouragement to their projects. Young priests for their part are to respect the age and experience of their elders; they ought to consult with them on matters concerning the care of souls and willingly cooperate with them.

Under the influence of the spirit of brotherhood priests should not forget hospitality,[47] and should cultivate kindness and the sharing of goods.[48] They should be particularly concerned about those who are sick,

about the afflicted, the overworked, the lonely, the exiled, the perse-
cuted.[49] They should also be delighted to gather together for relaxation,
remembering the words by which the Lord himself invited his weary
apostles: "Come apart into a desert place and rest a little" (Mk. 6.31).

Moreover, in order to enable priests to find mutual help in cultivating
the intellectual and spiritual life, to promote better cooperation amongst
them in the ministry, to safeguard them from possible dangers arising
from loneliness, it is necessary to foster some kind of community life or
social relations with them. This however can take different forms according to varying personal and pastoral needs: by priests' living together
where this is possible, or by their sharing a common table, or at least
meeting at frequent intervals. Associations of priests are also to be highly
esteemed and diligently promoted, when by means of rules recognized by
the competent authority they foster priestly holiness in the exercise of the
ministry through a suitable and properly approved rule of life and through
brotherly help, and so aim at serving the whole order of priests.

Finally, because of the same brotherly bond of priesthood, priests
ought to realize that they have an obligation towards those laboring under
difficulties. They should offer timely help to them, even by discreetly
warning them where necessary. They ought always to treat with fraternal
charity and compassion those who have failed in certain ways. They
should pray earnestly to God for them and never cease to show themselves
genuine brothers and friends to them.

Relation of Priests with Lay People

9. Even though the priests of the new law by reason of the sacrament of
Order fulfill the preeminent and essential function of father and teacher
among the People of God and on their behalf, still they are disciples of the
Lord along with all the faithful and have been made partakers of his
kingdom by God, who has called them by his grace.[50] Priests, in common
with all who have been reborn in the font of baptism, are brothers among
brothers[51] as members of the same Body of Christ which all are commanded to build up.[52]

Priests should, therefore, occupy their position of leadership as men
who do not seek the things that are their own but the things that are Jesus
Christ's.[53] They should unite their efforts with those of the lay faithful and
conduct themselves among them after the example of the Master, who
came amongst men "not to be served but to serve, and to give his life as a
ransom for many" (Mt. 20.28). Priests are to be sincere in their appreciation and promotion of lay people's dignity and of the special role the laity
have to play in the Church's mission. They should also have an unfailing
respect for the just liberty which belongs to everybody in civil society.
They should be willing to listen to lay people, give brotherly consideration to their wishes, and recognize their experience and competence in the
different fields of human activity. In this way they will be able to recognize along with them the signs of the times.

While trying the spirits if they be of God,[54] they must discover with
faith, recognize with joy, and foster with diligence the many and varied
charismatic gifts of the laity, whether these be of a humble or more exalted
kind. Among the other gifts of God which are found abundantly among
the faithful, special attention ought to be devoted to those graces by which
a considerable number of people are attracted to greater heights of the
spiritual life. Priests should also be confident in giving lay people charge

of duties in the service of the Church, giving them freedom and opportunity for activity and even inviting them, when opportunity occurs, to take the initiative in undertaking projects of their own.[55]

Finally, priests have been placed in the midst of the laity so that they may lead them all to the unity of charity, "loving one another with brotherly affection; outdoing one another in sharing honor" (Rom. 12.10). Theirs is the task, then, of bringing about agreement among divergent outlooks in such a way that nobody may feel a stranger in the Christian community. They are to be at once the defenders of the common good, for which they are responsible in the bishop's name; and at the same time the unwavering champions of truth lest the faithful be carried about with every wind of doctrine.[56] Those who have abandoned the practice of the sacraments, or even perhaps the faith, are entrusted to priests as special objects of their care. They will not neglect to approach these as good shepherds.

Priests should keep in mind what has been laid down in regard to ecumenism[57] and not forget those fellow Christians who do not enjoy complete ecclesiastical union with us.

They will regard as committed to their charge all those who fail to recognize Christ as their Saviour.

The faithful for their part ought to realize that they have obligations to their priests. They should treat them with filial love as being their fathers and pastors. They should also share their priests' anxieties and help them as far as possible by prayer and active work so that they may be better able to overcome difficulties and carry out their duties with greater success.[58]

III. The Distribution of Priests, Priestly Vocations

Proper Distribution of Priests

10. The spiritual gift which priests have received in ordination does not prepare them merely for a limited and circumscribed mission, but for the fullest, in fact the universal mission of salvation "to the end of the earth" (Acts 1.8). The reason is that every priestly ministry shares in the fullness of the mission entrusted by Christ to the apostles. For the priesthood of Christ, of which priests have been really made sharers, is necessarily directed to all peoples and all times, and is not confined by any bounds of blood, race, or age, as was already typified in a mysterious way by the figure of Melchizedek.[59]

Priests, therefore, should recall that the solicitude of all the churches ought to be their intimate concern. For this reason priests of those dioceses which are blessed with greater abundance of vocations should be prepared gladly to offer themselves — with the permission or encouragement of their own ordinary—for the exercise of their ministry in countries or mission or tasks that are hampered by shortage of clergy.

In addition, the rules about incardination and excardination should be revised in such a way that, while this ancient institution remains intact, it will answer better to the pastoral needs of today. Where the nature of the apostolate demands this, not only the proper distribution of priests should be made easier but also the carrying out of special pastoral projects for the benefit of different social groups in any region or among any race in any part of the world. For this purpose there can with advantages be set up some international seminaries, special dioceses, or personal prelacies and other institutions to which, by methods to be decided for the individual undertaking and always without prejudice to the rights of local ordinaries, priests can be attached or incardinated for the common good of the whole Church.

As far as possible, however, priests are not to be sent alone into a new territory, especially if they are not yet well versed in its language and customs. Rather, after the example of Christ's disciples,[60] they should be sent at least in groups of two or three so that they may be of mutual help to one another. It is advisable also to pay careful attention to their spiritual life and their mental and bodily health. Where possible, places and conditions of work are to be prepared for them to suit each one's personal circumstances.

It is also of the greatest advantage that those who go to a new territory should take the trouble to learn not only the language of the place but also the special psychological and social characteristics of the people they wish to serve in humility, and should establish the most perfect possible communication with them. In this way they will be following the example of St. Paul, who could say of himself: "For though I am free of all men, I made myself a slave to all, that I might win the more. To the Jews I became a Jew, in order to win Jews . . ." (1 Cor. 9.19-20).

Priests' Care for Priestly Vocations

11. The Shepherd and Bishop of our souls[61] set up his Church in such a way that the people whom he chose and acquired by his blood[62] should always and until the end of the world have its own priests, for fear Christians would ever be like sheep that have no shepherd.[63] The apostles realized this intention of Christ and under the guidance of the Holy Spirit considered it their duty to choose ministers who should "be able to teach others also" (2 Tm. 2.2). In fact this duty belongs to the very nature of the priestly mission which makes the priest share in the anxiety of the whole Church lest laborers should ever be wanting to the People of God here on earth.

However, since "a common interest exists . . . between the pilot of the ship and the passengers,"[64] the whole Christian people ought to be made aware that it is their duty to cooperate in their various ways, both by earnest prayer and by other means available to them,[65] to ensure that the Church will always have those priests who are needed for the fulfillment of her divine mission. First, then, priests are to make it their most cherished object to make clear to people the excellence and necessity of the priesthood. They do this by their preaching and by the personal witness of a life that shows clearly a spirit of service and a genuine paschal joy. Then they must spare no trouble or inconvenience in helping both youths and older men whom they prudently consider suitable for so great a ministry to prepare themselves properly so that they can be called at some time by the bishops—while preserving their full freedom, both external and internal. In the pursuit of this object diligent and prudent spiritual direction is of the greatest advantage.

Parents, teachers, and all who are in any way concerned in the education of boys and young men ought to train them in such a way that they will know the solicitude of the Lord for his flock and be alive to the needs of the Church. In this way they will be prepared when the Lord calls to answer generously with the prophet: "Here am I! Send me" (Is. 6.8). However, it is emphatically not to be expected that the voice of the Lord calling should come to the future priest's ears in some extraordinary way. Rather it must be perceived and judged through the signs by which God's will becomes known to prudent Christians in everyday life. And these signs are to be studied attentively by priests.[66]

Therefore organizations for the promotion of vocations, whether diocesan or national, are recommended highly to priests.[67] In sermons, in catechetical instruction and in periodicals the needs of the Church both local and universal are to be made known clearly. The meaning and excellence of the priestly ministry is to be highlighted — a ministry in which the many trials are balanced by such great joys, and especially one in which, as the Fathers teach, the greatest witness of love can be given to Christ.[68]

III. The Life of Priests

I. Priests' Call to Perfection

Call of Priests to Holiness

12. By the sacrament of Order priests are configured to Christ the priest as servants of the Head, so that as co-workers with the episcopal order they may build up the Body of Christ, the Church. Like all Christians they have already received in the consecration of baptism the sign and gift of their great calling and grace. So they are enabled and obliged even in the midst of human weakness[1] to seek perfection, according to the Lord's word: "You, therefore, must be perfect, as your heavenly Father is perfect" (Mt. 5.48).

But priests are bound by a special reason to acquire this perfection. They are consecrated to God in a new way in their ordination and are made the living instruments of Christ the eternal priest, and so are enabled to accomplish throughout all time that wonderful work of his which with supernatural efficacy restored the whole human race.[2] Since every priest in his own way assumes the person of Christ he is endowed with a special grace. By this grace the priest, through his service of the people committed to his care and all the People of God, is able the better to pursue the perfection of Christ, whose place he takes. The human weakness of his flesh is remedied by the holiness of him who became for us a high priest "holy, innocent, undefiled, separated from sinners" (Heb. 7.26).

Christ, whom the Father sanctified or consecrated and sent into the world,[3] "gave himself for us to redeem us from all iniquity and to purify for himself a people of his own who are zealous for good deeds" (Ti. 2.14), and in this way through his passion entered into his glory.[4] In a similar way, priests, who are consecrated by the anointing of the Holy Spirit and sent by Christ, mortify the works of the flesh in themselves and dedicate themselves completely to the service of people, and so are able, in the holiness with which they have been enriched in Christ, to make progress towards the perfect man.[5]

In this way they are made strong in the life of the spirit by exercising the ministration of the Spirit and of justice,[6] provided they are prepared to listen to the inspiration of the Spirit of Christ who gives them life and guidance. For it is through the sacred actions they perform every day, as through their whole ministry which they exercise in union with the bishop and their fellow priests, that they are set on the right course to perfection of life. The very holiness of priests is of the greatest benefit for the fruitful fulfillment of their ministry. While it is possible for God's grace to carry out the work of salvation through unworthy ministers, yet God ordinarily prefers to show his wonders through those men who are more submissive to the impulse and guidance of the Holy Spirit and who, because of their intimate union with Christ and their holiness of life, are able to say with St. Paul: "It is no longer I who live, but Christ who lives in me" (Gal. 2.20).

For this reason this sacred Council, in the hope of attaining its pastoral objectives of interior renewal, of worldwide diffusion of the Gospel, and of dialogue with the modern world, issues the strongest exhortation to all priests to strive always by the use of all suitable means commended by the Church[7] towards that greater holiness that will make them daily more effective instruments for the service of all God's people.

The Exercise of the Threefold Priestly Function Both Demands and Fosters Holiness

13. Priests will acquire holiness in their own distinctive way by exercising their functions sincerely and tirelessly in the Spirit of Christ.

Since they are ministers of the Word of God, they read and hear every day the Word of God which they must teach to others. If they strive at the same time to make it part of their own lives, they will become daily more perfect disciples of the Lord, according to the saying of the apostle Paul to Timothy: "Practice these duties, devote yourself to them; so that all may see your progress. Take heed to thyself and to your teaching; hold to that, for in doing so you will save both yourself and your hearers" (1 Tm. 4.15-16). For by seeking more effective ways of conveying to others what they have meditated on[8] they will savor more profoundly the "unsearchable riches of Christ" (Eph. 3.8) and the many-sided wisdom of God.[9] By keeping in mind that it is the Lord who opens hearts[10] and that the excellence comes not from themselves but from the power of God[11] they will be more intimately united with Christ the Teacher and will be guided by his Spirit in the very act of teaching the Word. And by this close union with Christ they share in the charity of God, the mystery of which was kept hidden from all ages[12] to be revealed in Christ.

Priests as ministers of the sacred mysteries, especially in the sacrifice of the Mass, act in a special way in the person of Christ who gave himself as a victim to sanctify men. And this is why they are invited to imitate what they handle, so that as they celebrate the mystery of the Lord's death they may take care to mortify their members from vices and concupiscences.[13]

In the mystery of the eucharistic sacrifice, in which priests fulfill their principal function, the work of our redemption is continually carried out.[14] For this reason the daily celebration of it is earnestly recommended. This celebration is an act of Christ and the Church even if it is impossible for the faithful to be present.[15] So when priests unite themselves with the act of Christ the Priest they daily offer themselves completely to God, and by being nourished with Christ's Body they share in the charity of him who gives himself as food to the faithful.

In the same way they are united with the intention and the charity of Christ when they administer the sacraments. They do this in a special way when they show themselves to be always available to administer the sacrament of Penance whenever it is reasonably requested by the faithful. In reciting the Divine Office they lend their voice to the Church which perseveres in prayer in the name of the whole human race, in union with Christ who "always lives to make intercession for them" (Heb. 7.25).

While they govern and shepherd the People of God they are encouraged by the love of the Good Shepherd to give their lives for their sheep.[16] They, too, are prepared for the supreme sacrifice, following the example of those priests who even in our own times have not shrunk from laying down their lives. Since they are the instructors in the faith and have themselves "confidence to enter the sanctuary by the blood of Jesus" (Heb. 10.19), they approach God "with a true heart in full assurance of faith" (Heb. 10.22). They set up a steadfast hope for their faithful people,[17] so that they may be able to comfort all who are in distress those by the exhortation wherewith God also exhorts them.[18] As rulers of the community they cultivate the form of asceticism suited to a pastor of souls, renouncing their own convenience, seeking not what is to their own advantage but what will benefit the many for salvation,[19] always making further progress towards a more perfect fulfillment of their pastoral work and, where the need arises, prepared to break new ground in pastoral methods under the guidance of the Spirit of love who breathes where he will.[20]

Unity and Harmony of Priests

14. In the world of today, with so many duties which people must undertake and the great variety of problems vexing them and very often demanding a speedy solution, there is often danger for those whose energies are divided by different activities. Priests who are perplexed and distracted by the very many obligations of their position may be anxiously enquiring how they can reduce to unity their interior life and their program of external activity. This unity of life cannot be brought about merely by an outward arrangement of the works of the ministry nor by the practice of spiritual exercises alone, though this may help to foster such unity. Priests can however achieve it by following in the fulfillment of their ministry the example of Christ the Lord, whose meat was to do the will of him who sent him that he might perfect his work.[21]

The fact of the matter is that Christ, in order ceaselessly to do that same will of his Father in the world through the Church, is working through his ministers and therefore remains always the principle and source of the unity of their life. Therefore priests will achieve the unity of their life by joining themselves with Christ in the recognition of the Father's will and in the gift of themselves to the flock entrusted to them.[22] In this way, by adopting the role of the good shepherd they will find in the practice of pastoral charity itself the bond of priestly perfection which will reduce to unity their life and activity. Now this pastoral charity[23] flows especially from the eucharistic sacrifice. This sacrifice is therefore the center and root of the whole life of the priest, so that the priestly soul strives to make its own what is enacted on the altar of sacrifice. But this cannot be achieved except through priests themselves penetrating ever more intimately through prayer into the mystery of Christ.

To enable them to make their unity of life a concrete reality they should consider all their projects to find what is God's will[24]—that is to say, how far their projects are in conformity with the standards of the Church's

Gospel mission. Faithfulness to Christ cannot be separated from faithfulness to his Church. Hence pastoral charity demands that priests, if they are not to run in vain,[25] should always work within the bond of union with the bishops and their fellow priests. If they act in this manner, priests will find unity of life in the unity of the Church's own mission. In this way they will be united with their Lord and through him with the Father in the Holy Spirit, and can be filled with consolation and exceedingly abound with joy.[26]

II. Special Spiritual Requirements in the Life of the Priest

Humility and obedience

15. Among the virtues especially demanded by the ministry of priests must be reckoned that disposition of mind by which they are always prepared to seek not their own will but the will of him who has sent them.[27] The divine task for the fulfillment of which they have been set apart by the Holy Spirit[28] transcends all human strength and human wisdom; for "God chose what is weak in the world to shame the strong" (1 Cor. 1.27).

Therefore the true minister of Christ is conscious of his own weakness and labors in humility. He proves what is well-pleasing to God[29] and, bound as it were in the Spirit,[30] he is guided in all things by the will of him who wishes all men to be saved. He is able to discover and carry out that will in the course of his daily routine by humbly placing himself at the service of all those who are entrusted to his care by God in the office that has been committed to him and the variety of events that make up his life.

The priestly ministry, being the ministry of the Church itself, can only be fulfilled in the hierarchical union of the whole body of the Church. Hence pastoral charity urges priests to act within this communion and by obedience to dedicate their own will to the service of God and their fellow Christians. They will accept and carry out in the spirit of faith the commands and suggestions of the Pope and of their bishop and other superiors. They will most gladly spend themselves and be spent[31] in whatever office is entrusted to them, even the humbler and poorer. By acting in this way they preserve and strengthen the indispensable unity with their brothers in the ministry and especially with those whom the Lord has appointed the visible rulers of his Church. They also work towards the building up of the Body of Christ, which grows "by what every joint supplieth."[32] This obedience, which leads to the more mature freedom of the sons of God, by its nature demands that priests in the exercise of their duties should be moved by charity prudently to seek new methods of advancing the good of the Church. At the same time it also demands that while putting forward their schemes with confidence and being insistent in making known the needs of the flock entrusted to them, they should always be prepared to submit to the judgment of those who exercise the chief function in ruling God's Church.

By this humility and by responsible and willing obedience priests conform themselves to Christ. They reproduce the sentiment of Jesus Christ who "emptied himself, taking the form of a servant . . . and became obedient unto death" (Phil. 2.7-9), and who by this obedience overcame and redeemed the disobedience of Adam, as the apostle declares: "For as by one man's disobedience many were made sinners, so by one man's obedience many will be made righteous" (Rom. 5.19).

Celibacy to be embraced and esteemed as a gift

16. Perfect and perpetual continence for the sake of the kingdom of heaven was recommended by Christ the Lord.[33] It has been freely accepted and laudably observed by many Christians down through the centuries as well as in our own time, and has always been highly esteemed in a special way by the Church as a feature of priestly life. For it is at once a sign of pastoral charity and an incentive to it as well as being in a special way a source of spiritual fruitfulness in the world.[34] It is true that it is not demanded of the priesthood by its nature. This is clear from the practice of the primitive Church[35] and the tradition of the Eastern Churches where in addition to those—including all bishops—who choose from the gift of grace to preserve celibacy, there are also many excellent married priests. While recommending ecclesiastical celibacy this sacred Council does not by any means aim at changing that contrary discipline which is lawfully practiced in the Eastern Churches. Rather the Council affectionately exhorts all those who have received the priesthood in the married state to persevere in their holy vocation and continue to devote their lives fully and generously to the flock entrusted to them.[36]

There are many ways in which celibacy is in harmony with the priesthood. For the whole mission of the priest is dedicated to the service of the new humanity which Christ, the victor over death, raises up in the world through his Spirit and which is born "not of blood nor of the will of the flesh nor of the will of man, but of God" (Jn. 1.13). By preserving virginity or celibacy for the sake of the kingdom of heaven[37] priests are consecrated in a new and excellent way to Christ. They more readily cling to him with undivided heart[38] and dedicate themselves more freely in him and through him to the service of God and of men. They are less encumbered in their service of his kingdom and of the task of heavenly regeneration. In this way they become better fitted for a broader acceptance of fatherhood in Christ.

By means of celibacy, then, priests profess before men their willingness to be dedicated with undivided loyalty to the task entrusted to them, namely that of espousing the faithful to one husband and presenting them as a chaste virgin to Christ.[39] They recall that mystical marriage, established by God and destined to be fully revealed in the future, by which the Church holds Christ as her only spouse.[40] Moreover they are made a living sign of that world to come, already present through faith and charity, a world in which the children of the resurrection shall neither be married nor take wives.[41]

For these reasons, based on the mystery of Christ and his mission, celibacy, which at first was recommended to priests, was afterwards in the Latin Church imposed by law on all who were to be promoted to holy Orders. This sacred Council approves and confirms this legislation so far as it concerns those destined for the priesthood, and feels confident in the Spirit that the gift of celibacy, so appropriate to the priesthood of the New Testament, is liberally granted by the Father, provided those who share Christ's priesthood through the sacrament of Order, and indeed the whole Church, ask for that gift humbly and earnestly.

This sacred Council also exhorts all priests who, with trust in God's grace, have of their own free choice accepted consecrated celibacy after the example of Christ, to hold fast to it with courage and enthusiasm, and to persevere faithfully in this state, appreciating that glorious gift that has been given them by the Father and is so clearly extolled by the Lord,[42] and keeping before their eyes the great mysteries that are signified and fulfilled in it. And the more that perfect continence is considered by many people to be impossible in the world of today, so much the more humbly and perseveringly in union with the Church ought priests demand the grace of fidelity, which is never denied to those who ask.

At the same time they will employ all the helps to fidelity both supernatural and natural, which are available to everybody. Especially they should never neglect to follow the rules of ascetical practice which are approved by the experience of the Church and are as necessary as ever in the modern world. So this sacred Council asks that not only priests but all the faithful would cherish this precious gift of priestly celibacy, and that all of them would beg of God always to lavish this gift abundantly on his Church.

Relation with the world and worldly goods: voluntary poverty

17. Priests can learn, by brotherly and friendly association with each other and with other people, to cultivate human values and appreciate created goods as gifts of God. While living in the world they should still realize that according to the Word of our Lord and Master they are not of the world.[43] By using the world, then, as those who do not use it[44] they will come to that liberty by which they will be freed from all inordinate anxiety and will become docile to the divine voice in their daily life. From this liberty and docility grows that spiritual insight through which is found a right attitude to the world and to earthly goods.

This attitude is of great importance for priests for this reason, that the Church's mission is carried out in the midst of the world and that created goods are absolutely necessary for man's personal progress. Let priests be thankful then for everything that the heavenly Father has given them towards a proper standard of living. However, they ought to judge everything they meet in the light of faith, so that they will be guided towards the right use of things in accordance with God's will and will reject anything that is prejudicial to their mission.

Priests as men whose "portion and inheritance" (Nm. 18.20) is the Lord ought to use temporal goods only for those purposes to which the teaching of Christ and the direction of the Church allow them to be devoted.

Priests are to manage ecclesiastical property, properly so called, according to the nature of the case and the norm of ecclesiastical laws and with the help, as far as possible, of skilled laymen. They are to apply this property always to those purposes for the achievement of which the Church is allowed to own temporal goods. These are: the organization of divine worship, the provision of decent support for the clergy, and the exercise of works of the apostolate and of charity, especially for the benefit of those in need.[45]

Priests, just like bishops (without prejudice to particular law),[46] are to use moneys acquired by them on the occasion of their exercise of some ecclesiastical office primarily for their own decent support and the fulfillment of the duties of their state. They should be willing to devote whatever is left over to the good of the Church or to works of charity. So they are not to regard an ecclesiastical office as a source of profit, and are not to spend the income accruing from it for increasing their own private fortunes.[47] Hence priests, far from setting their hearts on riches,[48] must always avoid all avarice and carefully refrain from all appearance of trafficking.

In fact priests are invited to embrace voluntary poverty. By it they become more clearly conformed to Christ and more ready to devote themselves to their sacred ministry. For Christ being rich became poor for our sakes, that through his poverty we might be rich.[49] The apostles by their example gave testimony that the free gift of God was to be given freely.[50] They knew both how to abound and to suffer need.[51] Even some kind of use of property in common, like the community of goods which is extolled in the history of the primitive Church,[52] provides an excellent opening for pastoral charity. By this way of life priests can laudably reduce to practice the spirit of poverty commended by Christ.

Guided then by the Spirit of the Lord, who anointed the Saviour and sent him to preach the Gospel to the poor, [53] priests and bishops alike are to avoid everything that might in any way antagonize the poor. More than the rest of Christ's disciples they are to put aside all appearance of vanity in their surroundings. They are to arrange their house in such a way that it never appears unapproachable to anyone and that nobody, even the humblest, is ever afraid to visit it.

III. Helps for the Priest's Life

Helps toward fostering interior life

18. To enable them to foster union with Christ in all circumstances of life, priests, in addition to the meaningful carrying out of their ministry, have at their disposal the means both common and particular, new and old, which the Holy Spirit has never ceased to raise up among the People of God and which the Church recommends and in fact sometimes commands[54] for the sanctification of her members. Those actions by which Christians draw nourishment through the Word of God from the double table of holy Scripture and the Eucharist hold a preeminent place above all spiritual aids.[55] Everybody knows how important their continuous use is for the personal sanctification of priests.

The ministers of sacramental grace are intimately united to Christ the Saviour and Pastor through the fruitful reception of Penance. If it is prepared for by a daily examination of conscience, it is a powerful incentive to the essential conversation of heart to the love of the Father of mercies. Under the light of a faith that has been nourished by spiritual reading, priests can diligently search for the signs of God's will and the inspirations of his grace in the varied events of life. In this way they will become daily more docile in the demands of the mission they have undertaken in the Holy Spirit. They always find a wonderful example of such docility in the Blessed Virgin Mary who under the guidance of the Holy Spirit made a total dedication of herself for the mystery of the redemption of men.[56] Priests should always venerate and love her, with a filial devotion and worship, as the Mother of the supreme and eternal Priest, as Queen of Apostles, and as protectress of their ministry.

As a help towards faithful fulfillment of their ministry priests should love to talk daily with Christ the Lord in their visit to the most blessed sacrament and in their personal devotion to it. They should be glad to take time for spiritual retreat and should have a high regard for spiritual direction. In various ways, in particular through the approved practice of mental prayer and the different forms of vocal prayer which they freely choose to practice, priests are to seek and perseveringly ask of God the true spirit of adoration. By this spirit they themselves, and with them the people entrusted to their care, will unite themselves with Christ the Mediator of the New Testament, and will be able as adopted sons to cry, "Abba! Father!" (Rom. 8.15).

Study and pastoral knowledge

19. Priests are warned by the bishop in the ceremony of ordination that they are to be "mature in knowledge" and that their teaching should be "a spiritual medicine for the People of God."[57] Now a sacred minister's knowledge ought to be sacred in the sense of being derived from a sacred source and directed to a sacred purpose. Primarily, then, it is drawn from the reading and meditation of sacred Scripture.[58] It is also fruitfully nourished by the study of the Fathers and Doctors of the Church and the other ancient records of Tradition. Moreover, if priests are to give adequate answers to the problems discussed by people at the present time, they should be well versed in the statements of the Church's magisterium and especially those of the Councils and the Popes. They should also consult the best approved writers on the science of theology.

Secular culture and even sacred science are advancing at an unprecedented rate in our time. Priests are therefore urged to adequate and continuous perfection of their knowledge of things divine and human. In this way they will prepare themselves to enter with greater advantage into dialogue with their contemporaries.

To facilitate study and the more effective learning of methods of evangelization and the apostolate, every attention is to be given to providing priests with suitable helps. Examples of these are the organization according to the conditions of each territory of courses or congresses, the setting up of centers designed for pastoral studies, the founding of libraries, and the proper direction of studies by suitable persons.

In addition bishops, either individually or in collaboration with others, should consider more effective ways of arranging that their priests would be able to attend a course of study at certain times, especially for a few years after ordination.[59] The aim of the course would be to give them an opportunity of increasing their knowledge of pastoral methods and theological science, and at the same time of strengthening their spiritual life and sharing their pastoral experiences with their brother priests.[60] By these and other suitable aids special attention may be given to helping newly appointed parish priests also, as well as priests assigned to new pastoral work or sent to another diocese or country.

Finally, bishops should be careful to see that some priests devote themselves to deeper study of the sacred sciences. This will ensure that there will never be any lack of suitable teachers for the education of clerics. It will also ensure that the rest of the priests and the faithful will be helped to acquire the knowledge of religion necessary for them, and that the sound progress in sacred studies so very necessary for the Church will be encouraged.

The provision of just remuneration for priests

20. Completely devoted as they are to the service of God in the fulfillment of the office entrusted to them, priests are entitled to receive a just remuneration. For "the laborer deserves his wages" (Lk. 10.7),[61] and "the Lord commanded that they who proclaim the Gospel should get their living by the Gospel" (1 Cor. 9.14). For this reason, insofar as provision is not made from some other source for the just remuneration of priests, the faithful are bound by a real obligation of seeing to it that the necessary provision for a decent and fitting livelihood for the priests is available. This obligation arises from the fact that it is for the benefit of the faithful that priests are working. Bishops are bound to warn the faithful of their obligation in this connection. They should also, either individually for their own dioceses or better still by several acting together for a common territory, see to it that rules are drawn up by which due provision is made for the decent support of those who hold or have held any office in the serving of God.

Taking into consideration the conditions of different places and times as well as the nature of the office they hold, the remuneration to be received by each of the priests should be fundamentally the same for all living in the same circumstances. It should be in keeping with their status and in addition should give priests the means not only of providing properly for the salary of those who devote themselves to their service but also of personally assisting in some way those who are in need. The Church has always from its very beginnings held this ministry to the poor in great honor. Moreover, priests' remuneration should be such as to allow the priest a proper holiday each year. The bishop should see to it that priests are able to have this holiday.

It is, however, to the office that sacred ministers fulfill that the greatest importance must be attached. For this reason the so-called system of benefices is to be abandoned or else reformed in such a way that the part that has to do with the benefice—that is, the right to the revenues attached to the endowment of the office—shall be regarded as secondary and the principal emphasis in law given to the ecclesiastical office itself. This should in future be understood as any office conferred in a permanent fashion and to be exercised for a spiritual purpose.

Common funds to be set up: social security for priests to be organized

21. The example of the faithful in the primitive Church of Jerusalem should be always kept in mind. There "they had everything in common" (Acts 4.32), and "distribution was made to each as any had need" (Acts 4.35). It is then an excellent arrangement, at least in places where the support of the clergy depends completely or to a great extent on the offerings of the faithful, that the money offered in this way should be collected by some kind of diocesan agency. The bishop would administer this agency with the help of priests appointed for this purpose and also lay experts in financial matters, where the advantage of such appointment may make it advisable.

It is also desirable that as far as possible there should be set up in each diocese or region a common fund to enable bishops to satisfy obligations to people employed in the service of the Church and to meet the various needs of the diocese. From this fund too, richer dioceses would be able to help poorer ones, so that the abundance of the one may supply the want of the other.[62] This common fund also should be made up mainly of moneys from the offerings of the faithful as well as from those coming from other sources to be determined by law.

Moreover, in countries where social security has not yet been adequately organized for the benefit of clergy, episcopal conferences are to make provision, in harmony with ecclesiastical and civil law, for the setting up of diocesan organizations (even federated with one another), or organizations for different dioceses grouped together, or an association catering for the whole territory: the purpose of these being that under the supervision of the hierarchy satisfactory provision should be made both for suitable insurance and what is called health assistance and for the proper support of priests who suffer from sickness, ill health or old age.

Priests should assist this organization when it has been set up, moved by a spirit of solidarity with their brother priests, sharing their hardships,[63] and at the same time realizing that in this way they can, without anxiety for their future, practice poverty with a readier appreciation of the Gospel and devote themselves completely to the salvation of souls. Those responsible should do their utmost to have such organizations combined on an international scale, so as to give them more stability and strength and promote their wider diffusion.

Conclusion and Exhortation

22. This sacred Council, while keeping in mind the joys of the priestly life, cannot pass over the difficulties too which priests encounter in the circumstances of their life today. It knows also how much economic and social conditions, and even men's morals, are being transformed, and how much men's sense of values is undergoing change. Hence it is that the Church's ministers, and even sometimes the faithful, in the midst of this world feel themselves estranged from it and are anxiously seeking suitable methods and words by which they may be able to communicate with it. The new obstacles opposing the faith, the apparent fruitlessness of the work done, the bitter loneliness they experience — these can bring for priests the danger of a feeling of frustration.

But this world as it is entrusted today to the Church as the object of its love and service, this is the world God has so loved as to give his only-begotten Son for it.[1] The truth is that this world, caught as it is in the grip of much sin yet enriched too with many possibilities, provides the Church with the living stones[2] which are built together into an habitation of God in the Spirit.[3] The same Holy Spirit, while urging the Church to open new avenues of approach to the modern world, also suggests and fosters suitable adaptations of the priestly ministry.

Let priests remember that in carrying out their task they are never alone but are supported by the almighty power of God. Believing in Christ who has called them to share in his priesthood, let them devote themselves to their office with all trust, knowing that God is powerful to increase charity in them.[4] Let them remember too that they have their brothers in the priesthood and indeed the faithful of the entire world, as allies.

For all priests are cooperating in carrying out God's saving plan, the mystery of Christ or the sacrament hidden from eternity in God.[5] Only gradually is this mystery carried into effect by the united efforts of the different ministries for the building up of the Body of Christ until the measure of its age be fulfilled. Since all these truths are hidden with Christ in God[6] it is by faith especially that they can be perceived. For the leaders of the People of God must needs walk by faith, following the example of the faithful Abraham who by faith "obeyed when he was called to go out to a place which he was to receive as an inheritance; and he went out, not knowing where he was to go" (Heb. 11.8).

Indeed the dispenser of the mysteries of God can be compared to the man who cast the seed into the earth, of whom the Lord said that he "should sleep and rise night and day, and the seed should sprout and grow, he knows not how" (Mk. 4.27). The Lord Jesus who said "Be of good cheer, I have overcome the world" (Jn. 16.23), did not by these words promise complete victory to his Church in this world. This sacred Council rejoices that the earth which has been sown with the seed of the Gospel is now bringing forth fruit in many places under the guidance of the Spirit of the Lord. This Spirit is filling the world and has stirred up a truly missionary spirit in the hearts of many priests and faithful. For all this the sacred Council affectionately offers its thanks to all the priests of the world: "Now to him who by the power of work within us is able to do far more abundantly than all that we ask or think, to him be glory in the church and in Christ Jesus . . ." (Eph. 3.20-21).

What has been set down in this Decree has been accepted by the Fathers of the Sacred Council in its entirety and in all its parts. And, together with the Venerable Council Fathers, we by the apostolic power granted to us by Christ, approve, decree and establish it, and we order that what has been established in synod be promulgated, for the glory of God.

Given at Rome, at St. Peter's, 7 December 1965.

I, Paul, Bishop of the Catholic Church
(The signatures of the Fathers then follow.)

Notes

a) Translated by Archbishop Joseph Cunnane of Tuam, and revised by Michael Mooney and Enda Lyons of St. Jarlath's College, Tuam, Co. Galway. The references to D. *46* at the end of certain sections indicate where the norms for their implementation are to be found, in *Ecclesiae Sanctae,* 1.

1. Conc. Vat. II, Const. *Sacrosanctum Concilium,* on the Sacred Liturgy, 4 December 1963: *AAS* 56 (1964) 97 ff.; Const. dogm. *Lumen gentium,* 21 November 1964: *AAS* 57 (1965) 5 ff.; Decree *Christus Dominus,* on the Pastoral Function of Bishops in the Church, 28 October 1965: Decree *Optatam totius,* on Priestly Training, 28 October 1965.

Chapter I

a) The subheadings are those of the final draft of the Decree presented to the Council Fathers after the debate in the aula, October 1965.

1. Cf. Mt. 3.16; Lk. 4.18; Acts 4.27; 10.38.
2. Cf. 1 Pt. 2.5 and 9.
3. Cf. 1 Pt. 3.15.
4. Cf. Apoc. 19.10; Conc. Vat. II, Const. dogm. *Lumen gentium,* 21 November 1964, n. 35: *AAS* 57 (1965) 40-41.
5. Conc. Trid., Session 23, cap. 1 and can. 1: *Denz.* 957 and 961 (17,64 and 1771).
6. Cf. John 20.21; Conc. Vat. II, Const. dogm. *Lumen gentium,* 21 November 1964, n. 18: *AAS* 57 (1965) 21-22.
7. Cf. Conc. Vat. II, Const. dogm. *Lumen gentium,* 21 November 1964, n. 28: *AAS* 57 (1965) 33-36.
8. Cf. ibid.
9. Cf. Roman Pontifical, "Ordination of a Priest," Preface. These words are already found in the *Sacramentary of Verona* (ed. L.C. Mohlberg, Rome 1956, 122); *Missale Francorum* (ed. L.C. Mohlberg, Rome 1957, 9); in the *Liber Sacramentorum Romanae Ecclesiae* (ed. L.C. Mohlberg, Rome 1960, 25); in the *Pontificale Romano-Germanicum* (ed. Vogel-Elze, Vatican City 1963, vol. 1, 34).
10. Cf. Conc. Vat. II, Const. dogm. *Lumen gentium,* 21 November 1964, n. 10: *AAS* 57 (1965) 14-15.
11. Cf. Rom. 15.16 Gr.
12. Cf. 1 Cor. 11.26.
13. St. Augustine, *De civitate Dei,* 10, 6: *PL* 41, 284.
14. Cf. 1 Cor. 15.24.
15. Cf. Heb. 5.1.
16. Cf. Heb. 2.17; 4-15.
17. Cf. 1 Cor. 9.19-23 Vg.
18. Cf. Acts 13.2.
19. "Such anxiety for religious and moral perfection is more and more demanded even by the external conditions in which the Church lives out her life. For she cannot remain immovable and indifferent to the changes in the human scene around her which in many ways influences her policy and imposes limits and conditions upon her. IT IS QUITE CLEAR THAT THE Church is not isolated from the human community, but is situated in it, and hence that her children are influenced and guided by it, and that they imbibe its culture, obey its laws, adopt its customs. Now this intercourse of the Church with human society is constantly giving rise to difficult problems. These are particularly serious at present. . . The Apostle of the Gentiles addressed this exhortation to the Christians of his time: 'Bear not the yoke with unbelievers. For what participation hath justice with injustice? Or what fellowship hath light with darkness? . . . Or what part hath the faithful with the unbeliever?' (2 Cor. 6.14-15). For this reason those who at present hold the position of educators and teachers in the Church must impress upon Catholic youth their outstanding dignity and the duty arising from this of living in this world but not according to the sentiments of this world. This will be in conformity with the prayer made by Christ for his disciples: 'I pray not that thou shouldst take them out of the world, but that thou shouldst keep them from evil. They are not of the world, as I am not of the world' (Jn. 17.15-16). The Church adopts this prayer as her own.

"At the same time however such a difference as this does not mean the same thing as separation. It does not profess neglect, nor fear, nor contempt. For when the Church makes a distinction between herself and the human race, so far is she from setting herself in opposition to it that she rather is joined with it" (Paul VI, Litt. Encycl. *Ecclesiam suam,* 6 August 1964: *AAS* 56 (1964) 627 and 638).
20. Cf. Rom. 12.2.
21. Cf. Jn. 10.14-16.
22. Cf. St. Polycarp, *Epist. ad Philippenses,* VI, I: "Let priests also be disposed to pity, merciful to all, leading back the erring, visiting all the sick, not neglecting the widow, the orphan or the poor. Rather let them be always solicitous for good in the sight of God and men, refraining from all anger, acceptance of persons, unjust judgment, completely avoiding all avarice, slow to believe evil against anyone. Let them not be over-severe in judgment, knowing that we are all debtors of sin" (ed. F. X. Funk, *Patres Apostolici,* I, 303).

CHAPTER II

1. Cf. 1 Pt. 1.23; Acts 6.7; 12.24, "(The apostles) preached the Word of truth and produced churches." (St. Augustine, *Comments on Ps.*, 44, 23: *PL* 36, 508).

2. Cf. Mal. 2.7; 1 Tm. 4.11-13; 2 Tm. 4.5; Ti.1.9.

3. Cf. Mk. 16.16.

4. Cf. 2 Cor. 11.7. What is said of bishops holds also for priests, since they are the co-workers of the bishops. Cf. *Statuta Ecclesiae Antiqua*, c. 3 (ed. Munier, Paris 1960, 79); *Decretum Gratiani*, C. 6, D. 88 (ed. Friedberg, I, 307); Conc. Trid., Decree *De reform.*, Session 5, c. 2, n. 9 (*Conc. Oec. Decreta*, ed. Herder, Rome 1963, 645); Session 24, c. 4 (739); Conc. Vat. II, Const. dogm. *Lumen gentium*, 21 November 1964, n. 25: *AAS* 57 (1965) 29-31.

5. Cf. *Constitutiones Apostolorum*, II, 26, 7: "Let (priests) be the teachers of divine knowledge, since the Lord himself also commanded us, says: Going teach ye, etc." (ed F.X. Funk, *Didascalia et Constitutiones Apostolorum*, I, Paderborn 1905, 105). *Leonine Sacramentary* and other sacramentaries down to the *Roman Pontifical*, Preface for the Ordination of a Priest: "By this providence, O Lord, you have added teachers of the faith to the apostles of your Son, and through them they filled the whole earth with preachers [or: preachings] of the second rank." *Book of Orders of the Mozarabic Liturgy*, Preface for the Ordination of a Priest: "The teacher of peoples and the ruler of subjects, let him keep the Catholic faith in well-ordered fashion, and announce true salvation to all" (ed. M. Ferotin, Paris 1904, col. 55).

6. Cf. Gal. 2.5.

7. Cf. 1 Pt. 2.12

8. Cf. the Rite of Ordination of a Priest in the Alexandrian Church of the Jacobites: ". . . Gather your people to the word of doctrine like a nurse who cherishes her children" (H. Denzinger, *Ritus Orientalium*, vol. II, Wurzberg 1863, 14).

9. Cf. Mt. 28.19; Mk. 16.16; Tertullian, *On baptism*, 14, 2 (Corpus Christianorum, Latin series, 1, 289, 11-13); St. Athanasius, *Adv. Arianos*, 2, 42 (*PG* 26, 237); St. Jerome, *Comment. on Mat.*, 28, 19 (*PL* 26, 218 BC): "First they teach all nations, then they baptize with water those who have been taught. For it cannot be that the body should receive the sacrament of Baptism unless the soul has previously received the truth of the faith"; St. Thomas, *Expositio primae Decretalis*, §1: "When our Saviour was sending his disciples to preach he gave them three injunctions. First, that they should teach the faith; secondly that they should initiate believers through the sacraments" (ed. Marietti, *Opuscula Theologica*, Turin-Rome 1954, 1138).

10. Cf. Conc. Vat. II, Const. *Sacrosanctum Concilium*, on the Sacred Liturgy, 4 December 1963, n. 35, 2: *AAS* 56 (1964) 109.

11. Cf. ibid., nn. 33, 35, 48, 52 (108-109, 113, 114).

12. Cf. ibid., n. 7 (100-101); Pius XII, Encycl. *Mystici Corporis*, 29 June 1943: *AAS* 35 (1943) 230.

13. St. Ignatius Martyr, *Smyrn.*, 8, 1-2 (ed. F. X. Funk, 282, 6-15); *Constitutiones Apostolorum*, VIII, 12, 3 (ed. F. X. Funk, 496); VIII, 29, 2 (532).

14. Cf. Conc. Vat. II, Const, dogm. *Lumen gentium*, 21 November 1964, n. 28: *AAS* 57 (1965) 33-36.

15. "The Eucharist is as it were the completion of the spiritual life and the end of all the sacraments" (St. Thomas, *Summa Theol.* III, q. 73, a. 3 c); cf. *Summa Theol.* III, q. 65, a. 3.

16. Cf. St. Thomas, *Summa Theol.* III, q. 65, a. 3, ad 1; q. 79, a. 1, c. et ad 1.

17. Cf. Eph. 5.19-20.

18. Cf. St. Jerome, *Epist.*, 114, 2: ". . . and consecrated chalices and sacred vestments and the other things that have to do with the worship of the Lord's passion. . . because of their association with the Body and Blood of the Lord are to be venerated with the same reverence as his Body and Blood" (*PL* 22, 934). See Conc. Vat. II, Const. *Sacrosanctum Concilium*, on Sacred Liturgy, 4 December 1963, nn. 122-127: *AAS* 56 (1964) 130-132.

19. "Moreover, let them not omit to make each day a visit to the most blessed sacrament, which is to be reserved in the most noble place and in the most honorable way possible in churches, according to liturgical laws, since this visit will be at once a proof of gratitude, a pledge of love and an act of the adoration due to Christ present in this same sacrament" (Paul VI, Encycl. *Mysterium Fidei*, 3 September 1965: *AAS* 57 [1965] 771).

20. Cf. Conc. Vat. II, Const. dogm. *Lumen gentium*, 21 November 1964, n. 28: *AAS* 57 (1965) 33-36.

21. Cf. 2 Cor. 10.8; 13.10.

22. Cf. Gal. 1.10.

23. Cf. 1 Cor. 4.14.

24. Cf. *Didascalia*, II, 34, 3; II, 46, 6; II, 47, 1; *Constitutiones Apostolorum*, II, 47, 1 (ed. F. X. Funk, *Didascalia et Constitutiones*, I, 116, 142 and 143).

25. Cf. Gal. 4.3; 5.1 and 13.

26. Cf. St. Jerome, *Epist.*, 58, 7: "What use is it that walls glitter with gems while Christ dies in the person of a poor man?" (*PL* 22, 584).

27. Cf. 1 Pt. 4.10 ff.

28. Cf. Mt. 25.34-35.

29. Cf. Lk. 4.18.

30. Other classes can be mentioned, e.g., migrants, itinerants, etc. These are dealt with in the Decree *Christus Dominus*, on the Pastoral Function of Bishops in the Church, 28 October 1965.

31. Cf. *Didascalia*, II, 59, 1-3: "In your teaching order and exhort the people to visit the church and never to be entirely absent, but to assemble always and not impoverish the church, by staying away, and

make the Body of Christ less a member. . . . Therefore since you are members of Christ do not separate yourselves from the Church by failing to be united; for having Christ your head according to his promise present and communicating with you, do not neglect yourselves or alienate the Saviour from his members or divide or disperse his Body. . . " (ed. F. X. Funk, I, 170); Paul VI, *Allocution* to the Italian clergy at the 13th "Week of pastoral renewal." at Orvieto, 6 September 1963: *AAS* 55 (1963) 750 ff.

32. Cf. Conc. Vat. II, Const. dogm. *Lumen gentium*, 21 November 1964, n. 28: *AAS* 57 (1965) 35.

33. Cf. the so-called *Ecclesiastical Constitution of the Apostles*, XVIII: Priests are fellow-participants in the mysteries and fellow-soldiers of the bishops (ed. Th. Schermann, *Die allgemeine Kirchenordnung*, I, Paderborn 1914, 26; A. Harnack, T. u. U., II, 4, 13, n. 18 and 19); Pseudo-Jerome, *On the Seven Orders of the Church:* ". . . in the blessing, they are sharers in the mysteries with the bishops" (ed. A. W. Kalff, Wurzburg 1937, 45); St. Isidore of Seville, *On Ecclesiastical Offices*, c. VII: "They are set over the Church of God and in the celebration of the Eucharist they are the associates of the bishops, as they are also in teaching the people and in the office of preaching" (*PL* 83, 787).

34. Cf. *Didascalia*, II, 28, 4 (ed. F. X. Funk, 108); *Apostolic Constitutions*, II, 28, 4; II, 34, 3 (ibid., 109 and 117).

35. *Apostolic Constitutions*, VIII, 16, 4 (ed. F. X. Funk, I, 522, 13); cf. *Summary of Apostolic Constitutions*, VI (ibid., 11, 80, 3-4); *Testament of the Lord:* ". . . give him the Spirit of grace, counsel, and magnanimity, the spirit of the priesthood . . . to help and govern your people in work, in fear, in a pure heart" (trans. I. E. Rahmani, Mainz 1899, 69). So also in *Apostolic Tradition* (ed. B. Botte, *La Tradition Apostolique*, Munster i. W. 1963, 20).

36. Cf. Nm. 11.16-25.

37. *Roman Pontifical*, "Ordination of a Priest," Preface; these words are already contained in the *Leonine*, *Gelasian* and *Gregorian Sacramentaries*. Similar expressions are found in the eastern liturgies; cf. *Apost. Trad.:* ". . . look upon your servant and impart to him the spirit of grace and counsel, that he may aid the priests and rule your people in a clean heart, as you looked upon the people of your choice and commanded Moses to choose elders whom you filled with your spirit which you have given to your servant" (from the ancient Latin version of Verona, ed. B. Botte, *La Tradition Apostolique de S. Hippolyte. Essai de reconstruction*, Munster i. W. 1963, 20); *Apost. Const.* VIII, 16, 4 (ed. F. X. Funk, I, 522, 16-17); *Summary of Apost. Const.* 6 (ed. F. X. Funk, II, 20, 5-7); *Testament of the Lord* (trans. I. E. Rahmani, Mainz 1899, 69), *Euchology of Serapion*, XXVII (ed. F. X. Funk, *Didascalia et Constitutiones*, II, 190, lin. 1-7); *Rite of Ordination in the Maronite Liturgy* (trans. H. Denzinger, *Ritus Orientalium*, II, Wurzburg 1863, 161). Among the Fathers can be cited: Theodore of Mopsuesta, *In I Tim.* 3, 8 (ed. Swete, II, 119-121); Theodore, *Questions on Numbers*, XVIII (*PG* 80, 372 b).

38. Cf. Conc. Vat. II, Const. dogm. *Lumen gentium*, 21 November 1964, n. 28: *AAS* 57 (1965) 35.

39. Cf. John XXIII, Encycl. *Sacerdotii Nostri primordia*, 1 August 1959: *AAS* 51 (1959) 576; St. Pius X, Exhortation to the Clergy *Haerent animo*, 4 August 1908: S. Pii X Acta, vol. IV (1908) 237 ff.

40. Cf. Conc. Vat. II, Decree *Christus Dominus*, on the Pastoral Function of Bishops in the Church, 28 October 1965, nn. 15 and 16.

41. In established law the Cathedral Chapter is regarded as the bishop's "senate and council" *C.I.C.*, c. 391), or in its absence the group of diocesan consultors (cf. *C.I.C.*, cc. 423-428). But it is desirable to reform these institutions in such a way as to make better provision for present-day needs. Clearly this group of priests differs from the pastoral council spoken of in the Decree *Christus Dominus* on the Pastoral Function of Bishops in the Church, 28 October 1965, n. 27, which includes laymen and whose function is confined to investigating question of pastoral activity. On the question of priests as counsellors of bishops see *Didascalia*, II, 28, 4 (ed. F. X. Funk, I, 108); also *Apost. Const.*, II, 2, 4 (ed. F. X. Funk, I, 109); St. Ignatius Martyr, *Magnesians*, 6, 1 (ed. F. X. Funk, 244, 10-12); Origen, *Against Celsus*, 3, 30: Priests are counsellors or *bouleutai* (*PG* 11, 157 d—960 a).

42. St. Ignatius Martyr, *Magnesians*, 6, 1: "I exhort you to strive to do all things in the peace of God, the bishop presiding in the place of God and the priests in the place of the senate of apostles, and the deacons who are so dear to me having entrusted to them the ministry of Jesus Christ who was with the Father before all ages and finally appeared" (ed. F. X. Funk, 244, 10-13); St. Ignatius Martyr, *Trallians*, 3, 1: "Likewise let all reverence the deacons as Jesus Christ, as also the bishop who is the image of the Father, the priests as the senate of God and the council of apostles: without these one cannot speak of a church" (ibid., 244, 10-13); St. Jerome, *Commentary on Isaias*, II, 3 (*PL* 24, 61 A): "We also have in the Church our senate, the group of priests. "

43. Cf. Paul VI, *Allocution* to the parish priests and Lenten preachers of Rome, in the Sistine Chapel, 1 March 1965: *AAS* 57 (1965), 326.

44. Cf. *Apost. Const.*, VIII, 47, 39: "Priests . . . should do nothing without the decision of the bishop; for it is to him that the people of the Lord has been entrusted and from him an account of their souls will be demanded" (ed. F. X. Funk, 577).

45. Cf. 3 Jn. 8.

46. Cf. Jn. 17.23.

47. Cf. Heb. 13.1-2.

48. Cf. Heb. 13.16.

49. Cf. Mt. 5.10.

50. Cf. 1 Thes. 2.12; Col. 1.13.

51. Cf. Mt. 23.8. "From the very fact that we wish to be the pastors, fathers and teachers of men it follows that we must act as their brothers" (Paul VI, Encycl. *Ecclesiam suam*, 6 August 1964: *AAS* 58 [1964] 647).

52. Cf. Eph. 4.7 and 16; *Apost. Const.,* VIII, 1, 20: "The bishop moreover should not set himself up over the deacons or priests, nor the priests over the people; for the structure of the assembly is made up of members of both" (ed. F. X. Funk, I, 467).

53. Cf. Phil. 2.21.

54. Cf. 1 Jn. 4.1.

55. Cf. Conc. Vat. II, Const. dogm. *Lumen gentium,* 21 November 1964, n. 37: *AAS* 57 (1965) 42-43.

56. Cf. Eph. 4.14.

57. Cf. Conc. Vat. II, Decree *Unitatis redintegratio,* on Ecumenism, 21 November 1964: *AAS* 57 (1965) 90 ff.

58. Cf. Conc. Vat. II, Const. dogm. *Lumen gentium,* 21 November 1964, n. 37: *AAS* 57 (1965) 42-43.

59. Cf. Heb. 7.3.

60. Cf. Lk. 10.1.

61. Cf. 1 Pt. 2.25.

62. Cf. Acts 20.28.

63. Cf. Mt. 9.36.

64. *Roman Pontifical,* "Ordination of a Priest."

65. Cf. Conc. Vat. II, Decree *Optatam totius,* on Priestly Training, 28 October 1965, n. 2.

66. "The voice of God which calls expresses itself in two different ways that are marvellous and converging: one interior, that of grace, that of the Holy Spirit, that inexpressible interior attraction which the silent and powerful voice of the Lord exercises in the unfathomable depths of the human soul; and the other one external, human, sensible, social, juridical, concrete, that of the qualified minister of the Word of God, that of the Apostle, that of the hierarchy, an indispensable instrument instituted and willed by Christ as a concrete means of translating into the language of experience the message of the Word and the divine precept. Such is the teaching of Catholic doctrine with St. Paul: *How shall they hear without a preacher... Faith comes from hearing* (Rom. 10.14 and 17)" (Paul VI, *Allocution,* 5 May 1965: *L'Osservatore Romano,* 6 May 1965, 1).

67. Cf. Conc. Vat. II, Decree *Optatam totius,* on Priestly Training, 28 October 1965, n. 2.

68. This is the teaching of the Fathers when they explain Christ's words to Peter: "Lovest thou me?... Feed my sheep" (Jn. 21.17): so St. John Chrysostom, *On the Priesthood,* II, 1-2 (*PG* 47-48, 633); St. Gregory the Great, *Pastoral Rule,* P. I. c. 5 (*PL* 77, 19 a).

Chapter III

1. Cf. 2 Cor. 12.9.

2. Cf. Pius XI, Encycl. *Ad catholici sacerdotii,* 20 December 1935: *AAS* 28 (1936) 10.

3. Cf. Jn. 10.36.

4. Cf. Lk. 24.26.

5. Cf. Eph. 4.13.

6. Cf. 2 Cor. 3.8-9.

7. Cf. among others: St. Pius X, Exhortation to the Clergy, *Haerent animo,* 4 August 1908: St. Pii X Acta, vol. IV (1908) 237 ff. Pius XI, Encycl. *Ad catholici sacerdotii,* 20 December 1935: *AAS* 28 (1936) 5 ff. Pius XII, Apostolic Exhortation, *Menti Nostrae,* 23 September 1950: *AAS* 42 (1950) 657 ff. John XXIII, Encycl. *Sacerdotii Nostri primordia,* 1 August 1959: *AAS* 51 (1959) 545 ff.

8. Cf. St. Thomas, *Summa Theol.,* II-II, q. 188, a. 7.

9. Cf. Heb. 3.9-10.

10. Cf. Acts 16.14.

11. Cf. 2 Cor. 4.7.

12. Cf. Eph. 3.9.

13. *Roman Pontifical,* "Ordination of a Priest."

14. Cf. *Roman Missal,* Prayer over the offerings, of Ninth Sunday after Pentecost.

15. "The Mass, even though it is celebrated privately is still not private, but is the act of Christ and the Church. The Church, in the sacrifice which she offers, learns to offer herself as a universal sacrifice and applies the unique and infinite redemptive power of the sacrifice of the cross to the whole world for its salvation. For every Mass that is celebrated is offered not merely for the salvation of some souls but for that of the whole world... Therefore we recommend with paternal insistence to priests, who are our especial joy and our crown in the Lord, that... they celebrate Mass worthily and devoutly every day" (Paul VI, Encycl. *Mysterium Fidei,* 3 September 1965: *AAS* 57 [1965] 761-762). Cf. Conc. Vat. II, Const. *Sacrosanctum Concilium,* on the Sacred Liturgy, 4 December 1963, nn. 26 and 27: *AAS* 56 (1964) 107.

16. Cf. Jn. 10.11.

17. Cf. 2 Cor. 1.7.

18. Cf. 2 Cor. 1.4.

19. Cf. 1 Cor. 10.33.

20. Cf. Jn. 3.8.

21. Cf. Jn. 4.34.

22. Cf. 1 Jn. 3.16.

23. "Let it be the duty of love to shepherd the Lord's flock" (St. Augustine, *Treatise on John,* 123, 5: *PL* 35, 1967).

24. Cf. Rom. 12.2.
25. Cf. Gal. 2.2.
26. Cf. 2 Cor. 7.4.
27. Cf. Jn. 4.34; 5.30; and 6.38.
28. Cf. Acts 13.2.
29. Cf. Eph. 5.10.
30. Cf. Acts 20.22.
31. Cf. 2 Cor. 12.15.
32. Cf. Eph. 4.11-16.
33. Cf. Mt. 19.12.
34. Cf. Conc. Vat. II, Const. dogm. *Lumen gentium,* 21 November 1964, n. 42: *AAS* 57 (1965) 47-49.
35. Cf. 1 Tm. 3.2-5; Ti. 1.6.
36. Cf. Pius XI, Encycl. *Ad catholici sacerdotii,* 20 December 1935; *AAS* 28 (1936) 28.
37. Cf. Mt. 19.12.
38. Cf. 1 Cor. 7.32-34.
39. Cf. 2 Cor. 11.2.
40. Cf. Conc. Vat. II, Const. dogm. *Lumen gentium,* 21 November 1964, nn. 42 and 44: *AAS* 57 (1965) 47-49 and 50-51; Decree *Perfectae caritatis,* on the Renewal of Religious Life, 28 October 1965, n. 12.
41. Cf. Lk. 20.35-36; Pius XI, Encycl. *Ad catholici sacerdotii,* 20 December 1935: *AAS* 28 (1936) 24-28; Pius XII, Encycl. *Sacra Virginitas,* 25 March 1954: *AAS* 46 (1954) 169-172.
42. Cf. Mt. 19.11.
43. Cf. Jn. 17.14-16.
44. Cf. 1 Cor. 7.31.
45. Council of Antioch, can. 25: Mansi 2, 1328; *Decree of Gratian,* c. 23, C. 12, q. 1 (ed. Friedberg, I, 684-685).
46. This is to be understood especially of the laws and customs in force in the Eastern Churches.
47. Council of Paris, a. 829, can. 15: M.G.H., sect. III, *Concilia,* t. 2, par. 6, 622; Council of Trent, Session 25, *De reform.,* cap. 1.
48. Cf. Ps. 62, 11 Vg. 61.
49. Cf. 2 Cor. 8.9.
50. Cf. Acts 8.18-25.
51. Cf. Phil. 4.12.
52. Cf. Acts 2.42-47.
53. Cf. Lk. 4.18.
54. Cf. *C.I.C.,* can. 125 ff.
55. Cf. Conc. Vat. II, Decree *Perfectae caritatis,* on the Renewal of Religious Life, 28 October 1965, n. 6; Const. dogm. *Dei verbum,* on Divine Revelation, 18 November 1965, n. 21.
56. Cf. Conc. Vat. II, Const. dogm. *Lumen gentium,* 21 November 1964, n. 65: *AAS* 57 (1965) 64-65.
57. *Roman Pontifical,* "Ordination of a Priest."
58. Cf. Conc. Vat. II, Const. dogm., *Dei verbum,* on Divine Revelation, 18 November 1965, n. 25.
59. This course is not the same as the pastoral course to be completed immediately after ordination and dealt with in the Decree *Optatam totius,* on Priestly Training, 28 October 1965, n. 22.
60. Cf. Conc. Vat. II, Decree *Christus Dominus,* on the Pastoral Function of Bishops in the Church, 28 October 1965, n. 16.
61. Cf. Mt. 10.10; 1 Cor. 9.7; 1 Tm. 5.18.
62. Cf. 2 Cor. 8.14.
63. Cf. Phil. 4.14.

Conclusion and Exhortation

1. Cf. Jn. 3.16.
2. Cf. 1 Pt. 2.5.
3. Cf. Eph. 2.22.
4. Cf. *Roman Pontifical,* "Ordination of a Priest."
5. Cf. Eph. 3.9.
6. Cf. Col. 3.3.

The Ministerial Priesthood

Synod of Bishops

1971

The Ministerial Priesthood

Introduction

In recent times, especially since the close of the Second Vatican Council, the Church is experiencing a profound movement of renewal, which all Christians should follow with great joy and with fidelity to the Gospel. The power of the Holy Spirit is present to illumine, strengthen and perfect our mission.

Every true renewal brings the Church undoubted benefits of great value. We well know that through the recent Council priests have been fired with new zeal and that they have contributed much to fostering this renewal by their daily solicitude. We have before our minds our many heroic brothers who, in fidelity of their ministry, live lives dedicated to God with joy, either among the peoples where the Church is subjected to a harsh yoke or in mission lands. At the same time, however, the renewal also entails difficulties, which are especially felt by all in the priesthood, whether bishops or priests.

We should all scrutinize the signs of the times in this age of renewal and interpret them in the light of the Gospel (cf. *GS* 4), in order that we may work together in distinguishing between spirits, to see if they come from God, lest ambiguity cloud the unity of the Church's mission or excessive uniformity hinder needed adaptation. Thus, by testing everything and holding fast to what is good, the present crisis can give occasion for an increase of faith.

In accordance with its importance, the Holy Father put forward the ministerial priesthood for discussion by this year's Synod. Before the Synod many episcopal conferences examined this theme together with priests and quite frequently with lay people. Some priests were also called to the Synod as "auditores," to assist the bishops in dealing with important questions.

We wish to fulfill our duty with the evangelical simplicity which befits pastors who are serving the Church. Considering our responsibility before the fraternal community of the Church, we desire to strengthen the faith, uplift the hope and stimulate the love both of our brothers in the ministerial priesthood and of all the faithful. May our words bring solace to the People of God and the priests dedicated to their service and renew their joy!

Description of the Situation

1. The extent of the Church's mission was illustrated at length by the Second Vatican Council. Indeed, the Church's relationship with the world was the subject especially of the pastoral constitution *Gaudium et Spes [GS, Pastoral Constitution on the Church in the Modern World]*. Many good results followed from a closer consideration of this matter: it is more clearly seen that salvation is not an abstract category outside, as it were, of history and time, but that it comes from God and ought to permeate the whole of man and the whole history of men and lead them freely to the Kingdom of God, so that at last "God may be all in all" (1 Cor. 15.28).

However, as is understandable, difficulties have also arisen: some priests feel themselves estranged from the movements which permeate society and unable to solve the problems which touch men deeply. Often too the problems and troubles of priests derive from their having, in their pastoral and missionary care, to use methods which are now perhaps obsolete to meet the modern mentality. Serious problems and several questions then arise, especially from real difficulties which they experience in exercising their function and not—although this is sometimes the case — from an exasperated spirit of protest or from selfish personal concerns. Is it possible to exhort the laity as if from the outside? Is the Church sufficiently present to certain groups without the active presence of the priest? If the situation characteristic of a priest consists in segregation from secular life, is not the situation of the layman better? What is to be thought of the celibacy of Latin-rite priests in present-day circumstances, and of the personal spiritual life of the priest immersed in the world?

2. Many priests, experiencing within themselves the questionings that have arisen with the secularization of the world, feel the need to sanctify worldly activities by exercising them directly and bring the leaven of the Gospel into the midst of events. Similarly, the desire is developing of cooperating with the joint efforts of men to build up a more just and fraternal society. In a world in which almost all problems have political aspects, participation in politics and even in revolutionary activity is by some considered indispensable.

3. The Council emphasized the pre-eminence of the proclamation of the Gospel, which should lead through faith to the fullness of the celebration of the sacraments. But current thinking about the religious phenomenon fosters doubts in many minds concerning the sense of a sacramental and cultic ministry. Many priests not suffering from a personal identity crisis ask themselves another question: What methods should be used so that sacramental practice may be an expression of faith really affecting the whole of personal and social life, in order that Christian worship should not be wrongly reduced to a mere external ritualism?

Since priests are very concerned with the image of herself that the Church seems to present to the world, and at the same time are deeply conscious of the singular dignity of the human person, they desire to bring about a change within the Church herself in interpersonal relationships, in relations between person and institutions, and in the very structures of authority.

4. And still, relationships between bishops and priests and between priests themselves are growing more difficult by the very fact that the exercise of the ministry is becoming more diversified. Present-day society is divided into many groups with different disciplines, which call for differing skills and forms of apostolate. This gives rise to problems concerning brotherhood, union and consistency in the priestly ministry.

Happily the recent Council recalled the traditional and fruitful teaching on the common priesthood of the faithful (cf. *LG [Dogmatic Constitution on the Church]*, 10). That, however, gives rise, as by a swing of the pendulum, to certain questions which seem to obscure the position of the priestly ministry in the Church and which deeply trouble the minds of some priests and faithful. Many activities which in the past were reserved to priests—for instance, catechetical work, administrative activity in the communities, and even liturgical activities—are today quite frequently carried out by lay people, while on the other hand many priests, for reasons already mentioned, are trying to involve themselves in the condition of life of lay persons. Hence a number of questions are being asked: Does the priestly ministry have any specific nature? Is this ministry necessary? Is the priesthood incapable of being lost? What does being a priest mean today? Would it not be enough to have for the service of the Christian communities presidents designated for the preservation of the common good, without sacramental ordination, and exercising their office for a fixed period?

5. Still more serious questions are posed, some of them as a result of exegetical and historical research, which show a crisis of confidence in the Church: Is the present-day Church too far removed from its origins to be able to proclaim the ancient Gospel credibly to modern man? Is it still possible to reach the reality of Christ after so many critical investigations? Are the essential structures of the early Church well enough known to us that they can and must be considered an invariable scheme for every age, including our own?

6. The above-mentioned questions, some of them new, others already long familiar but appearing in new forms today, cannot be understood outside of the whole context of modern culture, which has strong doubts about its meaning and value. New means of technology have stirred up a hope based excessively on enthusiasm and at the same time they have aroused profound anxiety. One rightly asks whether man will be capable of being master of his work and directing it towards progress.

Some, especially the young, despair of the meaning of this world and look for salvation in purely meditative systems and in artificial marginal paradises, abandoning the common striving of mankind.

Others dedicate themselves with ardent utopian hope devoid of reference to God to the attainment of some state of total liberation, and transfer the meaning of their whole personal lives from the present to the future.

There is therefore a profound cleavage between action and contemplation, work and recreation, culture and religion, and between the immanent and the transcendental aspects of human life.

Thus the world itself is obscurely awaiting a solution to this dilemma and is paving a way whereby the Church may go forward proclaiming the Gospel. Certainly, the only complete salvation offered to men is Christ himself, Son of God and Son of Man, who makes himself present in history through the Church. He joins inseparably together love for God and the love which God has until the end for men as they seek their way amid the shadows, and the value of human love whereby a man gives his life for his friends. In Christ, and only in him, do all of these become one whole, and in this synthesis the meaning of human life, both individual and social, shines forth. The mission of the Church, Christ's Body, far from being obsolete, is therefore rather of the highest relevance for the present and the future: the whole Church is the witness and effective sign of this union, especially through the priestly ministry. The minister's proper task in the Church's midst is to render present, by the word and sacrament, the love of God in Christ for us, and at the same time to promote the fellowship of men with God and with each other. All this of course demands that we should all, especially those who perform the sacred office, strive to renew ourselves daily in accordance with the Gospel.

7. We know that there are some parts of the world in which that profound cultural change has hitherto been less felt, and that the questions raised above are not being asked everywhere, nor by all priests, nor in the same way. But since communications between men and peoples have today become more frequent and more speedy, we judge it good and opportune to examine these questions in the light of faith and to give humbly but in the strength of the Holy Spirit some principles for finding more concrete answers to them. Although this response must be applied differently according to the circumstances of each region, it will have the force of truth for all those faithful and priests who live in situations of greater tranquillity. Therefore, ardently desiring to strengthen the witness of faith, we fraternally urge all the faithful to strive to contemplate the Lord Jesus living in his Church and to realize that he wishes to work in a special way through his ministers; they will thus be convinced that the Christian community cannot fulfull its complete mission without the ministerial priesthood. Let priests be aware that their anxieties are truly shared by the bishops, and that the bishops desire to share them still more.

* * *

Moved by this desire, the Synod Fathers, in the spirit of the Gospel, following closely the teaching of the Second Vatican Council, and considering also the documents and addresses of the Supreme Pontiff Paul VI, intend to set forth briefly some principles of the Church's teaching on the ministerial priesthood which are at present more urgent, together with some guidelines for pastoral practice.

Part One
Principles of Doctrine

1. Christ, Alpha and Omega

Jesus Christ, the Son of God and the Word, "whom the Father sanctified and sent into the world" (Jn. 10.36), and who was marked with the seal of the fullness of the Holy Spirit (cf. Lk. 4.1; 18-21; Acts 10.38), proclaimed to the world the Good News of reconciliation between God and men. His preaching as a prophet, confirmed by signs, reaches its summit in the paschal mystery, the supreme word of the divine love with which the Father addressed us. On the cross Jesus showed himself to the greatest possible extent to be the Good Shepherd who laid down his life for his sheep in order to gather them into that unity which depends on himself (cf. Jn. 10.15 ff.; 11.52). Exercising a supreme and unique priesthood by the offering of himself, he surpassed, by fulfilling them, all the ritual priesthoods and holocausts of the Old Testament and indeed of the pagans. In his sacrifice he took on himself the miseries and sacrifices of men of every age and also the efforts of those who suffer for the cause of justice or who are daily oppressed by misfortune. He took on himself the endeavors of those who abandon the world and attempt to reach God by asceticism and contemplation as well as the labors of those who sincerely devote their lives to a better present and future society. He bore the sins of us all on the cross; rising from the dead and being made Lord (cf. Phil. 2.9-11), he reconciled us to God; and he laid the foundation of the people of the New Covenant, which is the Church.

He is the "one mediator between God and men, the man Christ Jesus" (1 Tm. 2.5), "for in him were created all things" (Col. 1.16; cf. Jn. 1.3 ff.) and everything is brought together under him, as head (cf. Eph. 1.10). Since he is the image of the Father and manifestation of the unseen God (cf. Col. 1.15), by emptying himself and by being raised up he brought us into the fellowship of the Holy Spirit which he lives with the Father.

When therefore we speak of the priesthood of Christ, we should have before our eyes a unique, incomparable reality, which includes the prophetic and royal office of the Incarnate Word of God.

So Jesus Christ signifies and manifests in many ways the presence and effectiveness of the anticipatory love of God. The Lord himself, constantly influencing the Church by his Spirit, stirs up and fosters the response of all those who offer themselves to this freely given love.

2. Coming to Christ in the Church

The way to the person and mystery of Christ lies ever open in the Holy Spirit through the Scriptures understood in the living tradition of the Church. All the Scriptures, especially those of the New Testament, must be interpreted as intimately interlinked and interrelated by their single inspiration. The books of the New Testament are not of such differing value that some of them can be reduced to mere late inventions.

A personal and immediate relationship with Christ in the Church should still for the faithful of today sustain their whole spiritual lives.

3. The Church from Christ through the Apostles

The Church which he had declared would be built on Peter, Christ founded on the Apostles (cf. *LG* 18). In them are already manifested two aspects of the Church: in the Group of the Twelve Apostles there are already both fellowship in the Spirit and the origin of the hierarchical ministry (cf. *AG [Decree on the Church's Missionary Activity]*, 5). For that reason, the New Testament writings speak of the Church as founded on the Apostles (cf. Rv. 21.14; Mt. 16.18). This was concisely expressed by ancient tradition: "The Church from the Apostles, the Apostles from Christ, Christ from God." [1]

The Church, which was founded on the Apostles and sent into the world and is a pilgrim there, was established to be a sacrament of the salvation which came to us from God in Christ. In her, Christ is present and operative for the world as a saviour, so that the love offered by God to men and their response meet. The Holy Spirit stirs up in and through the Church impulses of generous free will by which man participates in the very work of creation and redemption.

4. The origin and nature of the hierarchical ministry

The Church, which through the gift of the Spirit is made up organically, participates in different ways in the functions of Christ as Priest, Prophet and King, in order to carry out her mission of salvation in his name and by his power, as a priestly people (cf. *LG* 10).

It is clear from the New Testament writings that an Apostle and a community of faithful united with one another by a mutual link under Christ as head and the influence of his Spirit belong to the original inalienable structure of the Church. The Twelve Apostles exercised their mission and functions, and "they not only had helpers in their ministry (cf. Acts 6.2-6; 11.30; 13.1; 14.23; 24.17; 1 Thes. 5.12-13; Phil. 1; Col. 4.11 and passim), but also, in order that the mission assigned to them might continue after their death, they passed on to their immediate cooperators, as a kind of testament, the duty of perfecting and consolidating the work begun by themselves (Acts 20.25-27; 2 Tm. 4.6 taken together with 1 Tm. 5.22; 2 Tm. 2.2; Ti. 1.5; Saint Clement of Rome to the Corinthians 44.3), charging them to attend to the whole flock in which the Holy Spirit placed them to shepherd the Church of God (cf. Acts 20.28). They appointed such men, and made provision that, when these men should die, other approved men would take up their ministry (cf. Saint Clement of Rome to the Corinthians 44.2)" (*LG* 20).

The letters of Saint Paul show that he was conscious of acting by Christ's mission and mandate (cf. 2 Cor. 5.18 ff.). The powers entrusted to the Apostles for the Churches were handed on to others insofar as they were communicable (cf. 2 Tm. 1.6), and these others were obliged to hand them on to yet others (cf. Ti. 1.5).

This essential structure of the Church — consisting of a flock and of pastors appointed for this purpose (cf. 1 Pt. 5.1-4) — according to the Tradition of the Church herself was always and remains the norm. Precisely as a result of this structure, the Church can never remain closed in on herself and is always subject to Christ as her origin and head.

Among the various charisms and services, the priestly ministry of the New Testament, which continues Christ's function as mediator, and which in essence and not merely in degree is distinct from the common priesthood of all the faithful (cf. *LG* 10), alone perpetuates the essential work of the Apostles: by effectively proclaiming the Gospel, by gathering together and leading the community, by remitting sins, and especially by celebrating the Eucharist, it makes Christ, the head of the community, present in the exercise of his work of redeeming mankind and glorifying God perfectly.

Bishops and, on a subordinate level, priests by virtue of the sacrament of Orders, which confers an anointing of the Holy Spirit and configures to Christ (cf. *PO [Decree on the Ministry and Life of Priests]* 2), become sharers in the functions of sanctifying, teaching and governing, and the exercise of these functions is determined more precisely by hierarchical communion (cf. *LG* 24, 27-28).

The priestly ministry reaches its summit in the celebration of the Eucharist, which is the source and center of the Church's unity. Only a priest is able to act in the person of Christ in presiding over and effecting the sacrificial banquet wherein the People of God are associated with Christ's offering (cf. *LG* 28).

The priest is a sign of the divine anticipatory plan proclaimed and effective today in the Church. He makes Christ, the Saviour of all men, sacramentally present among his brothers and sisters, in both their personal and social lives. He is a guarantor both of the first proclamation of the Gospel for the gathering together of the Church and of the ceaseless renewal of the Church which has already been gathered together. If the Church lacks the presence and activity of the ministry which is received by the laying on of hands with prayer, she cannot have full certainty of her fidelity and of her visible continuity.

5. Permanence of the priesthood

By the laying on of hands there is communicated a gift of the Holy Spirit which cannot be lost (cf. 2 Tm. 1.6). This reality configures the ordained minister to Christ the Priest, consecrates him (cf. *PO* 2) and makes him a sharer in Christ's mission under its two aspects of authority and service.

That authority does not belong to the minister as his own: it is a manifestation of the "exousia" (i.e. the power) of the Lord, by which the priest is an ambassador of Christ in the eschatological work of reconciliation (cf. 2 Cor. 5.18-20). He also assists the conversion of human freedom to God for the building up of the Christian community.

The lifelong permanence of this reality, which is a sign, and which is a teaching of the faith and is referred to in the Church's tradition as the priestly character, expresses the fact that Christ associated the Church with himself in an irrevocable way for the salvation of the world, and that the Church dedicates herself to Christ in a definitive way for the carrying out of his work. The minister whose life bears the seal of the gift received through the sacrament of Orders reminds the Church that the gift of God is irrevocable. In the midst of the Christian community which, in spite of its defects, lives by the Spirit, he is a pledge of the salvific presence of Christ.

This special participation in Christ's priesthood does not disappear even if a priest for ecclesial or personal reasons is dispensed or removed from the exercise of his ministry.

6. For the service of fellowship

Even if he exercises his ministry in a determined community, the priest nevertheless cannot be exclusively devoted to a particular group of faithful. His ministry always tends towards the unity of the whole Church and to the gathering together in her of all men. Each individual community of faithful needs fellowship with the bishop and the universal Church. In this way the priestly ministry too is essentially communitarian within the presbyterium and with the bishop who, preserving communion with the Successor of Peter, is a part of the body of bishops. This holds also for priests who are not in the immediate service of any community or who work in remote and isolated territories. Religious priests also, within the context of the special purpose and structure of their institute, are indissolubly part of a mission which is ecclesially ordered.

Let the whole life and activity of the priest be imbued with a spirit of catholicity, that is, with a sense of the universal mission of the Church, so that he will willingly recognize all the gifts of the Spirit, give them freedom and direct them towards the common good.

Let priests follow Christ's example and cultivate with the bishop and with each other that brotherhood which is founded on their ordination and the oneness of their mission so that their priestly witness may be more credible.

7. The priest and temporal matters

All truly Christian undertakings are related to the salvation of mankind, which, while it is of an eschatological nature, also embraces temporal matters. Every reality of this world must be subjected to the lordship of Christ. This however does not mean that the Church claims technical competence in the secular order, with disregard for the latter's autonomy.

The proper mission entrusted by Christ to the priest, as to the Church, is not of the political, economic or social order, but of the religious order (cf. *GS* 42); yet, in the pursuit of his ministry, the priest can contribute greatly to the establishment of a more just secular order, especially in places where the human problems of injustice and oppression are more serious. He must always, however, preserve ecclesial communion and reject violence in words or deeds as not being in accordance with the Gospel.

In fact, the word of the Gospel which he proclaims in the name of Christ and the Church, and the effective grace of sacramental life which he administers should free man from his personal and social egoism and foster among men conditions of justice, which would be a sign of the love of Christ present among us (cf. *GS* 58).

Part Two
Guidelines for the Priestly Life and Ministry

Considering the priestly mission in the light of the mystery of Christ and the communion of the Church, the Fathers of this Synod, united with the Roman Pontiff and conscious of the anxieties which bishops and priests are experiencing in the fulfillment of their common role today, present the following guidelines to clarify certain questions and to give encouragement.

I. Priests in the Mission of Christ and the Church

1. Mission: Evangelization and sacramental life

a) "By their vocation and ordination, the priests of the New Testament are indeed set apart in a certain sense within the midst of God's people. But this is so, not that they may be made distant from this people or from any man, but that they may be totally dedicated to the work for which the Lord has raised them up" *(PO* 3). Priests thus find their identity to the extent that they fully live the mission of the Church and exercise it in different ways in communion with the entire People of God, as pastors and ministers of the Lord in the Spirit, in order to fulfill by their work the plan of salvation in history. "By means of their own ministry, which deals principally with the Eucharist as the source of perfecting the Church, priests are in communion with Christ the Head and are leading others to this communion. Hence they cannot help realizing how much is yet wanting to the fullness of that Body, and how much therefore must be done if it is to grow from day to day." *(AG* 39).

b) Priests are sent to all men and their mission must begin with the preaching of God's Word. "Priests have as their duty the proclamation of the Gospel of Christ to all . . . For through the saving Word the spark of faith is struck in the hearts of unbelievers and fed in the hearts of the faithful" *(PO* 4). The goal of evangelization is "that all who are made sons of God by faith and baptism should come together to praise God in the midst of his Church, to take part in her sacrifice and to eat the Lord's supper" *(SC [The Constitution on the Sacred Liturgy]* 10). The ministry of the Word, if rightly understood, leads to the sacraments and to the Christian life, as it is practiced in the visible community of the Church and in the world.

The sacraments are celebrated in conjunction with the proclamation of the Word of God and thus develop faith by strengthening it with grace. They cannot be considered of slight importance, since through them the word is brought to fuller effect, namely communion in the mystery of Christ.

Let priests then perform their ministry in such a way that the faithful will "have recourse with great eagerness to the sacraments which were instituted to nourish the Christian life" *(SC* 59).

An enduring evangelization and a well-ordered sacramental life of the community demand, by their nature, a *diaconia* of authority, that is, a serving of unity and a presiding over charity. Thus the mutual relationship between evangelization and the celebration of the sacraments is clearly seen in the mission of the Church. A separation between the two would divide the heart of the Church to the point of imperilling the faith, and the priest, who is dedicated to the service of unity in the community, would be gravely distorting his ministry.

Unity between evangelization and sacramental life is always proper to the ministerial priesthood and must carefully be kept in mind by every priest. And yet the application of this principle to the life and ministry of individual priests must be made with discretion, for the exercise of the priestly ministry often in practice needs to take different forms in order better to meet special or new situations in which the Gospel is to be proclaimed.

c) Although the pedagogy of faith demands that man be gradually initiated into the Christian life, the Church must nevertheless always proclaim to the world the Gospel in its entirety. Each priest shares in the special responsibility of preaching the whole of the Word of God and of interpreting it according to the faith of the Church.

The proclamation of the Word of God is the announcement in the power of the Spirit of the wonders performed by God and the calling of men to share the paschal mystery and to introduce it as a leaven into concrete human history. It is the action of God in which the power of the Holy Spirit brings the Church together interiorly and exteriorly. The minister of the word by evangelization prepares the ways of the Lord with great patience and faith, conforming himself to the various conditions of individuals' and peoples' lives, which are evolving more or less rapidly.

Impelled by the need to keep in view both the personal and social aspects of the announcement of the Gospel, so that in it an answer may be given to all the more fundamental questions of men (cf. *CD [Decree on the Pastoral Office of Bishops in the Church]* 13), the Church not only preaches conversion to God to individual men, but also, to the best of her ability, as the conscience of humanity, she addresses society itself and performs a prophetic function in society's regard, always taking pains to effect her own renewal.

As regards the experiences of life, whether of men in general or of priests, which must be kept in mind and always interpreted in the light of the Gospel, these experiences cannot be either the sole or the principal norm of preaching.

d) Salvation, which is effected through the sacraments, does not come from us but from God; this demonstrates the primacy of action of Christ, the one priest and mediator, in his body, which is the Church.

Since the sacraments are truly sacraments of faith (cf. *SC* 59), they require conscious and free participation by every Christian who has the use of reason. This makes clear the great importance of preparation and of a disposition of faith on the part of the person who receives the sacraments; it also makes clear the necessity for a witness of faith on the part of the minister in his entire life and especially in the way he values and celebrates the sacraments themselves.

To bishops and, in the cases foreseen by law, to episcopal conferences is committed the role of authentically promoting, in accordance with the norms given by the Holy See, pastoral activity and liturgical renewal better adapted to each region, and also of determining the criteria for admission to the sacraments. These criteria, which must be applied by priests, are likewise to be explained to the faithful, so that a person who asks for a sacrament may become more aware of his own responsibility.

Let priests, with consciousness of their office of reconciling all men in the love of Christ and with attention to the dangers of divisions, strive with great prudence and pastoral charity to form communities which are imbued with apostolic zeal and which will make the Church's missionary spirit present everywhere. Small communities, which are not opposed to the parish or diocesan structure, ought to be inserted into the parochial or diocesan community in such a way that they may serve it as a leaven of missionary spirit. The need to find apt forms of effectively bringing the Gospel message to all men, who live in differing circumstances, furnishes a place for the multiple exercise of ministries lower than the priesthood.

2. Secular and political activity

a) The priestly ministry, even if compared with other activities, not only is to be considered as a fully valid human activity but indeed as more excellent than other activities, though this great value can be fully understood only in the light of faith. Thus, as a general rule, the priestly ministry shall be a full-time occupation. Sharing in the secular activities of men is by no means to be considered the principal end nor can such participation suffice to give expression to priests' specific responsibility. Priests, without being of the world and without taking it as their model, must nevertheless live in the world (cf. *PO* 3.17; Jn. 17.14-16), as witnesses and stewards of another life (cf. *PO* 3).

In order to determine in concrete circumstances whether secular activity is in accord with the priestly ministry, inquiry should be made whether and in what way those duties and activities serve the mission of the Church, those who have not yet received the Gospel message and finally the Christian community. This is to be judged by the local bishop with his presbyterium, and if necessary in consulation with the episcopal conference.

When activities of this sort, which ordinarily pertain to the laity, are as it were demanded by the priest's very mission to evangelize, they must be harmonized with his other ministerial activities, in those circumstances where they can be considered as necessary forms of true ministry (cf. *PO* 8).

b) Together with the entire Church, priests are obliged, to the utmost of their ability, to select a definite pattern of action, when it is a question of the defense of fundamental human rights, the promotion of the full development of persons and the pursuit of the cause of peace and justice; the means must indeed always be consonant with the Gospel. These principles are all valid not only in the individual sphere, but also in the social field; in this regard priests should help the laity to devote themselves to forming their consciences rightly.

In circumstances in which there legitimately exist different political, social and economic options, priests like all citizens have a right to select their personal options. But since political options are by nature contingent and never in an entirely adequate and perennial way interpret the Gospel, the priest, who is the witness of things to come, must keep a certain distance from any political office or involvement.

In order that he may remain a valid sign of unity and be able to preach the Gospel in its entirety, the priest can sometimes be obliged to abstain from the exercise of his own right in this matter. Moreover, care must be taken lest his option appear to Christians to be the only legitimate one or become a cause of division among the faithful. Let priests be mindful of the laity's maturity, which is to be valued highly when it is a question of their specific role.

Leadership or active militancy on behalf of any political party is to be excluded by every priest unless, in concrete and exceptional circumstances, this is truly required by the good of the community, and receives the consent of the bishop after consulation with the priests' council and, if circumstances call for it, with the episcopal conference.

The priority of the specific mission which pervades the entire priestly existence must therefore always be kept in mind so that, with great confidence, and having a renewed experience of the things of God, priests may be able to announce these things efficaciously and with joy to the men who await them.

3. The spiritual life of priests

Every priest will find in his very vocation and ministry the deep motivation for living his entire life in oneness and strength of spirit. Called like the rest of those who have been baptized to become a true image of Christ (cf. Rom. 8.29), the priest, like the Apostles, shares besides in a special way companionship with Christ and his mission as the Supreme Pastor: "And he appointed twelve; they were to be his companions and to be sent out to preach" (Mk. 3.14). Therefore in the priestly life there can be no dichotomy between love for Christ and zeal for souls.

Just as Christ, anointed by the Holy Spirit, was impelled by his deep love for his Father to give his life for men, so the priest, consecrated by the Holy Spirit, and in a special way made like to Christ the Priest, dedicates himself to the work of the Father performed through the Son. Thus the whole rule for the priest's life is expressed in the words of Jesus: "And for their sake I consecrate myself, that they also may be consecrated in truth" (Jn. 17.19).

Following the example of Christ who was continually in prayer, and led by the Holy Spirit in whom we cry, "Abba, Father," priests should give themselves to the contemplation of the Word of God and daily take the opportunity to examine the events of the life in the light of the Gospel, so that having become faithful and attentive hearers of the Word they may become true ministers of the Word. Let them be assiduous in personal prayer, in the Liturgy of the Hours, in frequent reception of the sacrament of penance and especially in devotion to the mystery of the Eucharist. Even if the Eucharist should be celebrated without participation by the faithful, it nevertheless remains the center of the life of the entire Chruch and the heart of priestly existence.

With his mind raised to heaven and sharing in the communion of saints, the priest should very often turn to Mary the Mother of God, who received the Word of God with perfect faith, and daily ask her for the grace of conforming himself to her Son.

The activities of the apostolate for their part furnish an indispensable nourishment for fostering the spiritual life of the priest: "By assuming the role of the Good Shepherd, they will find precisely in the pastoral exercise of love the bond of priestly perfection which will unify their lives and activities" *(PO 14)*. In the exercise of his ministry the priest is enlightened and strengthened by the action of the Church and the example of the faithful. The renunciations imposed by the pastoral life itself help him to acquire an ever greater sharing in Christ's Cross and hence a purer pastoral charity.

This same charity of priests will also cause them to adapt their spiritual lives to the modes and forms of sanctification which are more suitable and fitting for the men of their own times and culture. Desiring to be all things to all men, to save all (cf. Cor. 9.22), the priest should be attentive to the inspiration of the Holy Spirit in these days. Thus he will announce the Word of God not only by human means but he will be taken as a valid instrument by the Word himself, whose message is "living and active and sharper than any two-edged sword" (Heb. 4.12).

4. Celibacy

a) The basis for celibacy.

Celibacy for priests is in full harmony with the vocation to the apostolic following of Christ and also with the unconditional response of the person who is called and who undertakes pastoral service. Through celibacy, the priest, following his Lord, shows in a fuller way his availability, and embarking upon the way of the Cross with paschal joy he ardently desires to be consumed in an offering which can be compared to the Eucharist.

If celibacy is lived in the spirit of the Gospel, in prayer and vigilance, with poverty, joy, contempt of honours, and brotherly love, it is a sign which cannot long be hidden, but which effectively proclaims Christ to modern men also. For words today are scarcely heeded, but the witness of a life which displays the radical character to the Gospel has the power of exercising a strong attraction.

b) Convergence of motives.

Celibacy, as a personal option for some more important good, even a merely natural one, can promote the full maturity and integration of the human personality. This is all the more true in regard to celibacy undertaken for the Kingdom of heaven, as is evident in the lives of so many saints and of the faithful who, living the celibate life, dedicated themselves totally to promoting human and Christian progress for the sake of God and men.

Within modern culture, in which spiritual values are to a great extent obscured, the celibate priest indicates the presence of the Absolute God, who invites us to be renewed in his image. Where the value of sexuality is so exaggerated that genuine love is forgotten, celibacy for the sake of the Kingdom of Christ calls men back to the sublimity of faithful love and reveals the ultimate meaning of life.

Furthermore, one rightly speaks of the value of celibacy as an eschatological sign. By transcending every contingent human value, the celibate priest associates himself in a special way with Christ as the final and absolute good and shows forth, in anticipation, the freedom of the children of God. While the value of the sign and holiness of Christian marriage is fully recognized, celibacy for the sake of the Kingdom nevertheless more clearly displays that spiritual fruitfulness or generative power of the New Law by which the apostle knows that in Christ he is the father and mother of his communities.

From this special way of following Christ, the priest draws greater strength and power for the building up of the Church; and this power can be preserved and increased only by an intimate and permanent union with Christ's Spirit. The faithful people of God wish to see in their pastors this union with Christ, and they are able recognize it.

Through celibacy, priests are more easily able to serve God with undivided heart and spend themselves for their sheep, and as a result they are able more fully to be promoters of evangelization and of the Church's unity. For this reason, priests, even if they are fewer in number, but are resplendent with this outstanding witness of life, will enjoy greater apostolic fruitfulness.

Priestly celibacy, furthermore, is not just the witness of one person alone, but by reason of the special fellowship linking members of the presbyterium it also takes on a social character as the witness of the whole priestly order enriching the People of God.

c) Celibacy to be kept in the Latin Church.

The traditions of the Eastern Churches shall remain unchanged, as they are now in force in the various territories.

The Church has the right and duty to determine the concrete form of the priestly ministry and therefore to select more suitable candidates, endowed with certain human and supernatural qualities. When the Latin Church demands celibacy as a necessary condition for the priesthood (cf. *PO* 16), she does not do so out of a belief that this way of life is the only path to attaining sanctification. She does so while carefully considering the concrete form of exercising the ministry in the community for the building up of the Church.

Because of the intimate and multiple coherence between the pastoral function and a celibate life, the existing law upheld: one who freely wills total availability, the distinctive characteristic of this function, also freely undertakes a celibate life. The candidate should feel this form of living not as having been imposed from outside, but rather as a manifestation of his free self-giving, which is accepted and ratified by the Church through the bishop. In this way the law becomes a protection and safeguard of the freedom wherewith the priest gives himself to Christ, and it becomes "an easy yoke."

d) Conditions favoring celibacy.

We know well that in the world of today particular difficulties threaten celibacy from all sides; priests have indeed already repeatedly experienced them in the course of the centuries. But they can overcome these difficulties if suitable conditions are fostered, namely: growth of the interior life through prayer, renunciation and fervent love for God and one's neighbor and by other aids to the spiritual life; human balance through well-ordered integration into the fabric of social relationships; fraternal association and companionship with other priests and with the bishop, through pastoral structures better suited to this purpose and with the assistance also of the community of the faithful.

It must be admitted that celibacy, as a gift of God, cannot be preserved unless the candidate is adequately prepared for it. From the beginning, candidates should give attention to the positive reasons for choosing celibacy, without letting themselves be disturbed by objections, the accumulation and continual pressure of which are rather a sign that the original value of celibacy itself has been called in question. Let them also remember that the power with which God strengthens us is always for those who strive to serve him faithfully and entirely.

A priest who leaves the ministry should receive just and fraternal treatment; even though he can give assistance in the service of the Church, he is not however to be admitted to the exercise of priestly activities.

e) The law of celibacy.

The law of priestly celibacy existing in the Latin Church is to be kept in its entirety.[2]

f) The ordination of married men.

Two formulas were proposed to the vote of the Fathers:
Formula A: Excepting always the right of the Supreme Pontiff, the priestly ordination of married men is not permitted, even in particular cases.
Formula B: It belongs solely to the Supreme Pontiff, in particular cases, by reason of pastoral needs and the good of the universal Church to allow the priestly ordination of married men, who are of mature age and proven life.[3]

II. Priests in the Communion of the Church

1. Relations between priests and bishop

Priests will adhere more faithfully to their mission the more they know and show themselves to be faithful to ecclesial communion. Thus the pastoral ministry, which is exercised by bishops, priests and deacons, is an eminent sign of this ecclesial communion, in that they have received a special mandate to serve this communion.

But in order that this ministry may really become a sign of communion, the actual conditions in which it is exercised must be considered to be of the greatest importance.

The guiding principle expressed by the Second Vatican Council in the decree *Presbyterorum Ordinis [PO]*, namely that the very unity of consecration and mission requires the hierarchical communion of priests with the order of bishops, is considered fundamental to a practical restoration or renewal, with full confidence, of the mutual relationship between the bishop and the presbyterium over which the bishop presides. This principle is more concretely to be put into practice especially by the diligence of the bishops.

The service of authority on the one hand and the exercise of not merely passive obedience on the other should be carried out in a spirit of faith, mutual charity, filial and friendly confidence and constant and patient dialogue. Thus the collaboration and responsible cooperation of priests with the bishop will be sincere, human and at the same time supernatural (cf. *LG* 28; *CD* 15; *PO* 7).

Personal freedom, responding to the individual vocation and to the charisms received from God, and also the ordered solidarity of all for the service of the community and the good of the mission to be fulfilled are two conditions which should shape the Church's proper mode of pastoral action (cf. *PO* 7). The guarantee of these conditions is the bishop's authority, to be exercised in a spirit of service.

The Council of Priests, which is of its nature something diocesan, is an institutional manifestation of the brotherhood among priests which has its basis in the sacrament of Orders.

The activity of this council cannot be fully shaped by law. Its effectiveness depends especially on a repeated effort to listen to the opinions of all in order to reach a consensus with the bishop, to whom it belongs to make the final decision.

If this is done with the greatest sincerity and humility, and if all onesidedness is overcome, it will be easier to provide properly for the common good.

The Priests' Council is an institution in which priests recognize, at a time when variety in the exercise of their ministry increases every day, that they are mutually complementary in serving one and the same mission of the Church.

It is the task of this Council, among other things, to seek out clear and distinctly defined aims, to suggest priorities, to indicate methods of acting, to assist whatever the Spirit frequently stirs up through individuals or groups, and to foster the spiritual life, whence the necessary unity may more easily be attained.

New forms of hierarchical communion between bishops and priests (cf. *PO* 7) must be found, to facilitate contacts between local Churches. A search must be made for ways whereby priests may collaborate with bishops in supra-diocesan bodies and enterprises.

The collaboration of religious priests with the bishop in the presbyterium is necessary, though their work is of valuable assistance to the universal Church.

2. Relations of priests with each other

Since priests are bound together by an intimate sacramental brotherhood and by their mission, and since they work and plan together for the same task, some community of life or a certain association of life shall be encouraged among them and can take various forms, including non-institutional ones. This shall be allowed for by the law itself through opportune norms and by renewed or newly-discovered pastoral structures.

Priestly associations should also be fostered which in a spirit of ecclesial communion and being recognized by the competent ecclesiastical authority, "through an apt and properly approved rule of life and through brotherly assistance" *(PO* 8), seek to advance the aims which belong to their function and "holiness in the exercise of the ministry" (ibid.).

It is desirable that, as far as possible, ways be sought, even if they prove rather difficult, whereby associations which perhaps divide the clergy into factions may be brought back to communion and to the ecclesial structure.

There should be greater communication between religious priests and diocesan priests, so that true priestly fraternity may exist between them and that they may provide one another with mutual help, especially in spiritual matters.

3. Relations between priests and laity

Let priests remember "confidently to entrust to the laity duties in the service of the Church, allowing them freedom and room for action. In fact, on suitable occasions, they should invite them to undertake works on their own initiative" *(PO* 9). The laity, "likewise sharing their cares, should help their priests by prayer and work to the extent possible, so that their priests can more readily overcome difficulties and be able to fulfill their duties more fruitfully" (ibid.).

It is necessary to keep always in mind the special character of the Church's communion in order that personal freedom, in accordance with the recognized duties and charisms of each person, and the unity of life and activity of the People of God may be fittingly combined.

The pastoral council, in which specially chosen clergy, religious and lay people take part (cf. *CD* 27), furnishes by its study and reflection elements necessary for enabling the diocesan community to arrange its pastoral program organically and to fulfill it effectively.

In proportion as the co-responsibility of bishops and priests daily increases (especially through priests' councils), the more desirable it becomes that a pastoral council be established in each diocese.

4. Economic affairs

The economic questions of the Church cannot be adequately solved unless they are carefully examined within the context of the communion and mission of the People of God. All the faithful have the duty of assisting the Church's needs.

In treating these questions account must be taken not only of solidarity within the local Church, diocese or religious institute, but also of the condition of dioceses of the same region or nation, indeed of the whole world, especially of the Churches in the so-called mission territories, and of other poor regions.

The remuneration of priests, to be determined certainly in a spirit of evangelical poverty, but as far as possible equitable and sufficient, is a duty of justice and ought to include social security. Excessive differences in this matter must be removed, especially among priests of the same diocese or jurisdiction, account also being taken of the average condition of the people of the region.

It seems greatly to be desired that the Christian people be gradually instructed in such a way that priests' incomes may be separated from the acts of their ministry, especially sacramental ones.

Conclusion

To priests exercising the ministry of the Spirit (cf. 2 Cor. 3.4-12) in the midst of the communion of the entire Church, new ways are open for giving a profoundly renewed witness in today's world.

It is necessary therefore to look to the future with Christian confidence and to ask the Holy Spirit that by his guidance and inspiration doors may be opened to the Gospel, in spite of the dangers which the Church cannot overcome by merely human means.

Having always before our eyes the Apostles, especially Peter and Paul, as the examples for the renewal of the priesthood, we should give thanks to God the Father that he has given us all the opportunity of manifesting more faithfully the countenance of Christ.

Already there are true signs of a rebirth of spiritual life, while men everywhere, amid the uncertainties of modern times, look forward to fullness of life. This renewal certainly cannot take place without a sharing in the Lord's Cross, because the servant is not greater than his master (cf. Jn. 13.16). Forgetting the past let us strive for what is still to come (cf. Phil. 3.13).

With real daring we must show the world the fullness of the mystery hidden through all ages in God so that men through their sharing in it may be able to enter into the fullness of God (cf. Eph. 3.19).

"We proclaim to you the eternal life which was with the Father and was made manifest to us — that which we have seen and heard we proclaim also to you, so that you may have fellowship with us; and our fellowship is with the Father and with his Son Jesus Christ" (1 Jn. 1.23).

Rescript
of the Audience Given by the Holy Father
to the Cardinal Secretary of State
30 November 1971

The Holy Father has carefully examined the two documents containing the proposals expressed by the Second General Assembly of the Synod of Bishops on the themes, "The Ministerial Priesthood" and "Justice in the World," which had been put before the Assembly for study.

As he has already announced in his address at the General Audience of 24 November, the Holy Father desires that the aforementioned documents be made public.

His Holiness now accepts and confirms all the conclusions in the two documents that conform to the current norms: in particular, he confirms that in the Latin Church there shall continue to be observed in its entirety, with God's help, the present discipline of priestly celibacy.

The Holy Father reserves to himself to examine carefully in due course whether the proposals — and which of them — contained in the recommendations of the Synodal Assembly should be convalidated as directive guidelines or practical norms.

John Cardinal Villot
Secretary of State

Note: *The Ministerial Priesthood* has been deemed appropriate for inclusion in this work, but *Justice in the World* has not.

Notes

1. Tertullian, *De Praescr. Haer.* XXI, 4; cf. also 1 Letter of Clement *Ad Cor.* XLII, 1-4; Ignatius of Antioch *Ad Magn.* VI and passim; Irenaeus *Adv. Haer.* 4, 21, 3; Origen *De Princip.* IV, 2, 1; Serapion, Bishop of Antioch, in Eusebius *Hist. Eccl.* VI, 12.

2. Result of the vote on this proposition: *Placet* 168. *Non placet* 10. *Placet iuxta modum* 21. Abstentions 3.

3. According to the directives of the Presidents the vote was taken not by *Placet* or *Non placet,* but by the choice of the first or second formula. The first formula, *A,* obtained 107 votes; the second, *B,* obtained 87. There were 2 abstentions and also 2 null votes.

Relationship of the Local Ordinary (Bishop) to the Seminary Owned and Operated by Religious

Bishops' Committee on Priestly Formation

1981

Relationship of the Local Ordinary (Bishop) to the Seminary Owned and Operated by Religious

---

I. State of the Question

Ecumenical endeavor, liturgical renewal, theological investigation, controversy over the role and life-style of the priesthood today are major issues of divided opinion in priestly formation.

The NCCB Program for Priestly Formation is sometimes interpreted variously by some Ordinaries and seminaries.

The traditional confusion over the definitions of responsibility and competence and local Diocesan and Religious Ordinaries is a practical problem particularly where the above issues are concerned.

The problem is further complicated because the consultative and advisory role of the NCCB Committee on Priestly Formation is apparently misunderstood and sometimes thought or desired to be of determinative jurisdiction.

II. Communication—Approach to Cooperation

A general posture of open communication and discussion about matters of mutual concern to the local Diocesan Ordinary and the Rector of the Seminary is essential.

Regularly established meetings (e.g., end of semester) between Bishop and Rector seem advisable. Reports of plans, progress and problems for the Ordinary's information, reaction and suggestions are helpful. Consultation concerning major changes and programs seems advisable. Matters which relate directly to the Bishop's jurisdiction, e.g., certain Liturgical practices, matters which affect Diocesan policy, certainly ought to be part of regular communication and dialogue.

Opportunities for the Bishop to communicate with the Seminary Board of Trustees should be available to him and vice versa. In some cases it may be desirable that he be a member of the Board.

Opportunities for the Bishop to meet and dialogue with faculty members and the seminarians about the philosophy of priestly formation is likewise desirable.

In other words care should be taken to plan open communication and public relations between seminary and local Ordinaries.

III. Canonical Principles to Guide the Formal Relationship between Local Ordinaries and Religious in the Matter of Priestly Formation

A. Canonical Principles

1. General norms for relationship between religious and local Ordinaries.

a. "The privilege of exemption, by which religious are called to the service of the Supreme Pontiff or other ecclesiastical authority and are withdrawn from the jurisdiction of bishops, applies chiefly to the internal order of their communities so that in them all things may be more aptly coordinated and the growth and depth of religious life better served . . . this exemption however does not exclude religious in individual dioceses from the jurisdiction of the bishop in accordance with the norm of law, insofar as the performance of the pastoral office and the right ordering of the care of souls require" *(Christus Dominus [Decree on the Pastoral Office of Bishops in the Church], n. 35, 3).*

b. "All Religious, even the exempt, are bound by the laws, decrees and ordinances enacted by the local Ordinary for various activities, in those matters which touch upon the exercise of the sacred apostolate, as well as for pastoral and social action prescribed or recommended by the local Ordinary" *(Ecclesiae Sanctae,* n. 25, 1).

c. "Moreover, Religious are also bound by the laws and decrees issued by the local Ordinary according to the norm of the law regarding the public exercise of worship in their own churches and in public and semi-public oratories if the faithful ordinarily attend themselves. The proper rite of the Religious remains intact which they lawfully use for their own community alone, taking into consideration the order of the Divine Office in choir and the sacred functions which pertain to the special purpose of the institute" (ibid., n.26).

d. "Works proper or special to the institute, which are carried out in its own houses, even if these are rented, depend on the superiors of the institute who according to the constitutions rule and direct them. However, these works are also subject to the jurisdiction of the local Ordinary according to the norm of law.

"Works which have been entrusted to the institute by the local Ordinary, however, even if they may be proper or special to it, are under the authority and direction of the same Ordinary, without prejudice, however, to the right of the religious superiors to exercise vigilance over the life of the members of the institute, and in conjunction with the local Ordinary, over the fulfillment of duties committed to them" (ibid., n. 29, 1 and 2).

Note: The distinction between "works proper and special to the institute which are carried out in their own houses," and "works which have been entrusted to the institute by the local Ordinary, even if proper and special to the institute," is an important one. In the case of the former works, the religious superior has jurisdiction, and the local Ordinary coordinates the activity of the religious community with other apostolic activities in the diocese. In the case of the latter, the local Ordinary has jurisdiction over the work, and the religious superior's concern is confined for the most part to the internal affairs of the community.

How do we distinguish works which are "proper and carried out in its own houses," and those which are "entrusted to the institute, even though proper"? There is no definition of these works given in law. In practice, it seems we must take into consideration who instigated the work, and who finances it. Thus, if a high school were built and financed under the inspiration of a religious community, it would be a work "proper to the community and carried out in its own house." If the high school were part of the diocesan system, and built and financed by the diocese, it would be work which was "entrusted to the religious community, even though proper to it." (Cf. "Cooperation of Religious Local Ordinary," O'Rourke, *Jurist*, XXVII, 4, 1967.)

2. General norms which apply more specifically in the matter of Priestly Formation.

a. It is important to note that even in view of the provisions of *Ecclesiae Sanctae,* which are experimental (cf. Introduction), privileges of religious communities remain in effect because they are not specifically revoked.

Some religious communities of men have the privilege or right of immemorial custom of receiving students for the diocesan priesthood into their studia, and some even have the right to receive lay people.

b. The effect of the documents *The Basic Plan for Priestly Formation* and *The Program of Priestly Formation* of the NCCB is extremely important insofar as relations between seminaries and Ordinaries, whether religious or local, are concerned. These documents give guidelines, at times both detailed and definite, that must be followed by both seminary and the Ordinary. Hence, the Ordinary does not have an absolute right to determine goals, objectives and strategy for the seminary, nor do the seminary officials have an absolute right. Both must abide by the directives mentioned above. In these directives, there is some provision for due process of law, should there be disagreement between the Ordinary and the seminary officials.

These documents also provide for objective evaluation by a team of competent people acquainted with education and seminary formation, and for referral to higher authorities should there be some disagreement. These factors should eliminate some of the difficulties that might ordinarily occur in the relationships between Ordinaries and seminary officials.

c. In order to understand clearly the jurisdiction of the local Ordinary and the major superior of a religious seminary, it seems we must distinguish between the right of vigilance and the right of disposition. The right of vigilance enables the Ordinary in question to observe a situation, to ask questions about it, and make recommendations concerning it. If the Ordinary does not think that the situation is corrected, he has the right to bring the matter to a higher authority. The right of disposition enables one not only to observe and evaluate a situation, but it also gives the right and obligation to take steps necessary to correct the situation, such as changing policy or removing people from office. Hence, in a school conducted by religious, if it is a proper work, the local Ordinary would have the right of vigilance only; in a school operated by religious, but only "entrusted" to them, the local Ordinary would have the right of disposition as well.

Though this distinction between the right of vigilance and the right of disposition is not contained in the code, it seems to be presupposed, and it seems to be the working principle underlying statements of the Council and the practice of the Roman Congregations. (Cf. *Ecclesiae Sanctae,* n. 30, 31, 39); private letters of Congregation of Seminaries, April 27, 1964, November 25, 1970.)

The significance of this distinction is important in delineating the rights of local Ordinaries and religious major superiors in many different apostolic situations.

B. Specific Applications of the Principles

1. Seminaries which are conducted by religious for the training of religious candidates as well as candidates for the diocesan priesthood.

a. The Ordinary of such a seminary *qua* institution would be the religious major superior. The local Ordinary would have the right of vigilance *qua* institution.

b. Insofar as candidates for the religious priesthood are concerned, the Ordinary is the major superior of the religious community that conducts the seminary. The Ordinary of the students for the diocesan priesthood would be the local Ordinary of the place where the seminary is located, even if he does not have students from his own diocese studying there.

At first glance, it might seem strange to say that the local Ordinary of the place would be the Ordinary of the seminary, even if he does not have students there. Would it not be better to have the various Ordinaries of the diocesan students involved in the administration of the seminary? The reason the local Ordinary of the place where the seminary is located becomes involved is because of the nature of the school, not because he has students there. The local Ordinary has the general right to visitate schools conducted by religious if they educate students who do not belong to the religious institute (*Ecclesiae Sanctae*, n. 39). In the case of institutions which educate students for the priesthood, this right is more detailed and spelled out in the law, because of the importance of the work being done there. Thus, the right would extend to academic, spiritual, and disciplinary matters insofar as diocesan students are involved.

c. Does the local Ordinary have the right to appoint and remove people from the faculty of a seminary conducted by religious for both diocesan and religious candidates? In this case, we must use the distinction between works "proper and special to the institute which are carried out in their own houses," and works "entrusted to the institute by the local Ordinary." In the case of the former, it does not seem that the local Ordinary has the right to appoint people to the faculty, nor to remove them, since the apostolic work "depends upon the superiors of the institute who according to the constitutions rule and direct them" (*Ecclesiae Sanctae,* n. 29, n. 1). In the case of a seminary that is an "entrusted" apostolic work, however, it would seem that the local Ordinary would have more power. In this situation, members are appointed to this work by their own religious superior, "after mutual consultation with the local Ordinary" (ibid., n. 30). However, in this type of apostolic work the local Ordinary has the right to remove a person from office, having notified the religious superior (ibid., n. 32). In this case, the prudent way to proceed would be to define in writing the rights of the various Ordinaries and the people involved in the institutions (cf. ibid., n. 30).

How would one distinguish a seminary which is "proper" to a religious institute from one that is "entrusted"? Two factors should have to be considered: who exercised the apostolic initiative in founding the seminary; who finances and owns the seminary? If the religious community established the seminary, having obtained the necessary permission for founding a religious house, and owns and supports it, then it would seem

320

to be a "proper" work of the institute. If the local Ordinary, on the other hand, founded the seminary, owns and supports, it, and merely hires the religious to run it and teach in it, then it would be considered as "entrusted work."

2. Seminaries conducted by religious for the training of diocesan seminaries.

a. Some seminaries are conducted by religious, at the request of a local Ordinary, or a group of Ordinaries. Usually, this type of seminary would be considered an entrusted work, and the local Ordinary would be considered the Ordinary of the seminary in regard to its academic, spiritual and disciplinary preparation of the seminarians. The circumstances of the initial foundation, however, and the support of the seminary, might determine that the seminary is a proper work of the institute. If it is a "proper" work, then the norms outlined in the above section apply.

b. If it is an "entrusted" work, the major superior of the religious community would retain the right to appoint the members of his community who would serve as faculty members, after consultation with the local Ordinary (*Ecclesiae Sanctae,* n. 30, 2). Diocesan priests or lay people who would serve as members of the faculty would be appointed by the local Ordinary. "In this matter the superior and the authority are legally equal and the action of the one does not require the consent of the other, nor is the one bound to make known to the other the reason for his judgment, much less prove it, though recourse to the Apostolic See, without suspensive effect *(in devolutivo)* remains open." (Cf. ibid., n. 32.)

The ability to remove a man from office without giving reasons or without proving them, seems to violate the norms of due process of law, a natural right. Moreover, it is severely destructive of morale and perhaps of an individual's reputation. Since these seminary norms are experimental, it is suggested that the proper authorities be notified concerning the injustice of this type of procedure.

3. Seminary programs which are conducted by Schools of Theology, affiliated with universities or not.

a. A few schools of theology, some of them associated with universities, have programs for the education of diocesan seminarians. There are usually some other people enrolled in the School of Theology as well —priests, sisters, and lay men and women. The local Ordinary, it seems, would have the right to jurisdiction insofar as the academic, spiritual, and disciplinary matters are concerned for the diocesan students. However, he would not have the same right for other students. Rather, he would have the rights that are proper to local Ordinaries concerning schools, which are not as intensive as the rights concerning seminaries (right of vigilance).

As *Christus Dominus* states, "Catholic schools conducted by religious are also subject to the authority of the local Ordinaries as regards policy and supervision, but the right of religious to direct them remains intact" (n. 35, 4).

b. Complicating the matter a bit is the fact that some of the universities which have Schools of Theology have become "lay" institutions. Whether or not this removes them from the jurisdiction of the Ordinary is an interesting legal question.

c. When considering programs conducted by Schools of Theology for diocesan priests, we must once again determine whether or not the school is "proper" to the institute, or "entrusted" to it. As indicated, this makes a difference in the appointment and removal of professors and administrators. (Cf. *Ecclesiae Sanctae,* nn. 29, 30, 32.)

IV. Procedures for Resolving Problem Situations

a. A necessary preliminary to more formal procedures should be a personal discussion between the local Ordinary and the seminary rector to clarify and, if possible, to resolve any problem situation.

If discussions on the level of the local Ordinary and the seminary rector do not resolve the situation, then serious personal attempts at conciliation should be made in the spirit of charity between the local Ordinary and the proper Major Superior.

b. When all personal attempts at negotiation have failed, then the local Ordinary or the proper Major Superior or both may refer the problem to the Bishops' Committee on Priestly Formation which, with due consultation, will study and recommend a procedure for solving the difficulty. A representative (of the liaison committee) of the Conference of Major Superiors of Religious Men will be consulted by the Committee on making its study and recommendation.

c. The local Ordinary or the Major Superior, if dissatisfied with the final results of the referral to the Bishops' Committee on Priestly Formation, may have recourse to the appropriate Congregation in Rome.

Addendum

I. Other Canonical Principles Pertinent to the Formal Relationship Between Local Ordinaries and Religious

A. Right to Establish Religious Houses and Seminaries

1. "In order to establish a religious house of an exempt community in a particular diocese, the written consent of the local Ordinary is required." (Note: The permission of the Holy See is no longer required; cf. cong. rel., 6/4/70, *Ad Instituenda Experimenta.*)

2. "In the case of clerical institutes, the permission to establish a house implies the authorization for a Church or public oratory in connection with the house.... Moreover, in the case of clerical institutes, the permission for the opening of a house implies further the authorization for the celebration of sacred functions in conformity with the disposition of law. In the case of all institutes, it implies the authorization for the performance of all works proper to the respective institute, without prejudice to conditions that may have been inserted in the permission itself" (c. 497, § 2).

3. "Every clerical institute shall have houses of studies approved by the General Chapter or the superiors to which there shall be assigned only religious conspicuous for observance of religious discipline in accordance with c. 554, 3" (Canon 581, 1).

4. The definition of a seminary is not contained in law. There is a description of the various models of seminary in the 1981 *Program of Priestly Formation,* n. 17, several elements of which pertain to religious seminaries as well.

5. Perhaps the most accurate and concise description of seminary is: "an institution organized for the formation of priests, and provided with those educational features which, combined with others, can effectively promote the integral formation of future priests."

B. Additional Norms Pertinent to the Relationship of Religious and Local Ordinaries

1. "When a local Ordinary entrusts an apostolic work to an institute, observing what must be observed according to law, a written agreement should be entered into between the Ordinary and the competent superior of the institute by which, among other things, the matters pertaining to the carrying out of the work, the assignment of personnel for the work and finances are clearly defined" (ibid., n. 30, 1).

2. "For a grave reason any member of a religious institute can be removed from the position assigned to him either at the will of the authority who made the appointment, after he has advised the religious superior, or at the will of the superior after he has advised the one who made the appointment. In this matter the superior and the authority are legally equal and the action of the one does not require the consent of the other, nor is the one bound to make known to the other the reason for his judgment, much less prove it, though recourse to the Apostolic See, without suspensive effect *(in devolutivo),* remains open" (ibid., n. 32).

3. "The local Ordinary has the right, with respect to the observance of general laws and episcopal decrees concerning divine worship to conduct a visitation of the Churches of Religious, even exempt, and also their semi-public oratories, provided the faithful ordinarily frequent them. If he should discover abuses in this regard, and the religious superior has been admonished in vain, he can himself by his own authority make provisions" (ibid., n. 38).

4. "According to the norm of No. 35, 4 of the Decree *Christus Dominus,* in right of religious in regard to the direction of the schools remaining in effect, and observing the norms established there concerning the prior agreement to be mutually entered into between bishops and religious superiors, the general policy of the Catholic school of religious institutes involves the general distribution of all Catholic schools in a diocese, their common cooperation and supervision so that these schools no less than others may be adapted to pursue cultural and social aims.

"The local Ordinary can conduct a visitation, either personally or through a delegate, according to the norms of the sacred canons, of all schools, colleges, oratories, recreation centers, protectorates, hospitals, orphanages and other similar institutions of religious institutes devoted to works of religion or to the temporal or spiritual works of charity, except those schools of an institute which are open exclusively to the institute's own students" (ibid., n. 39, 1 and 2).

C. Competence of the Roman Curia and the NCCB

1. Prior to the revision of the Roman Curia (August 15, 1967), the Congregation of Religious was competent in the over-all formation of religious. Now, however, the Congregation of Catholic Education has competence over the academic preparation of people in religious life.

"Through the First Section the Congregation is in charge of affairs which pertain to religious institutes of the Latin Rite and of their members . . . therefore to this section pertains all matters which concern the founding, governing, and suppressing Institutes; the safeguarding and striving for their specific purpose, their rule and discipline, their possessions, privileges, training of the religious . . . with due regard for the competence of the Congregation of Catholic Education with respect to the systematic or academic arrangement of their studies in the Church" ("On the Roman Curia," August 15, 1967, n. 73).

"Through the First Office the Congregation watches . . . those things which have bearing on the promotion of the education of diocesan clergy and the systematic education of Religious and Secular Institutes; it examines especially, and approves, the statutes of regional and interregional seminaries which have been drawn up by the bishops concerned.

"Through the Second Office the Congregation oversees universities and faculties, atheneums, and any institute of higher learning which duly bear the name Catholic, insofar as they in any way depend on the authority of the Church, not excluding those which are conducted by religious or the laity" (ibid., n. 77).

2. a. Two documents have been drawn up under the direction of the Congregation for Catholic Education which are of interest to our study. *The Basic Plan for Priestly Formation* indicates to Episcopal Conferences "the solid foundations for carrying out the serious task of drawing up programs for priestly formation proper to each nation. It also supplies sure standards to the Congregation for Catholic Education in accordance with the decree *Optatam totius [Decree on the Training of Priests]*, n. 1.

"Since this document has been thoroughly treated by delegates of the Episcopal Conferences and approved by the Holy See, it is to be taken as obligatory as regards its principal points . . . so that it may become the norm for drawing up individual programs. . . ." (loc. cit., n. 1, 2).

The second document was composed by the Bishops' Committee on Priestly Formation of the United States National Conference of Catholic Bishops (NCCB) and approved by the Congregation for Catholic Education. This document is obligatory for all diocesan and inter-diocesan seminaries. It should also be followed by seminaries and schools owned and operated by religious in providing programs for the preparation of candidates for the diocesan priesthood. Finally, it should guide religious institutes in adapting their own formation programs to the conditions of education and pastoral ministry in the United States.

The Conference of Major Superiors of Men is strongly committed to ongoing close collaboration with the United States Bishops in the revision of the program of priestly formation. The omission of a special section dealing with religious in the present form of the program of priestly formation underlines the conviction that, while the priestly life and work of religious will differ from that of diocesan priests, the difference does not stem from their priesthood as such. Religious and diocesan priests share an increasingly pluriform priesthood; their needs for priestly formation as such do not differ.

At the same time, each religious community has its own foundational and renewal documents in which its distinctive charism is articulated, and for which no single section of a document on priestly formation in general can substitute.

Thus, the Conference of Major Superiors of Men adopted the 1981 *Program of Priestly Formation* as the one program for all United States religious seminaries. They did this at the suggestion of the Sacred Congregation for Catholic Education and at the invitation of the National Conference of Catholic Bishops, preserving the rights and privileges granted religious in Church law, especially regarding the religious and spiritual formation of their own candidates.

b. Another document of some consequence is the *Ecumenical Directory II*, which concerns ecumenism in higher education, and which was issued by the Secretariat for Promoting Christian Unity. The major points of this document have been incorporated into *The Program of Priestly Formation*.

II. Specific Applications of the Principles for the Seminary Owned and Operated by Religious Solely for Candidates of Religious Communities

a. The Ordinary of this seminary is the major superior of the community which owns and operates the seminary. In religious communities, major superiors carry out their responsibilities with the help of a provincial council. This council often has deliberative voice in important matters. Hence, the council of the major superior in question will also be involved in the governing of the religious seminary.

This type of seminary would be independent of the local Ordinary in academic, spiritual, and disciplinary matters.

b. If more than one religious community conducts the seminary, and the seminary educates only religious, for example, Catholic Theological Union in Chicago, the Ordinary is more difficult to determine. Though a Board of Directors is competent under civil law, it seems the various major superiors retain their rights under church law. Hence, the professors and students of the various communities would remain subject to their religious superiors in regard to most matters. If the seminaries are merely in *consortia*, and not in a full union, as they are in Washington, D.C., there is really no problem since all seminaries remain autonomous and under their major superiors.

c. Even though the seminary which educates religious students alone is not under the direct jurisdiction of the local Ordinary, it still must cooperate with the local Ordinary. Moreover, the local Ordinary retains the powers granted him in law concerning the sacred apostolate, pastoral and social action, the visiting of churches, and the soliciting of help from the religious community (right of vigilance) (cf. *Christus Dominus*, n. 35; *Ecclesiae Sanctae*, nn. 25, 26, 36, 37, 38, 39).

Index

Abbott, W. M., 13

Abraham, 286

academic degrees, in ecclesiastical universities and faculties, 238-239, 252-253

Acts, 32, 274, 284, 287, 288, 290, 291, 299, 300

Ad catholici sacerdotii, 12, 14, 50, 51, 205, 290, 291

Ad pascendum, 121, 138, 143

Adam, 280

administration, of the sacraments, 10

adulthood, particular difficulties of, 190

Aeterni Patris, 93

alpha and omega, 299

Ambrose, St., 13

annunciation, another name for incarnation, 222

anointing of the Holy Spirit, and baptism, give general priesthood, 20

Apocalypse, 287; *see* Revelation

apologetics, one should not neglect, 40

apostles, Christ founded the Church on, 300; sharers in the same priesthood, 20

Apostolic Constitutions, 134, 289, 290; *see Constitutiones apostolorum*

arts and sciences, seminary studies in, 38

asceticism, priestly, training in, 183-184

Athanasius, St., 288

atheism, becoming more common, 22

Athenaea, 288

auditores, 295

auditus fidei, 69

Augustine, St., 6, 13, 287, 288, 290

baptismal catecheses, of the Fathers, 137

Basic Plan for Priestly Formation, The, 15-60, 88, 93, 94, 95, 105, 107, 112, 142, 143, 150, 203, 204, 205, 209, 319, 325; *see Ratio fundamentalis institutionis sacerdotalis*

Bayard, Can., 217

bishop, bishops, as fathers, 4-5; authority of, 5; responsibility of, 10; priests are dependent on, 20; priests make him present, 20; relation between priests and, 271, 309-310; obedience should be shown to pope and to own, 33; sharers in the same priesthood, 20

Bishops' Committee on Priestly Formation, 315, 317, 322

Blessed Sacrament, visits are recommended to, 118, 119

Bonaventure, St., 13

Botte, B., 289

Buddhism, 87

Bultmann, R., 93, 104

bursar, in seminary, 28

canon law, 9, 12, 48-60, 72, 289, 291, 323; the function and role of, 148-149; the need for studying, 149-150; studies in seminaries, 261; faculty of, 242-243, 256; teaching those preparing to be priests, 145-151; practical directives, 150-151; how the system is in accord with the salvific will of God, 44

Capharnaum, 217

catechetics, 10; catechesis on vocations, 25; catecheses on the Fathers, 134

celibacy, specific nature of, 160; reason for, 162; no harm from, 7; gift of God, 32, 156; is rooted in Gospel, 32; is a lifelong offering, 182; for the

kingdom is falling in love,
171; guidelines, 156; the
specific reason for guidelines,
156-157; a guide to formation
in priestly, 153-205;
guidelines for seminary
formation in, 174-191;
modern difficulties with
clerical, 163; presuppositions
for training for, 163-164;
willing freely to embrace for
kingdom's sake, 32; to be
embraced and esteemed as a
gift, 280; relationship between
priesthood and, 162-163; a
convergence of motives for,
307-308; conditions favoring,
308-309; at first
recommended, then imposed
by law, 280; for priests, 307;
of Latin-rite priests, 296; to be
kept in the Latin church, 308;
in the life of the Church,
159-161; the meaning in
contemporary priestly life,
159-164; the apostolate and,
160-161

chastity, and love are actually the
same virtue, 189; governs the
use of sex, 170; to be seen as
something good, 180; the
theology of, 185; problems of
forming the student in, 174

Christology, is also mariology, 222

Church, universal sacrament of
salvation, 21, 300; tradition
and magisterium of, 20; hopes
of, 11; needs of the whole, 10,
27; magisterium of, 9; in the
spirit of, 25; of the Latin rite,
32; little by little even from
ancient times has forbidden
improvisation in composing
prayers of the liturgy, 132;
founded on the apostles, 300;
social doctrine of the, 41;
history of, 9, 41

Cicognani, A. G., 49

Clement of Rome, St., 134, 300,
313

clerical dress, the need and
meaning of, 218

Colossians, 35, 68, 182, 291, 299,
300

Communion, under both species is
recommended in seminaries,
118; received there daily, 34;
the admission of youngsters
to, 137; in the hierarchy with
order of bishops, 20

community of saints, 266

congregations:
Sacred Congregation of the
Holy Office, 54
Sacred Congregation of Rites,
13, 53, 56, 57, 58, 133,
142, 143
Sacred Congregation for
Catholic Education, 17,
18, 23, 47, 49, 50, 51, 52,
53, 54, 55, 56, 57, 58, 59,
60, 61, 63, 64, 91, 93, 94,
97, 99, 109, 111, 112, 113,
128, 145, 147, 150, 153,
155, 156, 203, 204, 205,
207, 209, 219, 223, 225,
231, 232, 245, 324, 325
Sacred Congregation for
Clergy, 55, 59, 60
Sacred Congregation for
Divine Worship, 142, 143
Sacred Congregation for
Religious, 12, 52
Sacred Congregation for
Religious and Secular
Institutes, 49, 50, 51, 52,
150
Sacred Congregation for
Seminaries and
Universities, 12, 48, 49
Sacred Congregation for the
Doctrine of the Faith, 47,
48, 51, 53, 54, 55, 56, 57,
58, 94, 138
Sacred Congregation for the
Evangelization of
Peoples, 94, 150
Sacred Congregation for the
Oriental Churches, 150
Sacred Congregation for the
Sacraments, 12, 50, 52, 53
Sacred Congregation for the
Sacraments and Divine
Worship, 53, 112

Liturgy of the Hours, 306; "so that
... the prayer of Christ might
ceaselessly continue in the
Church, " 119
love, the vocation of all, 170;
celibacy for the kingdom is
falling in, 171; and chastity are
actually the same virtue, 188;
and self-denial complement
each other, 183; of justice, 7
Luke, 7, 21, 25, 32, 157, 218, 222,
284, 287, 288, 290, 291, 299
Lumen ecclesiae, 93

magisterium, can be considered
both as authority and as
service, 72; a *conditio sine
qua non* of Catholic theology,
73; guards and authentically
interprets Scripture and
tradition, 68; well-versed in
statements of the, 283
Malachi, 288
Marialis cultus, 222
Marietti, 288
mariology, Christology is also, 222
Mark, 5, 22, 38, 157, 160, 268, 273
286, 306
marriage, Christian, duties and
dignity of, 7; which represents
love between Christ and the
Church, 7; is state of life that
is sacrificial, 184
Marx, 87
Mary, blessed virgin, 6, 215, 282; a
seminarian ought to have
fervent love for, 37; priests
should often turn to, 306
Mass, even without congregation is
action of Christ and the Church,
118; though it is celebrated
privately is still not private, 290;
two parts of the, 135; must be
work of the entire seminary,
118; it is desirable that some
parts be always sung, 118;
source and culmination of all
Christian life, 36
masturbation, sexual imbalance is
one of causes of, 188
Mater et Magistra, 14, 51, 57, 58,
60, 93

Matthew, 7, 25, 26, 34, 38, 159,
160, 230, 269, 273, 276, 287,
288, 289, 290, 291, 300
maturity, human, 7; formation in,
165-168; man's sexual, 167;
sexual, in a priest, 172; of a
Christian, 169-170; formation
in priestly, 170-173; formation
in Christian, 168-170;
emotional, in the priest, 171
Mediator Dei, 13, 14, 56
meditation, daily, 56; on the word
of God, 196
Melchizedek, 274
Menti nostrae, 12, 13, 14, 47, 49,
60, 204, 290
Ministeria quaedam, 121, 143
Ministerial Priesthood, The, 203
204, 293-313
mission, evangelization and
sacramental life in, 303
Mohlberg, L. C., 287
mortification, part of every Christian
and of every human life, 183
Moses, 271, 289
Musicae sacrae disciplina, 4
Musicam sacram, 57
Mysterii paschalis, 140
Mysterium fidei, 56, 118, 142, 288,
290
mystery of Christ and salvation
history, introductory course in
seminaries, 39
Mystici Corporis, 14, 56, 288

Nietzsche, 87
*Normae quaedam, 25; ad
constitutionem apostolicam
Deus scientiarum Dominus de
studiis academicis ecclesiasticis
recognoscendam,* 52, 94, 231
norms, of application, 225, 245
247-261; for the drawing up
of statutes, 258-259; practical,
for theology, 89-91
Numbers, 281, 289

obedience, is highest expression of
freedom, 221; should be shown
to pope and to own bishop, 36
Octogesima adveniens, 55, 56, 57,
59, 93

office, vocations, should be established in every diocese, region, or nation, 24

officials and staff assistants, in ecclesiastical universities and faculties, 237, 252

Officiorum omnium, 52

On Formation for the Priesthood, 18

On Priestly Celibacy, 156

order of priesthood, only they can fully exercise the ministerial ministry, 22

Orders, Holy, confers ministerial priesthood, which is different from priesthood bestowed by baptism, 159; age for, episcopal conferences should consider whether it should be raised, 8, 31

ordinations, to diaconate and priesthood involve whole diocese, 122; by it a priest takes on likeness of Christ, 6

Origen, 289, 313

Pacem in terris, 48, 93

Paenitemini, 54

Pater misericordiarum, 52

patristics, and theology, 83

Paul, St., 148, 212, 213, 221, 267, 275, 277, 290, 300, 311

Paul VI, pope, 11, 12, 13, 14, 47, 48, 49, 50, 51, 52, 53, 54, 55, 56, 57, 58, 59, 60, 93, 94, 142, 143, 148, 149, 203, 204, 205, 210, 222, 230, 232, 261, 263, 286, 287, 288, 289, 290

penance, priest must become teacher of, 219; private, 220; seminary will have to impart a sense of, 212; frequent recourse to, 35, 306; penitential celebrations were not designed gradually to eliminate individual confession, 219; *see* reconciliation

perfection, priests' call to, 276-279

Peter, 22, 24, 287, 288, 290, 291, 300, 302, 311

Petrum et Paulum, 93

Philippians, 33, 157, 196, 221, 267,

280, 290, 291, 299, 300, 312

philosophy, study in seminaries of, 97-107; constitutes soul of authentic culture, 103; is necessary for future priests, 102-104; in seminaries should be equivalent to at least two years, 37, 38, 90, 105; history of, 8, 39; and related subjects, 38-39; leads to a good knowledge of man, the world, and God, 8, 38; in seminaries may not be limited to teaching how to philosophize, 106; present situation demands real formation be given, 55-56; should be preparation for theological studies, 38; relations between theology and, 74; current difficulties in seminaries in, 100-102; is in itself a science, 103; faculty of, 243, 257; and theological studies, *see Normae quaedam*

Pilate, Pontius, 131

Pius X, pope, St., 12, 13, 14, 58, 216, 289, 290

Pius XI, pope, 12, 14, 51, 52, 60, 205, 228, 230, 290, 291

Pius XII, pope, 12, 13, 14, 47, 48, 49, 50, 51, 52, 53, 54, 55, 56, 57, 58, 59, 60, 204, 228, 290, 291

Pizzardo, cardinal, 50

pluralism, of theological expression, 77-78; no difficulty in admitting a healthy philosophical, 106; must not become pluralism of system that undermines unity of faith, 90, 106

Polycarp, St., 287

Pontifical Biblical Commission, 13, 56, 93, 94, 261

Pontifical Commission for Social Communication, 205

Pontifical French Seminary, 57

Pontifical Gregorian University, 13, 57, 58, 148

Pontificalis Romani, 138

pope, obedience should be shown to own bishop and to, 33

Populorum progressio, 55, 60, 93, 94, 203
prayer, the art of, 214; private, 25; in common, 25; there exists a general inclination to pray, 210
prefect of discipline, in seminary, 28
prefect of studies, in seminary, 28
Presbyterium, 27, 32
priest, priests, functions of, 268-271; the life of, 276-285; distribution of, 274-275; regrettable shortage of, 5; of the New Testament, 20; is a representative of Christ, 162; should regard seminary as heart of diocese, 5; as ministers of God's word, 268; human and Christian maturity in, 171; as ministers of the sacraments, 268; as father and teacher, 21; must preach the Gospel, 34; first duty is to preach the Gospel, 21, 268; and bishop are responsible for preaching in the Church, 65; as indispensable helpers in ministry and office of teaching, sanctifying and nourishing People of God, 20; train each of faithful to follow his vocation, 24; as rulers of God's people, 270-271; and economic affairs, 311; helps for the lives of, 282-285; priestly celibacy, 7; in modern life, 161-162; relations between bishop and, 309-310; relations with each other, 310; relations between bishops and body of, 271; relations between laity and, 273-274, 310-311; their relation with the world, and voluntary poverty, 281; their place in the world, 267; provision of just remuneration for, 283-284; reason for crises in lives of, 190; and secular and political activity, 305; priestly training should be continued after seminary, 11; guidelines for life and ministry, 303-311;

spiritual life of, 306-307; their call to perfection, 276-279; always available when penance is requested, 278; must become a "teacher of penance," 219; their care for priestly vocations, 275-276; to support seminarians, 12; are dependent on bishops for exercise of their power, 20; all share with bishops the one priesthood and ministry of Christ, 271; unity and harmony of, 278; bond and cooperation among, 272-273; associations of, are to be diligently promoted, 273
priesthood, permanence of, 301; in the Church's mission, 266-267; ministerial, surpasses the general, 20
Princeps pastorum, 14, 54, 55, 56, 57, 60
Profession of the Catholic Faith, summarizes the understanding the Church has of revelation, 82
professors, in seminaries, 11, 29-30; should be drawn from the best, 5; of sacred subjects in seminaries ought to be priests, 29; they teach in the Church's name, 43
Program of Priestly Training, The, 3, 17, 317, 319, 323, 325
Prosper of Aquitaine, St., 143
Providentissimus Deus, 13, 59
Psalms, 34, 157, 291

Quandoquidem, 14, 60
Quaracchi, V., 13
Queen of Apostles, 282
Quinque iam anni, 93

Rahmani, I. E., 289
Ratio fundamentalis institutionis sacerdotalis, 88, 105, 107, 112, 123, 129; *see* Basic Plan for Priestly Formation
reconciliation, sacrament of, seminarians should go often, 121; *see* penance

fundamentally different from animal mating, 169; a suitable education in matters of, 33

silence, in seminary, 7; interior, 213; interior silence demands and fosters, 215; keeping in seminaries of external, 36; must begin with cultivation of sense of interior, 212

sin, world caught as it is in much, 285; Jesus wills to be made like others in all things but, 267

social doctrine, so means may be learned of adapting teaching and Gospel principles to life of society, 41

spiritual formation, 6, 8, 12; given most important place of all, 209

staff assistants, and officials in ecclesiastical universities and faculties, 237, 251

students, of ecclesiastical universities and faculties, 236-237; in seminaries, 30-31; not a few difficulties come from, 101; should feel co-responsible for theological formation, 90; of theology should have an adequate knowledge of Latin and biblical languages, 90

Studia latinitatis, 55

study program, of ecclesiastical universities and faculties, 237-238, 252

Summi Dei Verbum, 12, 13, 14, 49, 51, 52, 53, 55, 203

Sunday, highest importance must be given to, 140; and main feasts become days of joy, 120

superiors, seminary, should be from the best, 5; are nominated by the bishop, 28

Swete, 289

Synod of Bishops, 17, 50, 156, 293, 295, 312

Tabernacle, devotional visits to, 54
teaching, in seminaries, 43; of

ecclesiastical universities and faculties, 235-236, 250-251

temple of the Holy Spirit, 21

Tertullian, 134, 288, 313

Theodore of Mopsuesta, 289

theology, function of, 66-69; and new ecumenical needs, 68; task of rediscovering ecumenical dimension of, 65; historical dimension of, 69-70; is science of Christian revelation, 68; and the magisterium, 72-73; cannot dispense with magisterium, 70; in seminaries should equal at least four years, 37, 39, 91; theological subjects should be renewed, 9; and the patrimony of Christianity, 73; systematic dimension of, 70-72; guidelines for teaching of, 77-88; Scripture is soul of, 9, 39, 81; fundamental theology, 86; biblical themes should have first place in dogmatic, 9; moral theology, 9; should be animated by Scripture, 40; renewal of, 84; must keep in contact with biblical and dogmatic, 85; teaching of moral theology finds its completion in spiritual, 40; affinity between pastoral ministry and competence in, 64; pastoral theology has to explain principles by which God's salvific will is realized, 41; teaching of pastoral theology must not be omitted, 86; philosophy should be preparation for, 38; relations between philosophy and, 74; speculative theologian must have special recourse to sound philosophy, 103-104; demands of teaching of, 67-76; seminary studies in, 39-41; faculty of, 241-242, 255-256

Theresa of Avila, St., 211

Thessalonians, 289, 300

Thomas Aquinas, St., 9, 40, 93, 94,

336